ESSAYS

FROM

FIVE CENTURIES

EDITED BY

WILLIAM THOMSON HASTINGS, A.M.
Associate Professor of English, Brown University

AND

KENNETH OLIVER MASON, A.M.
Assistant Professor of English, Brown University

HOUGHTON MIFFLIN COMPANY
BOSTON · NEW YORK · CHICAGO · DALLAS · SAN FRANCISCO
The Riverside Press Cambridge

Misc

29-10399
5/28/46

PREFACE

In this volume are gathered fifty-six characteristic specimens of the work of British and American essayists from the latter part of the sixteenth century to the present time. The inclusion of one of Ascham's prefaces and Montaigne's "Of the Cannibals" alongside the writings of Bacon, Overbury, and Earle provides material for a study of the origins of the essay form, and the liberal allotment of space to authors of the seventeenth and eighteenth centuries will enable the student to trace its historical evolution. No anthology of a form so marked with individuality as the essay can hope to be all-inclusive; it is enough, on this score, if the collection possesses the stimulus of diverse ideas and skillful writing, and exhibits quaint, subtle, and vigorous personalities for our delight.

In preparing the volume, furthermore, we have endeavored not to interfere with the indefeasible right of the student or the teacher to originate his own ideas and organize his own opinions. We have therefore avoided classifying the essays by types and we have refrained from providing study outlines; we have tried not to forestall the independent operation of thought by a tabulation of the standard comments on an author's character or the orthodox criticisms of his literary skill. Actuated by the same desire not to intervene between the author and his audience, we have restricted our notes as far as possible and have placed them at the bottom of the page, where they can be read with the slightest possible deflection of attention. We trust that these limitations of the editorial function will commend the volume to those who may use it.

The texts of the essays reprinted have been carefully prepared from first or subsequent authoritative editions, as indicated in the footnotes attached to the titles; in some cases with collation of two or more texts. For treating the text of essays earlier than the nineteenth century the following rules have been adopted. The spelling has been modernized except where the old spelling indicates a variant form of the word.

The use of capitals and italics has been made consistent with modern practice. The original sentence division has been preserved; except that some freedom has been assumed in handling the colon-capital sequence. The internal punctuation of the sentence has been made somewhat simpler and more logical; but in general it has been treated very conservatively. In a few cases, notably in Montaigne, very long paragraphs have been subdivided. The nineteenth and twentieth century essays are reproduced without change, except a slight normalizing of quotation marks and italics. It should, finally, be noted that to save space it was found necessary to omit short passages from three essays, and more extensive passages from three others. The substance of the omissions is indicated at the appropriate points.

The appendix contains compact information regarding each author: (1) an outline of his life; (2) the titles and dates of his chief works; (3) a selected list of books and articles about him. A brief bibliography of works on the essay is also included.

The thanks of the editors are due to those living authors who have permitted essays to be reprinted, and to their publishers; to the librarians of the John Hay Library and the John Carter Brown Library, Brown University, the Providence Athenæum, and the Widener Library, Harvard University, for textual and bibliographical assistance; and to a number of their colleagues for helpful information and advice.

CONTENTS

vi

CONTENTS

17.th Century ~ philosophical ideas which
18th century — bring out his own Character

CONTENTS

CONTENTS

Reader, loe here a well-meaning Booke. It doth at the first entrance forewarne thee, that in contriving the same, I have proposed unto my selfe no other than a familiar and private end: I have no respect or consideration at all, either to thy service, or to my glory: my forces are not capable of any such desseigne. I have vowed the same to the particular commodity of my kinsfolks and friends: to the end, that losing me (which they are likely to doe ere long) they may therein find some lineaments of my conditions and humours, and by that meanes reserve more whole, and more lively foster the knowledge and acquaintance they have had of me. Had my intention beene to forestal and purchase the worlds opinion and favour, I would surely have adorned my selfe more quaintly, or kept a more grave and solemne march. I desire therein to be delineated in mine owne genuine, simple and ordinarie fashion, without contention, art or study; for it is my selfe I pourtray. My imperfections shall therein be read to the life, and my naturall forme discerned, so farre-forth as publike reverence hath permitted me. For if my fortune had beene to have lived among those nations, which yet are said to live under the sweet liberty of Natures first and uncorrupted lawes, I assure thee, I would most willingly have pourtrayed my selfe fully and naked. Thus gentle Reader my selfe am the groundworke of my booke: It is then no reason thou shouldest employ thy time about so frivolous and vaine a Subject. Therefore farewell. From Montaigne, the first of March, 1580.

Florio's *Montaigne*: "The Author to the Reader."

ESSAYS FROM FIVE CENTURIES

.·.

MICHEL EYQUEM DE MONTAIGNE

OF THE CANNIBALS [1]

AT what time King Pyrrhus came into Italy, after he had sur-veyed the marshaling of the army which the Romans sent against him: "I wot not," said he, "what barbarous men these are" (for so were the Grecians wont to call all strange nations), "but the disposition of this army which I see is nothing barba-rous." So said the Grecians of that which Flaminius sent into their country; and Philip, viewing from a tower the order and distribution of the Roman camp, in his kingdom, under Pub-lius Sulpicius Galba. Lo, how a man ought to take heed, lest he overweeningly follow vulgar opinions, which should be measured by the rule of reason, and not by the common report. I have had long time dwelling with me a man who for the space of ten or twelve years had dwelt in that other world which in our age was lately discovered in those parts where Villegaignon first landed, and surnamed Antarctic France. This discovery of so infinite and vast a country seemeth worthy great consider-ation. I wot not whether I can warrant myself that some other be not discovered hereafter, sithence so many worthy men, and better learned than we are, have so many ages been deceived in this. I fear me our eyes be greater than our bellies, and that we have more curiosity than capacity. We embrace all, but we fasten nothing but wind. Plato maketh Solon to report that he had learnt of the priests of the city of Sais in Egypt, that whilom, and before the general Deluge, there was a great island called Atlantis, situated at the mouth of the strait of Gibraltar, which contained more firm land than Afric and Asia together. And that the kings of that country who did not only possess that island, but had so far entred into the main

[1] From John Florio's translation (1603) of the *Essais*, I, xxx.

land, that of the breadth of Afric they held as far as Egypt; and
of Europe's length, as far as Tuscany: and that they undertook to invade Asia, and to subdue all the nations that compass the Mediterranean Sea, to the gulf of Mare Maggiore,[1] and
to that end they traversed all Spain, France, and Italy, so far
as Greece, where the Athenians made head against them; but
that, a while after, both the Athenians themselves and that
great island were swallowed up by the Deluge.   It is very likely
this extreme ruin of waters wrought strange alterations in the
habitations of the earth: as some hold that the sea hath divided
Sicily from Italy, —

> *Haec loca vi quandam, et vasta convulsa ruina*
> *Dissiluisse ferunt, cùm protinus utraque tellus*
> *Una foret.*

> Men say, sometimes this land by that forsaken,
> And that by this, were split and ruin-shaken,
> Whereas till then both lands as one were taken —

Cyprus from Syria, the island of Negroponte from the main
land of Beotia; and in other places joined lands that were sun-
dred by the sea, filling with mud and sand the channels between them.

> *. . . sterilisque diu palus aptaque remis*
> *Vicinas urbes alit, et grave sentit aratrum.*

> The fen long barren, to be rowed in, now
> Both feeds the neighbor towns, and feels the plow.

But there is no great apparence[2] the said island should be
the new world we have lately discovered; for it well-nigh
touched Spain, and it were an incredible effect of inundation to
have removed the same more than twelve hundred leagues, as
we see it is.   Besides, our modern navigations have now almost
discovered that it is not an island, but rather firm land, and a
continent, with the East Indias on one side, and the countries
lying under the two Poles on the other; from which if it be divided, it is with so narrow a strait and interval, that it no way

---

[1] the Black Sea   [2] likelihood

deserveth to be named an island; for it seemeth there are certain motions in these vast bodies, some natural and other some febricitant,[1] as well as in ours. When I consider the impression my river of Dordoigne worketh in my time, toward the right shore of her descent, and how much it hath gained in twenty years, and how many foundations of divers houses it hath overwhelmed and violently carried away, I confess it to be an extraordinary agitation; for should it always keep one course, or had it ever kept the same, the figure of the world had ere this been overthrown. But they are subject to changes and alterations. Sometimes they overflow and spread themselves on one side, sometimes on another; and other times they contain themselves in their natural beds or channels. I speak not of sudden inundations, whereof we now treat the causes. In Medoc alongst the seacoast my brother, the Lord of Arsac, may see a town of his buried under the sands which the sea casteth up before it: the tops of some buildings are yet to be discerned. His rents and demains [2] have been changed into barren pastures. The inhabitants thereabouts affirm that, some years since, the sea encroacheth so much upon them that they have lost four leagues of firm land: these sands are her forerunners. And we see great hillocks of gravel moving, which march half a league before it, and usurp on the firm land.

The other testimony of antiquity, to which some will refer this discovery, is in Aristotle (if at least that little book of unheard-of wonders be his) where he reporteth that certain Carthaginians having sailed athwart the Atlantic Sea, without the strait of Gibraltar, after long time they at last discovered a great fertile island, all replenished with goodly woods and watered with great and deep rivers, far distant from all land, and that both they and others, allured by the goodness and fertility of the soil, went thither with their wives, children, and household, and there began to inhabit and settle themselves. The lords of Carthage, seeing their country by little and little to be dispeopled, made a law and express inhibition that upon pain of death no more men should go thither, and banished all that were gone thither to dwell, fearing (as they said) that in success of time they would so multiply as they might one day

---

[1] feverish; perhaps a reference to earthquakes   [2] demesnes

supplant them, and overthrow their own estate.[1] This narration of Aristotle hath no reference unto our new found countries.

This servant I had was a simple and rough-hewn fellow: a condition[2] fit to yield a true testimony. For subtile people may indeed mark more curiously, and observe things more exactly, but they amplify and glose them; and the better to persuade, and make their interpretations of more validity, they cannot choose but somewhat alter the story. They never represent things truly, but fashion and mask them according to the visage they saw them in; and to purchase credit to their judgment, and draw you on to believe them, they commonly adorn, enlarge, yea, and hyperbolize the matter. Wherein is required either a most sincere reporter, or a man so simple that he may have no invention to build upon, and to give a true likelihood unto false devices, and be not wedded to his own will. Such a one was my man; who, besides his own report, hath many times showed me divers mariners and merchants whom he had known in that voyage. So am I pleased with his information that I never inquire what cosmographers say of it. We had need of topographers to make us particular narrations of the places they have been in. For some of them, if they have the advantage of us that they have seen Palestine, will challenge [3] a privilege to tell us news of all the world besides. I would have every man write what he knows, and no more: not only in that, but in all other subjects. For one may have particular knowledge of the nature of one river, and experience of the quality of one fountain, that in other things knows no more than another man; who nevertheless, to publish this little scantling, will undertake to write of all the physics. From which vice proceed divers great inconveniences.

Now (to return to my purpose) I find (as far as I have been informed) there is nothing in that nation that is either barbarous or savage, unless men call that barbarism which is not common to them. As, indeed, we have no other aim [4] of truth and reason than the example and idea of the opinions and customs of the country we live in. There is ever perfect religion, perfect policy, perfect and complete use of all things. They

---

[1] government   [2] character   [3] lay claim to   [4] conjecture

are even savage, as we call those fruits wild which Nature of herself and of her ordinary progress hath produced; whereas, indeed, they are those which ourselves have altered by our artificial devices, and diverted from their common order, we should rather term savage. In those are the true and most profitable virtues, and natural properties most lively and vigorous, which in these we have bastardized, applying them to the pleasure of our corrupted taste. And if, notwithstanding, in divers fruits of those countries that were never tilled we shall find that in respect of ours they are most excellent, and as delicate unto our taste, there is no reason art should gain the point of honor of our great and puissant mother Nature. We have so much by our inventions surcharged the beauties and riches of her works, that we have altogether overchoked her; yet wherever her purity shineth, she makes our vain and frivolous enterprises wonderfully ashamed.

> *Et veniunt hederæ sponte sua melius,*
> *Surgit et in solis formosior arbutus antris,*
> *Et volucres nulla dulcius arte canunt.*

> Ivies spring better of their own accord,
> Unhanted [1] spots much fairer trees afford.
> Birds by no art much sweeter notes record.

All our endeavor or wit cannot so much as reach to represent the nest of the least birdlet, its contexture, beauty, profit, and use, no, nor the web of a seely [2] spider. "All things," saith Plato, "are produced either by nature, by fortune, or by art. The greatest and fairest by one or other of the two first, the least and imperfect by the last." Those nations seem therefore so barbarous unto me because they have received very little fashion from human wit, and are yet near their original naturality. The laws of nature do yet command them which are but little bastardized by ours, and that with such purity as I am sometimes grieved the knowledge of it came no sooner to light, at what time there were men that better than we could have judged of it. I am sorry Lycurgus and Plato had it not; for meseemeth that what in those nations we see by experience, doth not only exceed all the pictures wherewith licentious

---

[1] unhaunted, i.e., unfrequented   [2] silly, weak, frail

Poesy hath proudly embellished the Golden Age, and all her quaint inventions to feign a happy condition of man, but also the conception and desire of Philosophy. They could not imagine a genuity [1] so pure and simple as we see it by experience; nor ever believe our society might be maintained with so little art and human combination. It is a nation, would I answer Plato, that hath no kind of traffic, no knowledge of letters, no intelligence of numbers, no name of magistrate nor of politic superiority; [2] no use [3] of service, of riches, or of poverty; no contracts, no successions, no partitions, no occupation but idle; no respect of kinred, but common, [4] no apparel but natural, no manuring [5] of lands, no use of wine, corn, or metal. The very words that import lying, falsehood, treason, dissimulations, covetousness, envy, detraction, and pardon, were never heard of amongst them. How dissonant would he find his imaginary commonwealth from this perfection?

Hos natura modos primùm dedit.

Nature, at first uprise,
These manners did devise.

Furthermore, they live in a country of so exceeding pleasant and temperate situation that, as my testimonies have told me, it is very rare to see a sick body amongst them; and they have further assured me, they never saw any man there either shaking with the palsy, toothless, with eyes dropping, or crooked and stooping through age. They are seated alongst the seacoast, encompassed toward the land with huge and steepy mountains, having between both a hundred leagues or thereabout of open and champaign ground. They have great abundance of fish and flesh that have no resemblance at all with ours, and eat them without any sauces, or skill of cookery, but plain boiled or broiled. The first man that brought a horse thither, although he had in many other voyages conversed [6] with them, bred so great a horror in the land that, before they could take notice of him, they slew him with arrows. Their buildings are very long, and able to contain two or three hundred souls, covered with

---

[1] simplicity   [2] politic superiority = political overlordship
[3] experience   [4] i.e., "common respect," consideration for all alike
[5] tilling   [6] had dealings

barks of great trees, fastened in the ground at one end, inter-
laced and joined close together by the tops, after the manner
of some of our granges; the covering whereof hangs down to the
ground, and steadeth them as a flank. They have a kind of
wood so hard that, riving and cleaving the same, they make
blades, swords, and gridirons to broil their meat with. Their
beds are of a kind of cotton cloth, fastened to the house roof,
as our ship-cabins: every one hath his several couch; for the
women lie from their husbands. They rise with the sun, and
feed for all day as soon as they are up, and make no more meals
after that. They drink not at meat, as Suidas reporteth of some
other people of the East, which drank after meals, but drink
many times a day, and are much given to pledge carouses.
Their drink is made of a certain root, and of the color of our
claret wines, which lasteth but two or three days; they drink it
warm. It hath somewhat a sharp taste, wholesome for the
stomach, nothing heady, but laxative for such as are not used
unto it, yet very pleasing to such as are accustomed unto it.
In stead of bread they use a certain white composition, like
unto corianders confected. I have eaten some, the taste
whereof is somewhat sweet and wallowish.[1]

They spend the whole day in dancing. Their young men go
a hunting after wild beasts with bows and arrows. Their
women busy themselves therewhilst with warming of their
drink, which is their chiefest office. Some of their old men, in
the morning before they go to eating, preach in common to all
the household, walking from one end of the house to the other,
repeating one selfsame sentence many times, till he have ended
his turn (for their buildings are a hundred paces in length): he
commends but two things unto his auditory, first, valor against
their enemies, then, lovingness unto their wives. They never
miss (for their restraint) to put men in mind of this duty, that
it is their wives which keep their drink lukewarm and well-
seasoned. The form of their beds, cords, swords, blades, and
wooden bracelets wherewith they cover their hand wrists when
they fight, and great canes open at one end by the sound of
which they keep time and cadence in their dancing, are in
many places to be seen, and namely [2] in mine own house.

[1] insipidly sweet   [2] especially

They are shaven all over, much more close and cleaner than we are, with no other razors than of wood or stone.

They believe their souls to be eternal, and those that have deserved well of their gods to be placed in that part of heaven where the sun riseth, and the cursed toward the west in opposition. They have certain prophets and priests which commonly abide in the mountains, and very seldom show themselves unto the people; but when they come down, there is a great feast prepared, and a solemn assembly of many townships together (each grange as I have described maketh a village, and they are about a French league one from another). The prophet speaks to the people in public, exhorting them to embrace virtue, and follow their duty. All their moral discipline containeth but these two articles: first, an undismayed resolution to war; then, an inviolable affection to their wives. He doth also prognosticate of things to come, and what success they shall hope for in their enterprises: he either persuadeth or dissuadeth them from war; but if he chance to miss of his divination, and that it succeed otherwise than he foretold them, if he be taken, he is hewn in a thousand pieces, and condemned for a false prophet. And therefore he that hath once misreckoned himself is never seen again. Divination is the gift of God; the abusing whereof should be a punishable imposture. When the divines amongst the Scythians had foretold an untruth, they were couched along upon hurdles full of heath or brushwood, drawn by oxen, and so manacled hand and foot, burned to death. Those which manage matters subject to the conduct of man's sufficiency are excusable, although they show the utmost of their skill. But those that gull and conycatch [1] us with the assurance of an extraordinary faculty, and which is beyond our knowledge, ought to be double punished: first, because they perform not the effect of their promise; then, for the rashness of their imposture and unadvisedness of their fraud.

They war against the nations that lie beyond their mountains, to which they go naked, having no other weapons than bows, or wooden swords sharp at one end, as our broaches are. It is an admirable thing to see the constant resolution of their combats, which never end but by effusion of blood and mur-

[1] gull = coneycatch = cheat

ther; for they know not what fear or routs are. Every victor brings home the head of the enemy he hath slain, as a trophy of his victory, and fasteneth the same at the entrance of his dwelling place. After they have long time used and entreated their prisoners well, and with all commodities they can devise, he that is the master of them, summoning a great assembly of his acquaintance, tieth a cord to one of the prisoner's arms, by the end whereof he holds him fast, with some distance from him, for fear he might offend him,[1] and giveth the other arm, bound in like manner, to the dearest friend he hath, and both in the presence of all the assembly kill him with swords; which done, they roast and then eat him in common, and send some slices of him to such of their friends as are absent.

It is not, as some imagine, to nourish themselves with it (as anciently the Scythians wont to do), but to represent an extreme and inexpiable revenge. Which we prove thus: some of them, perceiving the Portugales, who had confederated themselves with their adversaries, to use another kind of death when they took them prisoners — which was, to bury them up to the middle, and against the upper part of the body to shoot arrows, and then being almost dead, to hang them up — they supposed that these people of the other world (as they who had sowed the knowledge of many vices amongst their neighbors, and were much more cunning in all kinds of evils and mischief than they) undertook not this manner of revenge without cause, and that consequently it was more smartful and cruel than theirs; and thereupon began to leave their old fashion to follow this. I am not sorry we note the barbarous horror of such an action, but grieved that, prying so narrowly into their faults, we are so blinded in ours. I think there is more barbarism in eating men alive than to feed upon them being dead; to mangle by tortures and torments a body full of lively sense, to roast him in pieces, to make dogs and swine to gnaw and tear him in mammocks (as we have not only read, but seen very lately, yea, and in our own memory, not amongst ancient enemies, but our neighbors and fellow citizens; and which is worse, under pretence of piety and religion), than to roast and eat him after he is dead. Chrysippus and Zeno, arch-pillars of the Stoic sect, have supposed that

[1] i.e., for fear the prisoner might hurt the master

it was no hurt at all in time of need, and to what end soever, to make use of our carrion bodies, and to feed upon them, as did our forefathers, who, being besieged by Cæsar in the city of Alexia,[1] resolved to sustain the famine of the siege with the bodies of old men, women, and other persons unserviceable and unfit to fight.

> *Vascones (fama est) alimentis talibus usi*
> *Produxere animas.*

> Gascoynes (as lame reports)
> Lived with meats of such sorts.

And physicians fear not, in all kinds of compositions availful to our health, to make use of it, be it for outward or inward applications: but there was never any opinion found so unnatural and immodest, that would excuse treason, treachery, disloyalty, tyranny, cruelty, and such like, which are our ordinary faults. We may then well call them barbarous, in regard of reason's rules, but not in respect of us, that exceed them in all kind of barbarism. Their wars are noble and generous, and have as much excuse and beauty as this human infirmity may admit: they aim at nought so much, and have no other foundation amongst them, but the mere jealousy of virtue. They contend not for the gaining of new lands; for to this day they yet enjoy that natural uberty and fruitfulness which, without laboring toil, doth in such plenteous abundance furnish them with all necessary things, that they need not enlarge their limits. They are yet in that happy estate as they desire no more than what their natural necessities direct them: whatsoever is beyond it, is to them superfluous. Those that are much about one age do generally inter-call one another brethren, and such as are younger they call children, and the aged are esteemed as fathers to all the rest. These leave this full possession of goods in common, and without division to their heirs, without other claim or title but that which Nature doth plainly impart unto all creatures, even as she brings them into the world.

If their neighbors chance to come over the mountains to assail or invade them, and that they get the victory over them,

---

[1] Alexia, in Gaul, defended by Vercingetorix

the victors' conquest is glory, and the advantage to be and remain superior in valor and virtue: else have they nothing to do with the goods and spoils of the vanquished, and so return into their country, where they neither want any necessary thing, nor lack this great portion, to know how to enjoy their condition happily, and are contented with what Nature affordeth them. So do these when their turn cometh. They require no other ransom of their prisoners but an acknowledgment and confession that they are vanquished. And in a whole age a man shall not find one that doth not rather embrace death than either by word or countenance remissly to yield one jot of an invincible courage. There is none seen that would not rather be slain and devoured than sue for life, or show any fear. They use their prisoners with all liberty, that they may so much the more hold their lives dear and precious, and commonly entertain them with threats of future death, with the torments they shall endure, with the preparations intended for that purpose, with mangling and slicing of their members, and with the feast that shall be kept at their charge. All which is done to wrest some remiss,[1] and exact some faint-yielding speech of submission, from them, or to possess them with a desire to escape or run away; that so they may have the advantage to have danted and made them afraid, and to have forced their constancy. For certainly true victory consisteth in that only point.

> *. . . Victoria nulla est*
> *Quâm quæ confessos animo quoque subjugat hostes.*

> No conquest such as to suppress
> Foes' hearts, the conquest to confess.

The Hungarians, a most war-like nation, were whilom wont to pursue their prey no longer than they had forced their enemy to yield unto their mercy. For, having wrested this confession from him, they set him at liberty without offence or ransom, except it were to make him swear never after to bear arms against them.

We get many advantages of our enemies that are but bor-

[1] surrender

rowed and not ours: it is the quality of porterly-rascal,[1] and not of virtue, to have stronger arms and sturdier legs: disposition [2] is a dead and corporal quality.   It is a trick of fortune to make our enemy stoop, and to blear his eyes with the sun's light: it is a prank of skill and knowledge to be cunning in the art of fencing, and which may happen unto a base and worthless man. The reputation and worth of a man consisteth in his heart and will: therein consists true honor.   Constancy is valor, not of arms and legs, but of mind and courage; it consisteth not in the spirit and courage of our horse, nor of our arms, but in ours. He that obstinately faileth in his courage, *Si succiderit, de genu pugnat*: "If he slip or fall, he fights upon his knee."   He that in danger of imminent death is no whit danted in his assuredness; he that in yielding up his ghost beholding his enemy with a scornful and fierce look, he is vanquished, not by us, but by fortune: he is slain, but not conquered.

The most valiant are often the most unfortunate.   So are there triumphant losses in envy [3] of victories.   Not those four sister victories, the fairest that ever the sun beheld with his all-seeing eye, of Salamis, of Platæa, of Mycale, and of Sicilia, durst ever dare to oppose all their glory together to the glory of the King Leonidas his discomfiture [4] and of his men, at the passage of Thermopylæ: what man did ever run with so glorious an envy or more ambitious desire to the goal of a combat, than Captain Ischolas to an evident loss and overthrow? who so ingeniously or more politicly did ever assure himself of his welfare than he of his ruin?   He was appointed to defend a certain passage of Peloponnesus against the Arcadians, which finding himself altogether unable to perform, seeing the nature of the place and inequality of the forces, and resolving that whatsoever should present itself unto his enemy must necessarily be utterly defeated: on the other side, deeming it unworthy both his virtue and magnanimity, and the Lacedemonian name, to fail or faint in his charge, between these two extremities he resolved upon a mean and indifferent course, which was this.   The youngest and best disposed of his troop

---

[1] the quality of porterly-rascal = the special characteristic of the low menial
[2] good physical condition   [3] rivalry
[4] Leonidas his discomfiture = Leonidas's discomfiture

he reserved for the service and defence of their country, to which he sent them back; and with those whose loss was least, and who might best be spared, he determined to maintain that passage, and by their death to force the enemy to purchase the entrance of it as dear as possibly he could; as indeed it followed. For being suddenly environed round by the Arcadians, after a great slaughter made of them, both himself and all his were put to the sword. Is any trophy assigned for conquerors that is not more duly due unto these conquered? A true conquest respecteth rather an undanted resolution, an honorable end, than a fair escape, and the honor of virtue doth more consist in combating than in beating.

But to return to our history, these prisoners, howsoever they are dealt withal, are so far from yielding, that contrariwise, during two or three months that they are kept, they ever carry a cheerful countenance, and urge their keepers to hasten their trial; they outrageously defy and injure them. They upbraid them with their cowardliness, and with the number of battles they have lost again[1] theirs. I have a song made by a prisoner, wherein is this clause, Let them boldly come altogether, and flock in multitudes, to feed on him; for with him they shall feed upon their fathers and grandfathers, that heretofore have served his body for food and nourishment: "These muscles," saith he, "this flesh, and these veins, are your own; fond[2] men as you are, know you not that the substance of your forefathers' limbs is yet tied unto ours? Taste them well, for in them shall you find the relish of your own flesh:" an invention that hath no show of barbarism. Those that paint them dying, and that represent this action when they are put to execution, delineate the prisoners spitting in their executioners' faces, and making mows[3] at them. Verily, so long as breath is in their body they never cease to brave and defy them, both in speech and countenance. Surely, in respect of us these are very savage men: for either they must be so in good sooth, or we must be so indeed; there is a wondrous distance between their form and ours.

Their men have many wives, and by how much more they are reputed valiant, so much the greater is their number. The manner and beauty in their marriages is wondrous strange and

[1] against   [2] foolish   [3] grimaces

remarkable; for, the same jealousy our wives have to keep us from the love and affection of other women, the same have theirs to procure it. Being more careful for their husbands' honor and content than of any thing else, they endeavor and apply all their industry to have as many rivals as possibly they can, forasmuch as it is a testimony of their husbands' virtue. Our women would count it a wonder, but it is not so: it is virtue properly matrimonial, but of the highest kind. And in the Bible, Leah, Rachel, Sarah, and Iacob's wives brought their fairest maiden servants unto their husbands' beds. And Livia seconded the lustful appetites of Augustus to her great prejudice. And Stratonica, the wife of King Deiotarus, did not only bring a most beauteous chamber-maid, that served her, to her husband's bed, but very carefully brought up the children he begot on her, and by all possible means aided and furthered them to succeed in their father's royalty.

And lest a man should think that all this is done by a simple and servile or awful duty unto their custom, and by the impression of their ancient custom's authority, without discourse [1] or judgment, and because they are so blockish and dull-spirited that they can take no other resolution, it is not amiss we allege some evidence of their sufficiency. Besides what I have said of one of their warlike songs, I have another amorous canzonet, which beginneth in this sense: "Adder stay, stay good adder, that my sister may by the pattern of thy parti-colored coat draw the fashion and work of a rich lace, for me to give unto my love; so may thy beauty, thy nimbleness or disposition be ever preferred before all other serpents." The first couplet is the burthen of the song. I am so conversant with poesy that I may judge this invention hath no barbarism at all in it, but is altogether Anacreontic. Their language is a kind of pleasant speech, and hath a pleasing sound, and some affinity with the Greek terminations.

Three of that nation, ignorant how dear the knowledge of our corruptions will one day cost their repose, security, and happiness, and how their ruin shall proceed from this commerce, which I imagine is already well advanced (miserable as they are to have suffered themselves to be so cozened by a desire of new-

[1] thought, reasoning

fangled novelties, and to have quit the calmness of their climate to come and see ours), were at Rouen in the time of our late King Charles the Ninth, who talked with them a great while. They were showed our fashions, our pomp, and the form of a fair city; afterward some demanded their advice, and would needs know of them what things of note and admirable they had observed amongst us: they answered three things, the last of which I have forgotten, and am very sorry for it; the other two I yet remember. They said, first, they found it very strange that so many tall men with long beards, strong and well armed, as it were about the King's person (it is very likely they meant the Switzers of his guard), would submit themselves to obey a beardless child, and that we did not rather choose one amongst them to command the rest. Secondly, (they have a manner of phrase whereby they call men but a moity [1] one of another) they had perceived there were men amongst us full gorged with all sorts of commodities, and others which, hunger-starved and bare with need and poverty, begged at their gates: and found it strange these moities so needy could endure such an injustice, and that they took not the others by the throat, or set fire on their houses.

I talked a good while with one of them, but I had so bad an interpreter, and who did so ill apprehend my meaning, and who through his foolishness was so troubled to conceive my imaginations, that I could draw no great matter from him. Touching that point wherein I demanded of him what good he received by the superiority he had amongst his countrymen (for he was a captain, and our mariners called him King), he told me it was to march foremost in any charge of war: further, I asked him how many men did follow him; he showed me a distance of place, to signify they were as many as might be contained in so much ground, which I guessed to be about four or five thousand men: moreover, I demanded if, when wars were ended, all his authority expired; he answered that he had only this left him, which was that when he went on progress, and visited the villages depending of him, the inhabitants prepared paths and highways athwart the hedges of their woods, for him to pass through at ease. All that is not very ill; but what of that? They wear no kind of breeches nor hosen.

[1] half, part

ROGER ASCHAM

A PREFACE TO THE READER [1]

WHEN the great plague was at London, the year 1563, the
Queen's Majesty, Queen Elizabeth, lay at her castle of Wind-
sor, where, upon the tenth day of December, it fortuned that
in Sir William Cecil's chamber, her Highness's principal secretary, there dined togither these personages: Mr. Secretary
himself, Sir William Peter, Sir J. Mason, D. Wotton, Sir Richard Sackville, treasurer of the exchequer, Sir Walter Mildmay,
chancellor of the exchequer, Mr. Haddon, master of requests,
Mr. John Astley, master of the jewel house, Mr. Bernard
Hampton, Mr. Nicasius, and I. Of which number the most
part were of her Majesty's most honorable Privy Council, and
the rest serving her in very good place. I was glad then, and
do rejoice yet to remember, that my chance was so happy to be
there that day, in the company of so many wise and good men
togither, as hardly then could have been picked out again out
of all England beside.

Mr. Secretary hath this accustomed manner, though his
head be never so full of most weighty affairs of the realm, yet
at dinner time he doth seem to lay them always aside; and
findeth ever fit occasion to talk pleasantly of other matters, but
most gladly of some matter of learning, wherein he will courteously hear the mind of the meanest at his table.

Not long after our sitting down, "I have strange news
brought me," saith Mr. Secretary, "this morning, that divers
scholars of Eton be run away from the school for fear of beating." Whereupon, Mr. Secretary took occasion to wish that
some more discretion were in many schoolmasters, in using
correction, than commonly there is. Who many times punish
rather the weakness of nature than the fault of the scholar.
Whereby many scholars, that might else prove well, be driven
to hate learning before they know what learning meaneth; and

[1] From *The Schoolmaster* (1570).

so are made willing to forsake their book, and be glad to be put to any other kind of living.

Mr. Peter, as one somewhat severe of nature, said plainly that the rod only was the sword that must keep the school in obedience, and the scholar in good order. Mr. Wotton, a man mild of nature, with soft voice and few words, inclined to Mr. Secretary's judgment, and said, "In mine opinion, the school-house should be in deed, as it is called by name, the house of play and pleasure, and not of fear and bondage; and, as I do remember, so saith Socrates in one place of Plato. And therefore, if a rod carry the fear of a sword, it is no marvel if those that be fearful of nature choose rather to forsake the play than to stand always within the fear of a sword in a fond [1] man's handling."

Mr. Mason, after his manner, was very merry with both parties, pleasantly playing both with the shrewd touches of many courste [2] boys, and with the small discretion of many lewd [3] schoolmasters. Mr. Haddon was fully of Mr. Peter's opinion, and said that the best schoolmaster of our time was the greatest beater, and named the person.[4] "Though," quoth I, "it was his good fortune to send from his school unto the University one of the best scholars indeed of all our time, yet wise men do think that that came so to pass rather by the great towardness of the scholar than by the great beating of the master: and whether this be true or no, you yourself are best witness." I said somewhat farder in the matter, how and why young children were sooner allured by love than driven by beating, to attain good learning; wherein I was the bolder to say my mind, because Mr. Secretary courteously provoked me thereunto; or else in such a company, and namely,[5] in his presence, my wont is to be more willing to use mine ears, than to occupy my tongue.

Sir Walter Mildmay, Mr. Astley, and the rest said very little;

---

[1] foolish

[2] shrewd touches of many courste boys = naughty traits of many mischievous boys

[3] ignorant

[4] i.e., Nicholas Udall, master of Eton and author of *Ralph Roister Doister*.

[5] especially

only Sir Rich. Sackville said nothing at all.   After dinner, I
went up to read with the Queen's Majesty.   We read then togither in the Greek tongue, as I well remember, that noble oration of Demosthenes against Aeschines, for his false dealing in
his ambassage to king Philip of Macedonie.   Sir Rich. Sackville came up soon after; and finding me in her Majesty's privy
chamber, he took me by the hand, and carrying me to a window, said: "Mr. Ascham, I would not for a good deal of money
have been this day absent from dinner.   Where, though I said
nothing, yet I gave as good ear, and do consider as well the talk
that passed, as any one did there.   Mr. Secretary said very
wisely, and most truly, that many young wits be driven to
hate learning before they know what learning is.   I can be
good witness to this myself; for a fond schoolmaster, before I
was fully fourteen years old, drave me so, with fear of beating,
from all love of learning, as now, when I know what difference
it is to have learning and to have little or none at all, I feel it my
greatest grief, and find it my greatest hurt that ever came to
me, that it was my so ill chance to light upon so lewd a schoolmaster.   But seeing it is but in vain to lament things past, and
also wisdom to look to things to come, surely, God willing, if God
lend me life, I will make this my mishap some occasion of good
hap to little Robert Sackville, my son's son.   For whose bringing up I would gladly, if it so please you, use specially your good
advice.   I hear say you have a son much of his age; we will deal
thus together.   Point you out a schoolmaster, who by your
order shall teach my son and yours, and for all the rest I will
provide, yea though they three do cost me a couple of hundred
pounds by year; and beside, you shall find me as fast a friend to
you and yours as perchance any you have."   Which promise
the worthy gentleman surely kept with me, until his dying
day.

We had then farther talk togither of bringing up of children,
of the nature of quick and hard wits, of the right choice of a
good wit, of fear and love in teaching children.   We passed
from children and came to young men, namely gentlemen: we
talked of their too much liberty to live as they lust; of their
letting loose too soon to overmuch experience of ill, contrary to
the good order of many good old commonwealths of the Per-

sians and Greeks; of wit gathered and good fortune gotten by some only by experience, without learning. And, lastly, he required of me very earnestly to show what I thought of the common going of Englishmen into Italy. "But," saith he, "because this place and this time will not suffer so long talk as these good matters require, therefore I pray you, at my request, and at your leisure, put in some order of writing the chief points of this our talk concerning the right order of teaching, and honesty of living, for the good bringing up of children and young men. And surely, beside contenting me, you shall both please and profit very many others." I made some excuse by lack of ability, and weakness of body: "Well," saith he, "I am not now to learn what you can do. Our dear friend, good Mr. Goodricke, whose judgment I could well believe, did once for all satisfy me fully therein. Again, I heard you say, not long ago, that you may thank Sir John Cheke for all the learning you have; and I know very well myself that you did teach the Queen. And therefore, seeing God did so bless you, to make you the scholar of the best master, and also the schoolmaster of the best scholar, that ever were in our time, surely you should please God, benefit your country, and honest your own name, if you would take the pains to impart to others what you learned of such a master, and how ye taught such a scholar. And in uttering[1] the stuff ye received of the one, in declaring the order ye took with the other, ye shall never lack neither matter nor manner, what to write nor how to write, in this kind of argument."[2]

I, beginning some farther excuse, suddenly was called to come to the Queen. The night following, I slept little, my head was so full of this our former talk, and I so mindful somewhat to satisfy the honest request of so dear a friend. I thought to prepare some little treatise for a new year's gift that Christmas. But, as it chanceth to busy builders, so in building this my poor schoolhouse (the rather because the form of it is somewhat new, and differing from others), the work rose daily higher and wider than I thought it would at the beginning.

And though it appear now, and be in very deed, but a small

[1] displaying (properly = expose for sale)   [2] subject

cottage, poor for the stuff and rude for the workmanship; yet, in going forward, I found the site so good as I was loth to give it over; but the making so costly, outreaching my ability, as many times I wished that some one of those three, my dear friends with full purses, Sir Tho. Smith, Mr. Haddon, or Mr. Watson, had had the doing of it. Yet, nevertheless, I myself spending gladly that little that I got at home by good Sir John Cheke, and that that I borrowed abroad of my friend Sturmius, beside somewhat that was left me in reversion by my old masters, Plato, Aristotle, and Cicero, I have at last patched it up, as I could, and as you see. If the matter be mean, and meanly handled, I pray you bear both with me and it; for never work went up in worse weather, with moe lets and stops, than this poor schoolhouse of mine. Westminster Hall can bear some witness, beside much weakness of body, but more trouble of mind, by some such sores as grieve me to touch them myself, and therefore I purpose not to open them to others. And in mids of outward injuries and inward cares, to increase them withal, good Sir Rich. Sackville dieth, that worthy gentleman; that earnest favorer and furtherer of God's true religion; that faithful servitor to his prince and country; a lover of learning and all learned men; wise in all doings; courteous to all persons; showing spite to none; doing good to many; and as I well found, to me so fast a friend as I never lost the like before. When he was gone, my heart was dead. There was not one that wore a black gown for him, who carried a heavier heart for him than I. When he was gone, I cast this book away: I could not look upon it but with weeping eyes, in remembering him who was the only setter on to do it, and would have been not only a glad commender of it, but also a sure and certain comfort to me and mine for it.

Almost two years togither this book lay scattered and neglected, and had been quite given over of me, if the goodness of one had not given me some life and spirit again. God, the mover of goodness, prosper always him and his, as he hath many times comforted me and mine, and, I trust to God, shall comfort more and more. Of whom most justly I may say, and very oft and always gladly I am wont to say, that sweet verse of Sophocles, spoken by Œdipus to worthy Theseus:

῎Εχω[γὰρ] ἄχω διὰ σὲ κοὐκ ἄλλον βροτῶν.[1]

This hope hath helped me to end this book; which, if he allow,[2] I shall think my labors well employed, and shall not much esteem the misliking of any others. And I trust he shall think the better of it, because he shall find the best part thereof to come out of his school whom he of all men loved and liked best.

Yet some men, friendly enough of nature, but of small judgment in learning, do think I take too much pains, and spend too much time, in setting forth these children's affairs. But those good men were never brought up in Socrates's school, who saith plainly that no man goeth about a more godly purpose than he that is mindful of the good bringing up both of his own and other men's children.

Therefore, I trust good and wise men will think well of this my doing. And of other, that think otherwise, I will think myself they are but men to be pardoned for their folly and pitied for their ignorance.

In writing this book, I have had earnest respect to three special points, troth of religion, honesty in living, right order in learning. In which three ways I pray God my poor children may diligently walk; for whose sake, as nature moved and reason required, and necessity also somewhat compelled, I was the willinger to take these pains.

For, seeing at my death I am not like to leave them any great store of living, therefore in my life time I thought good to bequeath unto them, in this little book, as in my will and testament, the right way to good learning; which if they follow, with the fear of God, they shall very well come to sufficiency of living.

I wish also, with all my heart, that young Mr. Rob. Sackville may take that fruct of this labor that his worthy grauntfather purposed he should have done: and if any other do take either profit or pleasure hereby, they have cause to thank Mr. Robert Sackville, for whom especially this my Schoolmaster was provided.

And one thing I would have the reader consider in reading this book, that, because no schoolmaster hath charge of any

[1] "For all I have I owe to thee and to no other mortal." *Œdipus at Colonus*, 1129.

[2] approve

child before he enter into his school, therefore, I leaving all former care of their good bringing up to wise and good parents, as a matter not belonging to the schoolmaster, I do appoint this my Schoolmaster then and there to begin, where his office and charge beginneth. Which charge lasteth not long, but until the scholar be made able to go to the university, to proceed in logic, rhetoric, and other kinds of learning.

Yet if my Schoolmaster, for love he beareth to his scholar, shall teach him somewhat for his furtherance and better judgment in learning, that may serve him seven year after in the university, he doth his scholar no more wrong, nor deserveth no worse name thereby, than he doth in London who, selling silk or cloth unto his friend, doth give him better measure than either his promise or bargain was.

Farewell in Christ.

FRANCIS BACON

OF BOLDNESS [1]

I⊤ is a trivial grammar school text, but yet worthy a wise man's consideration. Question was asked of Demosthenes, what was the chief part of an orator? He answered, "Action": what next? "Action": what next again? "Action." He said it that knew it best, and had by nature, himself, no advantage in that he commended. A strange thing, that that part of an orator which is but superficial, and rather the virtue of a player, should be placed so high, above those other noble parts, of invention, elocution, and the rest; nay almost alone, as if it were all in all. But the reason is plain. There is in human nature generally more of the fool than of the wise; and therefore those faculties by which the foolish part of men's minds is taken are most potent. Wonderful like is the case of boldness in civil business; what first? boldness: what second and third? boldness. And yet boldness is a child of ignorance and baseness, far inferior to other parts. But nevertheless it doth fascinate and bind hand and foot those that are either shallow in judgment or weak in courage, which are the greatest part; yea and prevaileth with wise men at weak times. Therefore we see it hath done wonders in popular states; but with senates and princes less; and more ever upon the first entrance of bold persons into action than soon after; for boldness is an ill keeper of promise. Surely, as there are mountebanks for the natural body, so are there mountebanks for the politic body: men that undertake great cures, and perhaps have been lucky in two or three experiments, but want the grounds of science, and therefore cannot hold out. Nay, you shall see a bold fellow many times do Mahomet's miracle. Mahomet made the people believe that he would call an hill to him, and from the top of it offer up his prayers for the observers of his law. The people assembled; Mahomet called the hill to come to him, again and

[1] The three essays which follow are from *Essays or Counsels, Civil and Moral* (1625).

again; and when the hill stood still, he was never a whit abashed, but said, "If the hill will not come to Mahomet, Mahomet will go to the hill." So these men, when they have promised great matters and failed most shamefully, yet (if they have the perfection of boldness) they will but slight it over, and make a turn, and no more ado. Certainly, to men of great judgment bold persons are a sport to behold; nay, and to the vulgar also boldness hath somewhat of the ridiculous. For if absurdity be the subject of laughter, doubt you not but great boldness is seldom without some absurdity. Especially it is a sport to see when a bold fellow is out of countenance; for that puts his face into a most shrunken and wooden posture; as needs it must; for in bashfulness the spirits do a little go and come; but with bold men, upon like occasion, they stand at a stay; like a stale at chess, where it is no mate, but yet the game cannot stir. But this last were fitter for a satire than for a serious observation. This is well to be weighed: that boldness is ever blind; for it seeth not dangers and inconveniences. Therefore it is ill in counsel, good in execution: so that the right use of bold persons is, that they never command in chief, but be seconds, and under the direction of others. For in counsel it is good to see dangers; and in execution not to see them, except they be very great.

OF TRAVEL

TRAVEL, in the younger sort, is a part of education; in the elder, a part of experience. He that traveleth into a country before he hath some entrance into the language, goeth to school, and not to travel. That young men travel under some tutor or grave servant I allow [1] well; so that he be such a one that hath the language and hath been in the country before; whereby he may be able to tell them what things are worthy to be seen in the country where they go; what acquaintances they are to seek; what exercises or disciplines the place yieldeth. For else young men shall go hooded,[2] and look abroad little. It is a strange thing that in sea voyages, where there is nothing to be seen but sky and sea, men should make diaries; but in land

[1] approve   [2] blindfold (a metaphor from falconry)

*devoid of personal inform-
ation*

travel, wherein so much is to be observed, for the most part they omit it; as if chance were fitter to be registered than observation. Let diaries, therefore, be brought in use. The things to be seen and observed are: the courts of princes, specially when they give audience to ambassadors; the courts of justice, while they sit and hear causes; and so of consistories ecclesiastic; the churches and monasteries, with the monuments which are therein extant; the walls and fortifications of cities and towns, and so the havens and harbors; antiquities and ruins; libraries; colleges, disputations, and lectures, where *Politics* any are; shipping and navies; houses and gardens of state and pleasure, near great cities; armories; arsenals; magazines; exchanges; burses; [1] warehouses; exercises of horsemanship, fencing, training of soldiers and the like; comedies, such whereunto the better sort of persons do resort; treasuries of jewels and robes; cabinets and rarities; and, to conclude, whatsoever is memorable in the places where they go. After all which the tutors or servants ought to make diligent inquiry. As for triumphs,[2] masks, feasts, weddings, funerals, capital executions, and such shows, men need not to be put in mind of them; yet are they not to be neglected. If you will have a young man to put his travel into a little room, and in short time to gather much, this you must do. First, as was said, he must have some entrance into the language before he goeth. Then he must have such a servant or tutor as knoweth the country, as was likewise said. Let him carry with him also some card or book describing the country where he traveleth; which will be a good key to his inquiry. Let him keep also a diary. Let him not stay long in one city or town; more or less as the place deserveth, but not long; nay, when he stayeth in one city or town, let him change his lodging from one end and part of the town to another; which is a great adamant [3] of acquaintance. Let him sequester himself from the company of his countrymen, and diet in such places where there is good company of the nation where he traveleth. I ʼhim, upon his removes from one place to another, procure re   nmendation to some person of quality residing in the place v   ther he removeth; that he may use his

---

[1] exchanges [2]   orate processions or festivities
[3] loadstone or magnet

favor in those things he desireth to see or know. Thus he may abridge his travel with much profit. As for the acquaintance which is to be sought in travel: that which is most of all profitable is acquaintance with the secretaries and employed men of ambassadors; for so in traveling in one country he shall suck the experience of many. Let him also see and visit eminent persons in all kinds which are of great name abroad; that he may be able to tell how the life agreeth with the fame. For quarrels, they are with care and discretion to be avoided: they are commonly for mistresses, healths,[1] place, and words. And let a man beware how he keepeth company with choleric and quarrelsome persons; for they will engage him into their own quarrels. When a traveler returneth home, let him not leave the countries where he hath traveled altogether behind him, but maintain a correspondence by letters with those of his acquaintance which are of most worth. And let his travel appear rather in his discourse than in his apparel or gesture; and in his discourse let him be rather advised [2] in his answers than forwards to tell stories; and let it appear that he doth not change his country manners for those of foreign parts; but only prick in some flowers of that he hath learned abroad into the customs of his own country.

OF DISPATCH

AFFECTED dispatch is one of the most dangerous things to business that can be. It is like that which the physicians call *predigestion*, or hasty digestion; which is sure to fill the body full of crudities and secret seeds of diseases. Therefore measure not dispatch by the times of sitting, but by the advancement of the business. And as in races it is not the large stride or high lift that makes the speed, so in business the keeping close to the matter, and not taking of it too much at once, procureth dispatch. It is the care of some only to come off speedily for the time; or to contrive some false periods of business because [3] they may seem men of dispatch. But it is one thing to abbreviate by contracting, another by cutting off: and business so

---

[1] *i.e.*, refusal to drink healths
[2] circumspect, cautious   [3] in order that

handled at several sittings or meetings goeth commonly backward and forward in an unsteady manner.

I knew a wise man that had it for a by-word, when he saw men hasten to a conclusion, "Stay a little, that we may make an end the sooner." [1]

On the other side, true dispatch is a rich thing. For time is the measure of business, as money is of wares; and business is bought at a dear hand where there is small dispatch. The Spartans and Spaniards have been noted to be of small dispatch; *Mi venga la muerte de Spagna*: [2] "Let my death come from Spain"; for then it will be sure to be long in coming.

Give good hearing to those that give the first information in business; and rather direct them in the beginning, than interrupt them in the continuance of their speeches; for he that is put out of his own order will go forward and backward, and be more tedious while he waits upon his memory, than he could have been if he had gone on in his own course. But sometimes it is seen that the moderator is more troublesome than the actor.

Iterations are commonly loss of time. But there is no such gain of time as to iterate often the state of the question; for it chaseth away many a frivolous speech as it is coming forth. Long and curious speeches are as fit for dispatch as a robe or mantle with a long train is for race. Prefaces, and passages,[3] and excusations, and other speeches of reference to the person, are great wastes of time; and though they seem to proceed of modesty, they are bravery.[4] Yet beware of being too material [5] when there is any impediment or obstruction in men's wills; for preoccupation of mind ever requireth preface of speech, like a fomentation to make the unguent enter.

Above all things, order, and distribution, and singling out of parts, is the life of dispatch; so as the distribution be not too subtle: for he that doth not divide will never enter well into business; and he that divideth too much will never come out of

---

[1] "Sir Amice Pawlet, when he saw too much haste made in any matter, was wont to say, *Stay a while, that we may make an end the sooner.*" Bacon: *Apophthegmes New and Old.*

[2] This proverb is a mixture of Italian and Spanish. It is an Italian saying and should read, *Mi venga la morte di Spagna.*

[3] digressions   [4] ostentation   [5] full of matter

it clearly. To choose time is to save time; and an unseasonable motion is but beating the air. There be three parts of business: the preparation, the debate or examination, and the perfection. Whereof, if you look for dispatch, let the middle only be the work of many, and the first and last the work of few. The proceeding upon somewhat conceived in writing doth for the most part facilitate dispatch; for though it should be wholly rejected, yet that negative is more pregnant of direction than an indefinite, as ashes are more generative than dust.

SIR THOMAS OVERBURY

A DEVILISH USURER [1]

Is sowed as cummin or hempseed, with curses, and he thinks he
thrives the better. He is better read in the penal statutes
than the Bible, and his evil angel persuades him he shall
sooner be saved by them. He can be no man's friend, for all
men he hath most interest in he undoes. And a double dealer
he is certainly, for by his good will he ever takes the forfeit.
He puts his money to the unnatural act of generation, and his
scrivener is the supervisor bawd to it. Good deeds he loves
none, but sealed and delivered; nor doth he wish anything to
thrive in the country but beehives, for they make him wax
rich. He hates all but law-Latin, yet thinks he might be
drawn to love a scholar, could he reduce the year to a shorter
compass, that his use money [2] might come in the faster. He
seems to be the son of a jailor, for all his estate is most heavy
and cruel bonds. He doth not give, but sell, days of payment,
and those at the rate of a man's undoing. He doth only fear
the Day of Judgment should fall sooner than the payment of
some great sum of money due to him. He removes his lodging
when a subsidy [3] comes; and if he be found out, and pay it, he
grumbles treason: but 'tis in such a deformed silence as witches
raise their spirits in. Gravity he pretends in all things but in
his private whore, for he will not in a hundred pound take one
light sixpence. And it seems he was at Tilbury Camp, for you
must not tell him of a Spaniard. He is a man of no conscience,
for (like the Jakes-farmer that swounded with going into Bucklersbury [4]) he falls into a cold sweat if he but look into the

---

[1] From *Characters; or Witty Descriptions of the Properties of Sundry Persons*,
included in the Second (1614) and subsequent editions of Overbury's poem,
A Wife. Not all the " Characters " are by Overbury. *A Devilish Usurer*,
which is not in the original group of sketches, is reprinted from the seventh
edition of *A Wife*, etc., 1616.

[2] interest   [3] tax

[4] Bucklersbury was a London street containing many druggists' shops and
hence permeated with perfumes.

Chancery; thinks, in his religion, we are in the right for every-thing, if that were abolished. He hides his money as if he thought to find it again at last day, and then begin's old trade with it. His clothes plead prescription, and whether they or his body are more rotten is a question. Yet, should he live to be hanged in them, this good they would do him: the very hangman would pity his case.[1] The table he keeps is able to starve twenty tall [2] men. His servants have not their living but their dying from him, and that's of hunger. A spare diet he commends in all men but himself. He comes to cathedrals only for love of the singing-boys, because they look hungry. He likes our religion best because 'tis best cheap,[3] yet would fain allow of purgatory, cause 'twas of his trade, and brought in so much money. His heart goes with the same snaphance [4] his purse doth: 'tis seldom open to any man. Friendship he ac-counts but a word without any signification; nay, he loves all the world so little, that an it were possible, he would make himself his own executor. For certain, he is made adminis-trator to his own good name while he is in perfect memory, for that dies long afore him; but he is so far from being at the charge of a funeral for it, that he lets it stink above ground. In conclusion, for neighbourhood you were better dwell by a contentious lawyer. And for his death, 'tis rather surfeit, the pox, or despair; for seldom such as he die of God's making, as honest men should do.

[1] A quibble on " case " = (1) situation (2) what encases him, *i.e.*, his clothing, which was a perquisite of the hangman.

[2] sturdy, vigorous, brave

[3] best cheap = best bargain, cheapest   [4] spring catch

JOHN EARLE

A CHILD [1]

Is a man in a small letter, yet the best copy of Adam before he tasted of Eve or the apple; and he is happy whose small practice in the world can only write this character. He is nature's fresh picture newly drawn in oil, which time and much handling dims and defaces. His soul is yet a white paper unscribbled with observations of the world, wherewith at length it becomes a blurred note-book. He is purely happy, because he knows no evil, nor hath made means by sin to be acquainted with misery. He arrives not at the mischief of being wise, nor endures evils to come by foreseeing them. He kisses and loves all, and when the smart of the rod is past, smiles on his beater. Nature and his parents alike dandle him, and tice him on with a bait of sugar to a draught of wormwood. He plays yet, like a young prentice the first day, and is not come to his task of melancholy. All the language he speaks yet is tears, and they serve him well enough to express his necessity.[2] His hardest labor is his tongue, as if he were loath to use so deceitful an organ; and he is best company with it when he can but prattle. We laugh at his foolish sports, but his game is our earnest: and his drums, rattles, and hobby-horses, but the emblems and mocking of man's business. His father hath writ him as his own little story, wherein he reads those days of his life that he cannot remember, and sighs to see what innocence he has outlived. The elder he grows, he is a stair lower from God; and, like his first father, much worse in his breeches.[3] He is the Christian's example, and the old man's relapse; the one imitates his pureness, and the other falls into his simplicity. Could he put off his body with his little coat, he had got eternity without a burthen, and exchanged but one heaven for another.

[1] From *Microcosmography; or A Piece of the World Discovered in Essays and Characters* (1628).

[2] This sentence is not in the first edition.

[3] *i.e.*, in morality.

A GOOD OLD MAN [1]

Is the best antiquity, and which we may with least vanity admire. One whom time hath been thus long a working, and like winter fruit, ripened when others are shaken down. He hath taken out as many lessons of the world as days, and learnt the best thing in it, the vanity of it. He looks o'er his former life as a danger well past, and would not hazard himself to begin again. His lust was long broken before his body, yet he is glad this temptation is broke too, and that he is fortified from it by this weakness. The next door of death sads him not, but he expects it calmly as his turn in nature: and fears more his recoiling back to childishness than dust. All men look on him as a common father, and on old age, for his sake, as a reverent thing. His very presence and face puts vice out of countenance, and makes it an indecorum in a vicious man. He practises his experience on youth [2] without the harshness of reproof, and in his counsel is good company. He has some old stories still of his own seeing to confirm what he says, and makes them better in the telling; yet is not troublesome neither with the same tale again, but remembers with them how oft he has told them. His old sayings and morals seem proper to his beard: and the poetry of Cato does well out of his mouth, and he speaks it as if he were the author. He is not apt to put the boy on [3] a younger man, nor the fool on a boy, but can distinguish gravity from a sour look; and the less testy he is, the more regarded. You must pardon him if he like his own times better than these, because those things are follies to him now that were wisdom then: yet he makes us of that opinion too when we see him, and conjecture those times by so good a relic. He is a man capable of a dearness [4] with the youngest men, yet he not youthfuller for them, but they older for him; and no man credits more his acquaintance. He goes away at last too soon whensoever, with all men's sorrow but his own; and his memory is fresh, when it is twice as old.

---

[1] From *Microcosmography*, 5th edition, 1629.
[2] *i.e.*, he gives young people the benefit of his experience
[3] to treat as a boy   [4] fondness, affection

SIR THOMAS BROWNE

A LETTER TO A FRIEND

UPON OCCASION OF THE DEATH OF HIS INTIMATE FRIEND[1]

GIVE me leave to wonder that news of this nature should have such heavy wings, that you should hear so little concerning your dearest friend, and that I must make that unwilling repetition to tell you, *Ad portam rigidos calces extendit*,[2] that he is dead and buried, and by this time no puny among the mighty nations of the dead; for tho he left this world not very many days past, yet every hour you know largely addeth unto that dark society; and considering the incessant mortality of mankind, you cannot conceive there dieth in the whole earth so few as a thousand an hour.

Altho at this distance you had no early account or particular of his death; yet your affection may cease to wonder that you had not some secret sense or intimation thereof by dreams, thoughtful whisperings, mercurisms,[3] airy nuncios[3] or sympathetical insinuations, which many seem to have had at the death of their dearest friends: for since we find in that famous story, that spirits themselves were fain to tell their fellows at a distance that the great Antonio was dead,[4] we have a sufficient excuse for our ignorance in such particulars, and must rest content with the common road and Appian Way of knowledge by information. Tho the uncertainty of the end of this world hath confounded all humane predictions; yet they who shall live to see the sun and moon darkned, and the stars to fall from heaven, will hardly be deceived in the advent of the Last Day; and therefore strange it is, that the common fallacy of con-

---

[1] Published in 1690. Except the glosses of individual words and the translations, the notes which follow are substantially those of the original edition. Some are omitted.

[2] " Toward the door he stretched his stiffened feet."

[3] messages

[4] In Plutarch his *Defect of Oracles*, wherein he relates that a voice was heard crying to mariners at sea, *Great Pan is dead.*

sumptive persons, who feel not themselves dying, and therefore still hope to live, should also reach their friends in perfect
health and judgment.   That you should be so little acquainted
with Plautus's sick complexion, or that almost an Hippocratical
face should not alarum you to higher fears, or rather despair of
his continuation in such an emaciated state, wherein medical
predictions fail not, as sometimes in acute diseases, and wherein
'tis as dangerous to be sentenced by a physician as a judge.

Upon my first visit I was bold to tell them who had not let
fall all hopes of his recovery, that in my sad opinion he was not
like to behold a grasshopper, much less to pluck another fig;
and in no long time after seemed to discover that odd mortal
symptom in him not mentioned by Hippocrates, that is, to lose
his own face and look like some of his near relations; for he
maintained not his proper countenance, but looked like his
uncle, the lines of whose face lay deep and invisible in his
healthful visage before: for as from our beginning we run
through variety of looks before we come to consistent and
settled faces, so before our end, by sick and languishing alterations, we put on new visages, and in our retreat to earth may
fall upon such looks which from community of seminal originals
were before latent in us.

He was fruitlessly put in hope of advantage by change of air,
and imbibing the pure aerial nitre of these parts; and therefore
being so far spent, he quickly found Sardinia in Tivoli,[1] and the
most healthful air of little effect, where death had set her broad
arrow;[2] for he lived not unto the middle of May, and confirmed
the observation of Hippocrates of that mortal time of the year
when the leaves of the fig-tree resemble a daw's claw.   He is
happily seated who lives in places whose air, earth, and water,
promote not the infirmities of his weaker parts, or is early removed into regions that correct them.   He that is tabidly inclined [3] were unwise to pass his days in Portugal; cholical per-

---

[1] Nullo fata loco possis excludere: cum mors
Venerit, in medio Tibure Sardinia est.   Mart. IV. lx. 5.
Tivoli was considered a healthful, Sardinia an unhealthful residence.

[2] In the King's forests they set the figure of a broad arrow upon trees that are
to be cut down.

[3] inclined to wasting diseases

sons will find little comfort in Austria or Vienna; he that is
weak-legged must not be in love with Rome, nor an infirm head
with Venice or Paris.   Death hath not only particular stars in
heaven, but malevolent places on earth, which single out our
infirmities, and strike at our weaker parts; in which concern,
passager and migrant birds have the great advantages; who are
naturally constituted for distant habitations, whom no seas nor
places limit, but in their appointed seasons will visit us from
Greenland and Mount Atlas, and, as some think, even from the
Antipodes.[1] *opposite place in the earth*.

Tho we could not have his life, yet we missed not our desires
in his soft departure, which was scarce an expiration; and his
end not unlike his beginning, when the salient point scarce
affords a sensible motion, and his departure so like unto sleep,
that he scarce needed the civil ceremony of closing his eyes;
contrary unto the common way wherein death draws up, sleep
lets fall, the eye-lids.   With what strife and pains we came into
the world we know not; but 'tis commonly no easy matter to
get out of it; yet if it could be made out that such who have
easy nativities have commonly hard deaths, and contrarily, his
departure was so easy that we might justly suspect his birth
was of another nature, and that some Juno sat cross-legged at
his nativity.

Besides his soft death, the incurable state of his disease might
somewhat extenuate [2] your sorrow, who know that monsters
but seldom happen, miracles more rarely, in physic.[3]   Angelus
Victorius gives a serious account of a consumptive, hectical,
phthisical woman, who was suddenly cured by the intercession
of Ignatius.   We read not of any Scripture who in this case
applied unto our Saviour, though some may be contained in
that large expression, that He went about Galilee healing all
manner of sickness, and all manner of diseases.[4]   Amulets,
spells, sigils,[5] and incantations, practised in other diseases, are

margin note: musical effective

[1] Bellonius: *De Avibus.*

[2] lessen

[3] Monstra contingunt in medicina.   Hippoc.: " Strange and rare escapes
there happen sometimes in physic."

[4] Matt. IV. 23.

[5] seals

seldom pretended in this; and we find no sigil in the *Archidoxis* of Paracelsus to cure an extreme consumption or marasmus, which, if other diseases fail, will put a period unto long livers, and at last make dust of all. And therefore the Stoics could not but think that the fiery principle would wear out all the rest, and at last make an end of the world, which notwithstanding without such a lingring period the Creator may effect at his pleasure: and to make an end of all things on earth, and our planetical system of the world, He need but put out the sun.

I was not so curious to entitle the stars unto any concern of his death, yet could not but take notice that he died when the moon was in motion from the meridian; at which time, an old Italian long ago would persuade me, that the greatest part of men died; but herein I confess I could never satisfy my curiosity; although from the time of tides in places upon or near the sea there may be considerable deductions; and Pliny [1] hath an odd and remarkable passage concerning the death of men and animals upon the recess or ebb of the sea. However, certain it is he died in the dead and deep part of the night, when Nox might be most apprehensibly said to be the daughter of Chaos, the mother of Sleep and Death, according to old genealogy; and so went out of this world about that hour when our blessed Saviour entered it, and about what time many conceive he will return again unto it. Cardan hath a peculiar and no hard observation from a man's hand, to know whether he was born in the day or night, which I confess holdeth in my own. And Scaliger to that purpose hath another from the tip of the ear: [2] most men are begotten in the night, most animals in the day; but whether more persons have been born in the night or the day, were a curiosity [3] undecidable, tho more have perished by violent deaths in the day; yet in natural dissolutions both times may hold an indifferency, at least but contingent inequality. The whole course of time runs out in the nativity and

---

[1] Aristoteles nullum animal nisi æstu recedente expirare affirmat; observatum id multum in Gallico Oceano et duntaxat in homine compertum. Pliny: *Natural History*, II.

[2] Auris pars pendula lobus dicitur, non omnibus ea pars est auribus; non enim iis qui noctu nati sunt, sed qui interdiu, maxima ex parte. *Com. in Aristot. de Animal*, lib. I.

[3] a nice point

death of things; which whether they happen by succession or coincidence, are best computed by the natural, not artificial day.

That Charles the Fifth was crowned upon the day of his nativity, it being in his own power so to order it, makes no singular animadversion; [1] but that he should also take King Francis prisoner upon that day, was an unexpected coincidence, which made the same remarkable. Antipater, who had an anniversary feast every year upon his birthday, needed no astrological revolution to know what day he should die on. When the fixed stars have made a revolution unto the points from whence they first set out, some of the ancients thought the world would have an end; which was a kind of dying upon the day of its nativity. Now the disease prevailing and swiftly advancing about the time of his nativity, some were of opinion that he would leave the world on the day he entred into it; but this being a lingring disease, and creeping softly on, nothing critical was found or expected, and he died not before fifteen days after. Nothing is more common with infants than to die on the day of their nativity, to behold the worldly hours and but the fractions thereof; and even to perish before their nativity, in the hidden world of the womb, and before their good angel is conceived to undertake them. But in persons who outlive many years, and when there are no less than three hundred and sixty-five days to determine [2] their lives in every year; that the first day should make the last, that the tail of the snake should return into its mouth precisely at that time, and they should wind up upon the day of their nativity,[3] is indeed a remarkable coincidence, which tho astrology hath taken witty pains to salve, yet hath it been very wary in making predictions of it.[4]

In this consumptive condition and remarkable extenuation [5] he came to be almost half himself, and left a great part behind him which he carried not to the grave. And tho that story of Duke John Ernestus Mansfield [6] be not so easily swallowed, that at his death his heart was found not to be so big as a nut;

---

[1] thing to notice   [2] end
[3] According to the Egyptian hieroglyphic.
[4] Browne himself died on his seventy-sixth birthday.
[5] loss of flesh   [6] Turkish history

yet if the bones of a good skeleton weigh little more than twenty pounds, his inwards and flesh remaining could make no bouffage,[1] but a light bit for the grave. I never more lively beheld the starved characters of Dante [2] in any living face; an aruspex might have read a lecture upon him without exenteration,[3] his flesh being so consumed that he might, in a manner, have discerned his bowels without opening of him: so that to be carried *sextâ cervice* [4] to the grave was but a civil unnecessity; and the complements of the coffin might outweigh the subject of it.

Omnibonus Ferrarius [5] in mortal dysenteries of children looks for a spot behind the ear; in consumptive diseases some eye the complexion of moles; Cardan eagerly views the nails, some the lines of the hand, the thenar or muscle of the thumb; some are so curious as to observe the depth of the throat-pit, how the proportion varieth of the small of the legs unto the calf, or the compass of the neck unto the circumference of the head: but all these, with many more, were so drowned in a mortal visage and last face of Hippocrates, that a weak physiognomist might say at first eye, this was a face of earth, and that Morta [6] had set her hard-seal upon his temples, easily perceiving what *caricatura* [7] draughts Death makes upon pined faces, and unto what an unknown degree a man may live backward.

Tho the beard be only made a distinction of sex and sign of masculine heat by Ulmus,[8] yet the precocity and early growth thereof in him was not to be liked in reference unto long life. Lewis, that virtuous but unfortunate king of Hungary, who lost his life in the battle of Mohacz, was said to be born without a skin, to have bearded at fifteen, and to have shewn some gray hairs about twenty; from whence the diviners conjectured that he would be spoiled of his kingdom, and have but a short life:

[1] satisfying meal [for the hungry grave]

[2] In the poet Dante's description [of an emaciated face. *Purgatorio*, XXIII. 32, 33.]

[3] disemboweling   [4] on the sixth shoulder, *i.e.*, by six bearers

[5] *De Morbis Puerorum*   [6] Morta, the deity of death or fate.

[7] When men's faces are drawn with resemblance to some other animals, the Italians call it, to be drawn *in caricatura*.

[8] Ulmus: *De Usu Barbæ Humanæ*

but hairs make fallible predictions, and many temples early gray have outlived the Psalmist's period.[1] Hairs which have most amused [2] me have not been in the face or head but on the back, and not in men but children, as I long ago observed in that endemial distemper of little children in Languedoc, called the *Morgellons*,[3] wherein they critically [4] break out with harsh hairs on their backs, which takes off the unquiet symptoms of the disease, and delivers them from coughs and convulsions.

The Egyptian mummies that I have seen have had their mouths open, and somewhat gaping, which affordeth a good opportunity to view and observe their teeth, wherein 'tis not easy to find any wanting or decayed: and therefore in Egypt, where one man practised but one operation, or the diseases but of single parts, it must needs be a barren profession to confine unto that of drawing of teeth, and little better than to have been tooth drawer unto King Pyrrhus,[5] who had but two in his head. How the Banyans of India maintain the integrity of those parts, I find not particularly observed; who notwithstanding have an advantage of their preservation by abstaining from all flesh, and employing their teeth in such food unto which they may seem at first framed, from their figure and conformation: but sharp and corroding rheums had so early mouldred those rocks and hardest parts of his fabric, that a man might well conceive that his years were never like to double, or twice tell over his teeth. Corruption had dealt more severely with them, than sepulchral fires and smart flames with those of burnt bodies of old; for in the burnt fragments of urns which I have enquired into, although I seem to find few incisors or shearers, yet the dog teeth and grinders do notably resist those fires.

[Affection had so blinded some of his nearest relations as to retain some hope of a postliminious [6] life, and that he might come to life again, and therefore would not have him coffined

---

[1] The life of a man is three-score and ten.

[2] puzzled, perplexed

[3] See Picotus: *De Rheumatismo*

[4] at the crisis of the disease

[5] His upper and lower jaw being solid, and without distinct rows of teeth.

[6] by way of appendix or epilogue (opposite of *preliminary*)

before the third day. Some such Virbiuses,[1] I confess, we find in story, and one or two I remember myself, but they lived not long after. Some contingent reanimations are to be hoped in diseases wherein the lamp of life is but puffed out and seemingly choked, and not where the oil is quite spent and exhausted. Though Nonnus will have it a fever, yet of what diseases Lazarus first died is uncertain from the text, as his second death from good authentic history; but since some persons conceived to be dead do sometimes return again unto evidence of life, that miracle was wisely managed by our Saviour; for had he not been dead four days and under corruption, there had not wanted enough who would have cavilled the same, which the Scripture now puts out of doubt: and tradition also confirmeth that he lived thirty years after, and being pursued by the Jews, came by sea into Provence, by Marseilles, with Mary Magdalen, Maximinus, and others; where remarkable places carry their names unto this day. But to arise from the grave to return again unto it, is but an uncomfortable reviction.[2] Few men would be content to cradle it once again; except a man can lead his second life better than the first, a man may be doubly condemned for living evilly twice, which were but to make the second death in Scripture the third, and to accumulate in the punishment of two bad livers at the last day. To have performed the duty of corruption in the grave, to live again as far from sin as death, and arise like our Saviour for ever, are the only satisfactions of well-weighed expectations.][3]

In the years of his childhood he had languished under the disease of his country, the rickets; after which, notwithstanding, many have become strong and active men; but whether any have attained unto very great years the disease is scarce so old as to afford good observation. Whether the children of the English plantations [4] be subject unto the same infirmity may be worth the observing. Whether lameness and halting do

---

[1] "Virbius[s]es " is a correction of the Bohn library editor's reading "virbiasses" (cf. note 3, below), for which we are indebted to Professor G. L. Kittredge. Virbius, a minor Latin deity, "is said to have been the same as Hippolytus, who was restored to life by Æsclepius."

[2] reconquest, recovery

[3] This paragraph is added from the manuscript, *Sloan 1862*, which contains three other passages not in the original edition.

[4] colonies

still encrease among the inhabitants of Rovigno in Istria I know not; yet scarce twenty years ago Monsieur du Loyr observed that a third part of that people halted: but too certain it is, that the rickets encreaseth among us; the small-pox grows more pernicious than the great: the king's purse knows that the king's evil[1] grows more common. Quartan agues are become no strangers in Ireland; more common and mortal in England: and though the ancients gave that disease very good words, yet now that bell makes no strange sound which rings out for the effects thereof.[2]

Some think there were few consumptions in the old world, when men lived much upon milk; and that the ancient inhabitants of this island were less troubled with coughs when they went naked, and slept in caves and woods, than men now in chambers and feather beds. Plato will tell us that there was no such disease as a catarrh in Homer's time, and that it was but new in Greece in his age. Polydore Virgil delivereth that pleurisies were rare in England, who lived but in the days of Henry the Eighth. Some will allow no diseases to be new, others think that many old ones are ceased, and that such which are esteemed new will have but their time: however, the mercy of God hath scattered the great heap of diseases, and not loaded any one country with all: some may be new in one country which have been old in another. New discoveries of the earth discover new diseases; for besides the common swarm, there are endemial and local infirmities proper unto certain regions, which in the whole earth make no small number; and if Asia, Africa, and America should bring in their list, Pandora's box would swell, and there must be a strange Pathology.

Most men expected to find a consumed kell,[3] empty and bladder-like guts, livid and marbled lungs, and a withered pericardium in this exuccous [4] corpse: but some seemed too much to wonder that two lobes of his lungs adhered unto his side; for the like I had often found in bodies of no suspected consumptions or difficulty of respiration. And the same more often happeneth in men than other animals, and, some think, in women than in men; but the most remarkable I have met with

---

[1] scrofula   [2] Pro febre quartana raro sonat campana.
[3] caul, omentum   [4] dry, sapless

was in a man, after a cough of almost fifty years, in whom all the lobes adhered unto the pleura, and each lobe unto another; who having also been much troubled with the gout, brake the rule of Cardan [1] and died of the stone in the bladder. Aristotle makes a query, why some animals cough as man; some not, as oxen. If coughing be taken as it consisteth of a natural and voluntary motion, including expectoration and spitting out, it may be as proper unto man as bleeding at the nose; otherwise we find that Vegetius and rural writers have not left so many medicines in vain against the coughs of cattle; and men who perish by coughs die the death of sheep, cats, and lions: and though birds have no midriff, yet we meet with divers remedies in Arrianus against the coughs of hawks. And tho it might be thought that all animals who have lungs do cough; yet in cetaceous fishes, who have large and strong lungs, the same is not observed; nor yet in oviparous quadrupeds: and in the greatest thereof, the crocodile, although we read much of their tears, we find nothing of that motion.[2]

From the thoughts of sleep, when the soul was conceived nearest unto divinity, the ancients erected an art of divination, wherein while they too widely expatiated in loose and inconsequent conjectures, Hippocrates [3] wisely considered dreams as they presaged alterations in the body, and so afforded hints toward the preservation of health, and prevention of diseases; and therein was so serious as to advise alteration of diet, exercise, sweating, bathing, and vomiting; and also so religious as to order prayers and supplications unto respective deities: in good dreams unto Sol, Jupiter Cœlestis, Jupiter Opulentus, Minerva, Mercurius, and Apollo; in bad unto Tellus and the Heroes.

And therefore I could not but take notice how his female friends were irrationally curious so strictly to examine his dreams, and in this low state to hope for the fantasms of health. He was now past the healthful dreams of the sun, moon, and stars in their clarity and proper courses. 'Twas too late to dream of flying, of limpid fountains, smooth waters, white

---

[1] Cardan in his *Encomium Podagræ* reckoneth this among the *Dona Podagræ*, that they are delivered thereby from the phthisis and stone in the bladder.

[2] tendency   [3] Hippoc.: *De Insomniis*

vestments, and fruitful green trees, which are the visions of healthful sleeps, and at good distance from the grave.

And they were also too deeply dejected that he should dream of his dead friends, inconsequently divining that he would not be long from them; for strange it was not that he should some-times dream of the dead whose thoughts run always upon death; beside, to dream of the dead, so they appear not in dark habits and take nothing away from us, in Hippocrates his sense was of good signification: for we live by the dead, and every thing is or must be so before it becomes our nourishment. And Cardan, who dreamed that he discoursed with his dead father in the moon, made thereof no mortal interpretation: and even to dream that we are dead was no condemnable fantasm in old oneirocriticism,[1] as having a signification of liberty, vacuity from cares, exemption and freedom from troubles, unknown unto the dead.

Some dreams I confess may admit of easy and feminine ex-position: he who dreamed that he could not see his right shoul-der, might easily fear to lose the sight of his right eye; he that before a journey dreamed that his feet were cut off, had a plain warning not to undertake his intended journey. But why to dream of lettuce should presage some ensuing disease, why to eat figs should signify foolish talk, why to eat eggs great trou-ble, and to dream of blindness should be so highly commended, according to the oneirocritical verses of Astrampsychus and Nicephorus, I shall leave unto your divination.

He was willing to quit the world alone and altogether, leav-ing no earnest [2] behind him for corruption or aftergrave,[3] hav-ing small content in that common satisfaction to survive or live in another, but amply satisfied that his disease should die with himself, nor revive in a posterity, to puzzle physic and make sad mementos of their parent hereditary. Leprosy awakes not sometimes before forty, the gout and stone often later; but

---

[1] interpretation of dreams

[2] earnest = money paid down as a binder, guarantee. The reference is to offspring, left as a sort of hostage to mortality.

[3] "Aftergrave" is possibly an Englishing of a spurious Latin derivative " posthume "(analogy of " exhume," " inhume "). It = subsequent burial (of his posterity), and is loosely equated with " corruption."

consumptive and tabid [1] roots spread more early, and at the fairest make seventeen years of our life doubtful before that age. They that enter the world with original diseases as well as sin, have not only common mortality but sick traductions [2] to destroy them, make commonly short courses, and live not at length but in figures; so that a sound Cæsarean nativity [3] may outlast a natural birth, and a knife may sometimes make way for a more lasting fruit than a midwife; which makes so few infants now able to endure the old test of the river,[4] and many to have feeble children who could scarce have been married at Sparta and those provident states who studied strong and healthful generations; which happen but contingently in mere pecuniary matches, or marriages made by the candle, wherein, notwithstanding, there is little redress to be hoped from an astrologer or a lawyer, and a good discerning physician were like to prove the most successful counsellor.

Julius Scaliger, who in a sleepless fit of the gout could make two hundred verses in a night, would have but five plain words upon his tomb.[5]   And this serious person, though no minor wit, left the poetry of his epitaph unto others; either unwilling to commend himself, or to be judged by a distich, and perhaps considering how unhappy great poets have been in versifying their own epitaphs; wherein Petrarca, Dante, and Ariosto have so unhappily failed, that if their tombs should outlast their works, posterity would find so little of Apollo on them as to mistake them for Ciceronian poets.

In this deliberate and creeping progress unto the grave, he was somewhat too young, and of too noble a mind, to fall upon that stupid symptom observable in divers persons near their journey's end, and which may be reckoned among the mortal symptoms of their last disease; that is, to become more narrow-

---

[1] Tabes maxime contingunt ab anno decimo octavo ad trigesimum quintum. Hippoc. [" The incidence of wasting diseases is chiefly between the eighteenth and the thirty-fifth year."]

[2] inheritance, inherited tendency

[3] A sound child cut out of the body of the mother.

[4] "Durum ab stirpe genus, natos ad flumina primum
Deferimus, saevoque gelu duramus et undis." Virgil: Æneid. IX. 603.

[5] Julii Caesaris Scaligeri quod fuit.   Joseph Scaliger: *In Vita Patris.*

minded, miserable, and tenacious, unready to part with anything when they are ready to part with all, and afraid to want
when they have no time to spend: meanwhile physicians, who
know that many are mad but in a single depraved imagination
and one prevalent decipiency,[1] and that beside and out of such
single deliriums a man may meet with sober actions and good
sense in Bedlam, cannot but smile to see the heirs and concerned relations gratulating themselves in the sober departure
of their friends; and though they behold such mad covetous
passages,[2] content to think they die in good understanding, and
in their sober senses.

Avarice, which is not only infidelity but idolatry,[3] either
from covetous progeny or questuary [4] education, had no root
in his breast, who made good works the expression of his faith,
and was big with desires unto public and lasting charities; and
surely where good wishes and charitable intentions exceed
abilities, theorical beneficency [5] may be more than a dream.
They build not castles in the air who would build churches on
earth: and tho they leave no such structures here, may lay good
foundations in Heaven.   In brief, his life and death were such
that I could not blame them who wished the like, and almost
to have been himself; almost, I say; for tho we may wish the
prosperous appurtenances of others, or to be another in his
happy accidents, yet so intrinsecal is every man unto himself,
that some doubt may be made, whether any would exchange
his being, or substantially [6] become another man.

He had wisely seen the world at home and abroad, and
thereby observed under what variety men are deluded in the
pursuit of that which is not here to be found.   And altho he
had no opinion of reputed felicities below, and apprehended
men widely out in the estimate of such happiness, yet his sober
contempt of the world wrought no Democratism or Cynicism,
no laughing or snarling at it, as well understanding there are
not felicities in this world to satisfy a serious mind; and therefore to soften the stream of our lives, we are fain to take in the

---

[1] hallucination   [2] acts
[3] Colossians, III. 5.   [4] studious of profit
[5] theorical beneficency = public philanthropy
[6] in substance, actually

reputed contentations [1] of this world, to unite with the crowd in their beatitudes,[2] and to make ourselves happy by consortion, opinion, or co-existimation: [3] for strictly to separate from received and customary felicities, and to confine unto the rigor of realities, were to contract the consolation of our beings unto too uncomfortable circumscriptions.

Not to fear death, nor desire it,[4] was short of his resolution: to be dissolved, and be with Christ, was his dying ditty. He conceived his thread long, in no long course of years, and when he had scarce outlived the second life of Lazarus; [5] esteeming it enough to approach the years of his Saviour, who so ordered his own humane state as not to be old upon earth.

But to be content with death may be better than to desire it: a miserable life may make us wish for death, but a virtuous one to rest in it; which is the advantage of those resolved Christians who, looking on death not only as the sting but the period and end of sin, the horizon and isthmus between this life and a better, and the death of this world but as a nativity of another, do contentedly submit unto the common necessity, and envy not Enoch or Elias.

Not to be content with life is the unsatisfactory state of those which destroy themselves; [6] who, being afraid to live, run blindly upon their own death, which no man fears by experience: and the Stoics had a notable doctrine to take away the fear thereof; that is, in such extremities, to desire that which is not to be avoided, and wish what might be feared; and so made evils voluntary and to suit with their own desires, which took off the terror of them.

But the ancient martyrs were not encouraged by such fallacies; who, though they feared not death, were afraid to be their own executioners; and therefore thought it more wisdom

---

[1] satisfactions   [2] (supposed) blessings

[3] by companionship, good reputation, and mutual esteem

[4] Summum nec metuas diem nec optes.

[5] Who upon some accounts, and tradition, is said to have lived thirty years after he was raised by our Saviour. Baronius.

[6] In the speech of Vulteius in Lucan, animating his soldiers in a great struggle to kill one another. — "Decernite Lethum, et metus omnis abest, cupias quodcunque necesse est." "All fear is over, do but resolve to die, and make your desires meet necessity."

to crucify their lusts than their bodies, to circumcise than stab
their hearts, and to mortify than kill themselves.

His willingness to leave this world about that age when most
men think they may best enjoy it, though paradoxical unto
worldly ears, was not strange unto mine, who have so often
observed that many, though old, oft stick fast unto the world,
and seem to be drawn, like Cacus his oxen, backward with great
struggling and reluctancy unto the grave. The long habit of
living makes mere men more hardly to part with life, and all to
be nothing but what is to come. To live at the rate of the old
world, when some could scarce remember themselves young,
may afford no better digested death than a more moderate
period. Many would have thought it an happiness to have had
their lot of life in some notable conjunctures of ages past; but
the uncertainty of future times hath tempted few to make a
part in ages to come. And surely, he that hath taken the true
altitude of things and rightly calculated the degenerate state of
this age, is not like to envy those that shall live in the next,
much less three or four hundred years hence, when no man can
comfortably imagine what face this world will carry: and therefore, since every age makes a step unto the end of all things,
and the Scripture affords so hard a character of the last times,
quiet minds will be content with their generations, and rather
bless ages past than be ambitious of those to come.

Tho age had set no seal upon his face, yet a dim eye might
clearly discover fifty in his actions; and therefore, since wisdom
is the gray hair, and an unspotted life old age, altho his years
came short, he might have been said to have held up with
longer livers, and to have been Solomon's [1] old man. And
surely, if we deduct all those days of our life which we might
wish unlived, and which abate the comfort of those we now
live, if we reckon up only those days which God hath accepted
of our lives, a life of good years will hardly be a span long: the
son in this sense may outlive the father, and none be climateri-
cally [2] old. He that early arriveth unto the parts and prudence
of age, is happily old without the uncomfortable attendants of

---

[1] Wisdom [of Solomon, V. 7–14].

[2] considering the climacterics, or supposed grand periods of change, in the
human life

it; and 'tis superfluous to live unto gray hairs, when in a precocious temper we anticipate the virtues of them. In brief, he cannot be accounted young who outliveth the old man. He that hath early arrived unto the measure of a perfect stature in Christ,[1] hath already fulfilled the prime and longest intention of his being: and one day lived after the perfect rule of piety, is to be preferred before sinning immortality.

Although he attained not unto the years of his predecessors, yet he wanted not those preserving virtues which confirm the thread of weaker constitutions. Cautelous [2] chastity and crafty sobriety were far from him; those jewels were paragon, without flaw, hair, ice, or cloud in him: which affords me a hint to proceed in these good wishes and few mementos [3] unto you.

[1] Ephesians, IV. 13.   [2] crafty, prompted by policy

[3] The original letter concludes with a series of "good wishes and ... mementos," now commonly omitted, which were included with some revision and considerable additions in his *Christian Morals*.

JOHN MILTON

OF EDUCATION: TO MASTER SAMUEL HARTLIB[1]

Master Hartlib,

I am long since persuaded that to say or do aught worth memory and imitation, no purpose or respect should sooner move us than simply the love of God and of mankind. Nevertheless, to write now the reforming of education, though it be one of the greatest and noblest designs that can be thought on, and for the want whereof this nation perishes, I had not yet at this time been induced, but by your earnest entreaties and serious conjurements; as having my mind for the present half diverted in the pursuance of some other assertions, the knowledge and the use of which cannot but be a great furtherance both to the enlargement of truth, and honest living, with much more peace. Nor should the laws of any private friendship have prevailed with me to divide thus or transpose my former thoughts, but that I see those aims, those actions, which have won you with me the esteem of a person sent hither by some good providence from a far country to be the occasion and the incitement of great good to this island.

And, as I hear, you have obtained the same repute with men of most approved wisdom, and some of highest authority among us. Not to mention the learned correspondence which you hold in foreign parts, and the extraordinary pains and diligence which you have used in this matter, both here and beyond the seas; either by the definite will of God so ruling, or the peculiar sway of nature, which also is God's working. Neither can I think that, so reputed and so valued as you are, you would, to the forfeit of your own discerning ability, impose upon me an unfit and overponderous argument, but that the satisfaction which you profess to have received from those incidental discourses which we have wandered into, hath pressed and almost constrained you into a persuasion that what you require from me in this point I neither ought nor can

[1] Published in 1644.

in conscience defer beyond this time both of so much need at once, and so much opportunity to try what God hath determined.

I will not resist, therefore, whatever it is either of divine or humane obligement that you lay upon me; but will forthwith set down in writing, as you request me, that voluntary idea, which hath long in silence presented itself to me, of a better education, in extent and comprehension far more large, and yet of time far shorter, and of attainment far more certain, than hath been yet in practice. Brief I shall endeavor to be; for that which I have to say, assuredly this nation hath extreme need should be done sooner than spoken. To tell you, therefore, what I have benefited herein among old renowned authors, I shall spare; and to search what many modern *Januas* and *Didactics* [1] more than ever I shall read have projected, my inclination leads me not. But if you can accept of these few observations which have flowered off, and are as it were the burnishing of many studious and contemplative years altogether spent in the search of religious and civil knowledge, and such as pleased you so well in the relating, I here give you them to dispose of.

The end, then, of learning is to repair the ruins of our first parents by regaining to know God aright, and out of that knowledge to love him, to imitate him, to be like him, as we may the nearest by possessing our souls of true virtue, which being united to the heavenly grace of faith makes up the highest perfection. But because our understanding cannot in this body found itself but on sensible things, nor arrive so clearly to the knowledge of God and things invisible as by orderly conning over the visible and inferior creature, the same method is necessarily to be followed in all discreet teaching. And seeing every nation affords not experience and tradition enough for all kind of learning, therefore we are chiefly taught the languages of those people who have at any time been most industrious after wisdom; so that language is but the instrument conveying to us things useful to be known. And though a linguist should pride himself to have all the tongues that Babel cleft the world into, yet if he have not studied the solid things

[1] *i.e.*, works of the type of these educational treatises of Comenius.

in them as well as the words and lexicons, he were nothing so much to be esteemed a learned man as any yeoman or tradesman competently wise in his mother dialect only.

Hence appear the many mistakes which have made learning generally so unpleasing and so unsuccessful; first, we do amiss to spend seven or eight years merely in scraping together so much miserable Latin and Greek as might be learnt otherwise easily and delightfully in one year. And that which casts our proficiency therein so much behind, is our time lost partly in too oft idle vacancies [1] given both to schools and universities; partly in a preposterous exaction, forcing the empty wits of children to compose themes, verses, and orations, which are the acts of ripest judgment, and the final work of a head filled, by long reading and observing, with elegant maxims and copious invention. These are not matters to be wrung from poor striplings, like blood out of the nose, or the plucking of untimely fruit: besides the ill habit which they get of wretched barbarising against the Latin and Greek idiom, with their untutored Anglicisms, odious to be read, yet not to be avoided without a well-continued and judicious conversing among pure authors digested, which they scarce taste; whereas, if after some preparatory grounds of speech by their certain forms got into memory they were led to the praxis [2] thereof in some chosen short book lessoned thoroughly to them, they might then forthwith proceed to learn the substance of good things, and arts in due order, which would bring the whole language quickly into their power. This I take to be the most rational and most profitable way of learning languages, and whereby we may best hope to give account to God of our youth spent herein.

And for the usual method of teaching arts, I deem it to be an old error of universities not yet well recovered from the scholastic grossness of barbarous ages, that instead of beginning with arts most easy — and those be such as are most obvious to the sense — they present their young unmatriculated novices, at first coming, with the most intellective abstractions of logic and metaphysics. So that they having but newly left those grammatic flats and shallows where they stuck unreason-

---

[1] vacations, holidays   [2] exercise, discipline, practice

ably to learn [1] a few words with lamentable construction, and now on the sudden transported under another climate to be tossed and turmoiled with their unballasted wits in fadomless and unquiet deeps of controversy, do for the most part grow into hatred and contempt of learning, mockt and deluded all this while with ragged notions and babblements, while they expected worthy and delightful knowledge; till poverty or youthful years call them importunately their several ways, and hasten them, with the sway of friends, either to an ambitious and mercenary or ignorantly zealous divinity; some allured to the trade of law, grounding their purposes not on the prudent and heavenly contemplation of justice and equity, which was never taught them, but on the promising and pleasing thoughts of litigious terms, fat contentions, and flowing fees; others betake them to state affairs, with souls so unprincipled in virtue and true generous breeding that flattery and court-shifts and tyrannous aphorisms appear to them the highest points of wisdom; instilling their barren hearts with a conscientious slavery, if, as I rather think, it be not feigned. Others, lastly, of a more delicious and airy spirit, retire themselves — knowing no better — to the enjoyments of ease and luxury, living out their days in feast and jollity; which indeed is the wisest and safest course of all these, unless they were with more integrity undertaken. And these are the errors, and these are the fruits of misspending our prime youth at the schools and universities as we do, either in learning mere words or such things chiefly as were better unlearned.

I shall detain you now no longer in the demonstration of what we should not do, but straight conduct ye to a hillside, where I will point ye out the right path of a virtuous and noble education; laborious indeed at the first ascent, but else so smooth, so green, so full of goodly prospect and melodious sounds on every side, that the harp of Orpheus was not more charming. I doubt not but ye shall have more ado to drive our dullest and laziest youth, our stocks and stubbs, from the infinite desire of such a happy nurture, than we have now to hale and drag our choicest and hopefullest wits to that asinine feast of sow-thistles and brambles which is commonly set before

[1] in learning

them as all the food and entertainment of their tenderest and
most docible [1] age. I call therefore a complete and generous
education that which fits a man to perform justly, skilfully, and
magnanimously all the offices both private and public of peace
and war.   And how all this may be done between twelve and
one and twenty, less time than is now bestowed in pure trifling
at grammar and sophistry, is to be thus ordered.

First, to find out a spacious house and ground about it fit for
an academy, and big enough to lodge a hundred and fifty persons, whereof twenty or thereabout may be attendants, all
under the government of one, who shall be thought of desert
sufficient and ability either to do all or wisely to direct and
oversee it done.   This place should be at once both school and
university, not needing a remove to any other house of scholarship, except it be some peculiar [2] college of law, or physic, where
they mean to be practitioners; but as for those general studies
which take up all our time from Lily [3] to the commencing, as
they term it, Master of Art, it should be absolute.   After this
pattern, as many edifices may be converted to this use as shall
be needful in every city throughout this land, which would
tend much to the increase of learning and civility everywhere.
This number, less or more thus collected, to the convenience
of a foot company, or interchangeably two troops of cavalry,
should divide their day's work into three parts as it lies orderly.
Their studies, their exercise, and their diet.

For their studies: First, they should begin with the chief and
necessary rules of some good grammar, either that now used or
any better; and while this is doing, their speech is to be fashioned to a distinct and clear pronunciation, as near as may be
to the Italian, especially in the vowels.   For we Englishmen
being far northerly, do not open our mouths in the cold air
wide enough to grace a Southern tongue; but are observed by
all other nations to speak exceeding close and inward: so that
to smatter Latin with an English mouth is as ill a hearing
as law French.   Next, to make them expert in the usefullest
points of grammar, and withal to season them and win them
early to the love of virtue and true labor, ere any flattering

---

[1] responsive to instruction   [2] special
[3] author of a Latin grammar widely used in the 16th and 17th centuries

seducement or vain principle seize them wandering, some easy and delightful book of education would be read to them; whereof the Greeks have store, as Cebes, Plutarch, and other Socratic discourses. But in Latin we have none of classic authority extant, except the two or three first books of Quintilian and some select pieces elsewhere.

But here the main skill and groundwork will be to temper [1] them such lectures and explanations, upon every opportunity, as may lead and draw them in willing obedience, inflamed with the study of learning and the admiration of virtue; stirred up with high hopes of living to be brave men and worthy patriots, dear to God and famous to all ages. That they may despise and scorn all their childish and ill-taught qualities, to delight in manly and liberal exercises: which he who hath the art and proper eloquence to catch them with, what with mild and effectual persuasions, and what with the intimation of some fear, if need be, but chiefly by his own example, might in a short space gain them to an incredible diligence and courage, infusing into their young breasts such an ingenuous and noble ardor, as would not fail to make many of them renowned and matchless men. At the same time, some other hour of the day, might be taught them the rules of arithmetic, and soon after the elements of geometry, even playing, as the old manner was. After evening repast, till bedtime their thoughts will be best taken up in the easy grounds of religion and the story of Scripture.

The next step would be to the authors of agriculture, Cato, Varro, and Columella, for the matter is most easy, and if the language be difficult, so much the better, it is not a difficulty above their years. And here will be an occasion of inciting and enabling them hereafter to improve the tillage of their country, to recover the bad soil, and to remedy the waste that is made of good: for this was one of Hercules' praises. Ere half these authors be read — which will soon be with plying hard and daily — they cannot choose but be masters of any ordinary prose. So that it will be then seasonable for them to learn in any modern author the use of the globes, and all the maps, first with the old names, and then with the new; or they might

[1] fashion, shape

be then capable to read any compendious method of natural philosophy.[1] And at the same time might be entring into the Greek tongue, after the same manner as was before prescribed in the Latin; whereby the difficulties of grammar being soon overcome, all the historical physiology of Aristotle and Theophrastus are open before them, and, as I may say, under contribution. The like access will be to Vitruvius, to Seneca's natural questions, to Mela, Celsus, Pliny, or Solinus. And having thus passed the principles of arithmetic, geometry, astronomy, and geography, with a general compact [2] of physics, they may descend in mathematics to the instrumental science of trigonometry, and from thence to fortification, architecture, enginery, or navigation. And in natural philosophy they may proceed leisurely from the history of meteors, minerals, plants, and living creatures, as far as anatomy.

Then also in course might be read to them out of some not tedious writer the institution of physic; that they may know the tempers, [3] the humors, [3] the seasons, and how to manage a crudity: [4] which he who can wisely and timely do, is not only a great physician to himself and to his friends, but also may at some time or other save an army by this frugal and expenseless means only; and not let the healthy and stout bodies of young men rot away under him for want of this discipline; [5] which is a great pity, and no less a shame to the commander. To set forward all these proceedings in nature and mathematics, what hinders but that they may procure, as oft as shall be needful, the helpful experiences of hunters, fowlers, fishermen, shepherds, gardeners, apothecaries; and in the other sciences, architects, engineers, mariners, anatomists; who doubtless would be ready, some for reward and some to favor such a hopeful seminary. And this will give them such a real tincture of natural knowledge as they shall never forget, but daily aug-

[1] physical science   [2] digest, summary

[3] According to medieval medical science the four humors — blood, bile, phlegm, and black bile — by virtue of the predominance of one or another of them in each individual, determined which of the corresponding tempers — sanguine, choleric, phlegmatic, and melancholy — should characterize the individual.

[4] indigestion

[5] knowledge acquired by training

ment with delight. Then also those poets which are now counted most hard, will be both facile and pleasant, Orpheus, Hesiod, Theocritus, Aratus, Nicander, Oppian, Dionysius; and in Latin, Lucretius, Manilius, and the rural part of Virgil.

By this time, years and good general precepts will have furnished them more distinctly with that act of reason which in ethics is called Proairesis; [1] that they may with some judgment contemplate upon moral good and evil. Then will be required a special reinforcement of constant and sound indoctrinating to set them right and firm, instructing them more amply in the knowledge of virtue and the hatred of vice; while their young and pliant affections are led through all the moral works of Plato, Xenophon, Cicero, Plutarch, Laertius, and those Locrian remnants; but still to be reduced in their nightward studies wherewith they close the day's work, under the determinate sentence [2] of David, or Solomon, or the Evangels and Apostolic Scriptures. Being perfect in the knowledge of personal duty, they may then begin the study of economies. [3] And either now or before this they may have easily learnt at any odd hour the Italian tongue. And soon after, but with wariness and good antidote, it would be wholesome enough to let them taste some choice comedies, Greek, Latin, or Italian; those tragedies also that treat of household matters, as *Trachiniae*, *Alcestis*, and the like.

The next remove must be to the study of politics; to know the beginning, end, and reasons of political societies; that they may not in a dangerous fit of the commonwealth be such poor, shaken, uncertain reeds, of such a tottering conscience, as many of our great counsellors have lately shown themselves, but steadfast pillars of the state. After this they are to dive into the grounds of law and legal justice; delivered first and with best warrant by Moses; and as far as humane prudence can be trusted, in those extolled remains of Grecian lawgivers, Lycurgus, Solon, Zaleucus, Charondas, and thence to all the Roman edicts and tables with their Justinian; and so down to the Saxon and common laws of England, and the statutes.

Sundays also and every evening may be now understandingly

[1] moral choice   [2] approved maxims, established truths
[3] the management of household expenses or private expenses

spent in the highest matters of theology, and church history ancient and modern; and ere this time the Hebrew tongue at a set hour might have been gained, that the Scriptures may be now read in their own original; whereto it would be no impossibility to add the Chaldee and the Syrian dialect. When all these employments are well conquered, then will the choice histories, heroic poems, and Attic tragedies of stateliest and most regal argument, with all the famous political orations, offer themselves; which if they were not only read, but some of them got by memory, and solemnly pronounced with right accent and grace, as might be taught, would endue them even with the spirit and vigor of Demosthenes or Cicero, Euripides or Sophocles.

And now, lastly, will be the time to read with them those organic arts which enable men to discourse and write perspicuously, elegantly, and according to the fitted style, of lofty, mean, or lowly. Logic, therefore, so much as is useful, is to be referred to this due place with all her well-coucht heads and topics, until it be time to open her contracted palm into a graceful and ornate rhetoric, taught out of the rule of Plato, Aristotle, Phalereus, Cicero, Hermogenes, Longinus. To which poetry would be made subsequent, or indeed rather precedent, as being less subtle and fine, but more simple, sensuous, and passionate. I mean not here the prosody of a verse, which they could not but have hit on before among the rudiments of grammar; but that sublime art which in Aristotle's *Poetics*, in Horace, and the Italian commentaries of Castlevetro, Tasso, Mazzoni, and others, teaches what the laws are of a true epic poem, what of a dramatic, what of a lyric; what decorum is, which is the grand masterpiece to observe. This would make them soon perceive what despicable creatures our common rhymers and play-writers be, and show them what religious, what glorious and magnificent use might be made of poetry, both in divine and humane things.

From hence, and not till now, will be the right season of forming them to be able writers and composers in every excellent matter, when they shall be thus fraught with an universal insight into things. Or whether they be to speak in parliament or council, honor and attention would be waiting on their lips.

There would then also appear in pulpits other visages, other gestures, and stuff otherwise wrought than what we now sit under, oft-times to as great a trial of our patience as any other that they preach to us. These are the studies wherein our noble and our gentle youth ought to bestow their time in a disciplinary way from twelve to one and twenty; unless they rely more upon their ancestors dead than upon themselves living. In which methodical course it is so supposed they must proceed by the steady pace of learning onward, as at convenient times, for memory's sake, to retire back into the middle ward and sometimes into the rear of what they have been taught, until they have confirmed and solidly united the whole body of their perfected knowledge, like the last embattling of a Roman legion. Now will be worth the seeing what exercises and what recreations may best agree and become these studies.

Their Exercise

The course of study hitherto briefly described is, what I can guess by reading, likest to those ancient and famous schools of Pythagoras, Plato, Isocrates, Aristotle, and such others, out of which were bred up such a number of renowned philosophers, orators, historians, poets, and princes all over Greece, Italy, and Asia, besides the flourishing studies of Cyrene and Alexandria. But herein it shall exceed them, and supply a defect as great as that which Plato noted in the commonwealth of Sparta; whereas that city trained up their youth most for war, and these in their academies and Lycæum all for the gown, this institution of breeding which I here delineate shall be equally good both for peace and war. Therefore, about an hour and a half ere they eat at noon should be allowed them for exercise, and due rest afterwards: but the time for this may be enlarged at pleasure, according as their rising in the morning shall be early.

The exercise which I commend first is the exact use of their weapon, to guard, and to strike safely with edge or point; this will keep them healthy, nimble, strong, and well in breath; is also the likeliest means to make them grow large and tall, and to inspire them with a gallant and fearless courage, which being tempered with seasonable lectures and precepts to them of true fortitude and patience, will turn into a native and heroic valor, and make them hate the cowardice of doing wrong. They must be also practised in all the locks and gripes of wrestling, wherein Englishmen were wont to excel, as need may often be in fight to tug, to grapple, and to close. And this perhaps will be enough wherein to prove and heat their single strength.

The interim of unsweating themselves regularly, and convenient rest before meat, may both with profit and delight be taken up in recreating and composing their travailed spirits with the solemn and divine harmonies of music, heard or learnt; either while the skilful organist plies his grave and fancied descant in lofty fugues, or the whole symphony with artful and unimaginable touches adorn and grace the well-studied chords of some choice composer; sometimes the lute or soft organ-stop waiting on elegant voices, either to religious, martial, or civil ditties; which, if wise men and prophets be not extremely out, have a great power over dispositions and manners, to smooth and make them gentle from rustic harshness and distempered passions. The like also would not be unexpedient after meat, to assist and cherish nature in her first concoction,[1] and send their minds back to study in good tune and satisfaction. Where having followed it close under vigilant eyes till about two hours before supper, they are, by a sudden alarum or watchword, to be called out to their military motions, under sky or covert, according to the season, as was the Roman wont; first on foot, then, as their age permits, on horseback, to all the art of cavalry; that having in sport, but with much exactness and daily muster, served out the rudiments of their soldiership in all the skill of embattling, marching, encamping, fortifying, besieging, and battering, with all the helps of ancient and modern stratagems, tactics, and warlike maxims, they may as it were out of a long war come forth renowned and perfect commanders in the service of their country. They would not then, if they were trusted with fair and hopeful armies, suffer them for want of just and wise discipline to shed away from about them like sick feathers, though they be never so oft supplied: they would not suffer their empty and unrecruitable colonels of twenty men in a company to quaff out or convey

---

[1] act of digestion

into secret hoards the wages of a delusive list, and a miserable remnant; yet in the meanwhile to be overmastered with a score or two of drunkards, the only soldiery left about them, or else to comply with all rapines and violences. No, certainly, if they knew aught of that knowledge that belongs to good men or good governors, they would not suffer these things.

But to return to our own institute: besides these constant exercises at home, there is another opportunity of gaining experience to be won from pleasure itself abroad; in those vernal seasons of the year when the air is calm and pleasant, it were an injury and sullenness against nature not to go out and see her riches, and partake in her rejoicing with heaven and earth. I should not therefore be a persuader to them of studying much then, after two or three year that they have well laid their grounds, but to ride out in companies, with prudent and staid guides, to all the quarters of the land: learning and observing all places of strength, all commodities of building and of soil, for towns and tillage, harbors and ports for trade. Sometimes taking sea as far as to our navy, to learn there also what they can in the practical knowledge of sailing and of seafight.

These ways would try all their peculiar gifts of nature, and if there were any secret excellence among them, would fetch it out, and give it fair opportunities to advance itself by, which could not but mightily redound to the good of this nation, and bring into fashion again those old admired virtues and excellencies, with far more advantage now in this purity of Christian knowledge. Nor shall we then need the monsieurs of Paris to take our hopeful youth into their slight and prodigal custodies, and send them over back again transformed into mimics, apes, and kickshows.[1] But if they desire to see other countries at three or four and twenty years of age, not to learn principles but to enlarge experience and make wise observation, they will by that time be such as shall deserve the regard and honor of all men where they pass, and the society and friendship of those in all places who are best and most eminent. And perhaps then other nations will be glad to visit us for their breeding, or else to imitate us in their own country.

---

[1] 1644, "Kicshoes."

Now, lastly, for their diet there cannot be much to say, save only that it would be best in the same house; for much time else would be lost abroad, and many ill habits got; and that it should be plain, healthful, and moderate, I suppose is out of controversy.

Thus, Master Hartlib, you have a general view in writing, as your desire was, of that which at several times I had discourst with you concerning the best and noblest way of education; not beginning, as some have done, from the cradle, which yet might be worth many considerations, if brevity had not been my scope; many other circumstances also I could have mentioned, but this, to such as have the worth in them to make trial, for light and direction may be enough. Only I believe that this is not a bow for every man to shoot in that counts himself a teacher; but will require sinews almost equal to those which Homer gave Ulysses; yet I am withal persuaded that it may prove much more easy in the assay than it now seems at distance, and much more illustrious: howbeit, not more difficult than I imagine, and that imagination presents me with nothing but very happy and very possible according to best wishes; if God have so decreed, and this age have spirit and capacity enough to apprehend.

JEREMY TAYLOR

OF MODESTY [1]

MODESTY is the appendage of sobriety, and is to chastity, to temperance, and to humility, as the fringes are to a garment. It is a grace of God, that moderates the over-activeness and curiosity of the mind, and orders the passions of the body and external actions, and is directly opposed to curiosity, to boldness, to undecency. The practice of modesty consists in these following rules.

Acts and Duties of Modesty as it is opposed to Curiosity

1. Inquire not into the secrets of God, but be content to learn thy duty according to the quality of thy person or employment: that is, plainly, if thou beest not concerned in the conduct of others; but if thou beest a teacher, learn it so as may best enable thee to discharge thy office. God's commandments were proclaimed to all the world, but God's counsels are to himself and to his secret ones, when they are admitted within the veil.

2. Inquire not into the things which are too hard for thee, but learn modestly to know thy infirmities and abilities,[2] and raise not thy mind up to inquire into mysteries of state, or the secrets of government, or difficulties theological, if thy employment really be, or thy understanding be judged to be, of a lower rank.

3. Let us not inquire into the affairs of others that concern us not, but be busied within ourselves and our own spheres; ever remembering that to pry into the actions or interests of other men not under our charge may minister to pride, to tyranny, to uncharitableness, to trouble, but can never consist

---

[1] From *The Rule and Exercises of Holy Living* (1650). Except the glosses of individual words, the notes are reprinted (with considerable omissions) from the original edition.

[2] Qui scrutator est majestatis, opprimetur à gloria. Prov. XXV. 27. . . . Epictetus: *Diss*. I. 26. 15. Et plus sapere interdum vulgus, quod quantum opus est sapiat. Lactant[ius.]

with modesty, unless where duty or the mere intentions of charity and relation [1] do warrant it.

4. Never listen at the doors or windows: [2] for, besides that it contains in it danger and a snare, it is also an invading my neighbor's privacy, and a laying that open which he therefore enclosed that it might not be open. Never ask what he carries covered so curiously; for it is enough that it is covered curiously. Hither, also, is reducible that we never open letters without public authority, or reasonably presumed leave, or great necessity, or charity.

Every man hath in his own life sins enough, in his own mind trouble enough, in his own fortune evils enough, and in performance of his offices failings more than enough, to entertain his own inquiry; so that curiosity after the affairs of others cannot be without envy and an evil mind. What is it to me, if my neighbor's grandfather were a Syrian, or his grandmother illegitimate; or that another is indebted five thousand pounds, or whether his wife be expensive? But commonly curious persons, or (as the Apostle's phrase is) "busybodies," are not solicitous or inquisitive into the beauty and order of a wellgoverned family, or after the virtues of an excellent person; but if there be any thing for which men keep locks and bars and porters, things that blush to see the light, and either are shameful in manners or private in nature, these things are their care and their business. But if great things will satisfy our inquiry, the course of the sun and moon, the spots in their faces, the firmament of heaven and the supposed orbs, [3] the ebbing and flowing of the sea, are work enough for us: or, if this be not, let him tell me whether the number of the stars be even or odd, and when they began to be so; since some ages have discovered new stars which the former knew not, but might have seen if they had been where now they are fixed. If these be too troublesome, search lower, and tell me why this turf this year brings forth a daisy, and the next year a plantain; why the apple

[1] the mere . . . relation = the pure motives of charity and kinship

[2] Eccles. VII. 21. Ne occhi in lettera, ne mano in tasca, ne orecchi in secreti altrui.

[3] the hollow, concentric spheres in which, according to the Ptolemaic astronomy, the planets were set

bears his seed in his heart, and wheat bears it in his head: let him tell why a graft, taking nourishment from a crab-stock, shall have a fruit more noble than its nurse and parent: let him say why the best of oil is at the top, the best of wine in the middle, and the best of honey at the bottom, otherwise than it is in some liquors that are thinner, and in some that are thicker. But these things are not such as please busybodies. They must feed upon tragedies, and stories of misfortunes and crimes; and yet tell them ancient stories of the ravishment of chaste maidens, or the debauchment of nations, or the extreme poverty of learned persons, or the persecutions of the old saints, or the changes of government, and sad accidents happing in royal families among the Arsacidæ, the Cæsars, the Ptolemies, these were enough to scratch the itch of knowing sad stories. But unless you tell them something *sad and new*, something that is done within the bounds of their own knowledge or relation, it seem tedious and unsatisfying; which shows plainly, it is an evil spirit: envy and idleness married together, and begot curiosity. Therefore Plutarch rarely well compares curious and inquisitive ears to the execrable gates of cities, out of which only malefactors and hangmen and tragedies pass, nothing that is chaste or holy. If a physician should go from house to house unsent for, and inquire what woman hath a cancer in her bowels, or what man hath a fistula in his colic-gut,[1] though he could pretend to cure it, he would be almost as unwelcome as the disease itself; and therefore it is inhumane to inquire after crimes and disasters without pretence[2] of amending them, but only to discover them. We are not angry with searchers and publicans when they look only on public merchandise; but when they break open trunks, and pierce vessels, and unrip packs, and open sealed letters.

Curiosity is the direct incontinency of the spirit: and adultery itself, in its principle, is many times nothing but a curious inquisition after, and envying of, another man's enclosed pleasures: and there have been many who refused fairer objects that they might ravish an enclosed woman from her retirement and single possessor. But these inquisitions are seldom without danger, never without baseness; they are

[1] colon   [2] intention

neither just, nor honest, nor delightful, and very often useless to the curious inquirer. For men stand upon their guards against them, as they secure their meat against harpies and cats, laying all their counsels and secrets out of their way; or as men clap their garments close about them when the searching and saucy winds would discover their nakedness: as knowing that what men willingly hear they do willingly speak of. Knock, therefore, at the door before you enter upon your neighbor's privacy; and remember that there is no difference between entring into his house and looking into it.

Acts of Modesty as it is opposed to Boldness

1. Let us always bear about us such impressions of reverence and fear of God as to tremble at his voice, to express our apprehensions of his greatness in all great accidents, in popular judgments, loud thunders, tempests, earthquakes; not only for fear of being smitten ourselves, or that we are concerned in the accident, but also that we may humble ourselves before his almightiness, and express that infinite distance between his infiniteness and our weaknesses, at such times especially when he gives such visible arguments of it. He that is merry and airy at shore when he sees a sad and a loud tempest on the sea, or dances briskly when God thunders from heaven, regards not when God speaks to all the world, but is possessed with a firm immodesty.

2. Be reverent, modest, and reserved in the presence of thy betters, giving to all according to their quality their titles of honor, keeping distance, speaking little, answering pertinently, not interposing without leave or reason, not answering to a question propounded to another; and ever present to thy superiors the fairest side of thy discourse, of thy temper, of thy ceremony, as being ashamed to serve excellent persons with unhandsome intercourse.

3. Never lie before a king or a great person, nor stand in a lie, when thou art accused, nor offer to justify what is indeed a fault, but modestly be ashamed of it, ask pardon, and make amends.[1]

---

[1] Quem Deus tegit verecundiæ pallio, hujus maculas hominibus non ostendit. Genz, *Annot. in Maimon. Can. Eth.* III.

4. Never boast of thy sin, but at least lay a veil upon thy nakedness and shame,[1] and put thy hand before thine eyes, that thou mayest have this beginning of repentance, to believe thy sin to be thy shame. For he that blushes not at his crime, but adds shamelessness to his shame, hath no instrument left to restore him to the hopes of virtue.

5. Be not confident and affirmative in an uncertain matter, but report things modestly and temperately, according to the degree of that persuasion which is, or ought to be, begotten in thee by the efficacy of the authority or the reason inducing thee.

6. Pretend not to more knowledge than thou hast, but be content to seem ignorant where thou art, lest thou beest either brought to shame, or retirest into shamelessness.

Acts of Modesty as it is opposed to Undecency

1. In your prayers in churches and places of religion use reverent postures, great attention, grave ceremony, the lowest gestures of humility; remembring that we speak to God, in our reverence to whom we cannot possibly exceed; but that the expression of this reverence be according to law and custom, and the example of the most prudent and pious persons; that is, let it be the best in its kind to the best of essences.

2. In all public meetings, private addresses, in discourses, in journeys, use those forms of salutation, reverence, and decency which the custom prescribes and is usual amongst the most sober persons; giving honor to whom honor belongeth, taking place of none of thy betters, and in all cases of question concerning civil precedency giving it to any one that will take it, if it be only thy own right that is in question.

3. Observe the proportion of affections in all meetings and to all persons: be not merry at a funeral, nor sad upon a festival; but "rejoice with them that rejoice, and weep with them that weep."

4. Abstain from wanton and dissolute laughter, petulant and uncomely jests, loud talking, jeering, and all such actions which in civil account are called undecencies and incivilities.

5. Towards your parents use all modesty of duty and hum-

---

[1] A Chione saltem vel ab Helide disce pudorem;
Abscondunt spurcas haec monumenta lupas. Mart. *Epigrams*, I. 34, 7.

ble carriage; towards them and all your kindred be severe in the modesties of chastity; ever fearing lest the freedoms of natural kindness should enlarge into any neighborhood of unhandsomeness. For all incestuous mixtures, and all circumstances and degrees towards it, are the highest violations of modesty in the world: for therefore incest is grown to be so high a crime, especially in the last periods of the world, because it breaks that reverence which the consent of all nations and the severity of humane laws hath enjoined towards our parents and nearest kindred, in imitation of that law which God give to the Jews in prosecution of modesty in this instance.

6. Be a curious observer of all those things which are of good report, and are parts of public honesty.[1] For public fame, and the sentence of prudent and public persons, is the measure of good and evil in things indifferent; and charity requires us to comply with those fancies and affections which are agreeable to nature, or the analogy of virtue, or public laws, or old customs. It is against modesty for a woman to marry a second husband as long as she bears a burden by the first, or to admit a second love while her funeral tears are not wiped from her cheeks. It is against public honesty to do some lawful actions of privacy in public theatres, and therefore in such cases retirement is a duty of modesty.[2]

7. Be grave, decent, and modest in thy clothing and ornament: never let it be above thy condition, not always equal to it, never light or amorous, never discovering a nakedness through a thin veil, which thou pretendest to hide: never to lay a snare for a soul, but remember what becomes a Christian professing holiness, chastity, and the discipline of the holy Jesus [: and the first effect of this let your servants feel by your gentleness and aptness to be pleased with their usual diligence, and ordinary conduct. For the man or woman that is dressed with anger and impatience,[3] wears pride under their robes, and immodesty above].[4]

8. Hither, also, is to be reduced singular and affected walking, proud, nice, and ridiculous gestures of body, painting, and lascivious dressings: all which together God reproves by the pro-

---

[1] Philippians, IV. 8.   [2] Martial: *Epigrams*, I. 34.5.

[3] Ovid: *Ars Amandi*, III. 239.   [4] Bracketed passage not in first edition.

phet: "The Lord saith, Because the daughters of Sion are
haughty, and walk with stretched-forth necks and wanton
eyes, walking and mincing as they go, and make a tinkling with
their feet; therefore the Lord will smite her with a scab of the
crown of the head, and will take away the bravery of their
tinkling ornaments."[1] And this duty of modesty, in this instance, is expressly enjoined to all Christian women by St.
Paul: "That women adorn themselves in modest apparel,
with shamefastness and sobriety, not with broidered hair, or
gold or pearl, or costly array, but (which becometh women
professing godliness) with good works."[2]

9. As those meats are to be avoided which tempt our
stomachs beyond our hunger, so also should prudent persons
decline all such spectacles, relations, theatres, loud noises, and
outcries which concern us not, and are besides our natural or
moral interest.   Our senses should not, like petulant and
wanton girls, wander into markets and theatres without just
employment; but when they are sent abroad by reason, return
quickly with their errand, and remain modestly at home under
their guide, till they be sent again.[3]

10. Let all persons be curious in observing modesty towards
themselves in the handsome treating their own body, and such
as are in their power, whether living or dead.   Against this rule
they offend who expose to others their own, or pry into others'
nakedness, beyond the limits of necessity, or where a leave is
not made holy by a permission from God.   It is also said that
God was pleased to work a miracle about the body of Epipha-
nius to reprove the immodest curiosity of an unconcerned person who pried too near when charitable people were composing it
to the grave.   In all these cases and particulars, although they
seem little, yet our duty and concernment is not little.   Concerning which I use the words of the son of Sirach, "He that
despiseth little things shall perish by little and little."

---

[1] Isaiah, III. 16–18.   [2] 1 Timothy, II. 9, 10.
[3] Œdipum curiositas in extremas conjecit calamitates. Plutarch: *De Curios.*

ABRAHAM COWLEY

THE DANGERS OF AN HONEST MAN IN MUCH COMPANY [1]

IF twenty thousand naked Americans were not able to resist the assaults of but twenty well-armed Spaniards, I see little possibility for one honest man to defend himself against twenty thousand knaves, who are all furnisht *cap à pe* with the defensive arms of worldly prudence, and the offensive, too, of craft and malice. He will find no less odds than this against him, if he have much to do in human affairs. The only advice therefore that I can give him is, to be sure not to venture his person any longer in the open campaign, to retreat and entrench himself, to stop up all avenues, and draw up all bridges against so numerous an enemy.

The truth of it is, that a man in much business must either make himself a knave, or else the world will make him a fool: and, if the injury went no farther than the being laught at, a wise man would content himself with the revenge of retaliation; but the case is much worse, for these civil cannibals too, as well as the wild ones, not only dance about such a taken stranger, but at last devour him. A sober man cannot get too soon out of drunken company, though they be never so kind and merry among themselves; 'tis not unpleasant only, but dangerous to him.

Do ye wonder that a virtuous man should love to be alone? It is hard for him to be otherwise; he is so, when he is among ten thousand: neither is the solitude so uncomfortable to be alone without any other creature, as it is to be alone in the midst of wild beasts. Man is to man all kind of beasts: a fawning dog, a roaring lion, a thieving fox, a robbing wolf, a dissembling crocodile, a treacherous decoy, and a rapacious vulture. The civilest, methinks, of all nations are those whom we account the most barbarous; there is some moderation and good nature in the Toupinambaltians, who eat no men but

[1] From *Several Discourses, by Way of Essays in Verse and Prose* (1668).

their enemies, whilst we learned and polite and Christian Europeans, like so many pikes and sharks prey upon every thing that we can swallow. It is the greatest boast of eloquence and philosophy, that they first congregated men disperst, united them into societies, and built up the houses and the walls of cities. I wish they could unravel all they had woven; that we might have our woods and our innocence again, instead of our castles and our policies.[1] They have assembled many thousands of scattered people into one body: 'tis true, they have done so, they have brought them together into cities to cozen, and into armies to murder one another. They found them hunters and fishers of wild creatures; they have made them hunters and fishers of their brethren; they boast to have reduced them to a state of peace, when the truth is, they have only taught them an art of war; they have framed, I must confess, wholesome laws for the restraint of vice, but they raised first that devil which now they conjure and cannot bind; though there were before no punishments for wickedness, yet there was less committed, because there were no rewards for it.

But the men who praise philosophy from this topic are much deceived; let oratory answer for itself, the tinkling perhaps of that may unite a swarm: it never was the work of philosophy to assemble multitudes, but to regulate only, and govern them, when they were assembled; to make the best of an evil, and bring them, as much as is possible, to unity again. Avarice and ambition only were the first builders of towns, and founders of empire; they said, "Go to, let us build us a city and a tower whose top may reach unto heaven, and let us make a name, lest we be scattered abroad upon the face of the earth." What was the beginning of Rome, the metropolis of all the world? what was it but a concourse of thieves and a sanctuary of criminals? It was justly named by the augury of no less than twelve vultures, and the founder cemented his walls with the blood of his brother; not unlike to this was the beginning even of the first town too in the world, and such is the original sin of most cities: their actual increase daily with their age and growth; the more people, the more wicked all of them; every one brings in his part to inflame the contagion,[2] which becomes

.   [1] enclosed parks   [2] 1669 edition reads *cogitation* at last so universal and so strong, that no precepts can be sufficient preservatives, nor any thing secure our safety, but flight from among the infected.

We ought, in the choice of a situation, to regard above all things the healthfulness of the place, and the healthfulness of it for the mind rather than for the body. But suppose (which is hardly to be supposed) we had antidote enough against this poison; nay, suppose farther we were always and at all pieces [1] armed and provided, both against the assaults of hostility, and the mines of treachery, 'twill yet be but an uncomfortable life to be ever in alarms: though we were compast round with fire to defend ourselves from wild beasts, the lodging would be unpleasant, because we must always be obliged to watch that fire, and to fear no less the defects of our guard than the diligences of our enemy. The sum of this is, that a virtuous man is in danger to be trod upon and destroyed in the crowd of his contraries, nay, which is worse, to be changed and corrupted by them; and that 'tis impossible to escape both these inconveniences without so much caution as will take away the whole quiet, that is, the happiness, of his life.

Ye see, then, what he may lose; but I pray, what can he get there?

Quid Romae faciam?   Mentiri nescio. [2]

What should a man of truth and honesty do at Rome? He can neither understand nor speak the language of the place; a naked man may swim in the sea, but 'tis not the way to catch fish there; they are likelier to devour him than he them, if he bring no nets, and use no deceits. I think, therefore, it was wise and friendly advice which Martial gave to Fabian, when he met him newly arrived at Rome:

> Honest and poor, faithful in word and thought;
> What has thee, Fabian, to the city brought?
> Thou neither the buffoon nor bawd canst play,
> Nor with false whispers th' innocent betray;
> Nor corrupt wives, nor from rich beldams get
> A living by thy industry and sweat;
> Nor with vain promises and projects cheat,
> Nor bribe or flatter any of the great.

---

[1] at all points (piece = piece of armor)   [2] Juvenal: *Satire* 3.

But you're a man of learning, prudent, just;
A man of courage, firm, and fit for trust.
Why, you may stay, and live unenvied here;
But (faith) go back, and keep you where you **were.**

Nay, if nothing of all this were in the case, yet the very sight of uncleanness is loathsome to the cleanly; the sight of folly and impiety vexatious to the wise and pious.

Lucretius, by his favor, though a good poet, was but an ill-natured man when he said it was delightful to see other men in a great storm: and no less ill-natured should I think Democritus, who laught at all the world, but that he retired himself so much out of it that we may perceive he took no great pleasure in that kind of mirth.   I have been drawn twice or thrice by company to go to Bedlam, and have seen others very much delighted with the fantastical extravagancy of so many various madnesses, which upon me wrought so contrary an effect, that I always returned, not only melancholy, but even sick with the sight.   My compassion there was perhaps too tender, for I meet a thousand madmen abroad without any perturbation; though, to weigh the matter justly, the total loss of reason is less deplorable than the total depravation of it.   An exact judge of human blessings, of riches, honors, beauty, even of wit itself, should pity the abuse of them more than the want.

Briefly, though a wise man could pass never so securely through the great roads of human life, yet he will meet perpetually with so many objects and occasions of compassion, grief, shame, anger, hatred, indignation, and all passions but envy (for he will find nothing to deserve that), that he had better strike into some private path; nay, go so far, if he could, out of the common way, *ut nec facta audiat Pelopidarum*; that he might not so much as hear of the actions of the sons of Adam.   But whither shall we fly, then? into the deserts, like the ancient Hermits?

> — *Quà terra patet, fera regnat Erinnys,*
> *In facinus jurâsse putes.*[1]

One would think that all mankind had bound themselves by an oath to do all the wickedness they can; that they had all (as

[1] *Metam.* 1

the Scripture speaks) "sold themselves to sin": the difference only is, that some are a little more crafty (and but a little, God knows) in making of the bargain. I thought, when I went first to dwell in the country, that without doubt I should have met there with the simplicity of the old poetical Golden Age: I thought to have found no inhabitants there but such as the shepherds of Sir Phil. Sidney in Arcadia, or of Monsieur D'Urfé upon the banks of Lignon; and began to consider with myself which way I might recommend no less to posterity the happiness and innocence of the men of Chertsea: but, to confess the truth, I perceived quickly, by infallible demonstrations, that I was still in Old England, and not in Arcadia, or La Forrest; that, if I could not content myself with any thing less than exact fidelity in human conversation,[1] I had almost as good go back and seek for it in the Court, or the Exchange, or Westminster Hall. I ask again, then, whither shall we fly, or what shall we do? The world may so come in a man's way that he cannot choose but salute it; he must take heed, though, not to go a whoring after it. If, by any lawful vocation, or just necessity, men happen to be married to it, I can only give them St. Paul's advice: "Brethren, the time is short; it remains that they that have wives be as though they had none. — But I would that all men were even as I myself."[2]

In all cases, they must be sure, that they do *mundum ducere*, and not *mundo nubere*.[3] They must retain the superiority and headship over it. Happy are they who can get out of the sight of this deceitful beauty, that they may not be led so much as into temptation; who have not only quitted the metropolis, but can abstain from ever seeing the next market town of their country.

[1] dealings, intercourse   [2] 1 Cor. VII. 29, 7.
[3] that they are masters of the world and not wedded to it

JOHN DRYDEN

PREFACE: FABLES, ANCIENT AND MODERN [1]

'TIS with a poet as with a man who designs to build, and is
very exact, as he supposes, in casting up the cost beforehand:
but, generally speaking, he is mistaken in his account, and
reckons short of the expense he first intended: he alters his
mind as the work proceeds, and will have this or that convenience more, of which he had not thought when he began.
So has it happened to me: I have built a house where I intended
but a lodge; yet with better success than a certain nobleman,
who, beginning with a dog-kennel, never lived to finish the
palace he had contrived.

From translating the first of Homer's *Iliads* (which I intended as an essay to the whole work) I proceeded to the
translation of the twelfth book of Ovid's *Metamorphoses*, because it contains, among other things, the causes, the beginning, and ending, of the Trojan War. Here I ought in reason
to have stopped; but the speeches of Ajax and Ulysses lying
next in my way, I could not balk 'em. When I had compassed
them, I was so taken with the former part of the Fifteenth
Book (which is the master-piece of the whole *Metamorphoses*)
that I enjoined myself the pleasing task of rendering it into
English. And now I found, by the number of my verses, that
they began to swell into a little volume; which gave me an occasion of looking backward on some beauties of my author, in
his former books. There occurred to me the Hunting of the
Boar, Cinyras and Myrrha, the good-natured story of Baucis
and Philemon, with the rest, which I hope I have translated
closely enough, and given them the same turn of verse which
they had in the original; and this, I may say without vanity, is
not the talent of every poet. He who has arrived the nearest
to it is the ingenious and learned Sandys, the best versifier of
the former age, if I may properly call it by that name, which
was the former part of this concluding century. For Spenser

[1] From *Fables, Ancient and Modern* (1700).

and Fairfax both flourished in the reign of Queen Elizabeth; great masters in our language, and who saw much farther into the beauties of our numbers than those who immediately followed them. Milton was the poetical son of Spenser, and Mr. Waller of Fairfax; for we have our lineal descents and clans as well as other families. Spenser more than once insinuates that the soul of Chaucer was transfused into his body, and that he was begotten by him two hundred years after his decease. Milton has acknowledged to me that Spenser was his original; and many besides myself have heard our famous Waller own that he derived the harmony of his numbers from the *Godfrey of Bulloign*,[1] which was turned into English by Mr. Fairfax.

But to return. Having done with Ovid for this time, it came into my mind that our old English poet, Chaucer, in many things resembled him, and that with no disadvantage on the side of the modern author, as I shall endeavor to prove when I compare them. And as I am, and always have been, studious to promote the honor of my native country, so I soon resolved to put their merits to the trial by turning some of the *Canterbury Tales* into our language as it is now refined; for by this means, both the poets being set in the same light and dressed in the same English habit, story to be compared with story, a certain judgment may be made betwixt them by the reader, without obtruding my opinion on him. Or if I seem partial to my countryman, and predecessor in the laurel, the friends of antiquity are not few; and besides many of the learned, Ovid has almost all the beaux, and the whole fair sex, his declared patrons. Perhaps I have assumed somewhat more to myself than they allow me, because I have adventured to sum up the evidence; but the readers are the jury, and their privilege remains entire to decide according to the merits of the cause, or, if they please, to bring it to another hearing before some other court.

In the mean time, to follow the thrid of my discourse (as thoughts, according to Mr. Hobbes, have always some connection), so from Chaucer I was led to think on Boccace, who was not only his contemporary but also pursued the same studies; wrote novels in prose, and many works in verse; par-

---

[1] *i.e.*, Tasso's *Jerusalem Delivered*.

ticularly is said to have invented the octave rhyme, or stanza
of eight lines, which ever since has been maintained by the
practice of all Italian writers who are, or at least assume the
title of, heroic poets. He and Chaucer, among other things,
had this in common, that they refined their mother tongues;
but with this difference, that Dante had begun to file their
language, at least in verse, before the time of Boccace, who
likewise received no little help from his master, Petrarch. But
the reformation of their prose was wholly owing to Boccace
himself, who is yet the standard of purity in the Italian tongue,
though many of his phrases are become obsolete, as in process
of time it must needs happen. Chaucer (as you have formerly
been told by our learned Mr. Rymer) first adorned and ampli-
fied our barren tongue from the Provençal, which was then the
most polished of all the modern languages; but this subject has
been copiously treated by that great critic, who deserves no
little commendation from us his countrymen. For these reasons of time and resemblance of genius in Chaucer and Boccace,
I resolved to join them in my present work; to which I have
added some original papers of my own, which, whether they
are equal or inferior to my other poems, an author is the most
improper judge; and therefore I leave them wholly to the mercy
of the reader. I will hope the best, that they will not be condemned; but if they should, I have the excuse of an old gentleman who, mounting on horseback before some ladies, when I
was present, got up somewhat heavily, but desired of the fair
spectators that they would count fourscore and eight before
they judged him. By the mercy of God I am already come
within twenty years of his number, a cripple in my limbs, but
what decays are in my mind the reader must determine. I
think myself as vigorous as ever in the faculties of my soul, excepting only my memory, which is not impaired to any great
degree; and if I lose not more of it, I have no great reason to
complain. What judgment I had increases rather than diminishes; and thoughts, such as they are, come crowding in so fast
upon me that my only difficulty is to choose or to reject, to run
them into verse or to give them the other harmony of prose.
I have so long studied and practised both that they are grown
into a habit and become familiar to me. In short, though I

may lawfully plead some part of the old gentleman's excuse, yet I will reserve it till I think I have greater need, and ask no grains of allowance for the faults of this my present work but those which are given of course to human frailty. I will not trouble my reader with the shortness of time in which I writ it, or the several intervals of sickness: they who think too well of their own performances are apt to boast in their prefaces how little time their works have cost them, and what other business of more importance interfered: but the reader will be as apt to ask the question, why they allowed not a longer time, to make their works more perfect; and why they had so despicable an opinion of their judges as to thrust their indigested stuff upon them, as if they deserved no better.

With this account of my present undertaking I conclude the first part of this discourse: in the second part, as at a second sitting, though I alter not the draught, I must touch the same features over again and change the dead coloring of the whole. In general, I will only say that I have written nothing which savors of immorality or profaneness; at least, I am not conscious to myself of any such intention. If there happen to be found an irreverent expression or a thought too wanton, they are crept into my verses through my inadvertency: if the searchers find any in the cargo, let them be staved or forfeited, like counterbanded goods; at least, let their authors be answerable for them, as being but imported merchandise and not of my own manufacture. On the other side, I have endeavored to choose such fables, both ancient and modern, as contain in each of them some instructive moral; which I could prove by induction, but the way is tedious, and they leap foremost into sight without the reader's trouble of looking after them. I wish I could affirm with a safe conscience that I had taken the same care in all my former writings; for it must be owned that, supposing verses are never so beautiful or pleasing, yet if they contain anything which shocks religion or good manners, they are at best what Horace says of good numbers without good sense, "*Versus inopes rerum, nugaeque canorae.*" [1] Thus far, I hope, I am right in court, without renouncing to my other

---

[1] "Lines poor in thought, melodious nothings." Horace: *De Arte Poetica*, 322.

right of self defence where I have been wrongfully accused and my sense wire-drawn into blasphemy or bawdry, as it has often been by a religious lawyer [1] in a late pleading against the stage, in which he mixes truth with falsehood, and has not forgotten the old rule of calumniating strongly that something may remain. . . .[2]

It remains that I say somewhat of Chaucer in particular.

In the first place, as he is the father of English poetry, so I hold him in the same degree of veneration as the Grecians held Homer or the Romans Virgil. He is a perpetual fountain of good sense, learned in all sciences, and therefore speaks properly on all subjects. As he knew what to say, so he knows also when to leave off; a continence which is practised by few writers, and scarcely by any of the ancients, excepting Virgil and Horace. One of our late great poets [3] is sunk in his reputation because he could never forgive [4] any conceit which came in his way, but swept, like a drag-net, great and small. There was plenty enough, but the dishes were ill sorted; whole pyramids of sweetmeats for boys and women, but little of solid meat for men. All this proceeded, not from any want of knowledge, but of judgment; neither did he want that in discerning the beauties and faults of other poets, but only indulged himself in the luxury of writing, and perhaps knew it was a fault but hoped the reader would not find it. For this reason, though he must always be thought a great poet, he is no longer esteemed a good writer; and for ten impressions which his works have had in so many successive years, yet at present a hundred books are scarcely purchased once a twelvemonth; for, as my last Lord Rochester said, though somewhat profanely, "Not being of God, he could not stand."

Chaucer followed nature everywhere, but was never so bold to go beyond her; and there is a great difference of being *poeta* and *nimis poeta*,[5] if we may believe Catullus,[6] as much as be-

---

[1] Jeremy Collier, in his *Short View of the Immorality and Profaneness of the English Stage*, 1698.

[2] A passage comparing Homer and Virgil, Ovid and Chaucer, is omitted.

[3] Cowley   [4] give over, forego

[5] poet and superpoet

[6] The reference should be to Martial (*Epigrams*. III. xliv), not to Catullus.

twixt a modest behavior and affectation. The verse of Chaucer, I confess, is not harmonious to us; but 'tis like the eloquence of one whom Tacitus commends: it was "*auribus istius temporis accommodata.*"[1] They who lived with him, and some time after him, thought it musical; and it continues so even in our judgment, if compared with the numbers of Lydgate and Gower, his contemporaries: there is the rude sweetness of a Scotch tune in it, which is natural and pleasing though not perfect. 'Tis true I cannot go so far as he who published the last edition of him, for he would make us believe the fault is in our ears, and that there were really ten syllables in a verse where we find but nine; but this opinion is not worth confuting; 'tis so gross and obvious an error that common sense (which is a rule in everything but matters of faith and revelation) must convince the reader that equality of numbers in every verse which we call heroic was either not known or not always practised in Chaucer's age. It were an easy matter to produce some thousands of his verses which are lame for want of half a foot and sometimes a whole one, and which no pronunciation can make otherwise. We can only say that he lived in the infancy of our poetry, and that nothing is brought to perfection at the first. We must be children before we grow men. There was an Ennius, and in process of time a Lucilius and a Lucretius, before Virgil and Horace; even after Chaucer there was a Spenser, a Harrington, a Fairfax, before Waller and Denham were in being; and our numbers were in their nonage till these last appeared. . . .[2]

He must have been a man of a most wonderful comprehensive nature, because, as it has been truly observed of him, he has taken into the compass of his *Canterbury Tales* the various manners and humors (as we now call them) of the whole English nation in his age. Not a single character has escaped him. All his pilgrims are severally distinguished from each other, and not only in their inclinations but in their very physiognomies and persons. Baptista Porta could not have described their natures better than by the marks which the poet gives them. The matter and manner of their tales and of their telling are so

[1] "suited to the ears of that age"

[2] A passage discussing Chaucer's life and his religious views is omitted.

suited to their different educations, humors, and callings that
each of them would be improper in any other mouth. Even
the grave and serious characters are distinguished by their
several[1] sorts of gravity: their discourses are such as belong to
their age, their calling, and their breeding, such as are becoming
of them and of them only. Some of his persons are vicious and
some virtuous; some are unlearned, or (as Chaucer calls them)
lewd, and some are learned. Even the ribaldry of the low
characters is different: the Reeve, the Miller, and the Cook are
several[1] men, and distinguished from each other as much as the
mincing Lady Prioress and the broad-speaking, gap-toothed
Wife of Bath. But enough of this: there is such a variety of
game springing up before me that I am distracted in my choice
and know not which to follow. 'Tis sufficient to say, according
to the proverb, that here is God's plenty. We have our forefathers and great-grandames all before us as they were in
Chaucer's days; their general characters are still remaining in
mankind, and even in England, though they are called by other
names than those of monks and friars and canons and lady ab-
besses and nuns; for mankind is ever .the same, and nothing lost
out of nature though everything is altered. . . . [2]

[1] individual
[2] The essay concludes with a defence of his translation from Chaucer, a criticism of Boccaccio, and an attack on three controversialists of the day, Mil-
bourn, Blackmore, and Collier.

DANIEL DEFOE

AN ACADEMY FOR WOMEN [1]

I HAVE often thought of it as one of the most barbarous customs in the world, considering us as a civilized and a Christian country, that we deny the advantages of learning to women. We reproach the sex every day with folly and impertinence, while I am confident, had they the advantages of education equal to us, they would be guilty of less than ourselves.

One would wonder, indeed, how it should happen that women are conversible at all, since they are only beholding to natural parts for all their knowledge. Their youth is spent to teach them to stitch and sew, or make baubles. They are taught to read, indeed, and perhaps to write their names or so, and that is the heighth of a woman's education. And I would but ask any who slight the sex for their understanding, What is a man (a gentleman, I mean) good for that is taught no more?

I need not give instances, or examine the character of a gentleman with a good estate and of a good family and with tolerable parts, and examine what figure he makes for want of education.

The soul is placed in the body like a rough diamond, and must be polished, or the lustre of it will never appear. And 'tis manifest that, as the rational soul distinguishes us from brutes, so education carries on the distinction and makes some less brutish than others. This is too evident to need any demonstration. But why, then, should women be denied the benefit of instruction? If knowledge and understanding had been useless additions to the sex, God Almighty would never have given them capacities; for He made nothing needless. Besides, I would ask such what they can see in ignorance that they should think it a necessary ornament to a woman. Or how much worse is a wise woman than a fool? Or what has the woman done to forfeit the privilege of being taught? Does she plague us with her pride and impertinence? Why did we not

[1] From *An Essay upon Projects* (1697).

let her learn, that she might have had more wit? Shall we upbraid women with folly, when 'tis only the error of this inhuman custom that hindered them being made wiser?

The capacities of women are supposed to be greater and their
senses quicker than those of the men; and what they might be
capable of being bred to is plain from some instances of female
wit which this age is not without; which upbraids us with injustice, and looks as if we denied women the advantages of education for fear they should vie with the men in their improvements.

To remove this objection, and that women might have at
least a needful opportunity of education in all sorts of useful
learning, I propose the draught of an academy for that purpose.

I know 'tis dangerous to make public appearances of the sex;
they are not either to be confined or exposed; the first will disagree with their inclinations, and the last with their reputations;
and therefore it is somewhat difficult; and I doubt a method
proposed by an ingenious lady, in a little book called *Advice to
the Ladies*, would be found impracticable. For, saving my respect to the sex, the levity which perhaps is a little peculiar to
them, at least in their youth, will not bear the restraint; and I
am satisfied nothing but the heighth of bigotry can keep up a
nunnery. Women are extravagantly desirous of going to
heaven, and will punish their pretty bodies to get thither; but
nothing else will do it; and even in that case sometimes it falls
out that *Nature will prevail*.

When I talk therefore of an academy for women, I mean
both the model, the teaching, and the government; different
from what is proposed by that ingenious lady, for whose proposal I have a very great esteem, and also a great opinion of
her wit; different, too, from all sorts of religious confinement,
and above all from *vows of celibacy*.

Wherefore the academy I propose should differ but little
from public schools, wherein such ladies as were willing to
study should have all the advantages of learning suitable to
their genius.

But since some severities of discipline more than ordinary
would be absolutely necessary to preserve the reputation of the
house, that persons of quality and fortune might not be afraid

to venture their children thither, I shall venture to make a small scheme by way of essay.

The house I would have built in a form
by itself, as well as in a place by itself.

The building should be of three plain fronts, without any jettings or bearing-work, that the eye might at a glance see from one coin [1] to the other; the gardens walled in the same triangular figure, with a large moat and but one entrance.

When thus every part of the situation was contrived as well as might be for discovery, and to render intriguing dangerous, I would have no guards, no eyes, no spies set over the ladies, but shall expect them to be tried by the principles of honor and strict virtue.

And if I am asked, "Why?" I must ask pardon of my own sex for giving this reason for it:

I am so much in charity with women, and so well acquainted with men, that 'tis my opinion there needs no other care to prevent intriguing than to keep the men effectually away. For though inclination, which we prettily call love, does sometimes move a little too visibly in the sex, and frailty often follows, yet I think verily custom, which we miscall modesty, has so far the ascendant over the sex that solicitation always goes before it. . . . [2]

Upon this ground I am persuaded such measures might be taken that the ladies might have all the freedom in the world within their own walls, and yet no intriguing, no indecencies, nor scandalous affairs happen; and, in order to this, the following customs and laws should be observed in the colleges, of which I would propose one at least in every county in England, and about ten for the city of London.

After the regulation of the form of the building as before:

1. All the ladies who enter into the house should set their hands to the orders of the house, to signify their consent to submit to them.

2. As no woman should be received but who declared herself willing, and that it was the act of her choice to enter herself, so no person should be confined to continue there a moment longer than the same voluntary choice inclined her.

[1] corner   [2] Some verses are omitted.

3. The charges of the house being to be paid by the ladies, every one that entered should have only this encumbrance: that she should pay for the whole year, though her mind should change as to her continuance.

4. An act of Parliament should make it felony, without clergy, for any man to enter by force or fraud into the house, or to solicit any woman, *though it were to marry*, while she was in the house. And this law would by no means be severe; because any woman who was willing to receive the addresses of a man might discharge herself of the house when she pleased; and, on the contrary, any woman who had occasion might discharge herself of the impertinent addresses of any person she had an aversion to, by entering into the house.

In this house the persons who enter should be taught all sorts of breeding suitable to both their genius and their quality; and, in particular, music and dancing, which it would be cruelty to bar the sex of, because they are their darlings; but, besides this, they should be taught languages, as particularly French and Italian; and I would venture the injury of giving a woman more tongues than one.

They should, as a particular study, be taught all the graces of speech and all the necessary air of conversation, which our common education is so defective in that I need not expose it. They should be brought to read books, and especially history, and so to read as to make them understand the world, and be able to know and judge of things when they hear of them.

To such whose genius would lead them to it I would deny no sort of learning; but the chief thing in general is to cultivate the understandings of the sex, that they may be capable of all sorts of conversation; that, their parts [1] and judgments being improved, they may be as profitable in their conversation as they are pleasant.

Women, in my observation, have little or no difference in them but as they are or are not distinguished by education. Tempers, indeed, may in some degree influence them, but the main distinguishing part is their breeding.

The whole sex are generally quick and sharp: I believe I may be allowed to say generally so; for you rarely see them lumpish

[1] endowments, natural gifts

and heavy when they are children, as boys will often be. If a woman be well bred, and taught the proper management of her natural wit, she proves generally very sensible and retentive; and, without partiality, a woman of sense and manners is the finest and most delicate part of God's creation, the glory of her Maker, and the great instance of His singular regard to man, His darling creature, to whom He gave the best gift either God could bestow or man receive; and 'tis the sordid'st piece of folly and ingratitude in the world to withhold from the sex the due lustre which the advantages of education gives to the natural beauty of their minds.

A woman well bred and well taught, furnished with the additional accomplishments of knowledge and behavior, *is a creature without comparison:* her society is the emblem of sublimer enjoyments; her person is angelic, and her conversation heavenly; she is all softness and sweetness, peace, love, wit, and delight; she is every way suitable to the sublimest wish; and the man that has such a one to his portion has nothing to do but to rejoice in her and be thankful.

On the other hand, suppose her to be the *very same* woman and rob her of the benefit of education, and it follows thus:

If her temper be good, want of education makes her soft and easy.

Her wit, for want of teaching, makes her impertinent and talkative.

Her knowledge, for want of judgment and experience, makes her fanciful and whimsical.

If her temper be bad, want of breeding makes her worse, and she grows haughty, insolent, and loud.

If she be passionate, want of manners makes her termagant and a scold, *which is much at one with lunatic.*

If she be proud, want of discretion (which still is breeding) makes her conceited, fantastic, and ridiculous.

And from these she degenerates to be turbulent, clamorous, noisy, nasty, *and the devil.*

Methinks mankind for their own sakes, since, say what we will of the women, we all think fit, one time or other, to be concerned with 'em, should take some care to breed them up to be suitable and serviceable, if they expected no such thing as delight from 'em. Bless us! What care do we take to breed up a good horse, and to break him well! and what a value do we put upon him when it is done! — and all because he should be fit for our use. And why not a woman? — since all her ornaments and beauty, without suitable behavior, is a cheat in nature, like the false tradesman who puts the best of his goods uppermost that the buyer may think the rest are of the same goodness.

Beauty of the body, which is the woman's glory, seems to be now unequally bestowed, and nature, or rather Providence, to lie under some scandal about it, as if 'twas given a woman for a snare to men, and so make a kind of she-devil of her: because, they say, exquisite beauty is rarely given with wit, more rarely with goodness of temper, and never at all with modesty. And some, pretending to justify the equity of such a distribution, will tell us 'tis the effect of the justice of Providence in dividing particular excellences among all His creatures, share and share alike, as it were, that all might for something or other be acceptable to one another, else some would be despised.

I think both these notions false; and yet the last, which has the show of respect to Providence, is the worst; for it supposes Providence to be indigent and empty, as if it had not wherewith to furnish all the creatures it had made, but was fain to be parsimonious in its gifts, and distribute them by piecemeal, for fear of being exhausted.

If I might venture my opinion against an almost universal notion, I would say most men mistake the proceedings of Providence in this case, and all the world at this day are mistaken in their practice about it. And because the assertion is very bold, I desire to explain myself.

That Almighty First Cause, Which made us all, is certainly the fountain of excellence, as It is of being, and by an invisible influence could have diffused equal qualities and perfections to all the creatures It has made, as the sun does its light, without the least ebb or diminution to Himself; and has given indeed to every individual sufficient to the figure His Providence had designed him in the world.

I believe it might be defended if I should say that I do suppose God has given to all mankind equal gifts and capacities, in that He has given them all souls equally capable, and that the whole difference in mankind proceeds either from accidental difference in the make of their bodies or from the foolish difference of education.

1. From accidental difference in bodies. I would avoid discoursing here of the philosophical position of the soul in the body: but if it be true, as philosophers do affirm, that the understanding and memory is dilated or contracted according to the accidental dimensions of the organ through which 'tis conveyed, then, though God has given a soul as capable to me as another, yet if I have any natural defect in those parts of the body by which the soul should act, I may have the same soul infused as another man, and yet he be a wise man and I a very fool. For example, if a child naturally have a defect in the organ of hearing, so that he could never distinguish any sound, that child shall never be able to speak or read, though it have a soul capable of all the accomplishments in the world. The brain is the centre of the soul's actings, where all the distinguishing faculties of it reside; and 'tis observable, a man who has a narrow, contracted head, in which there is not room for the due and necessary operations of nature by the brain, is never a man of very great judgment; and that proverb, "A great head and little wit," is not meant by nature, but is a reproof upon sloth, as if one should, by way of wonder, say, "Fie, fie, you that have a great head have but little wit; that's strange! that must certainly be your own fault." From this notion I do believe there is a great matter in the breed of men and women; not that wise men shall always get wise children, but I believe strong and healthy bodies have the wisest children, and sickly, weakly bodies affect the wits as well as the bodies of their children. We are easily persuaded to believe this in the breeds of horses, cocks, dogs, and other creatures; and I believe 'tis as visible in men.

[2.] But to come closer to the business: the great distinguishing difference which is seen in the world between men and women is in their education; and this is manifested by comparing it with the difference between one man or woman and another.

And herein it is that I take upon me to make such a bold assertion that all the world are mistaken in their practice about women; for I cannot think that God Almighty ever made them so delicate, so glorious creatures, and furnished them with such charms, so agreeable and so delightful to mankind, with souls capable of the same accomplishments with men, and all to be only stewards of our houses, *cooks, and slaves.*

Not that I am for exalting the female government in the least; but, in short, *I would have men take women for companions, and educate them to be fit for it.* A woman of sense and breeding will scorn as much to encroach upon the prerogative of the man as a man of sense will scorn to oppress the weakness of the woman. But if the women's souls were refined and improved by teaching, that word would be lost; to say "the weakness of the sex," as to judgment, would be nonsense; for ignorance and folly would be no more to be found among women than men. I remember a passage which I heard from a very fine woman. She had wit and capacity enough, an extraordinary shape and face, and a great fortune, but had been cloistered up all her time, and, for fear of being stolen, had not had the liberty of being taught the common necessary knowledge of women's affairs; and when she came to converse in the world, her natural wit made her so sensible of the want of education that she gave this short reflection on herself:

"I am ashamed to talk with my very maids," says she, "for I don't know when they do right or wrong. I had more need go to school than be married."

I need not enlarge on the loss the defect of education is to the sex, nor argue the benefit of the contrary practice; 'tis a thing will be more easily granted than remedied. This chapter is but an essay at the thing; and I refer the practice to those happy days, if ever they shall be, when men shall be wise enough to mend it.

JONATHAN SWIFT
A MODEST PROPOSAL [1]

FOR PREVENTING THE CHILDREN OF POOR PEOPLE FROM BEING A BURTHEN TO THEIR PARENTS OR COUNTRY, AND FOR MAKING THEM BENEFICIAL TO THE PUBLIC

IT is a melancholy object to those who walk through this great town [2] or travel in the country, when they see the streets, the roads, and cabin doors crowded with beggars of the female sex, followed by three, four, or six children, all in rags and importuning every passenger for an alms. These mothers, instead of being able to work for their honest livelihood, are forced to employ all their time in strolling to beg sustenance for their helpless infants, who, as they grow up, either turn thieves for want of work, or leave their dear native country to fight for the pretender in Spain, or sell themselves to the Barbadoes.

I think it is agreed by all parties that this prodigious number of children in the arms, or on the backs, or at the heels of their mothers, and frequently of their fathers, is, in the present deplorable state of the kingdom, a very great additional grievance; and therefore whoever could find out a fair, cheap, and easy method of making these children sound and useful members of the commonwealth would deserve so well of the public as to have his statue set up for a preserver of the nation.

But my intention is very far from being confined to provide only for the children of professed beggars: it is of a much greater extent, and shall take in the whole number of infants at a certain age, who are born of parents in effect as little able to support them as those who demand our charity in the streets.

As to my own part, having turned my thoughts for many years upon this important subject, and maturely weighed the several schemes of our projectors, I have always found them grossly mistaken in their computation. It is true, a child just dropt from its dam may be supported by her milk for a

[1] Published in 1729.   [2] Dublin

solar year, with little other nourishment, at most not above the value of two shillings, which the mother may certainly get, or the value in scraps, by her lawful occupation of begging; and it is exactly at one year old that I propose to provide for them in such a manner as, instead of being a charge upon their parents or the parish, or wanting food and raiment for the rest of their lives, they shall, on the contrary, contribute to the feeding, and partly to the clothing, of many thousands.

satire

There is likewise another great advantage in my scheme, that it will prevent those voluntary abortions, and that horrid practice of women murdering their bastard children, alas! too frequent among us, sacrificing the poor innocent babes, I doubt, more to avoid the expense than the shame, which would move tears and pity in the most savage and inhuman breast.

The number of souls in this kingdom being usually reckoned one million and a half, of these I calculate there may be about two hundred thousand couple whose wives are breeders; from which number I subtract thirty thousand couples who are able to maintain their own children, although I apprehend there cannot be so many, under the present distresses of the kingdom; but this being granted, there will remain an hundred and seventy thousand breeders. I again subtract fifty thousand for those women who miscarry, or whose children die by accident or disease within the year. There only remain an hundred and twenty thousand children of poor parents annually born. The question therefore is, how this number shall be reared and provided for, which, as I have already said, under the present situation of affairs is utterly impossible by all the methods hitherto proposed; for we can neither employ them in handicraft or agriculture; we neither build houses (I mean in the country), nor cultivate land: they can very seldom pick up a livelihood by stealing till they arrive at six years old, except where they are of towardly parts; although I confess they learn the rudiments much earlier; during which time they can however be properly looked upon only as probationers; as I have been informed by a principal gentleman in the county of Cavan, who protested to me that he never knew above one or two instances under the age of six, even in a part of the kingdom so renowned for the quickest proficiency in that art.

I am assured by our merchants that a boy or a girl before twelve years old is no salable commodity, and even when they come to this age, they will not yield above three pounds, or three pounds and half a crown at most, on the exchange, which cannot turn to account either to the parents or kingdom, the charge of nutriment and rags having been at least four times that value.

I shall now therefore humbly propose my own thoughts, which I hope will not be liable to the least objection.

I have been assured by a very knowing American of my acquaintance in London, that a young healthy child well nursed is at a year old a most delicious, nourishing, and wholesome food, whether stewed, roasted, baked, or boiled, and I make no doubt that it will equally serve in a fricassee, or a ragoust.

I do therefore humbly offer it to public consideration, that of the hundred and twenty thousand children already computed, twenty thousand may be reserved for breed, whereof only one fourth part to be males; which is more than we allow to sheep, black cattle, or swine; and my reason is, that these children are seldom the fruits of marriage, a circumstance not much regarded by our savages; therefore, one male will be sufficient to serve four females. That the remaining hundred thousand may, at a year old, be offered in sale to the persons of quality and fortune through the kingdom, always advising the mother to let them suck plentifully in the last month, so as to render them plump and fat for a good table. A child will make two dishes at an entertainment for friends, and when the family dines alone, the fore or hind quarter will make a reasonable dish, and seasoned with a little pepper or salt will be very good boiled on the fourth day, especially in winter.

I have reckoned, upon a medium, that a child just born will weigh 12 pounds, and in a solar year, if tolerably nursed, increaseth to 28 pounds.

I grant this food will be somewhat dear, and therefore very proper for landlords, who, as they have already devoured most of the parents, seem to have the best title to the children.

Infant's flesh will be in season throughout the year, but more plentiful in March, and a little before and after, for we are told by a grave author, an eminent French physician, that fish being a prolific diet, there are more children born in Roman Catholic countries about nine months after Lent than at any other season; therefore, reckoning a year after Lent, the markets will be more glutted than usual, because the number of popish infants is at least three to one in this kingdom; and therefore it will have one other collateral advantage, by lessening the number of papists among us.

I have already computed the charge of nursing a beggar's child (in which list I reckon all cottagers, laborers, and four fifths of the farmers) to be about two shillings per annum, rags included; and I believe no gentleman would repine to give ten shillings for the carcass of a good fat child, which, as I have said, will make four dishes of excellent nutritive meat, when he hath only some particular friend or his own family to dine with him. Thus the squire will learn to be a good landlord, and grow popular among his tenants; the mother will have eight shillings neat profit, and be fit for work till she produces another child.

Those who are more thrifty (as I must confess the times require) may flay the carcass; the skin of which, artificially dressed, will make admirable gloves for ladies and summer boots for fine gentlemen.

As to our city of Dublin, shambles may be appointed for this purpose in the most convenient parts of it, and butchers we may be assured will not be wanting, although I rather recommend buying the children alive, and dressing them hot from the knife, as we do roasting pigs.

A very worthy person, a true lover of his country and whose virtues I highly esteem, was lately pleased, in discoursing on this matter, to offer a refinement upon my scheme. He said that many gentlemen of this kingdom, having of late destroyed their deer, he conceived that the want of venison might be well supplied by the bodies of young lads and maidens, not exceeding fourteen years of age nor under twelve, so great a number of both sexes in every country being now ready to starve for want of work and service: and these to be disposed of by their parents if alive, or otherwise by their nearest relations. But with due deference to so excellent a friend and so deserving a patriot, I cannot be altogether in his sentiments; for as to the males, my American acquaintance assured me, from frequent experience, that their flesh was generally tough and lean, like that of our school-boys, by continual exercise, and their taste disagreeable, and to fatten them would not answer the charge. Then as to the females, it would, I think with humble submission, be a loss to the public, because they soon would become breeders themselves: and besides, it is not improbable that some scrupulous people might be apt to censure such a practice (although indeed very unjustly) as a little bordering upon cruelty, which, I confess, has always been with me the strongest objection against any project, how well soever intended.

But in order to justify my friend, he confessed that this expedient was put into his head by the famous Salmanaazar,[1] a native of the island Formosa, who came from thence to London above twenty years ago, and in conversation told my friend that in his country, when any young person happened to be put to death, the executioner sold the carcass to persons of quality as a prime dainty, and that in his time the body of a plump girl of fifteen, who was crucified for an attempt to poison the emperor, was sold to his imperial majesty's prime minister of state, and other great mandarins of the court, in joints from the gibbet, at four hundred crowns. Neither indeed can I deny that if the same use were made of several plump young girls in this town who, without one single groat to their fortunes, cannot stir abroad without a chair, and appear at a playhouse and assemblies in foreign fineries which they never will pay for, the kingdom would not be the worse.

Some persons of a desponding spirit are in great concern about that vast number of poor people who are aged, diseased, or maimed, and I have been desired to employ my thoughts what course may be taken to ease the nation of so grievous an incumbrance. But I am not in the least pain upon that matter, because it is very well known that they are every day dying and rotting, by cold and famine, and filth and vermin, as fast as can be reasonably expected. And as to the younger laborers, they are now in almost as hopeful a condition. They cannot get work, and consequently pine away for want of nourishment, to a degree that if at any time they are accidentally hired to

[1] *i.e.*, Psalmanaazar, author of *Description of Formosa* (1705)

common labor, they have not strength to perform it, and thus the country and themselves are happily delivered from the evils to come.

I have too long digressed, and therefore shall return to my subject. I think the advantages by the proposal which I have made are obvious and many, as well as of the highest importance.

For *first*, as I have already observed, it would greatly lessen the number of Papists, with whom we are yearly overrun, being the principal breeders of the nation, as well as our most dangerous enemies, and who stay at home on purpose with a design to deliver the kingdom to the Pretender, hoping to take their advantage by the absence of so many good Protestants, who have chosen rather to leave their country than stay at home and pay tithes against their conscience to an episcopal curate.

Secondly, the poorer tenants will have something valuable of their own which by law may be made liable to distress, and help to pay their landlord's rent, their corn and cattle being already seized, and money a thing unknown.

Thirdly, whereas the maintenance of a hundred thousand children, from two years old and upwards, cannot be computed at less than ten shillings apiece per annum, the nation's stock will be thereby increased fifty thousand pounds per annum, besides the profit of a new dish introduced to the tables of all gentlemen of fortune in the kingdom who have any refinement in taste, and the money will circulate among ourselves, the goods being entirely of our own growth and manufacture.

Fourthly, the constant breeders, besides the gain of eight shillings sterling per annum by the sale of their children, will be rid of the charge of maintaining them after the first year.

Fifthly, this food would likewise bring great custom to taverns, where the vintners will certainly be so prudent as to procure the best receipts for dressing it to perfection, and consequently have their houses frequented by all the fine gentlemen, who justly value themselves upon their knowledge in good eating; and a skilful cook, who understands how to oblige his guests, will contrive to make it as expensive as they please.

Sixthly, this would be a great inducement to marriage, which all wise nations have either encouraged by rewards, or enforced by laws and penalties. It would increase the care and tenderness of mothers towards their children, when they were sure of a settlement for life to the poor babes, provided in some sort by the public, to their annual profit instead of expense; we should soon see an honest emulation among the married women, which of them could bring the fattest child to the market. Men would become as fond of their wives during the time of their pregnancy as they are now of their mares in foal, their cows in calf, or sows when they are ready to farrow, nor offer to beat or kick them (as is too frequent a practice) for fear of a miscarriage.

Many other advantages might be enumerated. For instance, the addition of some thousand carcasses in our exportation of barreled beef. The propagation of swine's flesh, and improvement in the art of making good bacon, so much wanted among us by the great destruction of pigs, too frequent at our tables, which are no way comparable in taste or magnificence to a well grown, fat, yearly child, which roasted whole will make a considerable figure at a lord mayor's feast, or any other public entertainment. But this and many others I omit, being studious of brevity.

Supposing that one thousand families in this city would be constant customers for infants' flesh, besides others who might have it at merry meetings, particularly at weddings and christenings, I compute that Dublin would take off annually about twenty thousand carcasses, and the rest of the kingdom (where probably they will be sold somewhat cheaper) the remaining eighty thousand.

I can think of no one objection that will possibly be raised against this proposal, unless it should be urged that the number of people will be thereby much lessened in the kingdom. This I freely own, and 'twas indeed one principal design in offering it to the world. I desire the reader will observe that I calculate my remedy for this one individual kingdom of Ireland, and for no other that ever was, is, or, I think, ever can be upon earth. Therefore let no man talk to me of other expedients: of taxing our absentees at five shillings a pound; of using neither clothes nor household furniture, except what is of our own growth and manufacture; of utterly rejecting the materials and instruments that promote foreign luxury; of curing the expensiveness of pride, vanity, idleness, and gaming in our women; of introducing a vein of parsimony, prudence, and temperance; of learning to love our country, wherein we differ even from Laplanders, and the inhabitants of Topinamboo; of quitting our animosities and factions, nor act any longer like the Jews, who were murdering one another at the very moment their city was taken; of being a little cautious not to sell our country and consciences for nothing; of teaching landlords to have at least one degree of mercy towards their tenants. Lastly, of putting a spirit of honesty, industry, and skill into our shopkeepers, who, if a resolution could now be taken to buy only our native goods, would immediately unite to cheat and exact upon us in the price, the measure, and the goodness, nor could ever yet be brought to make one fair proposal of just dealing, though often and earnestly invited to it.

Therefore I repeat, let no man talk to me of these and the like expedients, till he hath at least some glimpse of hope that there will ever be some hearty and sincere attempt to put them in practice.

But, as to myself, having been wearied out for many years with offering vain, idle, visionary thoughts, and at length utterly despairing of success, I fortunately fell upon this proposal, which, as it is wholly new, so it hath something solid and real, of no expense and little trouble, full in our own power, and whereby we can incur no danger in disobliging England. For this kind of commodity will not bear exportation, the flesh being of too tender a consistence to admit a long continuance in salt, although perhaps I could name a country which would be glad to eat up our whole nation without it.

After all, I am not so violently bent upon my own opinion as to reject any offer, proposed by wise men, which shall be found equally innocent, cheap, easy, and effectual. But before something of that kind shall be advanced in contradiction to my scheme, and offering a better, I desire the author or authors will be pleased maturely to consider two points. First, as things now stand, how they will be able to find food and raiment for a hundred thousand useless mouths and backs. And secondly, there being a round million of creatures in human figure throughout this kingdom, whose whole subsistence put into a common stock would leave them in debt two millions of pounds sterling, adding those who are beggars by profession, to the bulk of farmers, cottagers, and laborers, with their wives and children, who are beggars in effect; I desire those politicians who dislike my overture and may perhaps be so bold to attempt an answer, that they will first ask the parents of these mortals whether they would not at this day think it a great happiness to have been sold for food at a year old, in the manner I prescribe, and thereby have avoided such a perpetual scene of misfortunes as they have since gone through, by the oppression of landlords, the impossibility of paying rent without money or trade, the want of common sustenance, with neither house nor clothes to cover them from the inclemencies of the weather, and the most inevitable prospect of entailing the like or greater miseries upon their breed for ever.

I profess, in the sincerity of my heart, that I have not the least personal interest in endeavoring to promote this necessary work, having no other motive than the public good of my country, by advancing our trade, providing for infants, relieving the poor, and giving some pleasure to the rich. I have no children by which I can propose to get a single penny; the youngest being nine years old, and my wife past child-bearing.

SIR RICHARD STEELE

LOVE OF GLORY [1]

Vera Gloria radices agit, atque etiam propagatur: Ficta omnia celeriter, tanquam flosculi, decidunt, nec simulatum potest quidquam esse diuturnum. Tull.[2]

OF all the affections which attend human life, the Love of Glory is the most ardent. According as this is cultivated in princes, it produces the greatest good or the greatest evil. Where sovereigns have it by impressions received from education only, it creates an ambitious rather than a noble mind; where it is the natural bent of the prince's inclination, it prompts him to the pursuit of things truly glorious. The two greatest men now in Europe (according to the common acceptation of the word *great*) are Lewis King of France and Peter Emperor of Russia. As it is certain that all fame does not arise from the practice of virtue, it is, methinks, no unpleasing amusement to examine the glory of these potentates, and distinguish that which is empty, perishing, and frivolous, from what is solid, lasting, and important. Lewis of France had his infancy attended by crafty and worldly men, who made extent of territory the most glorious instance of power, and mistook the spreading of fame for the acquisition of honor. The young monarch's heart was by such conversation easily deluded into a fondness for vainglory, and upon these unjust principles to form or fall in with suitable projects of invasion, rapine, murder, and all the guilts that attend war when it is unjust. At the same time this tyranny was laid, sciences and arts were encouraged in the most generous manner, as if men of higher faculties were to be bribed to permit the massacre of the rest of the world. Every superstructure which the court of France built upon their first designs, which were in themselves vicious, was suitable to its false foundation. The ostentation of riches, the vanity of equipage, shame of poverty, and ignorance of modesty, were the

[1] *The Spectator*, No. 139, Thursday, August 9, 1711.

[2] Cicero: *De Officiis*, II. xii.

common arts of life: the generous love of one woman was changed into gallantry for all the sex, and friendships among men turned into commerces of interest, or mere professions. *While these were the rules of life, perjuries in the prince, and a general corruption of manners in the subject, were the snares in which France has entangled all her neighbors.* With such false colors have the eyes of Lewis been enchanted, from the debauchery of his early youth to the superstition of his present old age. Hence it is that he has the patience to have statues erected to his prowess, his valor, his fortitude; and, in the softnesses and luxury of a court, to be applauded for magnanimity and enterprise in military achievements.

Peter Alexiwitz of Russia, when he came to the years of manhood, though he found himself emperor of a vast and numerous people, master of an endless territory, absolute commander of the lives and fortunes of his subjects, in the midst of this unbounded power and greatness turned his thoughts upon himself and people with sorrow. Sordid ignorance and a brute manner of life this generous prince beheld and contemned from the light of his own genius. His judgment suggested this to him, and his courage prompted him to amend it. In order to this he did not send to the nation from whence the rest of the world has borrowed its politeness, but himself left his diadem to learn the true way to glory and honor, and application to useful arts, wherein to employ the laborious, the simple, the honest part of his people. Mechanic employments and operations were very justly the first objects of his favor and observation. With this glorious intention he travelled into foreign nations in an obscure manner, above receiving little honors where he sojourned, but prying into what was of more consequence, their arts of peace and of war. By this means has this great prince laid the foundation of a great and lasting fame, by personal labor, personal knowledge, personal valor. It would be injury to any of antiquity to name them with him. Who but himself ever left a throne to learn to sit in it with more grace? Who ever thought himself mean in absolute power, till he had learned to use it?

If we consider this wonderful person, it is perplexity to know where to begin his encomium. Others may in a metaphorical or philosophic sense be said to command themselves, but this emperor is also literally under his own command. How generous and how good was his entring his own name as a private man in the army he raised, that none in it might expect to outrun the steps with which he himself advanced! By such measures this god-like prince learned to conquer, learned to use his conquests. How terrible has he appeared in battle, how gentle in victory? Shall then the base arts of the Frenchman be held polite, and the honest labors of the Russian barbarous? No: barbarity is the ignorance of true honor, or placing anything instead of it. The unjust prince is ignoble and barbarous, the good prince only renowned and glorious.

Though men may impose upon themselves what they please by their corrupt imaginations, truth will ever keep its station; and as glory is nothing else but the shadow of virtue, it will certainly disappear at the departure of virtue. But how carefully ought the true notions of it to be preserved, and how industrious should we be to encourage any impulses towards it? The Westminster schoolboy that said the other day he could not sleep or play for the colors in the Hall,[1] ought to be free from receiving a blow for ever.

But let us consider what is truly glorious according to the author I have today quoted in the front of my paper.

The perfection of glory, says Tully, consists in these three particulars: "that the people love us; that they have confidence in us; that being affected with a certain admiration towards us, they think we deserve honor." This was spoken of greatness in a commonwealth: but if one were to form a notion of consummate glory under our constitution, one must add to the above-mentioned felicities a certain necessary inexistence,[2] and disrelish of all the rest, without the prince's favor. He should, methinks, have riches, power, honor, command, glory; but riches, power, honor, command and glory should have no charms, but as accompanied with the affection of his prince. He should, methinks, be popular because a favorite, and a favorite because popular. Were it not to make the character too imaginary, I would give him sovereignty over some foreign

---

[1] The Colors taken at Blenheim hung in Westminster Hall.

[2] non-existence, unreality

territory, and make him esteem that an empty addition without the kind regards of his own prince. One may merely have an idea of a man thus composed and circumstantiated, and if he were so made for power without an incapacity of giving jealousy, he would be also glorious, without possibility of receiving disgrace. This humility and this importance must make his glory immortal.

These thoughts are apt [1] to draw me beyond the usual length of this paper, but if I could suppose such rhapsodies could outlive the common fate of ordinary things, I would say these sketches and faint images of glory were drawn in August, 1711, when John Duke of Marlborough made that memorable march wherein he took the French lines without bloodshed.

[1] such as, suitable

JOSEPH ADDISON

A SUPERSTITIOUS HOUSEHOLD [1]

Somnia, terrores magicos, miracula, sagas,
Nocturnos lemures, portentaque Thessala rides? [2]

Horace[: *Epistles,* II. ii. 208-09]

GOING yesterday to dine with an old acquaintance, I had the misfortune to find his whole family very much dejected. Upon asking him the occasion of it, he told me that his wife had dreamt a very strange dream the night before, which they were afraid portended some misfortune to themselves or to their children. At her coming into the room, I observed a settled melancholy in her countenance, which I should have been troubled for, had I not heard from whence it proceeded. We were no sooner sat down, but, after having looked upon me a little while, "My dear," says she, turning to her husband, "you may now see the stranger that was in the candle last night." Soon after this, as they began to talk of family affairs, a little boy at the lower end of the table told her that he was to go into join-hand [3] on Thursday. "Thursday?" says she, "no, child, if it please God, you shall not begin upon Childermas Day; tell your writing master that Friday will be soon enough." I was reflecting with myself on the oddness of her fancy, and wondering that anybody would establish it as a rule to lose a day in every week. In the midst of these my musings, she desired me to reach her a little salt upon the point of my knife, which I did in such a trepidation and hurry of obedience, that I let it drop by the way; at which she immediately startled, and said it fell towards her. Upon this I looked very blank; and, observing the concern of the whole table, began to consider myself, with some confusion, as a person that had brought a disaster upon the family. The lady however recovering herself,

---

[1] *The Spectator*, No. 7, Thursday, March 8, 1711.

[2] "Can you make sport of portents, gipsy crones,
Hobgoblins, dreams, raw head and bloody bones?"   John Conington.

[3] cursive writing, script

after a little space, said to her husband with a sigh, "My dear, misfortunes never come single." My friend, I found, acted but an under part at his table, and being a man of more good nature than understanding, thinks himself obliged to fall in with all the passions and humors of his yoke-fellow. "Do not you remember, child," says she, "that the pigeon-house fell the very afternoon that our careless wench spilt the salt upon the table?" "Yes," says he, "my dear, and the next post brought us an account of the battle of Almanza." The reader may guess at the figure I made, after having done all this mischief. I despatched my dinner as soon as I could, with my usual taciturnity; when, to my utter confusion, the lady seeing me cleaning my knife and fork, and laying them across one another upon my plate, desired me that I would humor her so far as to take them out of that figure, and place them side by side. What the absurdity was which I had committed I did not know, but I suppose there was some traditionary superstition in it; and therefore, in obedience to the lady of the house, I disposed of my knife and fork in two parallel lines, which is the figure I shall always lay them in for the future, though I do not know any reason for it.

It is not difficult for a man to see that a person has conceived an aversion to him. For my own part, I quickly found, by the lady's looks, that she regarded me as a very odd kind of fellow, with an unfortunate aspect: for which reason I took my leave immediately after dinner, and withdrew to my own lodgings. Upon my return home, I fell into a profound contemplation on the evils that attend these superstitious follies of mankind; how they subject us to imaginary afflictions, and additional sorrows, that do not properly come within our lot. As if the natural calamities of life were not sufficient for it, we turn the most indifferent circumstances into misfortunes, and suffer as much from trifling accidents as from real evils. I have known the shooting of a star spoil a night's rest; and have seen a man in love grow pale and lose his appetite upon the plucking of a merry-thought.[1] A screech owl at midnight has alarmed a family more than a band of robbers; nay, the voice of a cricket hath struck more terror than the roaring of a lion. There is

---

[1] wishbone

nothing so inconsiderable that may not appear dreadful to an imagination that is filled with omens and prognostics. A rusty nail, or a crooked pin, shoot up into prodigies.

I remember I was once in a mixed assembly that was full of noise and mirth, when on a sudden an old woman unluckily observed there were thirteen of us in company. This remark struck a panic terror into several that were present, insomuch that one or two of the ladies were going to leave the room; but a friend of mine, taking notice that one of our female companions was big with child, affirmed there were fourteen in the room, and that, instead of portending one of the company should die, it plainly foretold one of them should be born. Had not my friend found this expedient to break the omen, I question not but half the women in the company would have fallen sick that very night.

An old maid that is troubled with the vapors produces infinite disturbances of this kind among her friends and neighbors. I know a maiden aunt, of a great family, who is one of these antiquated sibyls, that forebodes and prophesies from one end of the year to the other. She is always seeing apparitions and hearing death watches; and was the other day almost frighted out of her wits by the great house dog, that howled in the stable at a time when she lay ill of the toothache. Such an extravagant cast of mind engages multitudes of people, not only in impertinent terrors, but in supernumerary duties of life; and arises from that fear and ignorance which are natural to the soul of man. The horror with which we entertain the thoughts of death (or indeed of any future evil) and the uncertainty of its approach fill a melancholy mind with innumerable apprehensions and suspicions, and consequently dispose it to the observation of such groundless prodigies and predictions. For as it is the chief concern of wise men to retrench the evils of life by the reasonings of philosophy, it is the employment of fools to multiply them by the sentiments of superstition.

For my own part, I should be very much troubled were I endowed with this divining quality, though it should inform me truly of every thing that can befall me. I would not anticipate the relish of any happiness, nor feel the weight of any misery, before it actually arrives.

I know but one way of fortifying my soul against these gloomy presages and terrors of mind, and that is by securing to myself the friendship and protection of that Being who disposes of events and governs futurity. He sees, at one view, the whole thread of my existence, not only that part of it which I have already passed through, but that which runs forward into all the depths of eternity. When I lay me down to sleep, I recommend myself to His care; when I awake, I give myself up to His direction. Amidst all the evils that threaten me, I will look up to Him for help, and question not but He will either avert them, or turn them to my advantage. Though I know neither the time nor the manner of the death I am to die, I am not at all solicitous about it; because I am sure that He knows them both, and that He will not fail to comfort and support me under them.

BENJAMIN FRANKLIN

RULES [1] FOR

Reducing a SMALL ONE; *presented to a* LATE
Minister, when he entered upon his Administration. [2]

AN ancient sage valued himself upon this, that though he
could not fiddle, he knew how to make a great city of a little
one. The science that I, a modern simpleton, am about to
communicate is the very reverse.

I address myself to all ministers who have the management
of extensive dominions which from their very greatness are
become troublesome to govern — because the multiplicity of
their affairs leaves no time for fiddling.

I. In the first place, gentlemen, you are to consider that a
great empire, like a great cake, is most easily diminished at the
edges. Turn your attention, therefore, first to the *remotest*
provinces, that, as you get rid of them, the next may follow in
order.

II. That the possibility of this separation may always exist,
take special care the provinces are *never incorporated with the
mother country*; that they do not enjoy the same common
rights, the same privileges in commerce; and that they are
governed by severer laws, all of your enacting, without allowing
them any share in the choice of the legislators. By carefully
making and preserving such distinctions, you will (to keep to
my simile of the cake) act like a wise gingerbread-baker; who,
to facilitate a division, cuts his dough half through in those
places where, when baked, he would have it broken to pieces.

---

[1] From the London edition of 1793. Originally published in the Philadelphia
Public Advertizer in October, 1773.

[2] The minister alluded to is supposed to be the Earl of H——h.
"The causes and motions of seditions " (says Lord Bacon) " are, innovation in
religion, taxes, alteration of laws and customs, breaking of privileges, general oppression, advancement of unworthy persons, strangers, dearths, disbanded soldiers, factions grown desperate, and whatsoever in offending people joineth and
knitteth them in a common cause." [Note in edition of 1793.]

III. These remote provinces have, perhaps, been acquired, purchased, or conquered, at the sole expense of the settlers their ancestors, without the aid of the mother country. If this should happen to increase her strength, by their growing numbers, ready to join in her wars; her commerce, by their growing demand for her manufactures; or her naval power, by greater employment for her ships and seamen. They may probably suppose some merit in this, and that it entitles them to some favor; you are therefore to *forget it all, or resent it,* as if they had done you injury. — If they happen to be zealous Whigs, friends of liberty, nurtured in revolution principles, remember all that to their prejudice, and contrive to punish it; for such principles, after a revolution is thoroughly established, are of no more use; they are even odious and abominable.

IV. However peaceably your colonies have submitted to your government, shown their affection to your interests, and patiently borne their grievances, you are to suppose them *always inclined to revolt,* and treat them accordingly. Quarter troops among them, who by their insolence may provoke the rising of mobs, and by their bullets and bayonets suppress them. By these means, like the husband who uses his wife ill from suspicion, you may in time convert your suspicions into realities.

V. Remote provinces must have governors and judges, to represent the royal person, and execute everywhere the delegated parts of his office and authority. You ministers know that much of the strength of government depends on the opinion of the people; and much of that opinion on the *choice of rulers* placed immediately over them. If you send them wise and good men for governors, who study the interests of the colonists, and advance their prosperity, they will think their king wise and good, and that he wishes the welfare of his subjects. If you send them learned and upright men for judges, they will think him a lover of justice. — This may attach your provinces more to his government. You are therefore to be careful who you recommend for those offices. — If you can find prodigals who have ruined their fortunes, broken gamesters or stock-jobbers, these may do well as Governors; for they will probably be rapacious, and provoke the people by their

extortions. Wrangling proctors and pettifogging lawyers too
are not amiss; for they will be for ever disputing and quarrelling
with their little parliaments. If withal they should be ignorant, wrong-headed, and insolent, so much the better. — At-
torneys' clerks and Newgate solicitors will do for Chief Jus-
tices, especially if they hold their places during your pleasure:
— and all will contribute to impress those ideas of your government that are proper for a people you would wish to renounce it.

VI. To confirm these impressions, and strike them deeper,
whenever the injured come to the capital with complaints of
mal-administration, oppression, or injustice, *punish such suitors* with long delay, enormous expense, and a final judgment in favor of the oppressor: this will have an admirable
effect every way. The trouble of future complaints will be
prevented, and governors and judges will be encouraged to
farther acts of oppression and injustice; and thence the people
may become more disaffected, and at length desperate.

VII. When such governors have crammed their coffers, and
made themselves so odious to the people that they can no
longer remain among them with safety to their persons, *recall
and reward them with pensions*. You may make them baronets,
too, if that respectable order should not think fit to resent it.
All will contribute to encourage new governors in the same
practice, and make the supreme government detestable.

VIII. If, when you are engaged in war, your colonies should
vie in liberal aids of men and money against the common
enemy, upon your simple requisition, and give far beyond their
abilities, — reflect that a penny taken from them by your
power, is more honorable to you than a pound presented by
their benevolence; *despise therefore their voluntary grants*, and
resolve to harass them with *novel taxes*. — They will probably
complain to your parliament that they are taxed by a body in
which they have no representative, and that this is contrary
to common right. They will petition for redress. Let the
parliament flout their claims, reject their petitions, refuse even
to suffer the reading of them, and treat the petitioners with the
utmost contempt. — Nothing can have a better effect in producing the alienation proposed; for though many can forgive
injuries, none ever forgave contempt.

IX. In laying these taxes *never regard the heavy burthens* those remote people already undergo; in defending their own frontiers, supporting their own provincial government, making new roads, building bridges, churches, and other public edifices, which in old countries have been done to your hands by your ancestors, but which occasion constant calls and demands on the purses of a new people. — Forget the restraint you lay on their trade for your own benefit, and the advantage a monopoly of this trade gives your exacting merchants. Think nothing of the wealth those merchants and your manufacturers acquire by the colony commerce; their increased ability thereby to pay taxes at home; their accumulating in the price of their commodities most of those taxes, and so levying them from their consuming customers: all this, and the employment and support of thousands of your poor by the colonists, you are entirely to forget. — But remember to make your arbitrary tax more grievous to your provinces by public declarations importing that your power of taxing them has *no limits*, so that when you take from them without their consent a shilling in the pound, you have a clear right to the other nineteen. This will probably weaken every idea of security in their property, and convince them that under such a government they have nothing they can call their own; which can scarce fail of producing the happiest consequences!

X. Possibly, indeed, some of them might still comfort themselves and say, "Though we have no property, we have yet something left that is valuable; we have constitutional *liberty both of person and of conscience*. This King, these Lords, and these Commons, who it seems are too remote from us to know us and to feel for us, cannot take from us our *habeas corpus* right, or our right of trial by a jury of our neighbors: they cannot deprive us of the exercise of our religion, alter our ecclesiastical constitution, and compel us to be Papists, if they please, or Mahometans." — To annihilate this comfort begin by laws to perplex their commerce with infinite regulations, impossible to be remembered and observed: ordain seizures of their property for every failure; take away the trial of such property by jury, and give it to arbitrary judges of your own appointing and of the lowest characters in the country, whose salaries and emoluments are to arise out of the duties or condemnations, and whose appointments are during pleasure. — Then let there be a formal declaration of both houses that opposition to your edicts is treason, and that persons suspected of treason in the provinces may, according to some obsolete law, be seized and sent to the metropolis of the empire for trial; and pass an act that those there charged with certain other offences shall be sent away in chains from their friends and country to be tried in the same manner for felony. Then erect a new court of inquisition among them, accompanied by an armed force, with instructions to transport all such suspected persons; to be ruined by the expense, if they bring over evidences to prove their innocence; or be found guilty and hanged if they cannot afford it. — And lest the people should think you cannot possibly go any farther, pass another solemn declaratory act, "that King, Lords, and Commons had, have, and of right ought to have, full power and authority to make statutes of sufficient force and validity to bind the unrepresented provinces *in all cases whatsoever.*" This will include spiritual with temporal, and taken together must operate wonderfully to your purpose; by convincing them that they are at present under a power something like that spoken of in the Scriptures, which can not only kill their bodies, but damn their souls to all eternity, by compelling them, if it pleases, to worship the devil.

XI. To make your taxes more odious, and more likely to procure resistance, send from the capital a *board of officers* to superintend the collection, *composed of the most indiscreet*, ill-bred, and insolent you can find. Let these have large salaries out of the extorted revenue, and live in open grating luxury upon the sweat and blood of the industrious; whom they are to worry continually with groundless and expensive prosecutions before the above-mentioned arbitrary revenue-judges; all at the cost of the party prosecuted, though acquitted, because the King is to pay no costs. — Let these men by your order be exempted from all the common taxes and burthens of the province, though they and their property are protected by its laws. — If any revenue officers are suspected of the least tenderness for the people, discard them. If others are justly complained of, protect and reward them. If any of the under officers behave so as to provoke the people to drub them, promote those to better offices: this will encourage others to procure for themselves such profitable drubbings, by multiplying and enlarging such provocations, and all will work towards the end you aim at.

XII. Another way to make your tax odious, is to *misapply the produce of it.* If it was originally appropriated for the defence of the provinces, and the better support of government, and the administration of justice where it may be necessary; then apply none of it to that defence, but bestow it where it is not necessary, in augmenting salaries or pensions to every governor who has distinguished himself by his enmity to the people, and by calumniating them to their sovereign. This will make them pay it more unwillingly, and be more apt to quarrel with those that collect it and those that imposed it; who will quarrel again with them; and all shall contribute to your own purpose, of making them weary of your government.

XIII. If the people of any province have been accustomed to *support their own governors and judges* to satisfaction, you are to apprehend that such governors and judges may be thereby influenced to treat the people kindly, and to do them justice. This is another reason for applying part of that revenue in larger salaries to such governors and judges, given, as their commissions are, during *your* pleasure only; forbidding them to take any salaries from their provinces: and thus the people may no longer hope any kindness from their governors, or (in Crown cases) any justice from their judges. And as the money thus misapplied in one province is extorted from all, probably all will resent the misapplication.

XIV. If the parliaments of your provinces should dare to claim rights, or complain of your administration, order them to be harassed with *repeated dissolutions.* — If the same men are continually returned by new elections, adjourn their meetings to some country village where they cannot be accommodated, and there keep them during pleasure; for this, you know, is your prerogative; and an excellent one it is, as you may manage it to promote discontents among the people, diminish their respect, and increase their disaffection.

XV. Convert the brave honest officers of your *navy* into

pimping tide-waiters and colony-officers of the *customs*. Let those who in time of war fought gallantly in defence of the commerce of their countrymen, in peace be taught to prey upon it. Let them learn to be corrupted by great and real smugglers; but (to shew their diligence) scour with armed boats every bay, harbor, creek, cove, or nook throughout the coast of your colonies; stop and detain every coaster, every woodboat, every fisherman; tumble their cargoes and even their ballast inside out, and upside down; and if a pennyworth of pins is found unentered, let the whole be seized and confiscated. Thus shall the trade of your colonists suffer more from their friends in time of peace than it did from their enemies in war. — Then let these boats' crews land upon every farm in their way, rob their orchards, steal their pigs and poultry, and insult the inhabitants. If the injured and exasperated farmers, unable to procure other justice, should attack the aggressors, drub them, and burn their boats; you are to call this *high treason and rebellion*, order fleets and armies into their country, and threaten to carry all the offenders three thousand miles to be hanged, drawn, and quartered. — O! this will work admirably!

XVI. If you are told of *discontents* in your colonies, never believe that they are general, or that you have given occasion for them; therefore do not think of applying any remedy, or of changing any offensive measure. — Redress no grievance, lest they should be encouraged to demand the redress of some other grievance. Grant no request that is just and reasonable, lest they should make another that is unreasonable. — Take all your informations of the state of the colonies from your governors and officers in enmity with them. Encourage and reward these leasing-makers; [1] secrete their lying accusations, lest they should be confuted; but act upon them as the clearest evidence — and believe nothing you hear from the friends of the people. Suppose all *their* complaints to be invented and promoted by a few factious demagogues, whom if you catch and hang, all would be quiet. — Catch and hang a few of them accordingly; and the blood of the martyrs shall work miracles in favor of your purpose.[2]

[1] makers of lies.

[2] One of the American writers affirms, "That there has not been a single in-

XVII. If you see *rival nations* rejoicing at the prospect of your disunion with your provinces, and endeavoring to promote it; if they translate, publish, and applaud all the complaints of your discontented colonists, at the same time privately stimulating you to severer measures; let not that alarm or offend you. Why should it? since you all mean the same thing.

XVIII. If any colony should *at their own charge erect a fortress* to secure their *port* against the fleets of a foreign enemy, get your governor to betray that fortress into your hands. Never think of paying what it cost the country, for that would look, at least, like some regard for justice; but turn it into a citadel, to awe the inhabitants, and curb their commerce. If they should have lodged in such fortress the very arms they bought and used to aid you in your conquests, seize them all; it will provoke like ingratitude added to robbery. — One admirable effect of these operations will be, to discourage every other colony from erecting such defences, and so their and your enemies may more easily invade them; to the great disgrace of your government, and of course the furtherance of your project.

XIX. Send armies into their country under pretence of protecting the inhabitants; but, instead of garrisoning the forts on their frontiers with those troops, to prevent incursions, demolish those forts, and order the troops into the heart of the country, that the savages may be encouraged to attack the frontiers, [1] and that the troops may be protected by the in-

---

stance in which *they* have complained without being rebuked; or in which they have been complained *against* without being punished." — A fundamental mistake in the minister occasioned this. Every individual in New England (the peccant country) was held a coward or a knave, and the disorders which spread abroad there, were treated as the result of the *too great lenity* of Britain! By the aid of this short and benevolent rule, judgment was ever wisely predetermined; to the shutting out redress on the one hand, and enforcing every rigor of punishment on the other. [Note in edition of 1793.]

[1] I am not versed in Indian affairs, but I find that in April, 1773, the assembled chiefs of the western nations told one of our Indian agents, "that they remembered their father, the King of Great Britain's message, delivered to them last fall; of demolishing Fort Pittsburg (on the Ohio) and removing the soldiers with their sharp-edged weapons out of the country; — this gave them great pleasure, as it was a strong proof of his paternal kindness towards them." (See *Considerations on the Agreement with Mr. T. Walpole for Lands upon the Ohio*, p. 9.) This is general history; I attempt no application of facts, personally invidious. [Note in edition of 1793.]

habitants: this will seem to proceed from your *ill-will or your ignorance*, and contribute farther to produce and strengthen an opinion among them, that you are no longer fit to govern them.[1]

XX. Lastly, invest the *general of your army in the provinces* with great and unconstitutional powers, and free him from the control of even your own civil governors. Let him have troops now [2] under his command, with all the fortresses in his possession; and who knows but (like some provincial generals in the Roman empire, and encouraged by the universal discontent you have produced) he may take it into his head to set up for himself? If he should, and you have carefully practised these few excellent rules of mine, take my word for it, all the provinces will immediately join him; — and you will that day (if you have not done it sooner) get rid of the trouble of governing them, and all the plagues attending their commerce and connection, from thenceforth and for ever.

[1] As the reader may be inclined to divide his belief between the wisdom of ministry and the candor and veracity of Dr. Franklin, I shall inform him, that two contrary objections may be made to the truth of this representation. The first is, that the conduct of Great Britain is made *too* absurd for possibility; and the second, that it is not made absurd *enough* for fact. If we consider that this piece does not include the measures subsequent to 1773, the latter difficulty is easily set aside. The former, I can only solve by the many instances in history, where the infatuation of individuals has brought the heaviest calamities upon nations. [Note in edition of 1793.]

[2] *i.e.*, in the situation and crisis into which things will *now* have been brought. [Note in edition of 1793.]

SAMUEL JOHNSON

PREFACE TO SHAKESPEARE [1]

. . . . THE poet of whose works I have undertaken the revision
may now begin to assume the dignity of an ancient, and claim
the privilege of established fame and prescriptive veneration.[2]
He has long outlived his century, the term commonly fixed as
the test of literary merit. Whatever advantages he might once
derive from personal allusions, local customs, or temporary
opinions, have for many years been lost; and every topic of
merriment, or motive of sorrow, which the modes of artificial
life afforded him, now only obscure the scenes which they once
illuminated. The effects of favor and competition are at an
end; the tradition of his friendships and his enmities has perished; his works support no opinion with arguments, nor supply any faction with invectives; they can neither indulge vanity, nor gratify malignity; but are read without any other reason than the desire of pleasure, and are therefore praised only
as pleasure is obtained; yet, thus unassisted by interest or
passion, they have passed through variations of taste and
changes of manners, and, as they devolved from one generation
to another, have received new honors at every transmission.

But because human judgment, though it be gradually gaining upon certainty, never becomes infallible; and approbation,
though long continued, may yet be only the approbation of
prejudice or fashion; it is proper to inquire, by what peculiarities of excellence Shakespeare has gained and kept the favor
of his countrymen.

Nothing can please many, and please long, but just repre-
sentations of general nature. Particular manners can be
known to few, and therefore few only can judge how nearly
they are copied. The irregular combinations of fanciful invention may delight awhile, by that novelty of which the com-

[1] This observation is preceded by a brief justification of "the reverence due to
writings that have long subsisted."

[2] From *Works of Shakespeare*, Vol. I, 1765.

mon satiety of life sends us all in quest; but the pleasures of sudden wonder are soon exhausted, and the mind can only repose on the stability of truth.

Shakespeare is, above all writers, at least above all modern writers, the poet of nature; the poet that holds up to his readers a faithful mirror of manners and of life. His characters are not modified by the customs of particular places, unpractised by the rest of the world; by the peculiarities of studies or professions, which can operate but upon small numbers; or by the accidents of transient fashions or temporary opinions: they are the genuine progeny of common humanity, such as the world will always supply, and observation will always find. His persons act and speak by the influence of those general passions and principles by which all minds are agitated, and the whole system of life is continued in motion. In the writings of other poets a character is too often an individual: in those of Shakespeare it is commonly a species.

It is from this wide extension of design that so much instruction is derived. It is this which fills the plays of Shakespeare with practical axioms and domestic wisdom. It was said of Euripides, that every verse was a precept; and it may be said of Shakespeare, that from his works may be collected a system of civil and economical prudence. Yet his real power is not shown in the splendor of particular passages, but by the progress of his fable, and the tenor of his dialogue: and he that tries to recommend him by select quotations, will succeed like the pedant in Hierocles,[1] who, when he offered his house to sale, carried a brick in his pocket as a specimen.

It will not easily be imagined how much Shakespeare excels in accommodating his sentiments to real life, but by comparing him with other authors. It was observed of the ancient schools of declamation that the more diligently they were frequented, the more was the student disqualified for the world, because he found nothing there which he should ever meet in any other place. The same remark may be applied to every stage but that of Shakespeare. The theatre, when it is under any other direction, is peopled by such characters as were never seen,

---

[1] A writer of the fifth century, reputed author of a collection of anecdotes about pedants.

conversing in a language which was never heard, upon topics which will never arise in the commerce of mankind. But the dialogue of this author is often so evidently determined by the incident which produces it, and is pursued with so much ease and simplicity, that it seems scarcely to claim the merit of fiction, but to have been gleaned by diligent selection out of common conversation, and common occurrences.

Upon every other stage the universal agent is love, by whose power all good and evil is distributed, and every action quickened or retarded. To bring a lover, a lady, and a rival into the fable; to entangle them in contradictory obligations, perplex them with oppositions of interest, and harass them with violence of desires inconsistent with each other; to make them meet in rapture, and part in agony; to fill their mouths with hyperbolical joy and outrageous sorrow; to distress them as nothing human ever was distressed; to deliver them as nothing human ever was delivered; is the business of a modern dramatist. For this, probability is violated, life is misrepresented, and language is depraved. But love is only one of many passions; and as it has no great influence upon the sum of life, it has little operation in the dramas of a poet who caught his ideas from the living world, and exhibited only what he saw before him. He knew that any other passion, as it was regular or exorbitant, was a cause of happiness or calamity.

Characters thus ample and general were not easily discriminated and preserved, yet perhaps no poet ever kept his personages more distinct from each other. I will not say with Pope, that every speech may be assigned to the proper speaker, because many speeches there are which have nothing characteristical; but, perhaps, though some may be equally adapted to every person, it will be difficult to find any that can be properly transferred from the present possessor to another claimant. The choice is right, when there is reason for choice.

Other dramatists can only gain attention by hyperbolical or aggravated characters, by fabulous and unexampled excellence or depravity, as the writers of barbarous romances invigorated the reader by a giant and a dwarf; and he that should form his expectations of human affairs from the play, or from the tale, would be equally deceived. Shakespeare has no heroes; his scenes are occupied only by men, who act and speak as the reader thinks that he should himself have spoken or acted on the same occasion: even where the agency is supernatural, the dialogue is level with life. Other writers disguise the most natural passions and most frequent incidents, so that he who contemplates them in the book will not know them in the world: Shakespeare approximates the remote, and familiarizes the wonderful; the event which he represents will not happen, but, if it were possible, its effects would probably be such as he has assigned; and it may be said, that he has not only shown human nature as it acts in real exigencies, but as it would be found in trials to which it cannot be exposed.

This therefore is the praise of Shakespeare, that his drama is the mirror of life; that he who has mazed his imagination, in following the phantoms which other writers raise up before him, may here be cured of his delirious ecstasies, by reading human sentiments in human language, by scenes from which a hermit may estimate the transactions of the world, and a confessor predict the progress of the passions.

His adherence to general nature has exposed him to the censure of critics, who form their judgments upon narrower principles. Dennis and Rymer think his Romans not sufficiently Roman; and Voltaire censures his kings as not completely royal. Dennis is offended that Menenius, a senator of Rome, should play the buffoon; and Voltaire perhaps thinks decency violated when the Danish usurper is represented as a drunkard. But Shakespeare always makes nature predominate over accident; and, if he preserves the essential character, is not very careful of distinctions superinduced and adventitious. His story requires Romans or kings, but he thinks only on men. He knew that Rome, like every other city, had men of all dispositions; and wanting a buffoon, he went into the senate-house for that which the senate-house would certainly have afforded him. He was inclined to show an usurper and a murderer not only odious, but despicable; he therefore added drunkenness to his other qualities, knowing that kings love wine like other men, and that wine exerts its natural power upon kings. These are the petty cavils of petty minds; a poet overlooks the casual distinction of country and condition, as a painter, satisfied with the figure, neglects the drapery. . . .¹

Shakespeare engaged in dramatic poetry with the world open before him; the rules of the ancients were yet known to few; the public judgment was unformed: he had no example of such fame as might force him upon imitation, nor critics of such authority as might restrain his extravagance; he therefore indulged his natural disposition; and his disposition, as Rymer has remarked, led him to comedy. In tragedy he often writes, with great appearance of toil and study, what is written at last with little felicity; but, in his comic scenes, he seems to produce, without labor, what no labor can improve. In tragedy he is always struggling after some occasion to be comic; but in comedy he seems to repose, or to luxuriate, as in a mode of thinking congenial to his nature. In his tragic scenes there is always something wanting, but his comedy often surpasses expectation or desire. His comedy pleases by the thoughts and the language, and his tragedy for the greater part by incident and action. His tragedy seems to be skill, his comedy to be instinct.

The force of his comic scenes has suffered little diminution from the changes made by a century and a half, in manners or in words. As his personages act upon principles arising from genuine passion, very little modified by particular forms, their pleasures and vexations are communicable to all times and to all places; they are natural and therefore durable: the adventitious peculiarities of personal habits are only superficial dyes, bright and pleasing for a little while, yet soon fading to a dim tinct, without any remains of former lustre; but the discriminations of true passion are the colors of nature: they pervade the whole mass and can only perish with the body that exhibits them. The accidental compositions of heterogeneous modes are dissolved by the chance which combined them; but the uniform simplicity of primitive qualities neither admits increase nor suffers decay. The sand heaped by one flood is scattered by another, but the rock always continues in its place. The stream of time, which is continually washing the

¹ A passage defending Shakspere from criticism for mingling tragic and comic scenes is omitted.

dissoluble fabrics of other poets, passes without injury by the adamant of Shakespeare.

If there be, what I believe there is, in every nation, a style which never becomes obsolete, a certain mode of phraseology so consonant and congenial to the analogy and principles of its respective language, as to remain settled and unaltered; this style is probably to be sought in the common intercourse of life, among those who speak only to be understood without ambition of elegance. The polite are always catching modish innovations, and the learned depart from established forms of speech, in hope of finding or making better: those who wish for distinction forsake the vulgar, when the vulgar is right; but there is a conversation above grossness, and below refinement, where propriety resides, and where this poet seems to have gathered his comic dialogue. He is therefore more agreeable to the ears of the present age than any other author equally remote, and among his other excellencies deserves to be studied as one of the original masters of our language.

These observations are to be considered not as unexceptionably constant, but as containing general and predominant truth. Shakespeare's familiar dialogue is affirmed to be smooth and clear, yet not wholly without ruggedness or difficulty; as a country may be eminently fruitful, though it has spots unfit for cultivation: his characters are praised as natural, though their sentiments are sometimes forced, and their actions improbable; as the earth upon the whole is spherical, though its surface is varied with protuberances and cavities.

Shakespeare with his excellencies has likewise faults, and faults sufficient to obscure and overwhelm any other merit. I shall show them in the proportion in which they appear to me, without envious malignity or superstitious veneration. No question can be more innocently discussed than a dead poet's pretensions to renown; and little regard is due to that bigotry which sets candor higher than truth.

His first defect is that to which may be imputed most of the evil in books or in men. He sacrifices virtue to convenience, and is so much more careful to please than to instruct that he seems to write without any moral purpose. From his writings, indeed, a system of social duty may be selected, for he that thinks reasonably must think morally; but his precepts and axioms drop casually from him; he makes no just distribution of good or evil, nor is always careful to show in the virtuous a disapprobation of the wicked; he carries his persons indifferently through right and wrong, and at the close dismisses them without further care, and leaves their examples to operate by chance. This fault the barbarity of his age cannot extenuate; for it is always a writer's duty to make the world better, and justice is a virtue independent on time or place.

The plots are often so loosely formed that a very slight consideration may improve them, and so carelessly pursued that he seems not always fully to comprehend his own design. He omits opportunities of instructing or delighting which the train of his story seems to force upon him, and apparently rejects those exhibitions which would be more affecting, for the sake of those which are more easy.

It may be observed, that in many of his plays the latter part is evidently neglected. When he found himself near the end of his work, and in view of his reward, he shortened the labor to snatch the profit. He therefore remits his efforts where he should most vigorously exert them, and his catastrophe is improbably produced or imperfectly represented.

He had no regard to distinction of time or place, but gives to one age or nation, without scruple, the customs, institutions, and opinions of another, at the expense not only of likelihood but of possibility. These faults Pope has endeavored, with more zeal than judgment, to transfer to his imagined interpolators. We need not wonder to find Hector quoting Aristotle, when we see the loves of Theseus and Hippolyta combined with the gothic mythology of fairies. Shakespeare, indeed, was not the only violator of chronology, for in the same age Sidney, who wanted not the advantages of learning, has, in his *Arcadia*, confounded the pastoral with the feudal times, the days of innocence, quiet, and security, with those of turbulence, violence, and adventure.

In his comic scenes he is seldom very successful when he engages his characters in reciprocations of smartness and contests of sarcasm: their jests are commonly gross, and their pleasantry licentious; neither his gentlemen nor his ladies have much delicacy, nor are sufficiently distinguished from his clowns by any appearance of refined manners. Whether he represented the real conversation of his time is not easy to determine: the reign of Elizabeth is commonly supposed to have been a time of stateliness, formality, and reserve; yet perhaps the relaxations of that severity were not very elegant. There must, however, have been always some modes of gaiety preferable to others, and a writer ought to choose the best.

In tragedy his performance seems constantly to be worse, as his labor is more. The effusions of passion, which exigence forces out, are for the most part striking and energetic; but whenever he solicits his invention, or strains his faculties, the offspring of his throes is tumor, meanness, tediousness, and obscurity.

In narration he affects a disproportionate pomp of diction, and a wearisome train of circumlocution, and tells the incident imperfectly in many words, which might have been more plainly delivered in few. Narration in dramatic poetry is naturally tedious, as it is unanimated and inactive, and obstructs the progress of the action; it should therefore always be rapid, and enlivened by frequent interruption. Shakespeare found it an encumbrance, and instead of lightening it by brevity, endeavored to recommend it by dignity and splendor.

His declamations or set speeches are commonly cold and weak, for his power was the power of nature; when he endeavored, like other tragic writers, to catch opportunities of amplification, and instead of inquiring what the occasion demanded, to show how much his stores of knowledge could supply, he seldom escapes without the pity or resentment of his reader.

It is incident to him to be now and then entangled with an unwieldy sentiment, which he cannot well express, and will not reject; he struggles with it a while, and, if it continues stubborn, comprises it in words such as occur, and leaves it to be disentangled and evolved by those who have more leisure to bestow upon it.

Not that always where the language is intricate the thought is subtle, or the image always great where the line is bulky; the equality of words to things is very often neglected, and trivial sentiments and vulgar ideas disappoint the attention, to which they are recommended by sonorous epithets and swelling figures.

But the admirers of this great poet have never less reason to indulge their hopes of supreme excellence, than when he seems fully resolved to sink them in dejection, and mollify them with tender emotions, by the fall of greatness, the danger of innocence, or the crosses of love.   [What he does best, he soon ceases to do.][1]   He is not long soft and pathetic without some idle conceit or contemptible equivocation.   He no sooner begins to move than he counteracts himself; and terror and pity, as they are rising in the mind, are checked and blasted by sudden frigidity.

A quibble is to Shakespeare what luminous vapors are to the traveller; he follows it at all adventures: it is sure to lead him out of his way, and sure to engulf him in the mire.   It has some malignant power over his mind, and its fascinations are irresistible.   Whatever be the dignity or profundity of his disquisition, whether he be enlarging knowledge or exalting affection, whether he be amusing attention with incidents, or enchaining it in suspense, let but a quibble spring up before him, and he leaves his work unfinished.   A quibble is the golden apple for which he will always turn aside from his career, or stoop from his elevation.   A quibble, poor and barren as it is, gave him such delight that he was content to purchase it by the sacrifice of reason, propriety, and truth.   A quibble was to him the fatal Cleopatra for which he lost the world, and was content to lose it.

It will be thought strange that, in enumerating the defects of this writer, I have not yet mentioned his neglect of the unities; his violation of those laws which have been instituted and established by the joint authority of poets and of critics.

For his other deviations from the art of writing I resign him to critical justice, without making any other demand in his favor than that which must be indulged to all human excellence — that his virtues be rated with his failings: but from the censure which this irregularity may bring upon him, I shall, with due reverence to that learning which I must oppose, adventure to try how I can defend him.

[1] Not in 1765 text; added in 1778.

His histories, being neither tragedies nor comedies, are not subject to any of their laws; nothing more is necessary to all the praise which they expect than that the changes of action be so prepared as to be understood; that the incidents be various and affecting, and the characters consistent, natural, and distinct. No other unity is intended, and therefore none is to be sought.

In his other works he has well enough preserved the unity of action. He has not, indeed, an intrigue regularly perplexed and regularly unravelled: he does not endeavor to hide his design only to discover it, for this is seldom the order of real events, and Shakespeare is the poet of nature: but his plan has commonly, what Aristotle requires, a beginning, a middle, and an end; one event is concatenated with another, and the conclusion follows by easy consequence. There are perhaps some incidents that might be spared, as in other poets there is much talk that only fills up time upon the stage; but the general system makes gradual advances, and the end of the play is the end of expectation.

To the unities of time and place he has shown no regard; and perhaps a nearer view of the principles on which they stand will diminish their value, and withdraw from them the veneration which, from the time of Corneille, they have very generally received, by discovering that they have given more trouble to the poet than pleasure to the auditor.

The necessity of observing the unities of time and place arises from the supposed necessity of making the drama credible. The critics hold it impossible that an action of months or years can be possibly believed to pass in three hours; or that the spectator can suppose himself to sit in the theatre, while ambassadors go and return between distant kings, while armies are levied and towns besieged, while an exile wanders and returns, or till he whom they saw courting his mistress shall lament the untimely fall of his son. The mind revolts from evident falsehood, and fiction loses its force when it departs from the resemblance of reality.

From the narrow limitation of time necessarily arises the contraction of place. The spectator, who knows that he saw the first act at Alexandria, cannot suppose that he sees the next at Rome, at a distance to which not the dragons of Medea could, in so short a time, have transported him; he knows with certainty that he has not changed his place; and he knows that place cannot change itself; that what was a house cannot become a plain; that what was Thebes can never be Persepolis.

Such is the triumphant language with which a critic exults over the misery of an irregular poet, and exults commonly without resistance or reply. It is time, therefore, to tell him by the authority of Shakespeare, that he assumes as an unquestionable principle a position which, while his breath is forming it into words, his understanding pronounces to be false. It is false that any representation is mistaken for reality; that any dramatic fable in its materiality was ever credible, or, for a single moment, was ever credited.

The objection arising from the impossibility of passing the first hour at Alexandria, and the next at Rome, supposes, that when the play opens, the spectator really imagines himself at Alexandria, and believes that his walk to the theatre has been a voyage to Egypt, and that he lives in the days of Antony and Cleopatra. Surely he that imagines this may imagine more. He that can take the stage at one time for the palace of the Ptolemies, may take it in half an hour for the promontory of Actium. Delusion, if delusion be admitted, has no certain limitation; if the spectator can be once persuaded that his old acquaintance are Alexander and Cæsar, that a room illuminated with candles is the plain of Pharsalia, or the bank of Granicus, he is in a state of elevation above the reach of reason, or of truth, and, from the heights of empyrean poetry, may despise the circumscriptions of terrestrial nature. There is no reason why a mind thus wandering in ecstasy should count the clock, or why an hour should not be a century in that calenture of the brain that can make the stage a field.

The truth is, that the spectators are always in their senses, and know, from the first act to the last, that the stage is only a stage, and that the players are only players. They come to hear a certain number of lines recited with just gesture and elegant modulation. The lines relate to some action, and an action must be in some place; but the different actions that complete a story may be in places very remote from each other;

and where is the absurdity of allowing that space to represent first Athens, and then Sicily, which was always known to be neither Sicily nor Athens, but a modern theatre?

By supposition, as place is introduced, time may be extended; the time required by the fable elapses for the most part between the acts; for, of so much of the action as is represented, the real and poetical duration is the same. If, in the first act, preparations for war against Mithridates are represented to be made in Rome, the event of the war may, without absurdity, be represented, in the catastrophe, as happening in Pontus; we know that there is neither war, nor preparation for war; we know that we are neither in Rome nor Pontus; that neither Mithridates nor Lucullus are before us. The drama exhibits successive imitations of successive actions; and why may not the second imitation represent an action that happened years after the first, if it be so connected with it, that nothing but time can be supposed to intervene? Time is, of all modes of existence, most obsequious to the imagination; a lapse of years is as easily conceived as a passage of hours. In contemplation we easily contract the time of real actions, and therefore willingly permit it to be contracted when we only see their imitation.

It will be asked how the drama moves, if it is not credited? It is credited with all the credit due to a drama. It is credited, whenever it moves, as a just picture of a real original; as representing to the auditor what he would himself feel, if he were to do or suffer what is there feigned to be suffered or to be done. The reflection that strikes the heart is not that the evils before us are real evils, but that they are evils to which we ourselves may be exposed. If there be any fallacy, it is not that we fancy the players, but that we fancy ourselves unhappy for a moment; but we rather lament the possibility than suppose the presence of misery, as a mother weeps over her babe, when she remembers that death may take it from her. The delight of tragedy proceeds from our consciousness of fiction; if we thought murders and treasons real, they would please no more. . . .[1]

---

[1] Johnson goes on to deny that observance of the classical unities is essential to an impression of truth, or nature; and comments on the dramatist's sources, etc.

The work of a correct and regular writer is a garden accurately formed and diligently planted, varied with shades, and scented with flowers; the composition of Shakespeare is a forest, in which oaks extend their branches, and pines tower in the air, interspersed sometimes with weeds and brambles, and sometimes giving shelter to myrtles and to roses; filling the eye with awful pomp, and gratifying the mind with endless diversity. Other poets display cabinets of precious rarities, minutely finished, wrought into shape, and polished unto brightness. Shakespeare opens a mine which contains gold and diamonds in unexhaustible plenty, though clouded by incrustations, debased by impurities, and mingled with a mass of meaner minerals. . . .[1]

[1] The essay concludes with remarks on Shakespeare's learning, his text, his editors before Johnson, and Johnson's editorial procedure.

OLIVER GOLDSMITH

BEAU TIBBS[1]

THE CHARACTER OF AN IMPORTANT TRIFLER

THOUGH naturally pensive, yet I am fond of gay company, and take every opportunity of thus dismissing the mind from duty. From this motive, I am often found in the centre of a crowd; and wherever pleasure is to be sold am always a purchaser. In those places, without being remarked by any, I join in whatever goes forward, work my passions into a similitude of frivolous earnestness, shout as they shout, and condemn as they happen to disapprove. A mind thus sunk for a while below its natural standard is qualified for stronger flights, as those first retire who would spring forward with greater vigor.

Attracted by the serenity of the evening, my friend and I lately went to gaze upon the company in one of the public walks near the city. Here we sauntered together for some time, either praising the beauty of such as were handsome, or the dresses of such as had nothing else to recommend them. We had gone thus deliberately forward for some time, when, stopping on a sudden, my friend caught me by the elbow, and led me out of the public walk. I could perceive by the quickness of his pace, and by his frequently looking behind, that he was attempting to avoid somebody who followed: we now turned to the right, then to the left; as we went forward he still went faster, but in vain; the person whom he attempted to escape hunted us through every doubling, and gained upon us each moment; so that at last we fairly stood still, resolving to face what we could not avoid.

Our pursuer soon came up, and joined us with all the familiarity of an old acquaintance. "My dear Drybone," cries he, shaking my friend's hand, "where have you been hiding this half-a-century? Positively I had fancied you were gone down

<hr />

[1] From the first collected edition of *The Citizen of the World*, Letters LIV–LV [incorrectly numbered LII–LIII], 1762. Series originally published in *The Public Ledger*, 1760–61.

to cultivate matrimony and your estate in the country."
During the reply, I had an opportunity of surveying the appearance of our new companion: his hat was pinched up with
peculiar smartness; his looks were pale, thin, and sharp; round
his neck he wore a broad black ribbon, and in his bosom a
buckle studded with glass; his coat was trimmed with tarnished
twist; he wore by his side a sword with a black hilt, and his
stockings of silk, though newly washed, were grown yellow by
long service. I was so much engaged with the peculiarity of
his dress, that I attended only to the latter part of my friend's
reply, in which he complimented Mr. Tibbs on the taste of his
clothes, and the bloom in his countenance: "Psha, psha, Will,"
cried the figure, "no more of that if you love me: you know I
hate flattery, on my soul I do; and yet, to be sure, an intimacy
with the great will improve one's appearance, and a course of
venison will fatten; and yet, faith, I despise the great as much
as you do: but there are a great many damned honest fellows
among them; and we must not quarrel with one half because
the other wants breeding.[1] If they were all such as my lord
Mudler, one of the most good-natured creatures that ever
squeezed a lemon, I should myself be among the number of
their admirers. I was yesterday to dine at the Duchess of
Piccadilly's. My lord was there. 'Ned,' says he to me,
'Ned,' says he, 'I'll hold gold to silver I can tell where you
were poaching last night.' 'Poaching, my lord,' says I; 'faith
you have missed already; for I staid at home, and let the girls
poach for me.' That's my way; I take a fine woman as some
animals do their prey — stand still, and swoop, they fall into
my mouth."

"Ah, Tibbs, thou art an happy fellow," cried my companion,
with looks of infinite pity; "I hope your fortune is as much
improved as your understanding in such company?" "Improved," replied the other; "you shall know — but let it go no
further — a great secret — five hundred a year to begin with.
My lord's word of honor for it — his lordship took me down in
his own chariot yesterday, and we had a *tête-à-tête* dinner in the
country; where we talked of nothing else." "I fancy you forget, sir," cried I, "you told us but this moment of your dining

[1] First edition reads "weeding."

yesterday in town." "Did I say so?" replied he, coolly; "to be sure if I said so, it was so — dined in town: egad, now I do remember, I did dine in town; but I dined in the country, too; for you must know, my boys, I eat two dinners. By the bye, I am grown as nice as the devil in my eating. I'll tell you a pleasant affair about that: we were a select party of us to dine at Lady Grogram's, an affected piece, but let it go no farther; a secret: well, there happened to be no assafœtida in the sauce to a turkey, upon which, says I, 'I'll hold a thousand guineas, and say done first, that —' but dear Drybone, you are an honest creature, lend me half-a-crown for a minute or two, or so, just till — but harkee, ask me for it the next time we meet, or it may be twenty to one but I forget to pay you."

When he left us, our conversation naturally turned upon so extraordinary a character. "His very dress," cries my friend, "is not less extraordinary than his conduct. If you meet him this day you find him in rags, if the next, in embroidery. With those persons of distinction of whom he talks so familiarly he has scarce a coffee-house acquaintance. However, both for interests of society, and perhaps for his own, Heaven has made him poor, and while all the world perceive his wants, he fancies them concealed from every eye. An agreeable companion, because he understands flattery; and all must be pleased with the first part of his conversation, though all are sure of its ending with a demand on their purse. While his youth countenances the levity of his conduct, he may thus earn a precarious subsistence, but when age comes on, the gravity of which is incompatible with buffoonery, then will he find himself forsaken by all; condemned in the decline of life to hang upon some rich family whom he once despised, there to undergo all the ingenuity of studied contempt, to be employed only as a spy upon the servants, or a bug-bear to fright the children into obedience. Adieu."

HIS CHARACTER CONTINUED; WITH THAT OF HIS WIFE, HIS HOUSE, AND FURNITURE

I am apt to fancy I have contracted a new acquaintance whom it will be no easy matter to shake off. My little beau yesterday overtook me again in one of the public walks, and slapping me on the shoulder, saluted me with an air of the most perfect familiarity. His dress was the same as usual, except that he had more powder in his hair, wore a dirtier shirt, a pair of temple spectacles, and his hat under his arm.

As I knew him to be an harmless, amusing little thing, I could not return his smiles with any degree of severity; so we walked forward on terms of the utmost intimacy, and in a few minutes discussed all the usual topics preliminary to particular conversation.

The oddities that marked his character, however, soon began to appear; he bowed to several well-dressed persons, who, by their manner of returning the compliment, appeared perfect strangers. At intervals he drew out a pocket-book, seeming to take memorandums before all the company, with much importance and assiduity. In this manner he led me through the length of the whole walk, fretting at his absurdities, and fancying myself laughed at not less than him by every spectator.

When we were got to the end of our procession, "Blast me," cries he with an air of vivacity, "I never saw the Park so thin in my life before! there's no company at all to-day; not a single face to be seen." "No company!" interrupted I peevishly; "no company where there is such a crowd? why man, there's too much. What are the thousand that have been laughing at us but company?" "Lord, my dear," returned he, with the utmost good humor, "you seem immensely chagrined; but, blast me, when the world laughs at me I laugh at the world, and so we are even. My Lord Trip, Bill Squash the Creolian, and I, sometimes make a party at being ridiculous; and so we say and do a thousand things for the joke sake. But I see you are grave, and if you are for a fine grave sentimental companion, you shall dine with me and my wife to-day; I must insist on't: I'll introduce you to Mrs. Tibbs, a lady of as elegant qualifications as any in nature; she was bred, but that's between ourselves, under the inspection of the Countess of Allnight. A charming body of voice; but no more of that, she shall give us a song. You shall see my little girl too, Carolina Wilhelmina Amelia Tibbs, a sweet pretty creature! I design her for my lord Drumstick's eldest son; but that's in friendship, let it go no farther: she's but six years old, and yet she walks a minuet, and plays on the guitar immensely already. I intend she shall be as perfect as possible in every accomplishment. In the first place, I'll make her a scholar; I'll teach her Greek myself, and learn that language purposely to instruct her; but let that be a secret."

Thus saying, without waiting for a reply, he took me by the arm, and hauled me along. We passed through many dark alleys and winding ways; for, from some motives to me unknown, he seemed to have a particular aversion to every frequented street; at last, however, we got to the door of a dismal-looking house in the outlets of the town, where he informed me he chose to reside for the benefit of the air.

We entered the lower door, which ever seemed to lie most hospitably open; and I began to ascend an old and creaking staircase, when, as he mounted to show me the way, he demanded whether I delighted in prospects; to which answering in the affirmative, "Then," says he, "I shall show you one of the most charming in the world, out of my windows; we shall see the ships sailing, and the whole country for twenty miles round, tip-top, quite high. My Lord Swamp would give ten thousand guineas for such a one; but, as I sometimes pleasantly tell him, I always love to keep my prospects at home, that my friends may see me the oftener."

By this time we were arrived as high as the stairs would permit us to ascend, till we came to what he was facetiously pleased to call the first floor down the chimney; and knocking at the door, a voice from within demanded, "Who's there?" My conductor answered that it was him. But this not satisfying the querist, the voice again repeated the demand: to which he answered louder than before; and now the door was opened by an old woman with cautious reluctance.

When we were got in, he welcomed me to his house with great ceremony, and turning to the old woman, asked where was her lady? "Good troth," replied she in a peculiar dialect, "she's washing your twa shirts at the next door, because they have taken an oath against lending out the tub any longer." "My two shirts," cries he in a tone that faltered with confusion, "what does the idiot mean?" "I ken what I mean well enough," replied the other; "she's washing your twa shirts at the next door, because ——" "Fire and fury! no more of thy stupid explanations," cried he; "go and inform her we have got company. Were that Scotch hag to be for ever in my family, she would never learn politeness, nor forget that absurd poisonous accent of hers, or testify the smallest specimen of breeding or high life; and yet it is very surprising, too, as I had her from a parliament man, a friend of mine from the Highlands, one of the politest men in the world; but that's a secret."

We waited some time for Mrs Tibbs's arrival, during which interval I had a full opportunity of surveying the chamber and all its furniture; which consisted of four chairs with old wrought bottoms, that he assured me were his wife's embroidery; a square table that had been once japanned; a cradle in one corner, a lumbering cabinet in the other; a broken shepherdess and a mandarin without an head were stuck over the chimney; and round the walls several paltry unframed pictures, which, he observed, were all his own drawing. "What do you think, Sir, of that head in the corner, done in the manner of Grisoni? there's the true keeping in it; it's my own face, and though there happens to be no likeness, a countess offered me an hundred for its fellow: I refused her, for, hang it, that would be mechanical, you know."

The wife at last made her appearance, at once a slattern and a coquet; much emaciated, but still carrying the remains of beauty. She made twenty apologies for being seen in such an odious dishabille, but hoped to be excused, as she had staid out all night at the Gardens with the countess, who was excessively fond of the horns. "And indeed, my dear," added she, turning to her husband, "his lordship drank your health in a bumper." "Poor Jack," cries he, "a dear good-natured creature, I know he loves me: but I hope, my dear, you have given orders for dinner; you need make no great preparations neither, there are but three of us; something elegant, and little will do; a turbot, an ortolan, or a ——" "Or what do you think, my dear," interrupts the wife, "of a nice pretty bit of ox-cheek, piping hot, and dressed with a little of my own sauce?" "The very thing," replies he, "it will eat best with some smart bottled beer; but be sure to let's have the sauce his grace was so fond of. I hate your immense loads of meat; that is country all over; extreme disgusting to those who are in the least acquainted with high life."

By this time my curiosity began to abate, and my appetite to increase: the company of fools may at first make us smile, but at last never fails of rendering us melancholy; I therefore pretended to recollect a prior engagement, and, after having shown my respect to the house, according to the fashion of the English, by giving the old servant a piece of money at the door, I took my leave; Mr. Tibbs assuring me that dinner, if I staid, would be ready at least in less than two hours.

JOSEPH DENNIE

FORTH INTO THE FIELD[1]

" Come, my beloved, let us go forth into the field; let us lodge in the villages."

THE hope of gain and the love of society have now, for centuries, incited men to risk many inconveniences, for the sake of congregating in cities. The simple would naturally conclude that where there was "much people" there would be much jollity. Desperate adventurers, bringing their craft to market, would have nothing to lose and every thing to gain in the throng. Ambition would find in every street a ladder lofty philosophy enough to reach the extent of many a project; and Avarice could find no place more convenient to drive a bargain than a frequented coffee house or an obscure alley. Schemes of wealth and aggrandizement, or pleasure, thus operating upon hope, the busiest and most sanguine passion, should we wonder to mark flocks of rovers, eager and upon the wing, expecting by a flight from the country to fly from themselves?

But wisely has the wise man said, "Better is a handful with *quietness*, than both hands full, with travail and vexation of spirit." Tranquility chooses the country for her favorite residence, and should you inquire for the peaceable personage in town, every cit would tell you he did not know her, and that she must be some outlandish person. In cities I grant there are many *agitations*, which are dignified by the name of pleasure, but they are a spurious brood, and felicity would not call them her own. The streams of pleasure in cities are like their common sewers: they are turbid, they are full of taint. He who quaffs liberally must soon be either sick or drunk; and such morbid influence have they on the brain that men go from them, like the apostle's gazer in the glass, "not knowing what manner of person they were."

They who wish never to be cloyed, to respire with freedom, to enjoy the pleasure of reading and reflection, and to sleep

[1] From *The Lay Preacher*, 1796.

sweetly, must *go forth into the field, and lodge in villages.*
Allowing that there are some genuine delights in the thronged
town, yet they tread too fast on each other, and weary by constant succession. A man will pray sometimes no less fervently
for a respite from pleasure than, in a fit of the gout, for a respite from pain. The pleasures of the country, pure, simple,
not dazzling, not boistrous, will gently stir the stream of life:
a stream which passion should not be suffered to vex into whirlpool, nor be "creamed over and mantled" by the stagnation of
sloth. To saunter along the banks of the brook and allure the
trout from his recess, to crop the fantastic flowers of May or
the strawberries of June, to climb the solemn mountain or
loiter in the valley's shade, are cheap and real pleasures, make
no man a criminal, and leave no sting behind.

Such is the influence of the atmosphere upon the human
body, that even robust constitutions are sensible of the changes
of the air, and invalids are "tremblingly alive" to them. A
fluid that, whether we are sheltered at home or exposed abroad,
we are obliged perpetually to dabble in, we should attempt to
find in the utmost purity. But in great towns, on the margin
of the main, reeking with the putrefaction of its shores: in
cities whose streets are defiled with frequent feet and scorched
by the dogstar, where every tenth house is a hospital, it is not
air which the sallow inhabitants breathe, but "a mass of
offensive things." Let the chain which binds willing prisoners
to the crowd be broken, let them "go forth to the field;" and
if the easy play of their lungs and alertness of limbs, if the
light slumber and the red cheek will not convince them whence
the mighty change in their health has proceeded, they deserve
to die soon, and in some dirty lane, as a punishment for their
incredulity.

Dissipation being the characteristic of cities, to travel its
round will require so much time that none will be left to cultivate the understanding or mend the heart. Whatever some
indolent fine ladies and fine gentlemen may suppose, we were
not sent into this world merely to go to assemblies, to saunter
at shops, to purchase of milliners, or undergo the three hours'
operation of a barber. He who wishes to read verses or write
them, he who means to instruct others or commune with him-

self, must seek the retirement of the "field" and the "village." In the city, protracted dinners and midnight revel will murder half, and more than, the day, and the long repose of the morning will be necessary to repair the wasted spirit. In solitude, as there are few incidents to enchain the mind, and few excesses to debase it, the student will bring a willing intellect to the complicated talk, and from a pen put to a rural desk all difficulty and hindrance will vanish away. He who in city and broken slumbers has a thousand times turned his pillow and himself, and, like SHAKESPEARE's king, has muttered, "O partial sleep, how have I frighted thee," will find that if he would sleep soundly he must "lodge in the village." That exercise which in the country is usually taken in the day, will induce that lassitude ever accompanied by delicious repose at night. He may be assured that *at the close of the day the hamlet is still*: no lumbering carts or chariots will banish his pleasant dreams, no outcry of midnight murder chill his palpitating heart. No noise will strike his ear but the distant waterfall, and no fires glitter in his eye but the innoxious one of the lucid insect of the meadows. At this genial period, when every June rose is broad blown, and the garniture of the fields is of the greenest hue, the emigrant from town may, perhaps, find some amusement not inferior to gambling all night, tracing dusty streets or visiting the sagacious dog. He will acknowledge the flavor of our strawberry equal to his pine apple, and the notes of the robin, and wren "of little quill," may soothe him as much and sound as sweet as those of the songstress of the theatre.

CHARLES LAMB

THE OLD BENCHERS OF THE INNER TEMPLE [1]

I WAS born, and passed the first seven years of my life in the Temple. Its church, its halls, its gardens, its fountain, its river, I had almost said — for in those young years, what was this king of rivers to me but a stream that watered our pleasant places? these are of my oldest recollections. I repeat, to this day, no verses to myself more frequently, or with kindlier emotion, than those of Spenser, where he speaks of this spot.

> There when they came, whereas those bricky towers,
> The which on Themmes brode aged back doth ride,
> Where now the studious lawyers have their bowers,
> There whylome wont the Templer knights to bide,
> Till they decayed through pride. [2]

Indeed, it is the most elegant spot in the metropolis. What a transition for a countryman visiting London for the first time — the passing from the crowded Strand or Fleet Street, by unexpected avenues, into its magnificent ample squares, its classic green recesses! What a cheerful, liberal look hath that portion of it, which, from three sides, overlooks the greater garden: that goodly pile

> Of building strong, albeit of Paper hight,

confronting, with massy contrast, the lighter, older, more fantastically shrouded one, named of Harcourt, with the cheerful Crown-office Row (place of my kindly engendure), right opposite the stately stream, which washes the garden-foot with her yet scarcely trade-polluted waters, and seems but just weaned from her Twickenham Naiades! a man would give something to have been born in such places. What a collegiate aspect has that fine Elizabethan hall, where the fountain plays, which I have made to rise and fall, how many times! to the as-

[1] From *Elia* (1823).   First published in *London Magazine*, September, 1821.
[2] *Prothalamion*, st. 8.

toundment of the young urchins, my contemporaries, who, not being able to guess at its recondite machinery, were almost tempted to hail the wondrous work as magic! What an antique air had the now almost effaced sun-dials, with their moral inscriptions, seeming coevals with that Time which they measured, and to take their revelations of its flight immediately from heaven, holding correspondence with the fountain of light! How would the dark line steal imperceptibly on, watched by the eye of childhood, eager to detect its movement, never catched, nice as an evanescent cloud, or the first arrests of sleep!

> Ah! yet doth beauty like a dial-hand
> Steal from his figure, and no pace perceived! [1]

What a dead thing is a clock, with its ponderous embowelments of lead and brass, its pert or solemn dulness of communication, compared with the simple altar-like structure, and silent heart-language of the old dial! It stood as the garden god of Christian gardens. Why is it almost everywhere vanished? If its business-use be superseded by more elaborate inventions, its moral uses, its beauty, might have pleaded for its continuance. It spoke of moderate labors, of pleasures not protracted after sunset, of temperance, and good hours. It was the primitive clock, the horologe of the first world. Adam could scarce have missed it in Paradise. It was the measure appropriate for sweet plants and flowers to spring by, for the birds to apportion their silver warblings by, for flocks to pasture and be led to fold by. The shepherd "carved it out quaintly in the sun;" [2] and, turning philosopher by the very occupation, provided it with mottoes more touching than tombstones. It was a pretty device of the gardener, recorded by Marvell, who, in the days of artificial gardening, made a dial out of herbs and flowers. I must quote his verses a little higher up, for they are full, as all his serious poetry was, of a witty delicacy. They will not come in awkwardly, I hope, in a talk of fountains and sun-dials. He is speaking of sweet garden scenes:

[1] Shakespeare, Sonnet 104.
[2] 3 Henry VI, II. v. 24.

What wondrous life in this I lead!
Ripe apples drop about my head.
The luscious clusters of the vine
Upon my mouth do crush their wine.
The nectarine, and curious peach,
Into my hands themselves do reach.
Stumbling on melons, as I pass,
Insnared with flowers, I fall on grass,
Meanwhile the mind from pleasure less
Withdraws into its happiness.
The mind, that ocean, where each kind
Does straight its own resemblance find;
Yet it creates, transcending these,
Far other worlds and other seas;
Annihilating all that's made
To a green thought in a green shade.
Here at the fountain's sliding foot,
Or at some fruit-tree's mossy root,
Casting the body's vest aside,
My soul into the boughs does glide:
There like a bird it sits and sings,
Then whets and claps its silver wings;
And, till prepared for longer flight,
Waves in its plumes the various light.
How well the skilful gardner drew,
Of flowers and herbs, this dial new!
Where, from above the milder sun
Does through a fragrant zodiac run;
And, as it works, the industrious bee
Computes its time as well as we.
How could such sweet and wholesome hours
Be reckon'd, but with herbs and flowers? [1]

The artificial fountains of the metropolis are, in like manner, fast vanishing. Most of them are dried up, or bricked over. Yet, where one is left, as in that little green nook behind the South-Sea House, what a freshness it gives to the dreary pile! Four little winged marble boys used to play their virgin fancies, spouting out ever fresh streams from their innocent wanton lips, in the square of Lincoln's Inn, when I was no bigger than they were figured. They are gone, and the spring choked up.

[1] From a copy of verses entitled *The Garden*.

The fashion, they tell me, is gone by, and these things are esteemed childish. Why not then gratify children, by letting them stand? Lawyers, I suppose, were children once. They are awakening images to them at least. Why must everything smack of man, and mannish? Is the world all grown up? Is childhood dead? Or is there not in the bosoms of the wisest and the best some of the child's heart left, to respond to its earliest enchantments? The figures were grotesque. Are the stiff-wigged living figures, that still flitter and chatter about that area, less Gothic in appearance? or is the splutter of their hot rhetoric one half so refreshing and innocent as the little cool playful streams those exploded cherubs uttered?

They have lately gothicised the entrance to the Inner Temple-hall, and the library front, to assimilate them, I suppose, to the body of the hall, which they do not at all resemble. What is become of the winged horse that stood over the former? a stately arms! and who has removed those frescoes of the Virtues, which Italianised the end of the Paper-buildings? — my first hint of allegory! They must account to me for these things, which I miss so greatly.

The terrace is, indeed, left, which we used to call the parade; but the traces are passed away of the footsteps which made its pavement awful! It is become common and profane. The old benchers had it almost sacred to themselves, in the fore part of the day at least. They might not be sided or jostled. Their air and dress asserted the parade. You left wide spaces betwixt you, when you passed them. We walk on even terms with their successors. The roguish eye of J——ll, ever ready to be delivered of a jest, almost invites a stranger to vie a repartee with it. But what insolent familiar durst have mated Thomas Coventry? — whose person was a quadrate, his step massy and elephantine, his face square as the lion's, his gait peremptory and path-keeping, indivertible from his way as a moving column, the scarecrow of his inferiors, the brow-beater of equals and superiors, who made a solitude of children wherever he came, for they fled his insufferable presence, as they would have shunned an Elisha bear.[1] His growl was as thunder in their ears, whether he spake to them in mirth or in

[1] 2 Kings, II. 24.

rebuke, his invitatory notes being, indeed, of all, the most repulsive and horrid. Clouds of snuff, aggravating the natural terrors of his speech, broke from each majestic nostril, darkening the air. He took it, not by pinches, but a palmful at once, diving for it under the mighty flaps of his old-fashioned waistcoat pocket; his waistcoat red and angry, his coat dark rappee, tinctured by dye original, and by adjuncts, with buttons of obsolete gold. And so he paced the terrace.

By his side a milder form was sometimes to be seen; the pensive gentility of Samuel Salt. They were coevals, and had nothing but that and their benchership in common. In politics Salt was a Whig, and Coventry a staunch Tory. Many a sarcastic growl did the latter cast out — for Coventry had a rough spinous humor — at the political confederates of his associate, which rebounded from the gentle bosom of the latter like cannonballs from wool. You could not ruffle Samuel Salt.

S. had the reputation of being a very clever man, and of excellent discernment in the chamber practice of the law. I suspect his knowledge did not amount to much. When a case of difficult disposition of money, testamentary or otherwise, came before him, he ordinarily handed it over with a few instructions to his man Lovel,[1] who was a quick little fellow, and would despatch it out of hand by the light of natural understanding, of which he had an uncommon share. It was incredible what repute for talents S. enjoyed by the mere trick of gravity. He was a shy man; a child might pose him in a minute — indolent and procrastinating to the last degree. Yet men would give him credit for vast application in spite of himself. He was not to be trusted with himself with impunity. He never dressed for a dinner-party but he forgot his sword — they wore swords then — or some other necessary part of his equipage. Lovel had his eye upon him on all these occasions, and ordinarily gave him his cue. If there was anything which he could speak unseasonably, he was sure to do it. — He was to dine at a relative's of the unfortunate Miss Blandy on the day of her execution; and L., who had a wary foresight of his probable hallucinations, before he set out, schooled him with great anxiety not in any possible manner to allude to her story that

[1] John Lamb, the father of the essayist.

day. S. promised faithfully to observe the injunction. He had not been seated in the parlor, where the company was expecting the dinner summons, four minutes, when, a pause in the conversation ensuing, he got up, looked out of the window, and pulling down his ruffles — an ordinary motion with him — observed, "it was a gloomy day," and added, "Miss Blandy must be hanged by this time, I suppose." Instances of this sort were perpetual. Yet S. was thought by some of the greatest men of his time a fit person to be consulted, not alone in matters pertaining to the law, but in the ordinary niceties and embarrassments of conduct — from force of manner entirely. He never laughed. He had the same good fortune among the female world, — was a known toast with the ladies, and one or two are said to have died for love of him — I suppose, because he never trifled or talked gallantry with them, or paid them, indeed, hardly common attentions. He had a fine face and person, but wanted, methought, the spirit that should have shown them off with advantage to the women. His eye lacked lustre. — Not so, thought Susan P——; who, at the advanced age of sixty, was seen, in the cold evening time, unaccompanied, wetting the pavement of B——d Row, with tears that fell in drops which might be heard, because her friend had died that day — he, whom she had pursued with a hopeless passion for the last forty years — a passion, which years could not extinguish or abate; nor the long resolved, yet gently enforced, puttings off of unrelenting bachelorhood dissuade from its cherished purpose. Mild Susan P——, thou hast now thy friend in heaven!

Thomas Coventry was a cadet of the noble family of that name. He passed his youth in contracted circumstances, which gave him early those parsimonious habits which in after-life never forsook him; so that, with one windfall or another, about the time I knew him he was master of four or five hundred thousand pounds; nor did he look, or walk, worth a moidore less. He lived in a gloomy house opposite the pump in Serjeants' Inn, Fleet Street. J., the counsel, is doing self-imposed penance in it, for what reason I divine not, at this day. C. had an agreeable seat at North Cray, where he seldom spent above a day or two at a time in the summer; but preferred, during the hot months, standing at his window in this damp, close, well-like mansion, to watch, as he said, "the maids drawing water all day long." I suspect he had his within-door reasons for the preference. *Hic currus et arma fuêre.* [1] He might think his treasures more safe. His house had the aspect of a strong box. C. was a close hunks — a hoarder rather than a miser — or, if a miser, none of the mad Elwes breed, who have brought discredit upon a character, which cannot exist without certain admirable points of steadiness and unity of purpose. One may hate a true miser, but cannot, I suspect, so easily despise him. By taking care of the pence, he is often enabled to part with the pounds, upon a scale that leaves us careless generous fellows halting at an immeasurable distance behind. C. gave away thirty thousand pounds at once in his lifetime to a blind charity. His housekeeping was severely looked after, but he kept the table of a gentleman. He would know who came in and who went out of his house, but his kitchen chimney was never suffered to freeze.

Salt was his opposite in this, as in all — never knew what he was worth in the world; and having but a competency for his rank, which his indolent habits were little calculated to improve, might have suffered severely if he had not had honest people about him. Lovel took care of everything. He was at once his clerk, his good servant, his dresser, his friend, his "flapper," [2] his guide, stop watch, auditor, treasurer. He did nothing without consulting Lovel, or failed in anything without expecting and fearing his admonishing. He put himself almost too much in his hands, had they not been the purest in the world. He resigned his title almost to respect as a master, if L. could ever have forgotten for a moment that he was a servant.

I knew this Lovel. He was a man of an incorrigible and losing honesty. A good fellow withal, and "would strike." [3] In the cause of the oppressed he never considered inequalities, or calculated the number of his opponents. He once wrested a sword out of the hand of a man of quality that had drawn upon

[1] "Here were his chariot and his arms." Virgil, *Æneid*, I. 17.
[2] Servants in Laputa (Swift's *Gulliver's Travels*).
[3] *King Lear*, V. iii. 283.

him; and pommelled him severely with the hilt of it. The swordsman had offered insult to a female — an occasion upon which no odds against him could have prevented the interference of Lovel. He would stand next day bare-headed to the same person, modestly to excuse his interference — for L. never forgot rank, where something better was not concerned. L. was the liveliest little fellow breathing, had a face as gay as Garrick's, whom he was said greatly to resemble (I have a portrait of him which confirms it), possessed a fine turn for humorous poetry — next to Swift and Prior — moulded heads in clay or plaster of Paris to admiration, by the dint of natural genius merely; turned cribbage-boards, and such small cabinet toys, to perfection; took a hand at quadrille or bowls with equal facility; made punch better than any man of his degree in England; had the merriest quips and conceits, and was altogether as brimful of rogueries and inventions as you could desire. He was a brother of the angle, moreover, and just such a free, hearty, honest companion as Mr. Izaak Walton would have chosen to go a-fishing with. I saw him in his old age and the decay of his faculties, palsy-smitten, in the last sad stage of human weakness — "a remnant most forlorn of what he was," — yet even then his eye would light up upon the mention of his favorite Garrick. He was greatest, he would say, in Bayes — "was upon the stage nearly throughout the whole performance, and as busy as a bee." At intervals, too, he would speak of his former life, and how he came up a little boy from Lincoln to go to service, and how his mother cried at parting with him, and how he returned, after some few years' absence, in his smart new livery to see her, and she blessed herself at the change, and could hardly be brought to believe that it was "her own bairn." And then, the excitement subsiding, he would weep, till I have wished that sad second-childhood might have a mother still to lay its head upon her lap. But the common mother of us all in no long time after received him gently into hers.

With Coventry, and with Salt, in their walks upon the terrace, most commonly Peter Pierson would join, to make up a third. They did not walk linked arm in arm in those days — "as now our stout triumvirs sweep the streets," — but gencrally with both hands folded behind them for state, or with one at least behind, the other carrying a cane. P. was a benevolent, but not a prepossessing man. He had that in his face which you could not term unhappiness; it rather implied an incapacity of being happy. His cheeks were colorless, even to whiteness. His look was uninviting, resembling (but without his sourness) that of our great philanthropist. I know that he *did* good acts, but I could never make out what he *was*. Contemporary with these, but subordinate, was Daines Barrington — another oddity — he walked burly and square — in imitation, I think, of Coventry — howbeit he attained not to the dignity of his prototype. Nevertheless, he did pretty well, upon the strength of being a tolerable antiquarian, and having a brother a bishop. When the account of his year's treasurership came to be audited, the following singular charge was unanimously disallowed by the bench: "Item, disbursed Mr. Allen, the gardener, twenty shillings, for stuff to poison the sparrows, by my orders." Next to him was old Barton — a jolly negation, who took upon him the ordering of the bills of fare for the parliament chamber, where the benchers dine — answering to the combination rooms at college — much to the easement of his less epicurean brethren. I know nothing more of him. — Then Read, and Twopenny — Read, good-humored and personable — Twopenny, good-humored, but thin, and felicitous in jests upon his own figure. If T. was thin, Wharry was attenuated and fleeting. Many must remember him (for he was rather of later date) and his singular gait, which was performed by three steps and a jump regularly succeeding. The steps were little efforts, like that of a child beginning to walk; the jump comparatively vigorous, as a foot to an inch. Where he learned this figure, or what occasioned it, I could never discover. It was neither graceful in itself, nor seemed to answer the purpose any better than common walking. The extreme tenuity of his frame, I suspect, set him upon it. It was a trial of poising. Twopenny would often rally him upon his leanness, and hail him as Brother Lusty; but W. had no relish of a joke. His features were spiteful. I have heard that he would pinch his cat's ears extremely, when anything had offended him. Jackson — the omniscient Jackson he was called

— was of this period. He had the reputation of possessing more multifarious knowledge than any man of his time. He was the Friar Bacon of the less literate portion of the Temple. I remember a pleasant passage, of the cook applying to him, with much formality of apology, for instructions how to write down *edge* bone of beef in his bill of commons. He was supposed to know, if any man in the world did. He decided the orthography to be — as I have given it — fortifying his authority with such anatomical reasons as dismissed the manciple (for the time) learned and happy. Some do spell it yet perversely, *aitch* bone, from a fanciful resemblance between its shape, and that of the aspirate so denominated. I had almost forgotten Mingay with the iron hand — but he was somewhat later. He had lost his right hand by some accident, and supplied it with a grappling hook, which he wielded with a tolerable adroitness. I detected the substitute, before I was old enough to reason whether it were artificial or not. I remember the astonishment it raised in me. He was a blustering, loud-talking person; and I reconciled the phenomenon to my ideas as an emblem of power — somewhat like the horns in the forehead of Michael Angelo's Moses. Baron Maseres, who walks (or did till very lately) in the costume of the reign of George the Second, closes my imperfect recollections of the old benchers of the Inner Temple.

Fantastic forms, whither are ye fled? Or, if the like of you exist, why exist they no more for me? Ye inexplicable, half-understood appearances, why comes in reason to tear away the preternatural mist, bright or gloomy, that enshrouded you? Why make ye so sorry a figure in my relation, who made up to me — to my childish eyes — the mythology of the Temple? In those days I saw Gods, as "old men covered with a mantle," walking upon the earth.[1] Let the dreams of classic idolatry perish, — extinct be the fairies and fairy trumpery of legendary fabling, — in the heart of childhood, there will, for ever, spring up a well of innocent or wholesome superstition — the seeds of exaggeration will be busy there, and vital — from everyday forms educing the unknown and the uncommon. In that little Goshen there will be light, when the grown world flounders

[1] 1 Samuel, XXVIII. 13-14.

about in the darkness of sense and materiality. While childhood, and while dreams, reducing childhood, shall be left, imagination shall not have spread her holy wings totally to fly the
earth.

P.S. — I have done injustice to the soft shade of Samuel
Salt. See what it is to trust to imperfect memory, and the erring notices of childhood! Yet I protest I always thought that
he had been a bachelor! This gentleman, R. N. informs me,
married young, and losing his lady in childbed, within the
first year of their union, fell into a deep melancholy, from the
effects of which, probably, he never thoroughly recovered. In
what a new light does this place his rejection (O call it by a
gentler name!) of mild Susan P——, unravelling into beauty
certain peculiarities of this very shy and retiring character! —
Henceforth let no one receive the narratives of Elia for true
records! They are, in truth, but shadows of fact — verisimili-
tudes, not verities — or sitting but upon the remote edges and
outskirts of history. He is no such honest chronicler as R. N.,
and would have done better perhaps to have consulted that
gentleman, before he sent these incondite reminiscences to
press. But the worthy sub-treasurer — who respects his old
and his new masters — would but have been puzzled at the in-
decorous liberties of Elia. The good man wots not, perad-
venture, of the licence which *Magazines* have arrived at in this
plain-speaking age, or hardly dreams of their existence beyond
the *Gentleman's* — his furthest monthly excursions in this nature having been long confined to the holy ground of honest
Urban's obituary. May it be long before his own name shall
help to swell those columns of unenvied flattery! — Meantime,
O ye New Benchers of the Inner Temple, cherish him kindly,
for he is himself the kindliest of human creatures. Should infirmities overtake him — he is yet in green and vigorous senility
— make allowances for them, remembering that "ye your-
selves are old." So may the Winged Horse, your ancient
badge and cognizance, still flourish! so may future Hookers
and Seldens illustrate your church and chambers! so may the
sparrows, in default of more melodious quiristers, unpoisoned
hop about your walks! so may the fresh-colored and cleanly

nursery-maid, who, by leave, airs her playful charge in your stately gardens, drop her prettiest blushing curtsey as ye pass, reductive of juvenescent emotion! so may the younkers of this generation eye you, pacing your stately terrace, with the same superstitious veneration, with which the child Elia gazed on the Old Worthies that solemnised the parade before ye!

WILLIAM HAZLITT

ON THE FEAR OF DEATH [1]

"And our little life is rounded with a sleep."

PERHAPS the best cure for the fear of death is to reflect that life has a beginning as well as an end. There was a time when we were not: this gives us no concern — why then should it trouble us that a time will come when we shall cease to be? I have no wish to have been alive a hundred years ago, or in the reign of Queen Anne: why should I regret and lay it so much to heart that I shall not be alive a hundred years hence, in the reign of I cannot tell whom?

When Bickerstaff wrote his Essays, I knew nothing of the subjects of them: nay, much later, and but the other day, as it were, in the beginning of the reign of George III., when Goldsmith, Johnson, Burke, used to meet at the Globe, when Garrick was in his glory, and Reynolds was over head and ears with his portraits, and Sterne brought out the volumes of *Tristram Shandy* year by year, it was without consulting me: I had not the slightest intimation of what was going on: the debates in the House of Commons on the American war, or the firing at Bunker's Hill, disturbed not me: yet I thought this no evil — I neither ate, drank, nor was merry, yet I did not complain: I had not then looked out into this breathing world, yet I was well; and the world did quite as well without me as I did without it! Why then should I make all this outcry about parting with it, and being no worse off than I was before? There is nothing in the recollection that at a certain time we were not come into the world, that "the gorge rises at" — why should we revolt at the idea that we must one day go out of it? To die is only to be as we were before we were born; yet no one feels any remorse or regret or repugnance in contemplating this last idea. It is rather a relief and disburthening of the mind: it seems to have been holiday-time with us then: we were not called to appear upon the stage of life, to wear robes

[1] From *Table Talk*, Part I (1821).

or tatters, to laugh or cry, be hooted or applauded; we had lain *perdus* all this while, snug, out of harm's way; and had slept out our thousands of centuries without wanting to be waked up; at peace and free from care, in a long nonage, in a sleep deeper and calmer than that of infancy, wrapped in the softest and finest dust. And the worst that we dread is, after a short, fretful, feverish being, after vain hopes and idle fears, to sink to final repose again, and forget the troubled dream of life!... Ye armed men, knights-templars, that sleep in the stone aisles of that old Temple Church, where all is silent above, and where a deeper silence reigns below (not broken by the pealing organ), are ye not contented where ye lie? Or would you come out of your long homes to go to the Holy War? Or do ye complain that pain no longer visits you, that sickness has done its worst, that you have paid the last debt to nature, that you hear no more of the thickening phalanx of the foe, or your lady's waning love; and that while this ball of earth rolls its eternal round, no sound shall ever pierce through to disturb your lasting repose, fixed as the marble over your tombs, breathless as the grave that holds you! And thou, oh! thou, to whom my heart turns, and will turn while it has feeling left, who didst love in vain, and whose first was thy last sigh, wilt not thou too rest in peace (or wilt thou cry to me complaining from thy clay-cold bed) when that sad heart is no longer sad, and that sorrow is dead, which thou wert only called into the world to feel!

It is certain that there is nothing in the idea of a pre-existent state, that excites our longing like the prospect of a posthumous existence. We are satisfied to have begun life when we did; we have no ambition to have set out on our journey sooner; and feel that we have quite enough to do to battle our way through since. We cannot say,

> "The wars we well remember of King Nine,
> Of old Assaracus and Inachus divine:"

neither have we any wish: we are contented to read of them in story, and to stand and gaze at the vast sea of time that separates us from them. It was early days then: the world was not *well-aired* enough for us: we have no inclination to have been up and stirring. We do not consider the six thousand years of the world before we were born as so much time lost to us: we are perfectly indifferent about the matter. We do not grieve and lament that we did not happen to be in time to see the grand mask and pageant of human life going on in all that period; though we are mortified at being obliged to quit our stand before the rest of the procession passes.

It may be suggested in explanation of this difference, that we know from various records and traditions what happened in the time of Queen Anne, or even in the reigns of the Assyrian monarchs: but that we have no means of ascertaining what is to happen hereafter but by awaiting the event, and that our eagerness and curiosity are sharpened in proportion as we are in the dark about it. This is not at all the case; for at that rate we should be constantly wishing to make a voyage of discovery to Greenland or to the Moon, neither of which we have, in general, the least desire to do. Neither, in truth, have we any particular solicitude to pry into the secrets of futurity, but as a pretext for prolonging our own existence. It is not so much that we care to be alive a hundred or a thousand years hence, any more than to have been alive a hundred or a thousand years ago: but the thing lies here, that we would all of us wish the present moment to last forever. We would be as we are, and would have the world remain just as it is, to please us.

"The present eye catches the present object"—

to have and to hold while it may; and abhors, on any terms, to have it torn from us, and nothing left in its room. It is the pang of parting, the unloosing our grasp, the breaking asunder some strong tie, the leaving some cherished purpose unfulfilled, that creates the repugnance to go, and "makes calamity of so long life," as it often is.

> ———"Oh! thou strong heart!
> There's such a covenant 'twixt the world and thee,
> They're loth to break!"

The love of life, then, is an habitual attachment, not an abstract principle. Simply *to be* does not "content man's natural desire:" we long to be in a certain time, place, and circumstance. We would much rather be now, "on this bank and shoal of time," than have our choice of any future period, than take a slice of fifty or sixty years out of the Millennium, for instance. This shows that our attachment is not confined either to *being* or to *well-being*; but that we have an inveterate prejudice in favour of our immediate existence, such as it is. The mountaineer will not leave his rock, nor the savage his hut; neither are we willing to give up our present mode of life, with all its advantages and disadvantages, for any other that could be substituted for it. No man would, I think, exchange his existence with any other man, however fortunate. We had as lief *not be*, as *not be ourselves*. There are some persons of that reach of soul that they would like to live two hundred and fifty years hence, to see to what height of empire America will have grown up in that period, or whether the English Constitution will last so long. These are points beyond me. But I confess I should like to live to see the downfall of the Bourbons. That is a vital question with me; and I shall like it the better, the sooner it happens!

No young man ever thinks he shall die. He may believe that others will, or assent to the doctrine that "all men are mortal" as an abstract proposition, but he is far enough from bringing it home to himself individually.[1] Youth, buoyant activity, and animal spirits hold absolute antipathy with old age as well as with death; nor have we, in the heyday of life, any more than in the thoughtlessness of childhood, the remotest conception how

> "This sensible warm motion can become
> A kneaded clod" ———

nor how sanguine, florid health and vigour shall "turn to withered, weak, and grey." Or if in a moment of idle speculation we indulge in this notion of the close of life as a theory, it is amazing at what a distance it seems; what a long, leisurely interval there is between; what a contrast its slow and solemn approach affords to our present gay dreams of existence! We eye the farthest verge of the horizon, and think what a way we shall have to look back upon, ere we arrive at our journey's

[1] "All men think all men mortal but themselves." Young.

end; and without our in the least suspecting it, the mists are at our feet, and the shadows of age encompass us. The two divisions of our lives have melted into each other: the extreme points close and meet with none of that romantic interval stretching out between them, that we had reckoned upon; and for the rich, melancholy, solemn hues of age, "the sear, the yellow leaf," the deepening shadows of an autumnal evening, we only feel a dank, cold mist encircling all objects, after the spirit of youth is fled. There is no inducement to look forward; and what is worse, little interest in looking back to what has become so trite and common. The pleasures of our existence have worn themselves out, are "gone into the wastes of time," or have turned their indifferent side to us: the pains by their repeated blows have worn us out, and have left us neither spirit nor inclination to encounter them again in retrospect. We do not want to rip up old grievances, nor to renew our youth like the phœnix, nor to live our lives twice over. Once is enough. As the tree falls, so let it lie. Shut up the book and close the account once for all!

It has been thought by some that life is like the exploring of a passage that grows narrower and darker the farther we advance, without a possibility of ever turning back, and where we are stifled for want of breath at last. For myself, I do not complain of the greater thickness of the atmosphere as I approach the *narrow house*. I felt it more formerly,[1] when the idea alone seemed to suppress a thousand rising hopes, and weighed upon the pulses of the blood. At present I rather feel a thinness and want of support, I stretch out my hand to some object and find none, I am too much in a world of abstraction; the naked map of life is spread out before me, and in the emptiness and desolation I see Death coming to meet me. In my youth I could not behold him for the crowd of objects and feelings, and Hope stood always between us, saying — "Never mind that old fellow!" If I had lived *indeed*, I should not care to die. But I do not like a contract of pleasure broken off unfulfilled, a marriage with joy unconsummated, a promise of happiness rescinded. My public and private hopes have been left a ruin,

---

[1] I remember, once in particular, having this feeling in reading Schiller's *Don Carlos*, where there is a description of death, in a degree that almost stifled me.

or remain only to mock me. I would wish them to be re-edified. I should like to see some prospect of good to mankind, such as my life began with. I should like to leave some sterling work behind me. I should like to have some friendly hand to consign me to the grave. On these conditions I am ready, if not willing, to depart. I could then write on my tomb — GRATEFUL AND CONTENTED! But I have thought and suffered too much to be willing to have thought and suffered in vain! — In looking back, it sometimes appears to me as if I had in a manner slept out my life in a dream or shadow on the side of the hill of knowledge, where I have fed on books, on thoughts, on pictures, and only heard in half-murmurs the trampling of busy feet, or the noises of the throng below. Waked out of this dim, twilight existence, and startled with the passing scene, I have felt a wish to descend to the world of realities, and join in the chase. But I fear too late, and that I had better return to my bookish chimeras and indolence once more! *Zanetto, lascia le donne, e studia la matematica.*[1] I will think of it.

It is not wonderful that the contemplation and fear of death become more familiar to us as we approach nearer to it: that life seems to ebb with the decay of blood and youthful spirits; and that as we find every thing about us subject to chance and change, as our strength and beauty die, as our hopes and passions, our friends and our affections leave us, we begin by degrees to feel ourselves mortal!

I have never seen death but once, and that was in an infant. It is years ago. The look was calm and placid, and the face was fair and firm. It was as if a waxen image had been laid out in the coffin, and strewed with innocent flowers. It was not like death, but more like an image of life! No breath moved the lips, no pulse stirred, no sight or sound would enter those eyes or ears more. While I looked at it, I saw no pain was there; it seemed to smile at the short pang of life which was over: but I could not bear the coffin-lid to be closed — it seemed to stifle me; and still as the nettles wave in a corner of the churchyard over his little grave, the welcome breeze helps to refresh me and ease the tightness at my breast!

[1] "Zanetto, relinquish love and study mathematics."

An ivory or marble image, like Chantry's monument of the two children, is contemplated with pure delight. Why do we not grieve and fret that the marble is not alive, or fancy that it has a shortness of breath? It never was alive; and it is the difficulty of making the transition from life to death, the struggle between the two in our imagination, that confounds their properties painfully together, and makes us conceive that the infant that is but just dead, still wants to breathe, to enjoy, and look about it, and is prevented by the icy hand of death, locking up its faculties and benumbing its senses; so that, if it could, it would complain of its own hard state. Perhaps religious considerations reconcile the mind to this change sooner than any others, by representing the spirit as fled to another sphere, and leaving the body behind it. So in reflecting on death generally, we mix up the idea of life with it, and thus make it the ghastly monster it is. We think how we should feel, not how the dead feel.

> "Still from the tomb the voice of nature cries;
> Even in our ashes live their wonted fires!"

There is an admirable passage on this subject in Tucker's *Light of Nature Pursued*, which I shall transcribe, as by much the best illustration I can offer of it.

"The melancholy appearance of a lifeless body, the mansion provided for it to inhabit, dark, cold, close and solitary, are shocking to the imagination; but it is to the imagination only, not the understanding: for whoever consults this faculty will see at first glance, that there is nothing dismal in all these circumstances: if the corpse were kept wrapped up in a warm bed, with a roasting fire in the chamber, it would feel no comfortable warmth therefrom; were store of tapers lighted up as soon as day shuts in, it would see no objects to divert it; were it left at large, it would have no liberty, nor if surrounded with company, would be cheered thereby; neither are the distorted features expressions of pain, uneasiness, or distress. This every one knows, and will readily allow upon being suggested, yet still cannot behold, nor even cast a thought upon those objects without shuddering; for knowing that a living person must suffer grievously under such appearances, they become habitually formidable to the mind, and strike a mechanical horror, which is increased by the customs of the world around us."

There is usually one pang added voluntarily and unnecessarily to the fear of death, by our affecting to compassionate the loss which others will have in us. If that were all, we might reasonably set our minds at rest. The pathetic exhortation on country tomb-stones, "Grieve not for me, my wife and children dear," &c., is for the most part speedily followed to the letter. We do not leave so great a void in society as we are inclined to imagine, partly to magnify our own importance, and partly to console ourselves by sympathy. Even in the same family the gap is not so great: the wound closes up sooner than we should expect. Nay, *our room* is not unfrequently thought better than *our company*. People walk along the streets the day after our deaths just as they did before, and the crowd is not diminished. While we were living, the world seemed in a manner to exist only for us, for our delight and amusement, because it contributed to them. But our hearts cease to beat, and it goes on as usual, and thinks no more about us than it did in our lifetime. The million are devoid of sentiment, and care as little for you or me as if we belonged to the moon. We live the week over in the Sunday's paper, or are decently interred in some obituary at the month's end! It is not surprising that we are forgotten so soon after we quit this mortal stage: we are scarcely noticed, while we are on it. It is not merely that our names are not known in China — they have hardly been heard of in the next street. We are hand and glove with the universe, and think the obligation is mutual. This is an evident fallacy. If this, however, does not trouble us now, it will not hereafter. A handful of dust can have no quarrel to pick with its neighbours or complaint to make against Providence, and might well exclaim, if it had but an understanding and a tongue, "Go thy ways, old world; swing round in blue ether, voluble to every age, you and I shall no more jostle!"

It is amazing how soon the rich and titled, and even some of those who have wielded great political power, are forgotten:

> "A little rule, a little sway,
> Is all the great and mighty have
> Betwixt the cradle and the grave"

and, after its short date, they hardly leave a name behind them. "A great man's memory may, at the common rate, survive him half a year." His heirs and successors take his titles, his power, and his wealth — all that made him considerable or courted by others; and he has left nothing else behind him either to delight or benefit the world. Posterity are not by any means so disinterested as they are supposed to be. They give their gratitude and admiration only in return for benefits conferred. They cherish the memory of those to whom they are indebted for instruction and delight; and they cherish it just in proportion to the instruction and delight they are conscious they receive. The sentiment of admiration springs immediately from this ground; and cannot be otherwise than well-founded.[1]

The effeminate clinging to life as such, as a general or abstract idea, is the effect of a highly civilized and artificial state of society. Men formerly plunged into all the vicissitudes and dangers of war, or staked their all upon a single die, or some one passion, which, if they could not have gratified, life became a burthen to them — now our strongest passion is to think, our chief amusement is to read new plays, new poems, new novels, and this we may do at our leisure, in perfect security, *ad infinitum*. If we look into the old histories and romances, before the *belles-lettres* neutralized human affairs and reduced passion to a state of mental equivocation, we find the heroes and heroines not setting their lives "at a pin's fee," but rather courting opportunities of throwing them away in very wantonness of spirit. They raise their fondness for some favorite pursuit to its height, to a pitch of madness, and think no price too dear to pay for its full gratification. Every thing else is dross. They go to death as to a bridal bed, and sacrifice themselves or others without remorse at the shrine of love, of honour, of re-

---

[1] It has been usual to raise a very unjust clamour against the enormous salaries of public singers, actors, and so on. This matter seems reducible to a *moral equation*. They are paid out of money raised by voluntary contributions in the strictest sense; and if they did not bring certain sums into the treasury, the Managers would not engage them. These sums are exactly in proportion to the number of individuals to whom their performance gives an extraordinary degree of pleasure. The talents of singer, actor, &c., are therefore worth just as much as they will fetch.

ligion, or any other prevailing feeling. Romeo runs his "sea-sick, weary bark upon the rocks" of death, the instant he finds himself deprived of his Juliet; and she clasps his neck in their last agonies, and follows him to the same fatal shore. One strong idea takes possession of the mind and overrules every other; and even life itself, joyless without that, becomes an object of indifference or loathing. There is at least more of imagination in such a state of things, more vigour of feeling and promptitude to act, than in our lingering, languid, protracted attachment to life for its own poor sake. It is perhaps also better, as well as more heroical, to strike at some daring or darling object, and if we fail in that, to take the consequences manfully, than to renew the lease of a tedious, spiritless, charmless existence, merely (as Pierre says) "to lose it after-wards in some vile brawl" for some worthless object. Was there not a spirit of martyrdom as well as a spice of the reck-less energy of barbarism in this bold defiance of death? Had not religion something to do with it: the implicit belief in a future life, which rendered this of less value, and embodied something beyond it to the imagination; so that the rough soldier, the infatuated lover, the valorous knight, &c., could afford to throw away the present venture, and take a leap into the arms of futurity, which the modern sceptic shrinks back from, with all his boasted reason and vain philosophy, weaker than a woman! I cannot help thinking so myself; but I have endeavored to explain this point before, and will not enlarge farther on it here.

A life of action and danger moderates the dread of death. It not only gives us fortitude to bear pain, but teaches us at every step the precarious tenure on which we hold our present being. Sedentary and studious men are the most apprehensive on this score. Dr. Johnson was an instance in point. A few years seemed to him soon over, compared with those sweeping contemplations on time and infinity with which he had been used to pose himself. In the *still-life* of a man of letters, there was no obvious reason for a change. He might sit in an arm-chair and pour out cups of tea to all eternity. Would it had been possible for him to do so! The most rational cure after all for the inordinate fear of death is to set a just value on life. If we merely wish to continue on the scene to indulge our head-strong humours and tormenting passions, we had better begone at once: and if we only cherish a fondness for existence according to the good we derive from it, the pang we feel at parting with it will not be very severe!

WASHINGTON IRVING

POPULAR SUPERSTITIONS[1]

Farewell rewards and fairies,
  Good housewives now may say;
For now fowle sluts in dairies
  Do fare as well as they:
And though they sweepe their hearths no lesse
  Than maids were wont to doe,
Yet who of late for cleanlinesse
  Finds sixpence in her shooe?

BISHOP CORBET.

I HAVE mentioned the Squire's fondness for the marvelous, and his predilection for legends and romances. His library contains a curious collection of old works of this kind, which bear evident marks of having been much read. In his great love for all that is antiquated, he cherishes popular superstitions, and listens, with very grave attention, to every tale, however strange; so that, through his countenance, the household, and, indeed, the whole neighborhood, is well stocked with wonderful stories; and if ever a doubt is expressed of any one of them, the narrator will generally observe, that "the Squire thinks there's something in it."

The Hall of course comes in for its share, the common people having always a propensity to furnish a great superannuated building of the kind with supernatural inhabitants. The gloomy galleries of such old family mansions; the stately chambers, adorned with grotesque carvings and faded paintings; the sounds that vaguely echo about them; the moaning of the wind; the cries of rooks and ravens from the trees and chimney-tops; all produce a state of mind favorable to superstitious fancies.

In one chamber of the Hall, just opposite a door which opens upon a dusky passage, there is a full length portrait of a warrior in armor; when, on suddenly turning into the passage, I have caught a sight of the portrait, thrown into strong relief by the dark paneling against which it hangs, I have more than

[1] From *Bracebridge Hall* (1822; revised edition, 1848-50).

once been startled, as though it were a figure advancing towards me.

To superstitious minds, therefore, predisposed by the strange and melancholy stories connected with family paintings, it needs but little stretch of fancy, on a moonlight night, or by the flickering light of a candle, to set the old pictures on the walls in motion, sweeping in their robes and trains about the galleries.

The Squire confesses that he used to take a pleasure in his younger days in setting marvelous stories afloat, and connecting them with the lonely and peculiar places of the neighborhood. Whenever he read any legend of a striking nature, he endeavored to transplant it, and give it a local habitation among the scenes of his boyhood. Many of these stories took root, and he says he is often amused with the odd shapes in which they come back to him in some old woman's narrative, after they have been circulating for years among the peasantry, and undergoing rustic additions and amendments. Among these may doubtless be numbered that of the crusader's ghost, which I have mentioned in the account of my Christmas visit; and another about the hard-riding squire of yore, the family Nimrod, who is sometimes heard on stormy winter nights, galloping, with hound and horn, over a wild moor a few miles distant from the Hall. This I apprehend to have had its origin in the famous story of the wild huntsman, the favorite goblin in German tales; though, by the by, as I was talking on the subject with Master Simon the other evening in the dark avenue, he hinted that he had himself once or twice heard odd sounds at night, very like a pack of hounds in cry; and that once, as he was returning rather late from a hunting dinner, he had seen a strange figure galloping along this same moor; but as he was riding rather fast at the time, and in a hurry to get home, he did not stop to ascertain what it was.

Popular superstitions are fast fading away in England, owing to the general diffusion of knowledge, and the bustling intercourse kept up throughout the country: still they have their strong-holds and lingering places, and a retired neighborhood like this is apt to be one of them. The parson tells me that he meets with many traditional beliefs and notions among the common people, which he has been able to draw from them in the course of familiar conversation, though they are rather shy of avowing them to strangers, and particularly to "the gentry," who are apt to laugh at them. He says there are several of his old parishioners who remember when the village had its bar-guest, or bar-ghost; a spirit supposed to belong to a town or village, and to predict any impending misfortune by midnight shrieks and wailings. The last time it was heard was just before the death of Mr. Bracebridge's father, who was much beloved throughout the neighborhood; though there are not wanting some obstinate unbelievers, who insisted that it was nothing but the howling of a watch-dog. I have been greatly delighted, however, at meeting with some traces of my old favorite, Robin Goodfellow, though under a different appellation from any of those by which I have heretofore heard him called. The parson assures me that many of the peasantry believe in household goblins, called Dobbies, which live about particular farms and houses, in the same way that Robin Goodfellow did of old. Sometimes they haunt the barns and outhouses, and now and then will assist the farmer wonderfully, by getting in all his hay or corn in a single night. In general, however, they prefer to live within doors, and are fond of keeping about the great hearths, and basking at night, after the family have gone to bed, by the glowing embers. When put in particular good humor by the warmth of their lodgings, and the tidiness of the housemaids, they will overcome their natural laziness, and do a vast deal of household work before morning; churning the cream, brewing the beer, or spinning all the good dame's flax. All this is precisely the conduct of Robin Goodfellow, described so charmingly by Milton:

> "Tells how the drudging goblin sweat
> To earn his cream-bowl duly set,
> When in one night, ere glimpse of morn,
> His shadowy flail had threshed the corn
> That ten day laborers could not end;
> Then lays him down the lubber-fiend,
> And stretch'd out all the chimney's length
> Basks at the fire his hairy strength,
> And crop-full, out of door he flings
> Ere the first cock his matin rings."

But beside these household Dobbies, there are others of a more gloomy and unsocial nature, which keep about lonely barns, at a distance from any dwelling-house, or about ruins and old bridges. These are full of mischievous, and often malignant tricks, and are fond of playing pranks upon benighted travelers. There is a story, among the old people, of one which haunted a ruined mill, just by a bridge that crosses a small stream; how that late one night, as a traveler was passing on horseback, the goblin jumped up behind him, and grasped him so close round the body that he had no power to help himself, but expected to be squeezed to death: luckily his heels were loose, with which he plied the sides of his steed, and was carried, with the wonderful instinct of a traveler's horse, straight to the village inn. Had the inn been at any greater distance, there is no doubt but he would have been strangled to death; as it was, the good people were a long time in bringing him to his senses, and it was remarked that the first sign he showed of returning consciousness was to call for a bottom of brandy.

These mischievous Dobbies bear much resemblance in their natures and habits to the sprites which Heywood, in his *Heirarchie*,[1] calls pugs or hobgoblins:

> "Their dwellings be
> In corners of old houses least frequented,
> Or beneath stacks of wood, and these convented,
> Make fearfull noise in butteries and in dairies;
> Robin Goodfellow some, some call them fairies.
> In solitarie rooms these uprores keep,
> And beate at doores, to wake men from their slepe,
> Seeming to force lockes, be they nere so strong,
> And keeping Christmasse gambols all night long.
> Pots, glasses, trenchers, dishes, pannes, and kettles
> They will make dance about the shelves and settles,
> As if about the kitchen tost and cast,
> Yet in the morning nothing found misplac't.
> Others such houses to their use have fitted
> In which base murthers have been once committed.
> Some have their fearful habitations taken
> In desolate houses, ruin'd and forsaken."

[1] Properly, this is *The Hierarchy of the Blessed Angels* (1635), by Thomas Heywood, the dramatist.

In the account of our unfortunate hawking expedition, I mentioned an instance of one of these sprites supposed to haunt the ruined grange that stands in a lonely meadow, and has a remarkable echo. The parson informs me, also, of a belief once very prevalent, that a household Dobbie kept about the old farmhouse of the Tibbets's. It has long been traditional, he says, that one of these good-natured goblins is attached to the Tibbets family, and came with them when they moved into this part of the country; for it is one of the peculiarities of these household sprites, that they attach themselves to the fortunes of certain families, and follow them in all their removals.

There is a large old-fashioned fireplace in the farmhouse, which affords fine quarters for a chimney-corner sprite that likes to lie warm; especially as Ready-Money Jack keeps up rousing fires in the winter time. The old people of the village recollect many stories about this goblin, current in their young days. It was thought to have brought good luck to the house, and to be the reason why the Tibbets's were always beforehand in the world; and why their farm was always in better order, their hay got in sooner, and their corn better stacked, than that of their neighbors. The present Mrs. Tibbets, at the time of her courtship, had a number of these stories told her by the country gossips; and when married, was a little fearful about living in a house where such a hobgoblin was said to haunt: Jack, however, who has always treated this story with great contempt, assured her that there was no spirit kept about his house that he could not at any time lay in the Red Sea with one flourish of his cudgel. Still his wife has never got completely over her notions on the subject; but has a horseshoe nailed on the threshold, and keeps a branch of rauntry, or mountain-ash, with its red berries, suspended from one of the great beams in the parlor — a sure protection from all evil spirits.

These stories, as I before observed, are fast fading away, and in another generation or two will probably be completely forgotten. There is something, however, about these rural superstitions extremely pleasing to the imagination; particularly those which relate to the good-humored race of household demons, and indeed to the whole fairy mythology. The

English have given an inexpressible charm to these superstitions, by the manner in which they have associated them
with whatever is most homefelt and delightful in nature. I do
not know a more fascinating race of beings than these little
fabled people who haunted the southern sides of hills and
mountains; lurked in flowers and about fountain-heads; glided
through keyholes into ancient halls; watched over farmhouses
and dairies; danced on the green by summer moonlight, and on
the kitchen hearth in winter. They accord with the nature of
English housekeeping and English scenery. I always have
them in mind when I see a fine old English mansion, with its
wide hall and spacious kitchen; or a venerable farmhouse, in
which there is so much fireside comfort and good housewifery.
There was something of national character in their love of
order and cleanliness; in the vigilance with which they watched
over the economy of the kitchen, and the functions of the
servants; munificently rewarding, with silver sixpence in shoe,
the tidy housemaid, but venting their direful wrath, in midnight bobs and pinches, upon the sluttish dairymaid. I think
I can trace the good effects of this ancient fairy sway over
household concerns, in the care that prevails to the present day
among English housemaids, to put their kitchens in order before they go to bed.

I have said that these fairy superstitions accord with the
nature of English scenery. They suit these small landscapes,
which are divided by honeysuckle hedges into sheltered fields
and meadows; where the grass is mingled with daisies, but-
tercups, and hare-bells. When I first found myself among
English scenery, I was continually reminded of the sweet
pastoral images which distinguish their fairy mythology; and
when for the first time a circle in the grass was pointed out to
me as one of the rings where they were formerly supposed to
have held their moonlight revels, it seemed for a moment as if
fairy-land were no longer a fable. Brown[e], in his *Britannia's
Pastorals*, gives a picture of the kind of scenery to which I allude:

"A pleasant mead
Where fairies often did their measures tread;
Which in the meadows make such circles green
As if with garlands it had crowned been.

Within one of these rounds was to be seen
A hillock rise, where oft the fairy queen
At twilight sat."

And there is another picture of the same, in a poem ascribed to Ben Jonson:

"By wells and rills in meadows green,
    We nightly dance our hey-day guise,
And to our fairy king and queen
    We chant our moonlight minstrelsies."

Indeed, it seems to me, that the older British poets, with that true feeling for nature which distinguishes them, have closely adhered to the simple and familiar imagery which they found in these popular superstitions; and have thus given to their fairy mythology those continual allusions to the farmhouse and the dairy, the green meadow and the fountain-head, which fill our minds with the delightful associations of rural life. It is curious to observe how the most beautiful fictions have their origin among the rude and ignorant. There is an indescribable charm about the illusions with which chimerical ignorance once clothed every subject. These twilight views of nature are often more captivating than any which are revealed by the rays of enlightened philosophy. The most accomplished and poetical minds, therefore, have been fain to search back into the accidental conceptions of what are termed barbarous ages, and to draw from them their finest imagery and machinery. If we look through our most admired poets, we shall find that their minds have been impregnated by these popular fancies, and that those have succeeded best who have adhered closest to the simplicity of their rustic originals. Such is the case with Shakspeare in his *Midsummer-Night's Dream*, which so minutely describes the employments and amusements of fairies, and embodies all the notions concerning them which were current among the vulgar. It is thus that poetry in England has echoed back every rustic note, softened into perfect melody; it is thus that it has spread its charms over every-day life, displacing nothing; taking things as it found them; but tinting them up with its own magical hues, until every green hill and fountain-head, every fresh meadow, **nay,** every humble flower, is full of song and story.

I am dwelling too long, perhaps, upon a threadbare subject; yet it brings up with it a thousand delicious recollections of those happy days of childhood, when the imperfect knowledge I have since obtained had not yet dawned upon my mind, and when a fairy tale was true history to me. I have often been so transported by the pleasure of these recollections, as almost to wish I had been born in the days when the fictions of poetry were believed. Even now I cannot look upon those fanciful creations of ignorance and credulity, without a lurking regret that they have all passed away. The experience of my early days tells me, they were sources of exquisite delight; and I sometimes question whether the naturalist who can dissect the flowers of the field, receives half the pleasure from contemplating them, that he did who considered them the abode of elves and fairies. I feel convinced that the true interests and solid happiness of man are promoted by the advancement of truth; yet I cannot but mourn over the pleasant errors which it has trampled down in its progress. The fauns and sylphs, the household sprite, the moonlight revel, Oberon, Queen Mab, and the delicious realms of fairy-land, all vanish before the light of true philosophy; but who does not sometimes turn with distaste from the cold realities of morning, and seek to recall the sweet visions of the night?

THOMAS DE QUINCEY

THE AFFLICTION OF CHILDHOOD [1]

ABOUT the close of my sixth year, suddenly the first chapter of my life came to a violent termination; that chapter which, even within the gates of recovered paradise, might merit a remembrance. *"Life is finished!"* was the secret misgiving of my heart; for the heart of infancy is as apprehensive as that of maturest wisdom in relation to any capital wound inflicted on the happiness. *"Life is finished! Finished it is!"* was the hidden meaning that, half unconsciously to myself, lurked within my sighs; and, as bells heard from a distance on a summer evening seem charged at times with an articulate form of words, some monitory message, that rolls round unceasingly, even so for me some noiseless and subterraneous voice seemed to chant continually a secret word, made audible only to my own heart — that "now is the blossoming of life withered forever." Not that such words formed themselves vocally within my ear, or issued audibly from my lips; but such a whisper stole silently to my heart. Yet in what sense could *that* be true? For an infant not more than six years old, was it possible that the promises of life had been really blighted, or its golden pleasures exhausted? Had I seen Rome? Had I read Milton? Had I heard Mozart? No. St. Peter's, the "Paradise Lost," the divine melodies of "Don Giovanni," all alike were as yet unrevealed to me, and not more through the accidents of my position than through the necessity of my yet imperfect sensibilities. Raptures there might be in arrear; but raptures are modes of *troubled* pleasure. The peace, the rest, the central security which belong to love that is past all understanding, — these could return no more. Such a love, so unfathomable, — such a peace, so unvexed by storms, or the fear of storms, — had brooded over those four latter years of my infancy, which brought me into special relations to my elder sister; she being at this period three years older than my-

[1] From *Autobiographic Sketches* (1853).

self. The circumstances which attended the sudden dissolution of this most tender connection I will here rehearse. . . .[1]

The earliest incidents in my life, which left stings in my memory so as to be remembered at this day, were two, and both before I could have completed my second year; namely, 1st, a remarkable dream of terrific grandeur about a favorite nurse, which is interesting to myself for this reason — that it demonstrates my dreaming tendencies to have been constitutional, and not dependent upon laudanum;[2] and, 2dly, the fact of having connected a profound sense of pathos with the reappearance, very early in the spring, of some crocuses. This I mention as inexplicable: for such annual resurrections of plants and flowers affect us only as memorials, or suggestions of some higher change, and therefore in connection with the idea of death; yet of death I could, at that time, have had no experience whatever.

This, however, I was speedily to acquire. My two eldest sisters — eldest of three *then* living, and also elder than myself — were summoned to an early death. The first who died was Jane, about two years older than myself. She was three and a half, I, one and a half, more or less by some trifle that I do not recollect. But death was then scarcely intelligible to me, and I could not so properly be said to suffer sorrow as a sad perplexity. There was another death in the house about the same time, namely, of a maternal grandmother; but, as she had come to us for the express purpose of dying in her daughter's society, and from illness had lived perfectly secluded, our nursery circle knew her but little, and were certainly more affected by the death (which I witnessed) of a beautiful bird, viz., a kingfisher, which had been injured by an accident. With my sister Jane's death (though otherwise, as I have said, less sorrowful than perplexing) there was, however, connected

---

[1] An account of De Quincey's family is omitted.

[2] It is true that in those days *paregoric elixir* was occasionally given to children in colds; and in this medicine there is a small proportion of laudanum. But no medicine was ever administered to any member of our nursery except under medical sanction; and this, assuredly, would not have been obtained to the exhibition of laudanum in a case such as mine. For I was then not more than twenty-one months old; at which age the action of opium is capricious, and therefore perilous.

an incident which made a most fearful impression upon myself, deepening my tendencies to thoughtfulness and abstraction beyond what would seem credible for my years. If there was one thing in this world from which, more than from any other, nature had forced me to revolt, it was brutality and violence. Now, a whisper arose in the family that a female servant, who by accident was drawn off from her proper duties to attend my sister Jane for a day or two, had on one occasion treated her harshly, if not brutally; and as this ill treatment happened within three or four days of her death, so that the occasion of it must have been some fretfulness in the poor child caused by her sufferings, naturally there was a sense of awe and indignation diffused through the family. I believe the story never reached my mother, and possibly it was exaggerated; but upon me the effect was terrific. I did not often see the person charged with this cruelty; but, when I did, my eyes sought the ground; nor could I have borne to look her in the face; not, however, in any spirit that could be called anger. The feeling which fell upon me was a shuddering horror, as upon a first glimpse of the truth that I was in a world of evil and strife. Though born in a large town, (the town of Manchester, even then amongst the largest of the island,) I had passed the whole of my childhood, except for the few earliest weeks, in a rural seclusion. With three innocent little sisters for playmates, sleeping always amongst them, and shut up forever in a silent garden from all knowledge of poverty, or oppression, or outrage, I had not suspected until this moment the true complexion of the world in which myself and my sisters were living. Henceforward the character of my thoughts changed greatly; for so *representative* are some acts, that one single case of the class is sufficient to throw open before you the whole theatre of possibilities in that direction. I never heard that the woman accused of this cruelty took it at all to heart, even after the event which so immediately succeeded had reflected upon it a more painful emphasis. But for myself, that incident had a lasting revolutionary power in colouring my estimate of life.

So passed away from earth one of those three sisters that made up my nursery playmates; and so did my acquaintance (if such it could be called) commence with mortality. Yet, in fact, I knew little more of mortality than that Jane had disappeared. She had gone away; but perhaps she would come back. Happy interval of heaven-born ignorance! Gracious immunity of infancy from sorrow disproportioned to its strength! I was sad for Jane's absence. But still in my heart I trusted that she would come again. Summer and winter came again — crocuses and roses; why not little Jane?

Thus easily was healed, then, the first wound in my infant heart. Not so the second. For thou, dear, noble Elizabeth, around whose ample brow, as often as thy sweet countenance rises upon the darkness, I fancy a *tiara* of light or a gleaming *aureola* [1] in token of thy premature intellectual grandeur, — thou whose head, for its superb developments, was the astonishment of science, [1] — thou next, but after an interval of happy years, thou also wert summoned away from our nursery; and the night, which for me gathered upon that event, ran after my steps far into life; and perhaps at this day I resemble little for good or for ill that which else I should have been. Pillar of fire that didst go before me to guide and to quicken, — pillar of darkness, when thy countenance was turned away to God, that didst too truly reveal to my dawning fears the secret shadow of death, — by what mysterious gravitation was it that *my* heart had been drawn to thine? Could a child, six years old, place any special value upon intellectual forwardness? Serene and capacious as my sister's mind appeared to me upon after review, was *that* a charm for stealing away the heart of an infant? O, no! I think of it *now* with interest, because it lends, in a stranger's ear, some justification to the excess of my fondness. But then it was lost upon me; or, if not lost, was perceived only through its effects. Hadst thou been an idiot, my sister, not the less I must have loved thee, having that capacious heart — overflowing, even as mine overflowed, with tenderness; stung, even as mine was stung, by the necessity of loving and being loved. This it was which crowned thee with beauty and power.

> "Love, the holy sense,
> Best gift of God, in thee was most intense."

[1] Notes by De Quincey are omitted.

That lamp of paradise was, for myself, kindled by reflection from the living light which burned so steadfastly in thee; and never but to thee, never again since *thy* departure, had I power or temptation, courage or desire, to utter the feelings which possessed me. For I was the shyest of children; and, at all stages of life, a natural sense of personal dignity held me back from exposing the least ray of feelings which I was not encouraged *wholly* to reveal.

It is needless to pursue, circumstantially, the course of that sickness which carried off my leader and companion. She (according to my recollection at this moment) was just as near to nine years as I to six. And perhaps this natural precedency in authority of years and judgment, united to the tender humility with which she declined to assert it, had been amongst the fascinations of her presence. It was upon a Sunday evening, if such conjectures can be trusted, that the spark of fatal fire fell upon that train of predispositions to a brain complaint which had hitherto slumbered within her. She had been permitted to drink tea at the house of a laboring man, the father of a favorite female servant. The sun had set when she returned, in the company of this servant, through meadows reeking with exhalations after a fervent day. From that time she sickened. In such circumstances, a child, as young as myself, feels no anxieties. Looking upon medical men as people privileged, and naturally commissioned, to make war upon pain and sickness, I never had a misgiving about the result. I grieved, indeed, that my sister should lie in bed; I grieved still more to hear her moan. But all this appeared to me no more than as a night of trouble, on which the dawn would soon arise. O moment of darkness and delirium, when the elder nurse awakened me from that delusion, and launched God's thunderbolt at my heart in the assurance that my sister MUST die! Rightly it is said of utter, utter misery, that it "cannot be *remembered*." [1] Itself, as a rememberable thing, is swallowed up in its own chaos. Blank anarchy and confusion of mind fell upon me. Deaf and blind I was, as I reeled under

[1] "I stood in unimaginable trance
And agony which cannot be remembered."
Speech of Alhadra, in Coleridge's *Remorse.*

the revelation. I wish not to recall the circumstances of that time, when *my* agony was at its height, and hers, in another sense, was approaching. Enough it is to say that all was soon over; and the morning of that day had at last arrived which looked down upon her innocent face, sleeping the sleep from which there is no awaking, and upon me sorrowing the sorrow for which there is no consolation.

On the day after my sister's death, whilst the sweet temple of her brain was yet unviolated by human scrutiny, I formed my own scheme for seeing her once more. Not for the world would I have made this known, nor have suffered a witness to accompany me. I had never heard of feelings that take the name of "sentimental," nor dreamed of such a possibility. But grief, even in a child, hates the light, and shrinks from human eyes. The house was large enough to have two staircases; and by one of these I knew that about midday, when all would be quiet, (for the servants dined at one o'clock,) I could steal up into her chamber. I imagine that it was about an hour after high noon when I reached the chamber door: it was locked, but the key was not taken away. Entering, I closed the door so softly, that, although it opened upon a hall which ascended through all the stories, no echo ran along the silent walls. Then, turning round, I sought my sister's face. But the bed had been moved, and the back was now turned towards myself. Nothing met my eyes but one large window, wide open, through which the sun of midsummer, at midday, was showering down torrents of splendor. The weather was dry, the sky was cloudless, the blue depths seemed the express types of infinity; and it was not possible for eye to behold, or for heart to conceive, any symbols more pathetic of life and the glory of life.

Let me pause for one instant in approaching a remembrance so affecting for my own mind, to mention, that, in the "Opium Confessions," I endeavored to explain the reason why death, other conditions remaining the same, is more profoundly affecting in summer than in other parts of the year — so far, at least, as it is liable to any modification at all from accidents of scenery or season. The reason, as I there suggested, lies in the antagonism between the tropical redundancy of life in summer and the frozen sterilities of the grave.   The summer we see, the grave we haunt with our thoughts; the glory is around us, the darkness is within us; and, the two coming into collision, each exalts the other into stronger relief.   But, in my case, there was even a subtler reason why the summer had this intense power of vivifying the spectacle or the thoughts of death. And, recollecting it, I am struck with the truth, that far more of our deepest thoughts and feelings pass to us through perplexed combinations of *concrete* objects, pass to us as *involutes* (if I may coin that word) in compound experiences incapable of being disentangled, than ever reach us *directly*, and in their own abstract shapes.   It had happened, that amongst our vast nursery collection of books was the Bible, illustrated with many pictures.   And in long dark evenings, as my three sisters, with myself, sat by the firelight round the *guard*[1] of our nursery, no book was so much in request among us.   It ruled us and swayed us as mysteriously as music.   Our younger nurse, whom we all loved, would sometimes, according to her simple powers, endeavor to explain what we found obscure.   We, the children, were all constitutionally touched with pensiveness: the fitful gloom and sudden lambencies of the room by firelight suited our evening state of feelings; and they suited, also, the divine revelations of power and mysterious beauty which awed us.   Above all, the story of a just man, — man, and yet *not* man, real above all things, and yet shadowy above all things, — who had suffered the passion of death in Palestine, slept upon our minds like early dawn upon the waters.   The nurse knew and explained to us the chief differences in Oriental climates; and all these differences (as it happens) express themselves, more or less, in varying relations to the great accidents and powers of summer.   The cloudless sunlights of Syria — those seemed to argue everlasting summer; the disciples plucking the ears of corn — that *must* be summer; but, above all, the very name of Palm Sunday (a festival in the English church) troubled me like an anthem.   "Sunday!" what was *that*? That was the day of peace which masked another peace deeper

---

[1] "*The guard.*" — I know not whether the word is a local one in this sense. What I mean is a sort of fender, four or five feet high, which locks up the fire from too near an approach on the part of children.

than the heart of man can comprehend. "Palms!" what were they? *That* was an equivocal word; palms, in the sense of trophies, expressed the pomps of life; palms, as a product of nature, expressed the pomps of summer. Yet still even this explanation does not suffice; it was not merely by the peace and by the summer, by the deep sound of rest below all rest and of ascending glory, that I had been haunted. It was also because Jerusalem stood near to those deep images both in time and in place. The great event of Jerusalem was at hand when Palm Sunday came; and the scene of that Sunday was near in place to Jerusalem. What then was Jerusalem? Did I fancy it to be the *omphalos* (navel) or physical centre of the earth? Why should *that* affect me? Such a pretension had once been made for Jerusalem, and once for a Grecian city; and both pretensions had become ridiculous, as the figure of the planet became known. Yes; but if not of the earth, yet of mortality; for earth's tenant, Jerusalem, had now become the *omphalos* and absolute centre. Yet how? There, on the contrary, it was, as we infants understood, that mortality had been trampled under foot. True; but, for that very reason, there it was that mortality had opened its very gloomiest crater. There it was, indeed, that the human had risen on wings from the grave; but, for that reason, there also it was that the divine had been swallowed up by the abyss; the lesser star could not rise before the greater should submit to eclipse. Summer, therefore, had connected itself with death, not merely as a mode of antagonism, but also as a phenomenon brought into intricate relations with death by scriptural scenery and events.

Out of this digression, for the purpose of showing how inextricably my feelings and images of death were entangled with those of summer, as connected with Palestine and Jerusalem, let me come back to the bed chamber of my sister. From the gorgeous sunlight I turned around to the corpse. There lay the sweet childish figure; there the angel face; and, as people usually fancy, it was said in the house that no features had suffered any change. Had they not? The forehead, indeed, — the serene and noble forehead, — *that* might be the same; but the frozen eyelids, the darkness that seemed to steal from beneath them, the marble lips, the stiffening hands, laid palm to

palm, as if repeating the supplications of closing anguish, —
could these be mistaken for life? Had it been so, wherefore
did I not spring to those heavenly lips with tears and never-
ending kisses? But so it was *not*. I stood checked for a moment; awe, not fear, fell upon me; and, whilst I stood, a solemn
wind began to blow — the saddest that ear ever heard. It was
a wind that might have swept the fields of mortality for a thousand centuries. Many times since, upon summer days, when
the sun is about the hottest, I have remarked the same wind
arising and uttering the same hollow, solemn, Memnonian,[1]
but saintly swell: it is in this world the one great *audible* symbol
of eternity. And three times in my life have I happened to
hear the same sound in the same circumstances — namely,
when standing between an open window and a dead body on a
summer day.

Instantly, when my ear caught this vast Æolian intonation,
when my eye filled with the golden fulness of life, the pomps of
the heavens above, or the glory of the flowers below, and turning when it settled upon the frost which overspread my sister's
face, instantly a trance fell upon me. A vault seemed to open
in the zenith of the far blue sky, a shaft which ran up forever.
I, in spirit, rose as if on billows that also ran up the shaft forever; and the billows seemed to pursue the throne of God; but
that also ran before us and fled away continually. The flight
and the pursuit seemed to go on forever and ever. Frost gathering frost, some Sarsar wind of death, seemed to repel me;
some mighty relation between God and death dimly struggled
to evolve itself from the dreadful antagonism between them;
shadowy meanings even yet continued to exercise and torment,
in dreams, the deciphering oracle within me. I slept — for
how long I cannot say: slowly I recovered my self-possession;

[1] *Memnonian.* For the sake of many readers, whose hearts may go along
earnestly with a record of infant sorrow, but whose course of life has not allowed them much leisure for study, I pause to explain — that the head of Mem-
non, in the British Museum, that sublime head which wears upon its lips a
smile coextensive with all time and all space, an Æonian smile of gracious love
and Pan-like mystery, the most diffusive and pathetically divine that the hand
of man has created, is represented, on the authority of ancient traditions, to
have uttered at sunrise, or soon after as the sun's rays had accumulated heat
enough to rarefy the air within certain cavities in the bust, a solemn and dirge-
like series of intonations. . . .

and, when I woke, found myself standing, as before, close to my sister's bed.

I have reason to believe that a *very* long interval had elapsed during this wandering or suspension of my perfect mind. When I returned to myself, there was a foot (or I fancied so) on the stairs. I was alarmed; for, if any body had detected me, means would have been taken to prevent my coming again. Hastily, therefore, I kissed the lips that I should kiss no more, and slunk, like a guilty thing, with stealthy steps from the room. Thus perished the vision, loveliest amongst all the shows which earth has revealed to me; thus mutilated was the parting which should have lasted forever; tainted thus with fear was that farewell sacred to love and grief, to perfect love and to grief that could not be healed.

O Ahasuerus, everlasting Jew![1] fable or not a fable, thou, when first starting on thy endless pilgrimage of woe, — thou, when first flying through the gates of Jerusalem, and vainly yearning to leave the pursuing curse behind thee, — couldst not more certainly in the words of Christ have read thy doom of endless sorrow, than I when passing forever from my sister's room. The worm was at my heart; and, I may say, the worm that could not die. Man is doubtless *one* by some subtle *nexus*, some system of links, that we cannot perceive, extending from the new-born infant to the superannuated dotard; but, as regards many affections and passions incident to his nature at different stages, he is *not* one, but an intermitting creature, ending and beginning anew: the unity of man, in this respect, is coextensive only with the particular stage to which the passion belongs. Some passions, as that of sexual love, are celestial by one half of their origin, animal and earthly by the other half. These will not survive their own appropriate stage. But love, which is *altogether* holy, like that between two children, is privileged to revisit by glimpses the silence and the darkness of declining years; and, possibly, this final experience in my sister's bed room, or some other in which her innocence was concerned, may rise again for me to illuminate the clouds of death.

---

[1] *Everlasting Jew.* — *Der ewige Jude* — which is the common German expression for "The Wandering Jew," and sublimer even than our own.

On the day following this which I have recorded came a body of medical men to examine the brain and the particular nature of the complaint, for in some of its symptoms it had shown perplexing anomalies. An hour after the strangers had withdrawn, I crept again to the room; but the door was now locked, the key had been taken away, and I was shut out forever.

Then came the funeral. I, in the ceremonial character of *mourner*, was carried thither. I was put into a carriage with some gentlemen whom I did not know. They were kind and attentive to me; but naturally they talked of things disconnected with the occasion, and their conversation was a torment. At the church, I was told to hold a white handkerchief to my eyes. Empty hypocrisy! What need had *he* of masks or mockeries, whose heart died within him at every word that was uttered? During that part of the service which passed within the church, I made an effort to attend; but I sank back continually into my own solitary darkness, and I heard little consciously, except some fugitive strains from the sublime chapter of St. Paul, which in England is always read at burials.[1]

Lastly came that magnificent liturgical service which the English church performs at the side of the grave; for this church does not forsake her dead so long as they continue in the upper air, but waits for her last "sweet and solemn [2] farewell" at the side of the grave. There is exposed once again, and for the last time, the coffin. All eyes survey the record of name, of sex, of age, and the day of departure from earth — records how shadowy! and dropped into darkness as if messages addressed to worms. Almost at the very last comes the symbolic ritual, tearing and shattering the heart with volleying discharges, peal after peal, from the final artillery of woe. The coffin is lowered into its home; it has disappeared from all eyes but those that look down into the abyss of the grave. The sacristan stands ready, with his shovel of earth and stones.

---

[1] 1 Corinthians, XV. 20, ff.

[2] This beautiful expression, I am pretty certain, must belong to Mrs. Trollope; I read it, probably, in a tale of hers connected with the backwoods of America, where the absence of such a farewell must unspeakably aggravate the gloom at any rate belonging to a household separation of that eternal character occurring amongst the shadows of those mighty forests.

The priest's voice is heard once more, — *earth to earth*, — and immediately the dread rattle ascends from the lid of the coffin; *ashes to ashes* — and again the killing sound is heard; *dust to dust* — and the farewell volley announces that the grave, the coffin, the face are sealed up forever and ever.

Grief! thou art classed amongst the depressing passions. And true it is that thou humblest to the dust, but also thou exaltest to the clouds. Thou shakest as with ague, but also thou steadiest like frost. Thou sickenest the heart, but also thou healest its infirmities. Among the very foremost of mine was morbid sensibility to shame. And, ten years afterwards, I used to throw my self-reproaches with regard to that infirmity into this shape, viz., that if I were summoned to seek aid for a perishing fellow-creature, and that I could obtain that aid only by facing a vast company of critical or sneering faces, I might, perhaps, shrink basely from the duty. It is true that no such case had ever actually occurred; so that it was a mere romance of casuistry to tax myself with cowardice so shocking. But, to feel a doubt, was to feel condemnation; and the crime that *might* have been was, in my eyes, the crime that *had* been. Now, however, all was changed; and for any thing which regarded my sister's memory, in one hour I received a new heart. Once in Westmoreland I saw a case resembling it. I saw a ewe suddenly put off and abjure her own nature, in a service of love — yes, slough it as completely as ever serpent sloughed his skin. Her lamb had fallen into a deep trench, from which all escape was hopeless without the aid of man. And to a man she advanced, bleating clamorously, until he followed her and rescued her beloved. Not less was the change in myself. Fifty thousand sneering faces would not have troubled me *now* in any office of tenderness to my sister's memory. Ten legions would not have repelled me from seeking her, if there had been a chance that she could be found. Mockery! it was lost upon me. Laughter! I valued it not. And when I was taunted insultingly with "my girlish tears," that word "*girlish*" had no sting for me, except as a verbal echo to the one eternal thought of my heart — that a girl was the sweetest thing which I, in my short life, had known; that a girl it was who had crowned the earth with beauty, and had opened to my thirst fountains of pure celestial love, from which, in this world, I was to drink no more.

Now began to unfold themselves the consolations of solitude, those consolations which only I was destined to taste; now, therefore, began to open upon me those fascinations of solitude, which, when acting as a co-agency with unresisted grief, end in the paradoxical result of making out of grief itself a luxury; such a luxury as finally becomes a snare, overhanging life itself, and the energies of life, with growing menaces. All deep feelings of a *chronic* class agree in this, that they seek for solitude, and are fed by solitude. Deep grief, deep love, how naturally do these ally themselves with religious feeling! and all three — love, grief, religion — are haunters of solitary places. Love, grief, and the mystery of devotion, — what were these without solitude? All day long, when it was not impossible for me to do so, I sought the most silent and sequestered nooks in the grounds about the house or in the neighboring fields. The awful stillness oftentimes of summer noons, when no winds were abroad, the appealing silence of gray or misty afternoons, — these were fascinations as of witchcraft. Into the woods, into the desert air, I gazed, as if some comfort lay hid in *them*. I wearied the heavens with my inquest of beseeching looks. Obstinately I tormented the blue depths with my scrutiny, sweeping them forever with my eyes, and searching them for one angelic face that might, perhaps, have permission to reveal itself for a moment.

At this time, and under this impulse of rapacious grief, that grasped at what it could not obtain, the faculty of shaping images in the distance out of slight elements, and grouping them after the yearnings of the heart, grew upon me in morbid excess. And I recall at the present moment one instance of that sort, which may show how merely shadows, or a gleam of brightness, or nothing at all, could furnish a sufficient basis for this creative faculty.

On Sunday mornings I went with the rest of my family to church: it was a church on the ancient model of England, having aisles, galleries,[1] organ, all things ancient and venerable,

---

[1] *Galleries.* — These, though condemned on some grounds by the restorers of authentic church architecture, have nevertheless, this one advantage — that,

and the proportions majestic. Here, whilst the congregation knelt through the long litany, as often as we came to that passage, so beautiful amongst many that are so, where God is supplicated on behalf of "all sick persons and young children," and that he would "show his pity upon all prisoners and captives," I wept in secret; and raising my streaming eyes to the upper windows of the galleries, saw, on days when the sun was shining, a spectacle as affecting as ever prophet can have beheld. The *sides* of the windows were rich with storied glass; through the deep purples and crimsons streamed the golden light; emblazonries of heavenly illumination (from the sun) mingling with the earthly emblazonries (from art and its gorgeous coloring) of what is grandest in man. *There* were the apostles that had trampled upon earth, and the glories of earth, out of celestial love to man. *There* were the martyrs that had borne witness to the truth through flames, through torments, and through armies of fierce, insulting faces. *There* were the saints who, under intolerable pangs, had glorified God by meek submission to his will. And all the time, whilst this tumult of sublime memorials held on as the deep chords from some accompaniment in the bass, I saw through the wide central field of the window, where the glass was *un*colored, white, fleecy clouds sailing over the azure depths of the sky: were it but a fragment or a hint of such a cloud, immediately under the flash of my sorrow-haunted eye, it grew and shaped itself into visions of beds with white lawny curtains; and in the beds lay sick children, dying children, that were tossing in anguish, and weeping clamorously for death. God, for some mysterious reason, could not suddenly release them from their pain; but he suffered the beds, as it seemed, to rise slowly through the clouds; slowly the beds ascended into the chambers of the air; slowly, also, his arms descended from the heavens, that he and his young children, whom in Palestine, once and forever, he had blessed, though they *must* pass slowly through the dreadful chasm of separation, might yet meet the sooner. These visions were self-sustained. These visions needed not that any sound should speak to me, or music mould my feelings.

when the *height* of a church is that dimension which most of all expresses its sacred character galleries expound and interpret that height.

The hint from the litany, the fragment from the clouds, — those and the storied windows were sufficient. But not the less the blare of the tumultuous organ wrought its own separate creations. And oftentimes in anthems, when the mighty instrument threw its vast columns of sound, fierce yet melodious, over the voices of the choir, — high in arches, when it seemed to rise, surmounting and overriding the strife of the vocal parts, and gathering by strong coercion the total storm into unity, — sometimes I seemed to rise and walk triumphantly upon those clouds which, but a moment before, I had looked up to as mementoes of prostrate sorrow; yes, sometimes under the transfigurations of music, felt of grief itself as of a fiery chariot for mounting victoriously above the causes of grief.

God speaks to children, also, in dreams, and by the oracles that lurk in darkness. But in solitude, above all things, when made vocal to the meditative heart by the truths and services of a national church, God holds with children "communion undisturbed." Solitude, though it may be silent as light, is, like light, the mightiest of agencies; for solitude is essential to man. All men come into this world *alone*; all leave it *alone*. Even a little child has a dread, whispering consciousness, that, if he should be summoned to travel into God's presence, no gentle nurse will be allowed to lead him by the hand, nor mother to carry him in her arms, nor little sister to share his trepidations. King and priest, warrior and maiden, philosopher and child, all must walk those mighty galleries alone. The solitude, therefore, which in this world appalls or fascinates a child's heart, is but the echo of a far deeper solitude, through which already he has passed, and of another solitude, deeper still, through which he *has* to pass: reflex of one solitude — prefiguration of another.

O burden of solitude, that cleavest to man through every stage of his being! in his birth, which *has* been — in his life, which *is* — in his death, which *shall* be — mighty and essential solitude! that wast, and art, and art to be; thou broodest, like the Spirit of God moving upon the surface of the deeps, over every heart that sleeps in the nurseries of Christendom. Like the vast laboratory of the air, which, seeming to be nothing, or less than the shadow of a shade, hides within itself the principles of all things, solitude for the meditating child is the Agrippa's mirror of the unseen universe. Deep is the solitude of millions who, with hearts welling forth love, have none to love them. Deep is the solitude of those who, under secret griefs, have none to pity them. Deep is the solitude of those who, fighting with doubts or darkness, have none to counsel them. But deeper than the deepest of these solitudes is that which broods over childhood under the passion of sorrow — bringing before it, at intervals, the final solitude which watches for it, and is waiting for it within the gates of death. O mighty and essential solitude, that wast, and art, and art to be, thy kingdom is made perfect in the grave; but even over those that keep watch outside the grave, like myself, an infant of six years old, thou stretchest out a sceptre of fascination.

THOMAS CARLYLE

BIOGRAPHY [1]

MAN'S sociality of nature evinces itself, in spite of all that can be said, with abundant evidence by this one fact, were there no other: the unspeakable delight he takes in Biography. It is written, "The proper study of mankind is man;" to which study, let us candidly admit, he, by true or by false methods, applies himself, nothing loth. "Man is perennially interesting to man; nay, if we look strictly to it, there is nothing else interesting." How inexpressibly comfortable to know our fellow-creature; to see into him, understand his goings-forth, decipher the whole heart of his mystery: nay, not only to see into him, but even to see out of him, to view the world altogether as he views it; so that we can theoretically construe him, and could almost practically personate him; and do now thoroughly discern both what manner of man he is, and what manner of thing he has got to work on and live on!

A scientific interest and a poetic one alike inspire us in this matter. A scientific: because every mortal has a Problem of Existence set before him, which, were it only, what for the most it is, the Problem of keeping soul and body together, must be to a certain extent *original*, unlike every other; and yet, at the same time, so *like* every other; like our own, therefore; instructive, moreover, since we also are indentured to *live*. A poetic interest still more: for precisely this same struggle of human Freewill against material Necessity, which every man's Life, by the mere circumstance that the man continues alive, will more or less victoriously exhibit, — is that which above all else, or rather inclusive of all else, calls the Sympathy of mortal hearts into action; and whether as acted, or as represented and written of, not only is Poetry, but is the sole Poetry possible. Borne onwards by which two all-embracing interests, may the

[1] From *Critical and Miscellaneous Essays*, Vol. III. First published in *Fraser's Magazine*, April, 1832, as a review of Croker's edition (1831) of Boswell's *Life of Johnson*.

earnest Lover of Biography expand himself on all sides, and indefinitely enrich himself. Looking with the eyes of every new neighbour, he can discern a new world different for each: feeling with the heart of every neighbour, he lives with every neighbour's life, even as with his own. Of these millions of living men, each individual is a mirror to us; a mirror both scientific and poetic; or, if you will, both natural and magical; — from which one would so gladly draw aside the gauze veil; and, peering therein, discern the image of his own natural face, and the supernatural secrets that prophetically lie under the same!

Observe, accordingly, to what extent, in the actual course of things, this business of Biography is practised and relished. Define to thyself, judicious Reader, the real significance of these phenomena, named Gossip, Egoism, Personal Narrative (miraculous or not), Scandal, Raillery, Slander, and such like; the sum-total of which (with some fractional addition of a better ingredient, generally too small to be noticeable), constitutes that other grand phenomenon still called "Conversation." Do they not mean wholly: *Biography* and *Autobiography*? Not only in the common Speech of men; but in all Art too, which is or should be the concentrated and conserved essence of what men can speak and show, Biography is almost the one thing needful.

Even in the highest works of Art, our interest, as the critics complain, is too apt to be strongly or even mainly of a Biographic sort. In the Art, we can nowise forget the Artist: while looking on the *Transfiguration*, while studying the *Iliad*, we ever strive to figure to ourselves what spirit dwelt in Raphael; what a head was that of Homer, wherein, woven of Elysian light and Tartarean gloom, that old world fashioned itself together, of which these written Greek characters are but a feeble though perennial copy. The Painter and the Singer are present to us; we partially and for the time become the very Painter and the very Singer, while we enjoy the Picture and the Song. Perhaps too, let the critic say what he will, this is the highest enjoyment, the clearest recognition, we can have of these. Art indeed is Art; yet Man also is Man. Had the *Transfiguration* been painted without human hand; had it grown merely on the canvas, say by atmospheric influences, as lichen-pictures do on rocks, — it were a grand Picture doubtless; yet nothing like so grand as *the* Picture, which, on opening our eyes, we everywhere in Heaven and in Earth see painted; and everywhere pass over with indifference, — because the Painter was not a Man. Think of this; much lies in it. The Vatican is great; yet poor to Chimborazo or the Peak of Teneriffe: its dome is but a foolish Big-endian or Little-endian chip of an egg-shell, compared with that star-fretted Dome where Arcturus and Orion glance forever; which latter, notwithstanding, who looks at, save perhaps some necessitous stargazer bent to make Almanacs; some thick-quilted watchman, to see what weather it will prove? The Biographic interest is wanting: no Michael Angelo was He who built that "Temple of Immensity;" therefore do we, pitiful Littlenesses as we are, turn rather to wonder and to worship in the little toybox of a Temple built by our like.

Still more decisively, still more exclusively does the Biographic interest manifest itself, as we descend into lower regions of spiritual communication; through the whole range of what is called Literature. Of History, for example, the most honoured, if not honourable species of composition, is not the whole purport Biographic? "History," it has been said, "is the essence of innumerable Biographies." Such, at least, it should be: whether it is, might admit of question. But, in any case, what hope have we in turning over those old interminable Chronicles, with their garrulities and insipidities; or still worse, in patiently examining those modern Narrations, of the Philosophic kind, where "Philosophy, teaching by Experience," has to sit like owl on housetop, *seeing* nothing, *understanding* nothing, uttering only, with solemnity enough, her perpetual most wearisome *hoo-hoo*: — what hope have we, except the for most part fallacious one of gaining some acquaintance with our fellow-creatures, though dead and vanished, yet dear to us; how they got along in those old days, suffering and doing; to what extent, and under what circumstances, they resisted the Devil and triumphed over him, or struck their colours to him, and were trodden under foot by him; how, in short, the perennial Battle went, which men name Life, which we also in these

new days, with indifferent fortune, have to fight, and must bequeath to our sons and grandsons to go on fighting, — till the
Enemy one day be quite vanquished and abolished, or else the
great Night sink and part the combatants; and thus, either by
some Millennium, or some new Noah's Deluge, the Volume of
Universal History wind itself up! Other hope, in studying
such Books, we have none: and that it is a deceitful hope, who
that has tried knows not? A feast of widest Biographic insight
is spread for us; we enter full of hungry anticipations: alas, like
so many other feasts, which Life invites us to, a mere Ossian's
"feast of *shells*," — the food and liquor being all emptied out
and clean gone, and only the vacant dishes and deceitful emblems thereof left! Your modern Historical Restaurateurs
are indeed little better than high-priests of Famine; that keep
choicest china dinner-sets, only no dinner to serve therein.
Yet such is our Biographic appetite, we run trying from shop
to shop, with ever new hope; and, unless we could eat the wind,
with ever new disappointment.

Again, consider the whole class of Fictitious Narratives; from
the highest category of epic or dramatic Poetry, in Shakspeare
and Homer, down to the lowest of froth Prose, in the Fashionable Novel. What are all these but so many mimic Biographies? Attempts, here by an inspired Speaker, there by an
uninspired Babbler, to deliver himself, more or less ineffectually, of the grand secret wherewith all hearts labour oppressed:
The significance of Man's Life; — which deliverance, even as
traced in the unfurnished head, and printed at the Minerva
Press, finds readers. For, observe, though there is *a* greatest
Fool, as a superlative in every kind; and *the* most Foolish man
in the Earth is now indubitably living and breathing, and did
this morning or lately eat breakfast, and is even now digesting
the same; and looks out on the world, with his dim horn-eyes,
and inwardly forms some unspeakable theory thereof: yet
where shall the authentically Existing be personally met with!
Can one of us, otherwise than by guess, know that we have got
sight of him, have orally communed with him? To take even
the narrower sphere of this our English Metropolis, can any one
confidently say to himself, that he has conversed with the
identical, individual Stupidest man now extant in London?

No one. Deep as we dive in the Profound, there is ever a new depth opens: where the ultimate bottom may lie, through what new scenes of being we must pass before reaching it (except that we know it does lie somewhere, and might by human faculty and opportunity be reached), is altogether a mystery to us. Strange, tantalising pursuit! We have the fullest assurance, not only that there is a Stupidest of London men actually resident, with bed and board of some kind, in London; but that several persons have been or perhaps are now speaking face to face with him: while for us, chase it as we may, such scientific blessedness will too probably be forever denied! — But the thing we meant to enforce was this comfortable fact, that no known Head was so wooden, but there might be other heads to which it were a genius and Friar Bacon's Oracle. Of no given Book, not even of a Fashionable Novel, can you predicate with certainty that its vacuity is absolute; that there are not other vacuities which shall partially replenish themselves therefrom, and esteem it a *plenum*. How knowest thou, may the distressed Novelwright exclaim, that I, here where I sit, am the Foolishest of existing mortals; that this my Long-ear of a Fictitious Biography shall not find one and the other, into whose still longer ears it may be the means, under Providence, of instilling somewhat? We answer, None knows, none can certainly know: therefore, write on, worthy Brother, even as thou canst, even as it has been given thee.

Here, however, in regard to "Fictitious Biographies," and much other matter of like sort, which the greener mind in these days inditeth, we may as well insert some singular sentences on the importance and significance of *Reality*, as they stand written for us in Professor Gottfried Sauerteig's *Æsthetische Springwürzel*. . . . [1]

Meanwhile, quitting these airy regions, let any one bethink him how impressive the smallest historical *fact* may become, as contrasted with the grandest *fictitious event*; what an incalculable force lies for us in this consideration: The Thing which I here hold imaged in my mind did actually occur; was, in very truth, an element in the system of the All, whereof I too form part; had therefore, and has, through all time, an authentic

---

[1] The supposed quotation is omitted.

being; is not a dream, but a reality! We ourselves can remember reading, in *Lord Clarendon*,[1] with feelings perhaps somehow accidentally opened to it, — certainly with a depth of impression strange to us then and now, — that insignificant-looking passage, where Charles, after the battle of Worcester, glides down, with Squire Careless, from the Royal Oak, at nightfall, being hungry: how, "making a shift to get over hedges and ditches, after walking at least eight or nine miles, which were the more grievous to the King by the weight of his boots (for he could not put *them* off when he cut off his hair, for want of shoes), before morning they came to *a poor cottage, the owner whereof being a Roman Catholic was known to Careless.*" How this poor drudge, being knocked up from his snoring, "carried them into a little barn full of hay, which was a better lodging than he had for himself;" and by and by, not without difficulty, brought his Majesty "a piece of bread and a great pot of buttermilk," saying candidly that "he himself lived by his daily labour, and that what he had brought him was the fare he and his wife had:" on which nourishing diet his Majesty, "staying upon the haymow," feeds thankfully for two days; and then departs, under new guidance, having first changed clothes, down to the very shirt and "old pair of shoes," with his landlord; and so, as worthy Bunyan has it, "goes on his way, and sees him no more." Singular enough, if we will think of it! This then was a genuine flesh-and-blood Rustic of the year 1651: he did actually swallow bread and buttermilk (not having ale and bacon), and do field-labour: with these hobnailed "shoes" has sprawled through mud-roads in winter, and, jocund or not, driven his team a-field in summer: he made bargains; had chafferings and higglings, now a sore heart, now a glad one; was born; was a son, was a father; toiled in many ways, being forced to it, till the strength was all worn out of him: and then — lay down "to rest his galled back," and sleep there till the long-distant morning! — How comes it, that he alone of all the British rustics who tilled and lived along with him, on whom the blessed sun on that same "fifth day of September" was shining, should have chanced to rise on us; that this poor pair of clouted Shoes, out of the million million

[1] *History of the Rebellion*, III. 625.

hides that have been tanned, and cut, and worn, should still subsist, and hang visibly together?   We see him but for a moment; for one moment, the blanket of the Night is rent asunder, so that we behold and see, and then closes over him — forever.

So too, in some *Boswell's Life of Johnson*, how indelible, and magically bright, does many a little *Reality* dwell in our remembrance!   There is no need that the personages on the scene be a King and Clown; that the scene be the Forest of the Royal Oak, "on the borders of Staffordshire:" need only that the scene lie on this old firm Earth of ours, where we also have so surprisingly arrived; that the personages be *men*, and *seen* with the eyes of a man.   Foolish enough, how some slight, perhaps mean and even ugly incident, if *real* and well presented, will fix itself in a susceptive memory, and lie ennobled there; silvered over with the pale cast of thought, with the pathos which belongs only to the Dead.   For the Past is all holy to us; the Dead are all holy, even they that were base and wicked while alive.   Their baseness and wickedness was not *They*, was but the heavy and unmanageable Environment that lay round them, with which they fought unprevailing: *they* (the ethereal god-given Force that dwelt in them, and was their *Self*) have now shuffled-off that heavy Environment, and are free and pure: their life-long Battle, go how it might, is all ended, with many wounds or with fewer; they have been recalled from it, and the once harsh-jarring battle-field has become a silent awe-inspiring Golgotha, and *Gottesacker* (Field of God)! — Boswell relates this in itself smallest and poorest of occurrences: "As we walked along the Strand to-night, arm in arm, a woman of the town accosted us in the usual enticing manner. 'No, no, my girl,' said Johnson; 'it won't do.'   He, however, did not treat her with harshness; and we talked of the wretched life of such women."   Strange power of *Reality*!   Not even this poorest of occurrences, but now, after seventy years are come and gone, has a meaning for us.   Do but consider that it is *true*; that it did in very deed occur!   That unhappy Outcast, with all her sins and woes, her lawless desires, too complex mischances, her wailings and her riotings, has departed utterly; alas! her siren finery has got all besmutched, ground, generations since, into dust and smoke; of her degraded body, and whole miserable earthly existence, all is away: *she* is no longer here, but far from us, in the bosom of Eternity, — whence we too came, whither we too are bound! Johnson said, "No, no, my girl; it won't do;" and then "we talked;" — and herewith the wretched one, seen but for the twinkling of an eye, passes on into the utter Darkness. No high Calistâ, that ever issued from Story-teller's brain, will impress us more deeply than this meanest of the mean; and for a good reason: That *she* issued from the Maker of Men.

It is well worth the Artist's while to examine for himself what it is that gives such pitiful incidents their memorableness; his aim likewise is, above all things, to be *memorable*. Half the effect, we already perceive, depends on the object; on its being *real*, on its being really *seen*. The other half will depend on the observer; and the question now is: How are real objects to be *so* seen; on what quality of observing, or of style in describing, does this so intense pictorial power depend? Often a slight circumstance contributes curiously to the result: some little, and perhaps to appearance accidental, feature is presented; a light-gleam, which instantaneously *excites* the mind, and urges it to complete the picture, and evolve the meaning thereof for itself. By critics, such light-gleams and their almost magical influence have frequently been noted: but the power to produce such, to select such features as will produce them, is generally treated as a knack, or trick of the trade, a secret for being "graphic;" whereas these magical feats are, in truth, rather inspirations; and the gift of performing them, which acts unconsciously, without forethought, and as if by nature alone, is properly a *genius* for description.

One grand, invaluable secret there is, however, which includes all the rest, and, what is comfortable, lies clearly in every man's power: *To have an open loving heart, and what follows from the possession of such!* Truly it has been said, emphatically in these days ought it to be repeated: A loving Heart is the beginning of all Knowledge. This it is that opens the whole mind, quickens every faculty of the intellect to do its fit work, that of *knowing*; and therefrom, by sure consequence, of *vividly uttering forth*. Other secret for being "graphic" is there none, worth having: but this is an all-sufficient one. See, for example, what a small Boswell can do! Hereby, indeed, is the whole man made a living mirror, wherein the wonders of this ever-wonderful Universe are, in their true light (which is ever a magical, miraculous one) represented, and reflected back on us. It has been said, "the heart sees farther than the head:" but, indeed, without the seeing heart, there is no true seeing for the head so much as possible; all is mere *oversight*, hallucination and vain superficial phantasmagoria, which can permanently profit no one.

Here, too, may we not pause for an instant, and make a practical reflection? Considering the multitude of mortals that handle the Pen in these days, and can mostly spell, and write without glaring violations of grammar, the question naturally arises: How is it, then, that no Work proceeds from them, bearing any stamp of authenticity and permanence; of worth for more than one day? Ship-loads of Fashionable Novels, Sentimental Rhymes, Tragedies, Farces, Diaries of Travel, Tales by flood and field, are swallowed monthly into the bottomless Pool: still does the Press toil; innumerable Papermakers, Compositors, Printers' Devils, Bookbinders, and Hawkers grown hoarse with loud proclaiming, rest not from their labour; and still, in torrents, rushes on the great array of Publications, unpausing, to their final home; and still Oblivion, like the Grave, cries, Give! Give! How is it that of all these countless multitudes, no one can attain to the smallest mark of excellence, or produce aught that shall endure longer than "snow-flake on the river," or the foam of penny-beer? We answer: Because they *are* foam; because there is no *Reality* in them. These Three Thousand men, women and children, that make up the army of British Authors, do not, if we will well consider it, *see* anything whatever; consequently *have* nothing that they can record and utter, only more or fewer things that they can plausibly pretend to record. The Universe, of Man and Nature, is still quite shut-up from them; the "open secret" still utterly a secret; because no sympathy with Man or Nature, no love and free simplicity of heart has yet unfolded the same. Nothing but a pitiful Image of their own pitiful Self, with its vanities, and grudgings, and ravenous hunger of all kinds, hangs forever painted in the retina of these unfortunate persons; so that the starry ALL, with whatsoever it embraces, does but appear as some expanded magic-lantern shadow of that same Image, — and naturally looks pitiful enough.

It is vain for these persons to allege that they are naturally without gift, naturally stupid and sightless, and so *can* attain to no knowledge of anything; therefore, in writing of anything, must needs write falsehoods of it, there being in it no truth for them. Not so, good Friends. The stupidest of you has a certain faculty; were it but that of articulate speech (say, in the Scottish, the Irish, the Cockney dialect, or even in "Governess-English"), and of physically discerning what lies under your nose. The stupidest of you would perhaps grudge to be compared in faculty with James Boswell; yet see what he has produced! You do not use your faculty honestly; your heart is shut up; full of greediness, malice, discontent; so your intellectual sense cannot be opened. It is vain also to urge that James Boswell had opportunities; saw great men and great things, such as you can never hope to look on. What make ye of Parson White in Selborne? He had not only no great men to look on, but not even men; merely sparrows and cock-chafers: yet has he left us a *Biography* of these; which, under its title *Natural History of Selborne*, still remains valuable to us; which has copied a little sentence or two *faithfully* from the Inspired Volume of Nature, and so is itself not without inspiration. Go ye and do likewise. Sweep away utterly all frothiness and falsehood from your heart; struggle unweariedly to acquire, what is possible for every god-created Man, a free, open, humble soul: *speak not at all, in any wise, till you have somewhat to speak;* care not for the *reward* of your speaking, but simply and with undivided mind for the *truth* of your speaking: then be placed in what section of Space and of Time soever, do but open your eyes, and they shall actually *see*, and bring you real *knowledge*, wondrous, worthy of *belief*; and instead of one Boswell and one White, the world will rejoice in a thousand, — stationed on their thousand several watch-towers, to instruct us by indubitable documents, of whatsoever in our so stupendous World comes to light and *is!* O, had the Editor of this

Magazine but a magic rod to turn all that not inconsiderable Intellect, which now deluges us with artificial fictitious soap-lather, and mere Lying, into the faithful study of Reality, — what knowledge of great, everlasting Nature, and of Man's ways and doings therein, would not every year bring us in! Can we but change one single soap-latherer and mountebank Juggler, into a true Thinker and Doer, who even *tries* honestly to think and do, — great will be our reward.

But to return; or rather from this point to begin our journey! If now, what with Herr Sauerteig's *Springwürzel*, what with so much lucubration of our own, it have become apparent how deep, immeasurable is the "worth that lies in *Reality*," and farther, how exclusive the interest which man takes in Histories of Man, — may it not seem lamentable, that so few genuinely good *Biographies* have yet been accumulated in Literature; that in the whole world, one cannot find, going strictly to work, above some dozen, or baker's dozen, and those chiefly of very ancient date?   Lamentable: yet, after what we have just seen, accountable.   Another question might be asked: How comes it that in England we have simply one good Biography, this *Boswell's Johnson*; and of good, indifferent, or even bad attempts at Biography, fewer than any civilised people?   Consider the French and Germans, with their Moreris, Bayles, Jördenses, Jöchers, their innumerable *Mémoires*, and *Schilderungen*, and *Biographies Universelles*; not to speak of Rousseaus, Goethes, Schubarts, Jung-Stillings: and then contrast with these our poor Birches and Kippises and Pecks; the whole breed of whom, moreover, is now extinct!

With this question, as the answer might lead us far, and come out unflattering to patriotic sentiment, we shall not intermeddle; but turn rather, with great pleasure, to the fact, that one excellent Biography *is* actually English; — and even now lies, in Five new Volumes, at our hand, soliciting a new consideration from us; such as, age after age (the Perennial showing ever new phases as *our* position alters), it may long be profitable to bestow on it; — to which task we here, in this position, in this age, gladly address ourselves.

First, however, let the foolish April-fool-day pass by; and our Reader, during these twenty-nine days of uncertain weather that will follow, keep pondering, according to convenience, the purport of BIOGRAPHY in general: then, with the blessed dew of May-day, and in unlimited convenience of space, shall all that we have written on *Johnson* and *Boswell's Johnson* and *Croker's Boswell's Johnson* be faithfully laid before him.

THOMAS BABINGTON MACAULAY

SOUTHEY'S EDITION OF THE *PILGRIM'S PROGRESS* [1]

THIS is an eminently beautiful and splendid edition of a book which well deserves all that the printer and the engraver can do for it. The life of Bunyan is, of course, not a performance which can add much to the literary reputation of such a writer as Mr. Southey. But it is written in excellent English, and, for the most part, in an excellent spirit. Mr. Southey propounds, we need not say, many opinions from which we altogether dissent; and his attempts to excuse the odious persecution to which Bunyan was subjected have sometimes moved our indignation. But we will avoid this topic. We are at present much more inclined to join in paying homage to the genius of a great man, than to engage in a controversy concerning church government and toleration.

We must not pass without notice the engravings with which this beautiful volume is decorated. Some of Mr. Heath's woodcuts are admirably designed and executed. Mr. Martin's illustrations do not please us quite so well. His Valley of the Shadow of Death is not that Valley of the Shadow of Death which Bunyan imagined. At all events, it is not that dark and horrible glen which has from childhood been in our mind's eye. The valley is a cavern: the quagmire is a lake: the straight path runs zigzag; and Christian appears like a speck in the darkness of the immense vault. We miss, too, those hideous forms which make so striking a part of the description of Bunyan, and which Salvator Rosa would have loved to draw. It is with unfeigned diffidence that we pronounce judgment on any question relating to the art of painting. But it appears to us that Mr. Martin has not of late been fortunate in his choice of subjects. He should never have attempted to illustrate the *Paradise Lost*. There can be no two manners more directly

---

[1] From *Critical and Miscellaneous Essays*, Vol. I. First published in the *Edinburgh Review*, December, 1831.

opposed to each other, than the manner of his painting and the manner of Milton's poetry. Those things which are mere accessaries in the descriptions, become the principal objects in the pictures; and those figures which are most prominent in the descriptions can be detected in the pictures only by a very close scrutiny. Mr. Martin has succeeded perfectly in representing the pillars and candelabras of Pandemonium; but he has forgotten that Milton's Pandemonium is merely the background to Satan. In the picture, the Archangel is scarcely visible amidst the endless colonnades of his infernal palace. Milton's Paradise, again, is merely the background to his Adam and Eve. But in Mr. Martin's picture, the landscape is everything. Adam, Eve, and Raphael attract much less notice than the lake and the mountains, the gigantic flowers and the giraffes which feed upon them. We have read, we forget where, that James the Second sat to Verelst, the great flower-painter. When the performance was finished, his Majesty appeared in the midst of sunflowers and tulips, which completely drew away all attention from the central figure. All who looked at the portrait took it for a flower-piece. Mr. Martin, we think, introduces his immeasurable spaces, his innumerable multitudes, his gorgeous prodigies of architecture and landscape, almost as unseasonably as Verelst introduced his flower-pots and nosegays. If Mr. Martin were to paint Lear in the storm, the blazing sky, the sheets of rain, the swollen torrents, and the tossing forest, would draw away all attention from the agonies of the insulted king and father. If he were to paint the death of Lear, the old man, asking the bystanders to undo his button, would be thrown into the shade by a vast blaze of pavilions, standards, armour, and herald's coats. He would illustrate the *Orlando Furioso* well, the *Orlando Innamorato* still better, the *Arabian Nights* best of all. Fairy palaces and gardens, porticoes of agate, and groves flowering with emeralds and rubies, inhabited by people for whom nobody cares, these are his proper domain. He would succeed admirably in the enchanted ground of Alcina, or the mansion of Aladdin. But he should avoid Milton and Bunyan.

The characteristic peculiarity of the *Pilgrim's Progress* is, that it is the only work of its kind which possesses a strong human interest. Other allegories only amuse the fancy. The allegory of Bunyan has been read by many thousands with tears. There are some good allegories in Johnson's works, and some of still higher merit by Addison. In these performances there is, perhaps, as much wit and ingenuity as in the *Pilgrim's Progress*. But the pleasure which is produced by the *Vision of Mirza*, or the *Vision of Theodore*,[1] the genealogy of Wit,[2] or the contest between Rest and Labour,[3] is exactly similar to the pleasure which we derive from one of Cowley's *Odes*, or from a Canto of *Hudibras*. It is a pleasure which belongs wholly to the understanding, and in which the feelings have no part whatever. Nay, even Spenser himself, though assuredly one of the greatest poets that ever lived, could not succeed in the attempt to make allegory interesting. It was in vain that he lavished the riches of his mind on the House of Pride and the House of Temperance. One unpardonable fault, the fault of tediousness, pervades the whole of the *Faerie Queene*. We become sick of Cardinal Virtues and Deadly Sins, and long for the society of plain men and women. Of the persons who read the first Canto, not one in ten reaches the end of the First Book, and not one in a hundred perseveres to the end of the poem. Very few and very weary are those who are in at the death of the Blatant Beast. If the last six books, which are said to have been destroyed in Ireland, had been preserved, we doubt whether any heart less stout than that of a commentator would have held out to the end.

It is not so with the *Pilgrim's Progress*. That wonderful book, while it obtains admiration from the most fastidious critics, is loved by those who are too simple to admire it. Doctor Johnson, all whose studies were desultory, and who hated, as he said, to read books through, made an exception in favour of the *Pilgrim's Progress*. That work, he said, was one of the two or three works which he wished longer. It was by no common merit that the illiterate sectary extracted praise like this from the most pedantic of critics and the most bigoted of Tories. In the wildest parts of Scotland the *Pilgrim's Progress* is the delight of the peasantry. In every nursery the *Pilgrim's Progress* is a greater favourite then *Jack the Giant-Killer*.

[1] By Dr. Johnson, 1748.   [2] *Spectator*, No. 63.   [3] *Rambler*, No. 33.

Every reader knows the straight and narrow path, as well as he knows a road in which he has gone backward and forward a hundred times. This is the highest miracle of genius — that things which are not should be as though they were, that the imaginations of one mind should become the personal recollections of another. And this miracle the tinker has wrought. There is no ascent, no declivity, no resting-place, no turn-stile, with which we are not perfectly acquainted. The wicket-gate, and the desolate swamp which separates it from the City of Destruction; the long line of road, as straight as a rule can make it; the Interpreter's house, and all its fair shows; the prisoner in the iron cage; the palace, at the doors of which armed men kept guard, and on the battlements of which walked persons clothed all in gold; the cross and the sepulchre; the steep hill and the pleasant arbour; the stately front of the House Beautiful by the wayside; the low green valley of Humiliation, rich with grass and covered with flocks, all are as well known to us as the sights of our own street. Then we come to the narrow place where Apollyon strode right across the whole breadth of the way, to stop the journey of Christian, and where afterwards the pillar was set up to testify how bravely the pilgrim had fought the good fight. As we advance, the valley becomes deeper and deeper. The shade of the precipices on both sides falls blacker and blacker. The clouds gather overhead. Doleful voices, the clanking of chains, and the rushing of many feet to and fro, are heard through the darkness. The way, hardly discernible in gloom, runs close by the mouth of the burning pit, which sends forth its flames, its noisome smoke, and its hideous shapes, to terrify the adventurer. Thence he goes on, amidst the snares and pitfalls, with the mangled bodies of those who have perished lying in the ditch by his side. At the end of the long dark valley, he passes the dens in which the old giants dwelt, amidst the bones and ashes of those whom they had slain.

Then the road passes straight on through a waste moor, till at length the towers of a distant city appear before the traveller; and soon he is in the midst of the innumerable multitudes of Vanity Fair. There are the jugglers and the apes, the shops and the puppet-shows. There are Italian Row, and French

Row, and Spanish Row, and Britain Row, with their crowds of buyers, sellers, and loungers, jabbering all the languages of the earth.

Thence we go on by the little hill of the silver mine, and through the meadow of lilies, along the bank of that pleasant river which is bordered on both sides by fruit-trees. On the left side, branches off the path leading to that horrible castle, the court-yard of which is paved with the skulls of pilgrims; and right onward are the sheepfolds and orchards of the Delectable Mountains.

From the Delectable Mountains, the way lies through the fogs and briers of the Enchanted Ground, with here and there a bed of soft cushions spread under a green arbour. And beyond is the land of Beulah, where the flowers, the grapes, and the songs of birds never cease, and where the sun shines night and day. Thence are plainly seen the golden pavements and streets of pearl, on the other side of that black and cold river over which there is no bridge.

All the stages of the journey, all the forms which cross or overtake the pilgrims, — giants and hobgoblins, ill-favoured ones, and shining ones; the tall, comely, swarthy Madam Bubble, with her great purse by her side, and her fingers playing with the money; the black man in the bright vesture; Mr. Worldly-Wiseman, and my Lord Hategood; Mr. Talkative, and Mrs. Timorous — are all actually existing beings to us. We follow the travellers through their allegorical progress with interest not inferior to that with which we follow Elizabeth from Siberia to Moscow, or Jeanie Deans from Edinburgh to London. Bunyan is almost the only writer that ever gave to the abstract the interest of the concrete. In the works of many celebrated authors, men are mere personifications. We have not an Othello, but jealousy; not an Iago, but perfidy; not a Brutus, but patriotism. The mind of Bunyan, on the contrary, was so imaginative, that personifications, when he dealt with them, became men. A dialogue between two qualities, in his dream, has more dramatic effect than a dialogue between two human beings in most plays. In this respect, the genius of Bunyan bore a great resemblance to that of a man who had very little else in common with him, Percy Bysshe

Shelley.   The strong imagination of Shelley made him an idolater in his own despite.   One of the most indefinite terms of a hard, cold, dark, metaphysical system, he made a gorgeous Pantheon, full of beautiful, majestic, and lifelike forms. He turned atheism itself into a mythology, rich with visions as glorious as the gods that live in the marble of Phidias, or the virgin saints that smile on us from the canvas of Murillo.   The Spirit of Beauty, the Principle of Good, the Principle of Evil, when he treated of them, ceased to be abstractions.   They took shape and colour.   They were no longer mere words; but "intelligible forms;" "fair humanities;" objects of love, of adoration, or of fear.   As there can be no stronger signs of a mind destitute of the poetical faculty than that tendency, which was so common among the writers of the French school, to turn images into abstractions — Venus, for example, into Love, Minerva into Wisdom, Mars into War, and Bacchus into Festivity — so there can be no stronger sign of a mind truly poetical, than a disposition to reverse this abstracting process, and to make individuals out of generalities.   Some of the metaphysical and ethical theories of Shelley were certainly most absurd and pernicious.   But we doubt whether any modern poet has possessed in an equal degree the highest qualities of the great ancient masters.   The words bard and inspiration, which seem so cold and affected when applied to other modern writers, have a perfect propriety when applied to him.   He was not an author, but a bard.   His poetry seems not to have been an art, but an inspiration.   Had he lived to the full age of man, he might not improbably have given to the world some great work of the very highest rank in design and execution. But, alas!

$$\delta \; \Delta\acute{\alpha}\phi\nu\iota\varsigma \; \acute{\epsilon}\beta\alpha \; \dot{\rho}\acute{o}o\nu \; \acute{\epsilon}\kappa\lambda\upsilon\sigma\epsilon \; \delta\acute{\iota}\nu\alpha$$
$$\tau\grave{o}\nu \; \mathrm{Mo}\acute{\iota}\sigma\alpha\iota\varsigma \; \phi\acute{\iota}\lambda o\nu \; \mathring{\alpha}\nu\delta\rho\alpha, \; \tau\grave{o}\nu \; o\grave{\upsilon} \; \mathrm{N}\acute{\upsilon}\mu\phi\alpha\iota\sigma\iota\nu \; \mathring{\alpha}\pi\epsilon\chi\theta\mathring{\eta}.[1]$$

But we must return to Bunyan.   The *Pilgrim's Progress* undoubtedly is not a perfect allegory.   The types are often inconsistent with each other; and sometimes the allegorical disguise is altogether thrown off.   The river, for example, is emblematic of death, and we are told that every human being

---

[1] "Daphnis trod the stream; the whirlpool closed over the man dear to the Muses, not hateful to the Nymphs."

must pass through the river. But Faithful does not pass through it. He is martyred, not in shadow, but in reality, at Vanity Fair. Hopeful talks to Christian about Esau's birthright, and about his own convictions of sin, as Bunyan might have talked with one of his own congregation. The damsels at the House Beautiful catechise Christiana's boys, as any good ladies might catechise any boys at a Sunday-school. But we do not believe that any man, whatever might be his genius, and whatever his good luck, could long continue a figurative history without falling into many inconsistencies. We are sure that inconsistencies, scarcely less gross than the worst into which Bunyan has fallen, may be found in the shortest and most elaborate allegories of the *Spectator* and the *Rambler*. *The Tale of a Tub* and the *History of John Bull* swarm with similar errors, if the name of error can be properly applied to that which is unavoidable. It is not easy to make a simile go on all-fours. But we believe that no human ingenuity could produce such a centipede as a long allegory, in which the correspondence between the outward sign and the thing signified should be exactly preserved. Certainly no writer, ancient or modern, has yet achieved the adventure. The best thing, on the whole, that an allegorist can do, is to present to his readers a succession of analogies, each of which may separately be striking and happy, without looking very nicely to see whether they harmonize with each other. This Bunyan has done; and, though a minute scrutiny may detect inconsistencies in every page of his tale, the general effect which the tale produces on all persons, learned and unlearned, proves that he has done well. The passages which it is most difficult to defend, are those in which he altogether drops the allegory, and puts into the mouth of his pilgrims religious ejaculations and disquisitions, better suited to his own pulpit at Bedford or Reading, than to the Enchanted Ground or the Interpreter's Garden. Yet even these passages, though we will not undertake to defend them against the objections of critics, we feel that we could ill spare. We feel that the story owes much of its charms to these occasional glimpses of solemn and affecting subjects, which will not be hidden, which force themselves through the veil, and appear before us in their native aspect. The effect is not unlike that which is said to have been produced on the ancient stage, when the eyes of the actor were seen flaming through his mask, and giving life and expression to what would else have been inanimate and uninteresting disguise.

It is very amusing and very instructive to compare the *Pilgrim's Progress* with the *Grace Abounding*. The latter work is indeed one of the most remarkable pieces of autobiography in the world. It is a full and open confession of the fancies which passed through the mind of an illiterate man, whose affections were warm, whose nerves were irritable, whose imagination was ungovernable, and who was under the influence of the strongest religious excitement. In whatever age Bunyan had lived, the history of his feelings would, in all probability, have been very curious. But the time in which his lot was cast was the time of a great stirring of the human mind. A tremendous burst of public feeling, produced by the tyranny of the hierarchy, menaced the old ecclesiastical institutions with destruction. To the gloomy regularity of one intolerant church had succeeded the license of innumerable sects, drunk with the sweet and heady must of their new liberty. Fanaticism, engendered by persecution, and destined to engender fresh persecution in turn, spread rapidly through society. Even the strongest and most commanding minds were not proof against this strange taint. Any time might have produced George Fox and James Naylor; but to one time alone belong the frantic delusions of such a statesman as Vane, and the hysterical tears of such a soldier as Cromwell.

The history of Bunyan is the history of a most excitable mind in an age of excitement. By most of his biographers he has been treated with gross injustice. They have understood in a popular sense all those strong terms of self-condemnation which he employed in a theological sense. They have, therefore, represented him as an abandoned wretch, reclaimed by means almost miraculous; or, to use their favourite metaphor, "as a brand plucked from the burning." Mr. Ivimey calls him the depraved Bunyan, and the wicked tinker of Elstow. Surely Mr. Ivimey ought to have been too familiar with the bitter accusations which the most pious people are in the habit of bringing against themselves, to understand literally all the strong expressions which are to be found in the *Grace Abounding*. It is quite clear, as Mr. Southey most justly remarks, that Mr. Bunyan never was a vicious man. He married very early; and he solemnly declares that he was strictly faithful to his wife. He does not appear to have been a drunkard. He owns, indeed, that when a boy, he never spoke without an oath. But a single admonition cured him of this bad habit for life; and the cure must have been wrought early: for at eighteen he was in the army of the Parliament; and if he had carried the vice of profaneness into that service, he would doubtless have received something more than an admonition from Sergeant Bind-their-kings-in-chains, or Captain Hew-Agag-in-pieces-before-the-Lord. Bell-ringing and playing at hockey on Sundays seem to have been the worst vices of this depraved tinker. They would have passed for virtues with Archbishop Laud. It is quite clear that, from a very early age, Bunyan was a man of a strict life, and of a tender conscience. "He had been," says Mr. Southey, "a blackguard." Even this we think too hard a censure. Bunyan was not, we admit, so fine a gentleman as Lord Digby; yet he was a blackguard no otherwise than as every tinker that ever lived has been a blackguard. Indeed, Mr. Southey acknowledges this: "Such he might have been expected to be by his birth, breeding, and vocation. Scarcely, indeed, by possibility could he have been otherwise." A man, whose manners and sentiments are decidedly below those of his class, deserves to be called a blackguard. But it is surely unfair to apply so strong a word of reproach to one who is only what the great mass of every community must inevitably be.

Those horrible internal conflicts, which Bunyan has described with so much power of language, prove, not that he was a worse man than his neighbors, but that his mind was constantly occupied by religious considerations, that his fervour exceeded his knowledge, and that his imagination exercised despotic power over his body and mind. He heard voices from heaven; he saw strange visions of distant hills, pleasant and sunny as his own Delectable Mountains; from those seats he was shut out and placed in a dark and horrible wilderness, where he wandered through ice and snow, striving to make his way into the happy region of light. At one time he was seized with an inclination to work miracles. At another time he thought himself actually possessed by the devil; he could distinguish the blasphemous whispers; he felt his infernal enemy pulling at his clothes behind him; he spurned with his feet, and struck with his hands at the destroyer. Sometimes he was tempted to sell his part in the salvation of mankind. Sometimes a violent impulse urged him to start up from his food, to fall on his knees and break forth into prayer. At length he fancied that he had committed the unpardonable sin; his agony convulsed his robust frame. He was, he says, as if his breastbone would split; and this he took for a sign that he was destined to burst asunder like Judas. The agitation of his nerves made all his movements tremulous; and this trembling, he supposed, was a visible mark of his reprobation, like that which had been set on Cain. At one time, indeed, an encouraging voice seemed to rush in at the window, like the noise of wind, but very pleasant, and commanded, as he says, a great calm in his soul. At another time, a word of comfort "was spoke loud unto him; it showed a great word; it seemed to be writ in great letters." But these intervals of ease were short. His state, during two years and a half, was generally the most horrible that the human mind can imagine. "I walked," says he, with his own peculiar eloquence, "to a neighbouring town, and sat down upon a settle in the street, and fell into a very deep pause about the most fearful state my sin had brought me to; and after long musing, I lifted up my head; but methought I saw as if the sun that shineth in the heavens did grudge to give me light; and as if the very stones in the streets and tiles upon the houses did band themselves against me. Methought that they all combined together to banish me out of the world! I was abhorred of them, and unfit to dwell among them, because I had sinned against the Saviour. Oh, how happy now was every creature over I! for they stood fast and kept their station; but I was gone and lost." Scarcely any madhouse could produce an instance of delusion so strong, or of misery so acute.

It was through this Valley of the Shadow of Death, overhung by darkness, peopled with devils, resounding with blasphemy and lamentation, and passing amidst quagmires, snares, and pitfalls, close by the very mouth of hell, that Bunyan journeyed to that bright and fruitful land of Beulah, in which he sojourned during the latter days of his pilgrimage. The only trace which his cruel sufferings and temptations seem to have left behind them, was an affectionate compassion for those who were still in the state in which he had once been. Religion has scarcely ever worn a form so calm and soothing as in his allegory. The feeling which predominates through the whole book is a feeling of tenderness for weak, timid, and harassed minds. The character of Mr. Fearing, of Mr. Feeble-Mind, of Mr. Despondency and his daughter Miss Muchafraid; the account of poor Littlefaith, who was robbed by the three thieves of his spending-money; the description of Christian's terror in the dungeons of Giant Despair, and in his passage through the river, all clearly show how strong a sympathy Bunyan felt, after his own mind had become clear and cheerful, for persons afflicted with religious melancholy.

Mr. Southey, who has no love for the Calvinists, admits that, if Calvinism had never worn a blacker appearance than in Bunyan's works, it would never have become a term of reproach. In fact, those works of Bunyan with which we are acquainted are by no means more Calvinistic than the homilies of the Church of England. The moderation of his opinions on the subject of predestination gave offence to some zealous persons. We have seen an absurd allegory, the heroine of which is named Hephzibah, written by some raving supralapsarian preacher, who was dissatisfied with the mild theology of the *Pilgrim's Progress*. In this foolish book, if we recollect rightly, the Interpreter is called the Enlightener, and the House Beautiful is Castle Strength. Mr. Southey tells us that the Catholics had also their *Pilgrim's Progress* without a Giant Pope, in which the Interpreter is the Director, and the House Beautiful Grace's Hall. It is surely a remarkable proof of the power of Bunyan's genius, that two religious parties, both of which regarded his opinions as heterodox, should have had recourse to him for assistance.

There are, we think, some characters and scenes in the *Pilgrim's Progress* which can be fully comprehended and enjoyed only by persons familiar with the history of the times through which Bunyan lived. The character of Mr. Greatheart, the guide, is an example. His fighting is, of course, allegorical; but the allegory is not strictly preserved. He delivers a sermon on imputed righteousness to his companions; and, soon after, he gives battle to Giant Grim, who had taken upon him to back the lions. He expounds the fifty-third chapter of *Isaiah* to the household and guests of Gaius; and then sallies out to attack Slaygood, who was of the nature of flesh-eaters, in his den. These are inconsistencies; but they are inconsistencies which add, we think, to the interest of the narrative. We have not the least doubt that Bunyan had in view some stout old Greatheart of Naseby and Worcester, who prayed with his men before he drilled them; who knew the spiritual state of every dragoon in his troop; and who, with the praises of God in his mouth, and a two-edged sword in his hand, had turned to flight on many fields of battle the swearing, drunken bravoes of Rupert and Lunsford.

Every age produces such men as By-ends; but the middle of the seventeenth century was eminently prolific of such men. Mr. Southey thinks that the satire was aimed at some particular individual, and this seems by no means improbable. At all events, Bunyan must have known many of those hypocrites who followed religion only when religion walked in silver slippers, when the sun shone, and when the people applauded. Indeed, he might have easily found all the kindred of By-ends among the public men of his time. He might have found among the peers, my Lord Turn-about, my Lord Time-server, and my Lord Fair-speech; in the House of Commons, Mr. Smooth-man, Mr. Any-thing, and Mr. Facing-both-ways; nor would "the parson of the parish, Mr. Two-Tongues," have been wanting. The town of Bedford probably contained more than one politician, who, after contriving to raise an estate by seeking the Lord during the reign of the saints, contrived to keep what he had got by persecuting the saints during the reign of the strumpets, and more than one priest who, during repeated changes in the discipline and doctrines of the church, had remained constant to nothing but his benefice.

One of the most remarkable passages in the *Pilgrim's Progress* is that in which the proceedings against Faithful are described. It is impossible to doubt that Bunyan intended to satirize the mode in which state trials were conducted under Charles the Second. The license given to the witnesses for the prosecution, the shameless partiality and ferocious insolence of the judge, the precipitancy and the blind rancour of the jury, remind us of those odious mummeries which, from the Restoration to the Revolution, were merely forms preliminary to hanging, drawing, and quartering. Lord Hategood performs the office of counsel for the prisoners as well as Scroggs himself could have performed it.

"JUDGE. Thou runagate, heretic, and traitor, hast thou heard what these honest gentlemen have witnessed against thee?

"FAITHFUL. May I speak a few words in my own defence?

"JUDGE. Sirrah, sirrah! thou deservest to live no longer, but to be slain immediately upon the place; yet, that all men may see our gentleness to thee, let us hear what thou, vile runagate, hast to say."

No person who knows the state trials can be at a loss for parallel cases. Indeed, write what Bunyan would, the baseness and cruelty of the lawyers of those times "sinned up to it still," and even went beyond it. The imaginary trial of Faithful before a jury composed of personified vices was just and merciful when compared with the real trial of Lady Alice Lisle before that tribunal where all the vices sat in the person of Jeffries.

The style of Bunyan is delightful to every reader, and invaluable as a study to every person who wishes to obtain a wide command over the English language. The vocabulary is the vocabulary of the common people. There is not an expression, if we except a few technical terms of theology, which would puzzle the rudest peasant. We have observed several pages which do not contain a single word of more than two syllables; yet no writer has said more exactly what he meant to say. For magnificence, for pathos, for vehement exhortation, for subtle disquisition, for every purpose of the poet, the orator, and the divine, this homely dialect, the dialect of plain workingmen, was perfectly sufficient. There is no book in our literature on which we could so readily stake the fame of the old unpolluted English language; no book which shows so well how rich that language is in its own proper wealth, and how little it has been improved by all that it has borrowed.

Cowper said, forty or fifty years ago, that he dared not name John Bunyan in his verse, for fear of moving a sneer. To our refined forefathers, we suppose Lord Roscommon's *Essay on Translated Verse*, and the Duke of Buckinghamshire's *Essay on Poetry*, appeared to be compositions infinitely superior to the allegory of the preaching tinker. We live in better times; and we are not afraid to say that, though there were many clever men in England during the latter half of the seventeenth century, there were only two great creative minds. One of those minds produced the *Paradise Lost*, the other the *Pilgrim's Progress*.

JOHN HENRY NEWMAN

WHAT IS A UNIVERSITY?[1]

IF I were asked to describe as briefly and popularly as I could, what a University was, I should draw my answer from its ancient designation of a *Studium Generale*, or "School of University Learning." This description implies the assemblage of strangers from all parts in one spot; — *from all parts*; else, how will you find professors and students for every department of knowledge? and *in one spot*; else, how can there be any school at all? Accordingly, in its simple and rudimental form, it is a school of knowledge of every kind, consisting of teachers and learners from every quarter. Many things are requisite to complete and satisfy the idea embodied in this description; but such as this a University seems to be in its essence, a place for the communication and circulation of thought, by means of personal intercourse, through a wide extent of country.

There is nothing far-fetched or unreasonable in the idea thus presented to us; and if this be a University, then a University does but contemplate a necessity of our nature, and is but one specimen in a particular medium, out of many which might be adduced in others, of a provision for that necessity. Mutual education, in a large sense of the word, is one of the great and incessant occupations of human society, carried on partly with set purpose, and partly not. One generation forms another; and the existing generation is ever acting and reacting upon itself in the persons of its individual members. Now, in this process, books, I need scarcely say, that is, the *litera scripta*, are one special instrument. It is true; and emphatically so in this age. Considering the prodigious powers of the press, and how they are developed at this time in the never-intermitting issue of periodicals, tracts, pamphlets, works in series, and light literature, we must allow there never was a time which prom-

---

[1] From *Historical Sketches*, Vol. III. Originally published with other papers in the *Catholic University Gazette* (Dublin, 1854); the first collected edition bore the title *The Office and Work of Universities* (1856).

ised fairer for dispensing with every other means of information and instruction. What can we want more, you will say, for the intellectual education of the whole man, and for every man, than so exuberant and diversified and persistent a promulgation of all kinds of knowledge? Why, you will ask, need we go up to knowledge, when knowledge comes down to us? The Sibyl wrote her prophecies upon the leaves of the forest, and wasted them; but here such careless profusion might be prudently indulged, for it can be afforded without loss, in consequence of the almost fabulous fecundity of the instrument which these latter ages have invented. We have sermons in stones, and books in the running brooks; works larger and more comprehensive than those which have gained for ancients an immortality, issue forth every morning, and are projected onwards to the ends of the earth at the rate of hundreds of miles a day. Our seats are strewed, our pavements are powdered, with swarms of little tracts; and the very bricks of our city walls preach wisdom, by informing us by their placards where we can at once cheaply purchase it.

I allow all this, and much more; such certainly is our popular education, and its effects are remarkable. Nevertheless, after all, even in this age, whenever men are really serious about getting what, in the language of trade, is called "a good article," when they aim at something precise, something refined, something really luminous, something really large, something choice, they go to another market; they avail themselves, in some shape or other, of the rival method, the ancient method, of oral instruction, of present communication between man and man, of teachers instead of learning, of the personal influence of a master, and the humble initiation of a disciple, and, in consequence, of great centres of pilgrimage and throng, which such a method of education necessarily involves. This, I think, will be found to hold good in all those departments or aspects of society, which possess an interest sufficient to bind men together, or to constitute what is called "a world." It holds in the political world, and in the high world, and in the religious world; and it holds also in the literary and scientific world.

If the actions of men may be taken as any test of their convictions, then we have reason for saying this, viz.: that the province and the inestimable benefit of the *litera scripta* is that of being a record of truth, and an authority of appeal, and an instrument of teaching in the hands of a teacher; but that, if we wish to become exact and fully furnished in any branch of knowledge which is diversified and complicated, we must consult the living man and listen to his living voice. I am not bound to investigate the cause of this, and anything I may say will, I am conscious, be short of its full analysis; — perhaps we may suggest, that no books can get through the number of minute questions which it is possible to ask on any extended subject, or can hit upon the very difficulties which are severally felt by each reader in succession. Or again, that no book can convey the special spirit and delicate peculiarities of its subject with that rapidity and certainty which attend on the sympathy of mind with mind, through the eyes, the look, the accent, and the manner, in casual expressions thrown off at the moment, and the unstudied turns of familiar conversation. But I am already dwelling too long on what is but an incidental portion of my main subject. Whatever be the cause, the fact is undeniable. The general principles of any study you may learn by books at home; but the detail, the colour, the tone, the air, the life which makes it live in us, you must catch all these from those in whom it lives already. You must imitate the student in French or German, who is not content with his grammar, but goes to Paris or Dresden: you must take example from the young artist, who aspires to visit the great Masters in Florence and in Rome. Till we have discovered some intellectual daguerreotype, which takes off the course of thought, and the form, lineaments, and features of truth, as completely and minutely, as the optical instrument reproduces the sensible object, we must come to the teachers of wisdom to learn wisdom, we must repair to the fountain, and drink there. Portions of it may go from thence to the ends of the earth by means of books; but the fulness is in one place alone. It is in such assemblages and congregations of intellect that books themselves, the masterpieces of human genius, are written, or at least originated.

The principle on which I have been insisting is so obvious,

and instances in point are so ready, that I should think it tiresome to proceed with the subject, except that one or two illustrations may serve to explain my own language about it, which may not have done justice to the doctrine which it has been intended to enforce.

For instance, the polished manners and high-bred bearing which are so difficult of attainment, and so strictly personal when attained, — which are so much admired in society, from society are acquired. All that goes to constitute a gentleman, — the carriage, gait, address, gestures, voice; the ease, the self-possession, the courtesy, the power of conversing, the talent of not offending; the lofty principle, the delicacy of thought, the happiness of expression, the taste and propriety, the generosity and forbearance, the candour and consideration, the openness of hand; — these qualities, some of them come by nature, some of them may be found in any rank, some of them are a direct precept of Christianity; but the full assemblage of them, bound up in the unity of an individual character, do we expect they can be learned from books? are they not necessarily acquired, where they are to be found, in high society? The very nature of the case leads us to say so; you cannot fence without an antagonist, nor challenge all comers in disputation before you have supported a thesis; and in like manner, it stands to reason, you cannot learn to converse till you have the world to converse with; you cannot unlearn your natural bashfulness, or awkwardness, or stiffness, or other besetting deformity, till you serve your time in some school of manners. Well, and is it not so in matter of fact? The metropolis, the court, the great houses of the land, are the centres to which at stated times the country comes up, as to shrines of refinement and good taste; and then in due time the country goes back again home, enriched with a portion of the social accomplishments, which those very visits serve to call out and heighten in the gracious dispensers of them. We are unable to conceive how the "gentlemanlike" can otherwise be maintained; and maintained in this way it is.

And now a second instance: and here, too, I am going to speak without personal experience of the subject I am introducing. I admit I have not been in Parliament, any more than

I have figured in the *beau monde*; yet I cannot but think that statesmanship, as well as high breeding, is learned, not by books, but in certain centres of education. If it be not presumption to say so, Parliament puts a clever man *au courant* with politics and affairs of state in a way surprising to himself. A member of the Legislature, if tolerably observant, begins to see things with new eyes, even though his views undergo no change. Words have a meaning now, and ideas a reality, such as they had not before. He hears a vast deal in public speeches and private conversation, which is never put into print. The bearings of measures and events, the action of parties, and the persons of friends and enemies, are brought out to the man who is in the midst of them with a distinctness, which the most diligent perusal of newspapers will fail to impart to them. It is access to the fountain-heads of political wisdom and experience, it is daily intercourse, of one kind or another, with the multitude who go up to them, it is familiarity with business, it is access to the contributions of fact and opinion thrown together by many witnesses from many quarters, which does this for him. However, I need not account for a fact, to which it is sufficient to appeal; that the Houses of Parliament and the atmosphere around them are a sort of University of politics.

As regards the world of science, we find a remarkable instance of the principle which I am illustrating, in the periodical meetings for its advance, which have arisen in the course of the last twenty years, such as the British Association. Such gatherings would to many persons appear at first sight simply preposterous. Above all subjects of study, Science is conveyed, is propagated, by books, or by private teaching; experiments and investigations are conducted in silence; discoveries are made in solitude. What have philosophers to do with festive celebrities, and panegyrical solemnities with mathematical and physical truth? Yet on a closer attention to the subject, it is found that not even scientific thought can dispense with the suggestions, the instruction, the stimulus, the sympathy, the intercourse with mankind on a large scale, which such meetings secure. A fine time of year is chosen, when days are long, skies are bright, the earth smiles, and all nature rejoices; a city or town is taken by turns, of ancient name or modern opulence, where buildings are spacious and hospitality hearty. The novelty of place and circumstance, the excitement of strange, or the refreshment of well-known faces, the majesty of rank or of genius, the amiable charities of men pleased both with themselves and with each other; the elevated spirits, the circulation of thought, the curiosity; the morning sections, the outdoor exercise, the well-furnished, well-earned board, the not ungraceful hilarity, the evening circle; the brilliant lecture, the discussions or collisions or guesses of great men one with another, the narratives of scientific processes, of hopes, disappointments, conflicts, and successes, the splendid eulogistic orations; these and the like constituents of the annual celebration are considered to do something real and substantial for the advance of knowledge which can be done in no other way. Of course they can but be occasional; they answer to the Annual Act, or Commencement, or Commemoration, of a University, not to its ordinary condition; but they are of a University nature; and I can well believe in their utility. They issue in the promotion of a certain living and, as it were, bodily communication of knowledge from one to another, of a general interchange of ideas, and a comparison and adjustment of science with science, of an enlargement of mind, intellectual and social, of an ardent love of the particular study which may be chosen by each individual, and a noble devotion to its interests.

Such meetings, I repeat, are but periodical, and only partially represent the idea of a University. The bustle and whirl which are their usual concomitants, are in ill keeping with the order and gravity of earnest intellectual education. We desiderate means of instruction which involve no interruption of our ordinary habits; nor need we seek it long, for the natural course of things brings it about, while we debate over it. In every great country, the metropolis itself becomes a sort of necessary University, whether we will or no. As the chief city is the seat of the court, of high society, of politics, and of law, so as a matter of course is it the seat of letters also; and at this time, for a long term of years, London and Paris are in fact and in operation Universities, though in Paris its famous University is no more, and in London a University scarcely exists except as a board of administration. The newspapers, magazines, reviews, journals, and periodicals of all kinds, the publishing trade, the libraries, museums, and academies there found, the learned and scientific societies, necessarily invest it with the functions of a University; and that atmosphere of intellect, which in a former age hung over Oxford or Bologna or Salamanca, has, with the change of times, moved away to the centre of civil government. Thither come up youths from all parts of the country, the students of law, medicine, and the fine arts, and the *employés* and *attachés* of literature. There they live, as chance determines; and they are satisfied with their temporary home, for they find in it all that was promised to them there. They have not come in vain, as far as their own object in coming is concerned. They have not learned any particular religion, but they have learned their own particular profession well. They have, moreover, become acquainted with the habits, manners, and opinions of their place of sojourn, and done their part in maintaining the tradition of them. We cannot then be without virtual Universities; a metropolis is such: the simple question is, whether the education sought and given should be based on principle, formed upon rule, directed to the highest ends, or left to the random succession of masters and schools, one after another, with a melancholy waste of thought and an extreme hazard of truth.

Religious teaching itself affords us an illustration of our subject to a certain point. It does not, indeed, seat itself merely in centres of the world; this is impossible from the nature of the case. It is intended for the many, not the few; its subject-matter is truth necessary for us, not truth recondite and rare; but it concurs in the principle of a University so far as this, that its great instrument, or rather organ, has ever been that which nature prescribes in all education, the personal presence of a teacher, or, in theological language, Oral Tradition. It is the living voice, the breathing form, the expressive countenance, which preaches, which catechises. Truth, a subtle, invisible, manifold spirit, is poured into the mind of the scholar by his eyes and ears, through his affections, imagination, and reason; it is poured into his mind and is sealed up there in perpetuity, by propounding and repeating it, by questioning and requestioning, by correcting and explaining, by progressing and then recurring to first principles, by all those ways which are implied in the word "catechising." In the first ages, it was a work of long time; months, sometimes years, were devoted to the arduous task of disabusing the mind of the incipient Christian of its pagan errors, and of moulding it upon the Christian faith. The Scriptures, indeed, were at hand for the study of those who could avail themselves of them; but St. Irenæus does not hesitate to speak of whole races, who had been converted to Christianity, without being able to read them. To be unable to read or write was in those times no evidence of want of learning: the hermits of the deserts were, in this sense of the word, illiterate; yet the great St. Anthony, though he knew not letters, was a match in disputation for the learned philosophers who came to try him. Didymus again, the great Alexandrian theologian, was blind. The ancient discipline, called the *Disciplina Arcani*, involved the same principle. The more sacred doctrines of Revelation were not committed to books but passed on by successive tradition. The teaching on the Blessed Trinity and the Eucharist appears to have been so handed down for some hundred years; and when at length reduced to writing, it has filled many folios, yet has not been exhausted.

But I have said more than enough in illustration; I end as I began; — a University is a place of concourse, whither students come from every quarter for every kind of knowledge. You cannot have the best of every kind everywhere; you must go to some great city or emporium for it. There you have all the choicest productions of nature and art all together, which you find each in its own separate place elsewhere. All the riches of the land, and of the earth, are carried up thither; there are the best markets, and there the best workmen. It is the centre of trade, the supreme court of fashion, the umpire of rival talents, and the standard of things rare and precious. It is the place for seeing galleries of first-rate pictures, and for hearing wonderful voices and performers of transcendent skill. It is the place for great preachers, great orators, great nobles, great statesmen. In the nature of things, greatness and unity go together; excellence implies a centre. And such, for the third or fourth time, is a University; I hope I do not weary out the reader by repeating it. It is the place to which a thousand schools make contributions; in which the intellect may safely range and speculate, sure to find its equal in some antagonist activity, and its judge in the tribunal of truth. It is a place where inquiry is pushed forward, and discoveries verified and perfected, and rashness rendered innocuous, and error exposed, by the collision of mind with mind, and knowledge with knowledge. It is the place where the professor becomes eloquent, and is a missionary and a preacher, displaying his science in its most complete and most winning form, pouring it forth with the zeal of enthusiasm, and lighting up his own love of it in the breasts of his hearers. It is the place where the catechist makes good his ground as he goes, treading in the truth day by day into the ready memory, and wedging and tightening it into the expanding reason. It is a place which wins the admiration of the young by its celebrity, kindles the affections of the middle-aged by its beauty, and rivets the fidelity of the old by its associations. It is a seat of wisdom, a light of the world, a minister of the faith, an Alma Mater of the rising generation. It is this and a great deal more, and demands a somewhat better head and hand than mine to describe it well.

Such is a University in its idea and in its purpose; such in good measure has it before now been in fact. Shall it ever be again? We are going forward in the strength of the Cross, under the patronage of the Blessed Virgin, in the name of St. Patrick, to attempt it.

RALPH WALDO EMERSON

SELF–RELIANCE [1]

I READ the other day some verses written by an eminent painter which were original and not conventional. The soul always hears an admonition in such lines, let the subject be what it may. The sentiment they instil is of more value than any thought they may contain. To believe your own thought, to believe that what is true for you in your private heart is true for all men, — that is genius. Speak your latent conviction, and it shall be the universal sense; for the inmost in due time becomes the outmost, and our first thought is rendered back to us by the trumpets of the Last Judgment. Familiar as the voice of the mind is to each, the highest merit we ascribe to Moses, Plato and Milton is that they set at naught books and traditions, and spoke not what men, but what *they* thought. A man should learn to detect and watch that gleam of light which flashes across his mind from within, more than the lustre of the firmament of bards and sages. Yet he dismisses without notice his thought, because it is his. In every work of genius we recognize our own rejected thoughts; they come back to us with a certain alienated majesty. Great works of art have no more affecting lesson for us than this. They teach us to abide by our spontaneous impression with good-humored inflexibility then most when the whole cry of voices is on the other side. Else to-morrow a stranger will say with masterly good sense precisely what we have thought and felt all the time, and we shall be forced to take with shame our own opinion from another.

There is a time in every man's education when he arrives at the conviction that envy is ignorance; that imitation is suicide; that he must take himself for better for worse as his portion;

[1] From *The Complete Works of Ralph Waldo Emerson*, Centenary Edition, Vol. II. Copyright, 1903, by Edward W. Emerson. Originally published in *Essays: First Series* (1841). By permission of the publishers, Houghton Mifflin Company.

that though the wide universe is full of good, no kernel of nourishing corn can come to him but through his toil bestowed on that plot of ground which is given to him to till. The power which resides in him is new in nature, and none but he knows what that is which he can do, nor does he know until he has tried. Not for nothing one face, one character, one fact, makes much impression on him, and another none. This sculpture in the memory is not without preëstablished harmony. The eye was placed where one ray should fall, that it might testify of that particular ray. We but half express ourselves, and are ashamed of that divine idea which each of us represents. It may be safely trusted as proportionate and of good issues, so it be faithfully imparted, but God will not have his work made manifest by cowards. A man is relieved and gay when he has put his heart into his work and done his best; but what he has said or done otherwise shall give him no peace. It is a deliverance which does not deliver. In the attempt his genius deserts him; no muse befriends; no invention, no hope.

Trust thyself: every heart vibrates to that iron string. Accept the place the divine providence has found for you, the society of your contemporaries, the connection of events. Great men have always done so, and confided themselves childlike to the genius of their age, betraying their perception that the absolutely trustworthy was seated at their heart, working through their hands, predominating in all their being. And we are now men, and must accept in the highest mind the same transcendent destiny; and not minors and invalids in a protected corner, not cowards fleeing before a revolution, but guides, redeemers and benefactors, obeying the Almighty effort and advancing on Chaos and the Dark.

What pretty oracles nature yields us on this text in the face and behavior of children, babes, and even brutes! That divided and rebel mind, that distrust of a sentiment because our arithmetic has computed the strength and means opposed to our purpose, these have not. Their mind being whole, their eye is as yet unconquered, and when we look in their faces we are disconcerted. Infancy conforms to nobody; all conform to it; so that one babe commonly makes four or five out of the adults who prattle and play to it. So God has armed youth and puberty and manhood no less with its own piquancy and charm, and made it enviable and gracious and its claims not to be put by, if it will stand by itself. Do not think the youth has no force, because he cannot speak to you and me. Hark! in the next room his voice is sufficiently clear and emphatic. It seems he knows how to speak to his contemporaries. Bashful or bold then, he will know how to make us seniors very unnecessary.

The nonchalance of boys who are sure of a dinner, and would disdain as much as a lord to do or say aught to conciliate one, is the healthy attitude of human nature. A boy is in the parlor what the pit is in the playhouse; independent, irresponsible, looking out from his corner on such people and facts as pass by, he tries and sentences them on their merits, in the swift, summary way of boys, as good, bad, interesting, silly, eloquent, troublesome. He cumbers himself never about consequences, about interests; he gives an independent, genuine verdict. You must court him; he does not court you. But the man is as it were clapped into jail by his consciousness. As soon as he has once acted or spoken with *éclat* he is a committed person, watched by the sympathy or the hatred of hundreds, whose affections must now enter into his account. There is no Lethe for this. Ah, that he could pass again into his neutrality! Who can thus avoid all pledges and, having observed, observe again from the same unaffected, unbiased, unbribable, unaffrighted innocence, — must always be formidable. He would utter opinions on all passing affairs, which being seen to be not private but necessary, would sink like darts into the ear of men and put them in fear.

These are the voices which we hear in solitude, but they grow faint and inaudible as we enter into the world. Society everywhere is in conspiracy against the manhood of every one of its members. Society is a joint-stock company, in which the members agree, for the better securing of his bread to each shareholder, to surrender the liberty and culture of the eater. The virtue in most requests is conformity. Self-reliance is its aversion. It loves not realities and creators, but names and customs.

Whoso would be a man, must be a nonconformist. He who

would gather immortal palms must not be hindered by the name of goodness, but must explore if it be goodness. Nothing is at last sacred but the integrity of your own mind. Absolve you to yourself, and you shall have the suffrage of the world. I remember an answer which when quite young I was prompted to make to a valued adviser who was wont to importune me with the dear old doctrines of the church. On my saying, "What have I to do with the sacredness of traditions, if I live wholly from within?" my friend suggested, — "But these impulses may be from below, not from above." I replied, "They do not seem to me to be such; but if I am the Devil's child, I will live then from the Devil." No law can be sacred to me but that of my nature. Good and bad are but names very readily transferable to that or this; the only right is what is after my constitution; the only wrong what is against it. A man is to carry himself in the presence of all opposition as if every thing were titular and ephemeral but he. I am ashamed to think how easily we capitulate to badges and names, to large societies and dead institutions. Every decent and well-spoken individual affects and sways me more than is right. I ought to go upright and vital, and speak the rude truth in all ways. If malice and vanity wear the coat of philanthropy, shall that pass? If an angry bigot assumes this bountiful cause of Abolition, and comes to me with his last news from Barbadoes, why should I not say to him, "Go love thy infant; love thy wood-chopper; be good-natured and modest; have that grace; and never varnish your hard, uncharitable ambition with this incredible tenderness for black folk a thousand miles off. Thy love afar is spite at home." Rough and graceless would be such greeting, but truth is handsomer than the affectation of love. Your goodness must have some edge to it, — else it is none. The doctrine of hatred must be preached, as the counteraction of the doctrine of love, when that pules and whines. I shun father and mother and wife and brother when my genius calls me. I would write on the lintels of the door-post, *Whim*. I hope it is somewhat better than whim at last, but we cannot spend the day in explanation. Expect me not to show cause why I seek or why I exclude company. Then again, do not tell me, as a good man did to-day, of my obligation to put all poor men in good situations. Are they *my* poor? I tell thee thou foolish philanthropist that I grudge the dollar, the dime, the cent I give to such men as do not belong to me and to whom I do not belong. There is a class of persons to whom by all spiritual affinity I am bought and sold; for them I will go to prison if need be; but your miscellaneous populaɪ charities; the education at college of fools; the building oɪ meeting-houses to the vain end to which many now stand; alms to sots, and the thousand-fold Relief Societies; — though I confess with shame I sometimes succumb and give the dollar, it is a wicked dollar, which by and by I shall have the manhood to withhold.

Virtues are, in the popular estimate, rather the exception than the rule. There is the man *and* his virtues. Men do what is called a good action, as some piece of courage or charity, much as they would pay a fine in expiation of daily non-appearance on parade. Their works are done as an apology or extenuation of their living in the world, — as invalids and the insane pay a high board. Their virtues are penances. I do not wish to expiate, but to live. My life is for itself and not for a spectacle. I much prefer that it should be of a lower strain, so it be genuine and equal, than that it should be glittering and unsteady. I wish it to be sound and sweet, and not to need diet and bleeding. I ask primary evidence that you are a man, and refuse this appeal from the man to his actions. I know that for myself it makes no difference whether I do or forbear those actions which are reckoned excellent. I cannot consent to pay for a privilege where I have intrinsic right. Few and mean as my gifts may be, I actually am, and do not need for my own assurance or the assurance of my fellows any secondary testimony.

What I must do is all that concerns me, not what the people think. This rule, equally arduous in actual and in intellectual life, may serve for the whole distinction between greatness and meanness. It is the harder because you will always find those who think they know what is your duty better than you know it. It is easy in the world to live after the world's opinion; it is easy in solitude to live after our own; but the great man is he who in the midst of the crowd keeps with perfect sweetness the independence of solitude.

The objection to conforming to usages that have become dead to you is that it scatters your force. It loses your time and blurs the impression of your character. If you maintain a dead church, contribute to a dead Bible-society, vote with a great party either for the government or against it, spread your table like base housekeepers,—under all these screens I have difficulty to detect the precise man you are: and of course so much force is withdrawn from your proper life. But do your work, and I shall know you. Do your work, and you shall reinforce yourself. A man must consider what a blindman's-buff is this game of conformity. If I know your sect I anticipate your argument. I hear a preacher announce for his text and topic the expediency of one of the institutions of his church. Do I not know beforehand that not possibly can he say a new and spontaneous word? Do I not know that with all this ostentation of examining the grounds of the institution he will do no such thing? Do I not know that he is pledged to himself not to look but at one side, the permitted side, not as a man, but as a parish minister? He is a retained attorney, and these airs of the bench are the emptiest affectation. Well, most men have bound their eyes with one or another handkerchief, and attached themselves to some one of these communities of opinion. This conformity makes them not false in a few particulars, authors of a few lies, but false in all particulars. Their every truth is not quite true. Their two is not the real two, their four not the real four; so that every word they say chagrins us and we know not where to begin to set them right. Meantime nature is not slow to equip us in the prison-uniform of the party to which we adhere. We come to wear one cut of face and figure, and acquire by degrees the gentlest asinine expression. There is a mortifying experience in particular, which does not fail to wreak itself also in the general history; I mean "the foolish face of praise," the forced smile which we put on in company where we do not feel at ease, in answer to conversation which does not interest us. The muscles, not spontaneously moved but moved by a low usurping wilfulness, grow tight about the outline of the face, with the most disagreeable sensation.

For nonconformity the world whips you with its displeasure.

And therefore a man must know how to estimate a sour face. The by-standers look askance on him in the public street or in the friend's parlor. If this aversation had its origin in contempt and resistance like his own he might well go home with a sad countenance; but the sour faces of the multitude, like their sweet faces, have no deep cause, but are put on and off as the wind blows and a newspaper directs. Yet is the discontent of the multitude more formidable than that of the senate and the college. It is easy enough for a firm man who knows the world to brook the rage of the cultivated classes. Their rage is decorous and prudent, for they are timid, as being very vulnerable themselves. But when to their feminine rage the indignation of the people is added, when the ignorant and the poor are aroused, when the unintelligent brute force that lies at the bottom of society is made to growl and mow, it needs the habit of magnanimity and religion to treat it godlike as a trifle of no concernment.

The other terror that scares us from self-trust is our consistency; a reverence for our past act or word because the eyes of others have no other data for computing our orbit than our past acts, and we are loath to disappoint them.

But why should you keep your head over your shoulder? Why drag about this corpse of your memory, lest you contradict somewhat you have stated in this or that public place? Suppose you should contradict yourself; what then? It seems to be a rule of wisdom never to rely on your memory alone, scarcely even in acts of pure memory, but to bring the past for judgment into the thousand-eyed present, and live ever in a new day. In your metaphysics you have denied personality to the Deity, yet when the devout motions of the soul come, yield to them heart and life, though they should clothe God with shape and color. Leave your theory, as Joseph his coat in the hand of the harlot, and flee.

A foolish consistency is the hobgoblin of little minds, adored by little statesmen and philosophers and divines. With consistency a great soul has simply nothing to do. He may as well concern himself with his shadow on the wall. Speak what you think now in hard words and to-morrow speak what to-morrow thinks in hard words again, though it contradict everything you said to-day. — "Ah, so you shall be sure to be misunderstood." — Is it so bad then to be misunderstood? Pythagoras was misunderstood, and Socrates, and Jesus, and Luther, and Copernicus, and Galileo, and Newton, and every pure and wise spirit that ever took flesh. To be great is to be misunderstood.

I suppose no man can violate his nature. All the sallies of his will are rounded in by the law of his being, as the inequalities of Andes and Himmaleh are insignificant in the curve of the sphere. Nor does it matter how you gauge and try him. A character is like an acrostic or Alexandrian stanza; — read it forward, backward, or across, it still spells the same thing. In this pleasing contrite wood-life which God allows me, let me record day by day my honest thought without prospect or retrospect, and, I cannot doubt, it will be found symmetrical, though I mean it not and see it not. My book should smell of pines and resound with the hum of insects. The swallow over my window should interweave that thread or straw he carries in his bill into my web also. We pass for what we are. Character teaches above our wills. Men imagine that they communicate their virtue or vice only by overt actions, and do not see that virtue or vice emit a breath every moment.

There will be an agreement in whatever variety of actions, so they be each honest and natural in their hour. For of one will, the actions will be harmonious, however unlike they seem. These varieties are lost sight of at a little distance, at a little height of thought. One tendency unites them all. The voyage of the best ship is a zigzag line of a hundred tacks. See the line from a sufficient distance, and it straightens itself to the average tendency. Your genuine action will explain itself and will explain your other genuine actions. Your conformity explains nothing. Act singly, and what you have already done singly will justify you now. Greatness appeals to the future. If I can be firm enough to-day to do right and scorn eyes, I must have done so much right before as to defend me now. Be it how it will, do right now. Always scorn appearances and you always may. The force of character is cumulative. All the foregone days of virtue work their health into this. What makes the majesty of the heroes of the senate and the field, which so fills the imagination? The consciousness of a train of great days and victories behind. They shed an united light on the advancing actor. He is attended as by a visible escort of angels. That is it which throws thunder into Chatham's voice, and dignity into Washington's port, and America into Adams's eye. Honor is venerable to us because it is no ephemera. It is always ancient virtue. We worship it to-day because it is not of to-day. We love it and pay it homage because it is not a trap for our love and homage, but is self-dependent, self-derived, and therefore of an old immaculate pedigree, even if shown in a young person.

I hope in these days we have heard the last of conformity and consistency. Let the words be gazetted and ridiculous henceforward. Instead of the gong for dinner, let us hear a whistle from the Spartan fife. Let us never bow and apologize more. A great man is coming to eat at my house. I do not wish to please him; I wish that he should wish to please me. I will stand here for humanity, and though I would make it kind, I would make it true. Let us affront and reprimand the smooth mediocrity and squalid contentment of the times, and hurl in the face of custom and trade and office, the fact which is the upshot of all history, that there is a great responsible Thinker and Actor working wherever a man works; that a true man belongs to no other time or place, but is the centre of things. Where he is, there is nature. He measures you and all men and all events. Ordinarily, every body in society reminds us of somewhat else, or of some other person. Character, reality, reminds you of nothing else; it takes place of the whole creation. The man must be so much that he must make all circumstances indifferent. Every true man is a cause, a country, and an age; requires infinite spaces and numbers and time fully to accomplish his design; — and posterity seem to follow his steps as a train of clients. A man Cæsar is born, and for ages after we have a Roman Empire. Christ is born, and millions of minds so grow and cleave to his genius that he is confounded with virtue and the possible of man. An institution is the lengthened shadow of one man; as, Monachism, of the Hermit Antony; the Reformation, of Luther; Quakerism, of Fox; Methodism, of Wesley; Abolition, of Clarkson. Scipio,

Milton called "the height of Rome"; and all history resolves itself very easily into the biography of a few stout and earnest persons.

Let a man then know his worth, and keep things under his feet. Let him not peep or steal, or skulk up and down with the air of a charity-boy, a bastard, or an interloper in the world which exists for him. But the man in the street, finding no worth in himself which corresponds to the force which built a tower or sculptured a marble god, feels poor when he looks on these. To him a palace, a statue, or a costly book have an alien and forbidding air, much like a gay equipage, and seem to say like that, "Who are you, Sir?" Yet they all are his, suitors for his notice, petitioners to his faculties that they will come out and take possession. The picture waits for my verdict; it is not to command me, but I am to settle its claims to praise. . . .[1]

And truly it demands something godlike in him who has cast off the common motives of humanity and has ventured to trust himself for a taskmaster. High be his heart, faithful his will, clear his sight, that he may in good earnest be doctrine, society, law, to himself, that a simple purpose may be to him as strong as iron necessity is to others!

If any man consider the present aspects of what is called by distinction *society*, he will see the need of these ethics. The sinew and heart of man seem to be drawn out, and we are become timorous, desponding whimperers. We are afraid of truth, afraid of fortune, afraid of death and afraid of each other. Our age yields no great and perfect persons. We want men and women who shall renovate life and our social state, but we see that most natures are insolvent, cannot satisfy their own wants, have an ambition out of all proportion to their practical force and do lean and beg day and night continually. Our housekeeping is mendicant, our arts, our occupations, our marriages, our religion we have not chosen, but society has chosen for us. We are parlor soldiers. We shun the rugged battle of fate, where strength is born.

---

[1] A passage is omitted in which Emerson sets forth a theoretical justification of self-reliance, in the existence of Instinct or Intuition, the "primary wisdom" of the soul, and in the relation of the individual soul to "the ever-blessed ONE."

If our young men miscarry in their first enterprises they lose all heart. If the young merchant fails, men say he is *ruined*. If the finest genius studies at one of our colleges and is not installed in an office within one year afterwards in the cities or suburbs of Boston or New York, it seems to his friends and to himself that he is right in being disheartened and in complaining the rest of his life. A sturdy lad from New Hampshire or Vermont, who in turn tries all the professions, who *teams it, farms it, peddles,* keeps a school, preaches, edits a newspaper, goes to Congress, buys a township, and so forth, in successive years, and always like a cat falls on his feet, is worth a hundred of these city dolls. He walks abreast with his days and feels no shame in not "studying a profession," for he does not postpone his life, but lives already. He has not one chance, but a hundred chances. Let a Stoic open the resources of man and tell men they are not leaning willows, but can and must detach themselves; that with the exercise of self-trust, new powers shall appear; that a man is the word made flesh, born to shed healing to the nations; that he should be ashamed of our compassion, and that the moment he acts from himself, tossing the laws, the books, idolatries and customs out of the window, we pity him no more but thank and revere him; — and that teacher shall restore the life of man to splendor and make his name dear to all history.

It is easy to see that a greater self-reliance must work a revolution in all the offices and relations of men; in their religion; in their education; in their pursuits; their modes of living; their association; in their property; in their speculative views.

1. In what prayers do men allow themselves! That which they call a holy office is not so much as brave and manly. Prayer looks abroad and asks for some foreign addition to come through some foreign virtue, and loses itself in endless mazes of natural and supernatural, and mediatorial and miraculous. Prayer that craves a particular commodity, anything less than all good, is vicious. Prayer is the contemplation of the facts of life from the highest point of view. It is the soliloquy of a beholding and jubilant soul. It is the spirit of God pronouncing his works good. But prayer as a means to effect a private end is meanness and theft. It supposes dualism and

not unity in nature and consciousness. As soon as the man is at one with God, he will not beg. He will then see prayer in all action. The prayer of the farmer kneeling in his field to weed it, the prayer of the rower kneeling with the stroke of his oar, are true prayers heard throughout nature, though for cheap ends. Caratach, in Fletcher's *Bonduca*, when admonished to inquire the mind of the god Audate, replies,

> " His hidden meaning lies in our endeavors;
> Our valors are our best gods."

Another sort of false prayers are our regrets. Discontent is the want of self-reliance: it is infirmity of will. Regret calamities if you can thereby help the sufferer; if not, attend your own work and already the evil begins to be repaired. Our sympathy is just as base. We come to them who weep foolishly and sit down and cry for company, instead of imparting to them truth and health in rough electric shocks, putting them once more in communication with their own reason. The secret of fortune is joy in our hands. Welcome evermore to gods and men is the self-helping man. For him all doors are flung wide; him all tongues greet, all honors crown, all eyes follow with desire. Our love goes out to him and embraces him because he did not need it. We solicitously and apologetically caress and celebrate him because he held on his way and scorned our disapprobation. The gods love him because men hated him. "To the persevering mortal," said Zoroaster, "the blessed Immortals are swift."

As men's prayers are a disease of the will, so are their creeds a disease of the intellect. They say with those foolish Israelites, "Let not God speak to us, lest we die. Speak thou, speak any man with us, and we will obey." Everywhere I am hindered of meeting God in my brother, because he has shut his own temple doors and recites fables merely of his brother's, of his brother's brother's God. Every new mind is a new classification. If it prove a mind of uncommon activity and power, a Locke, a Lavoisier, a Hutton, a Bentham, a Fourier, it imposes its classification on other men, and lo! a new system. In proportion to the depth of the thought, and so to the number of the objects it touches and brings within reach of the pupil, is his complacency.   But chiefly is this apparent in creeds and churches, which are also classifications of some powerful mind acting on the elemental thought of duty and man's relation to the Highest.   Such is Calvinism, Quakerism, Swedenborgism. The pupil takes the same delight in subordinating every thing to the new terminology as a girl who has just learned botany in seeing a new earth and new seasons thereby.   It will happen for a time that the pupil will find his intellectual power has grown by the study of his master's mind.   But in all unbalanced minds the classification is idolized, passes for the end and not for a speedily exhaustible means, so that the walls of the system blend to their eye in the remote horizon with the walls of the universe; the luminaries of heaven seem to them hung on the arch their master built.   They cannot imagine how you aliens have any right to see, — how you can see; "It must be somehow that you stole the light from us."   They do not yet perceive that light, unsystematic, indomitable, will break into any cabin, even into theirs.   Let them chirp awhile and call it their own.   If they are honest and do well, presently their neat new pinfold will be too strait and low, will crack, will lean, will rot and vanish, and the immortal light, all young and joyful, million-orbed, million-colored, will beam over the universe as on the first morning.

2. It is for want of self-culture that the superstition of Travelling, whose idols are Italy, England, Egypt, retains its fascination for all educated Americans.   They who made England, Italy, or Greece venerable in the imagination, did so by sticking fast where they were, like an axis of the earth.   In manly hours we feel that duty is our place.   The soul is no traveller; the wise man stays at home, and when his necessities, his duties, on any occasion call him from his house, or into foreign lands, he is at home still and shall make men sensible by the expression of his countenance that he goes, the missionary of wisdom and virtue, and visits cities and men like a sovereign and not like an interloper or a valet.

I have no churlish objection to the circumnavigation of the globe for the purposes of art, of study, and benevolence, so that the man is first domesticated, or does not go abroad with the hope of finding somewhat greater than he knows.   He who travels to be amused, or to get somewhat which he does not carry, travels away from himself, and grows old even in youth among old things. In Thebes, in Palmyra, his will and mind have become old and dilapidated as they. He carries ruins to ruins.

Travelling is a fool's paradise. Our first journeys discover to us the indifference of places. At home I dream that at Naples, at Rome, I can be intoxicated with beauty and lose my sadness. I pack my trunk, embrace my friends, embark on the sea and at last wake up in Naples, and there beside me is the stern fact, the sad self, unrelenting, identical, that I fled from. I seek the Vatican and the palaces. I affect to be intoxicated with sights and suggestions, but I am not intoxicated. My giant goes with me wherever I go.

3. But the rage of travelling is a symptom of a deeper unsoundness affecting the whole intellectual action. The intellect is vagabond, and our system of education fosters restlessness. Our minds travel when our bodies are forced to stay at home. We imitate; and what is imitation but the travelling of the mind? Our houses are built with foreign taste; our shelves are garnished with foreign ornaments; our opinions, our tastes, our faculties, lean, and follow the Past and the Distant. The soul created the arts wherever they have flourished. It was in his own mind that the artist sought his model. It was an application of his own thought to the thing to be done and the conditions to be observed. And why need we copy the Doric or the Gothic model? Beauty, convenience, grandeur of thought and quaint expression are as near to us as to any, and if the American artist will study with hope and love the precise thing to be done by him, considering the climate, the soil, the length of the day, the wants of the people, the habit and form of the government, he will create a house in which all these will find themselves fitted, and taste and sentiment will be satisfied also.

Insist on yourself; never imitate. Your own gift you can present every moment with the cumulative force of a whole life's cultivation; but of the adopted talent of another you have only an extemporaneous half possession. That which each can do best, none but his Maker can teach him. No man yet knows

what it is, nor can, till that person has exhibited it. Where is
the master who could have taught Shakspeare? Where is the
master who could have instructed Franklin, or Washington, or
Bacon, or Newton? Every great man is a unique. The Scip-
ionism of Scipio is precisely that part he could not borrow.
Shakspeare will never be made by the study of Shakspeare.
Do that which is assigned you, and you cannot hope too much
or dare too much. There is at this moment for you an utterance brave and grand as that of the colossal chisel of Phidias,
or trowel of the Egyptians, or the pen of Moses or Dante, but
different from all these. Not possibly will the soul, all rich, all
eloquent, with thousand-cloven tongue, deign to repeat itself;
but if you can hear what these patriarchs say, surely you can
reply to them in the same pitch of voice; for the ear and the
tongue are two organs of one nature. Abide in the simple and
noble regions of thy life, obey thy heart and thou shalt reproduce the Foreworld again.

4. As our Religion, our Education, our Art look abroad, so
does our spirit of society. All men plume themselves on the
improvement of society, and no man improves.

Society never advances. It recedes as fast on one side as it
gains on the other. It undergoes continual changes; it is barbarous, it is civilized, it is christianized, it is rich, it is scientific;
but this change is not amelioration. For every thing that is
given something is taken. Society acquires new arts and loses
old instincts. What a contrast between the well-clad, reading,
writing, thinking American, with a watch, a pencil and a bill
of exchange in his pocket, and the naked New Zealander,
whose property is a club, a spear, a mat and an undivided
twentieth of a shed to sleep under! But compare the health
of the two men and you shall see that the white man has lost
his aboriginal strength. If the traveller tell us truly, strike
the savage with a broad axe and in a day or two the flesh shall
unite and heal as if you struck the blow into soft pitch, and
the same blow shall send the white to his grave.

The civilized man has built a coach, but has lost the use of
his feet. He is supported on crutches, but lacks so much support of muscle. He has a fine Geneva watch, but he fails of the
skill to tell the hour by the sun. A Greenwich nautical almanac

he has, and so being sure of the information when he wants it, the man in the street does not know a star in the sky.   The solstice he does not observe; the equinox he knows as little; and the whole bright calendar of the year is without a dial in his mind.   His note-books impair his memory; his libraries overload his wit; the insurance-office increases the number of accidents; and it may be a question whether machinery does not encumber; whether we have not lost by refinement some energy, by a Christianity entrenched in establishments and forms some vigor of wild virtue.   For every Stoic was a Stoic; but in Christendom where is the Christian?

There is no more deviation in the moral standard than in the standard of height or bulk.   No greater men are now than ever were.   A singular equality may be observed between the great men of the first and of the last ages; nor can all the science, art, religion, and philosophy of the nineteenth century avail to educate greater men than Plutarch's heroes, three or four and twenty centuries ago.   Not in time is the race progressive. Phocion, Socrates, Anaxagoras, Diogenes, are great men, but they leave no class.   He who is really of their class will not be called by their name, but will be his own man, and in his turn the founder of a sect.   The arts and inventions of each period are only its costume and do not invigorate men.   The harm of the improved machinery may compensate its good.   Hudson and Behring accomplished so much in their fishing-boats as to astonish Parry and Franklin, whose equipment exhausted the resources of science and art.   Galileo, with an opera-glass, discovered a more splendid series of celestial phenomena than any one since.   Columbus found the New World in an undecked boat.   It is curious to see the periodical disuse and perishing of means and machinery which were introduced with loud laudation a few years or centuries before.   The great genius returns to essential man.   We reckoned the improvements of the art of war among the triumphs of science, and yet Napoleon conquered Europe by the bivouac, which consisted of falling back on naked valor and disencumbering it of all aids.   The Emperor held it impossible to make a perfect army, says Las Casas, "without abolishing our arms, magazines, commissaries and carriages, until, in imitation of the Roman custom, the soldier should receive his supply of corn, grind it in his hand-mill and bake his bread himself."

Society is a wave. The wave moves onward, but the water of which it is composed does not. The same particle does not rise from the valley to the ridge. Its unity is only phenomenal. The persons who make up a nation to-day, next year die, and their experience dies with them.

And so the reliance on Property, including the reliance on governments which protect it, is the want of self-reliance. Men have looked away from themselves and at things so long that they have come to esteem the religious, learned and civil institutions as guards of property, and they deprecate assaults on these, because they feel them to be assaults on property. They measure their esteem of each other by what each has, and not by what each is. But a cultivated man becomes ashamed of his property, out of new respect for his nature. Especially he hates what he has if he see that it is accidental, — came to him by inheritance, or gift, or crime; then he feels that it is not having; it does not belong to him, has no root in him and merely lies there because no revolution or no robber takes it away. But that which a man is, does always by necessity acquire; and what the man acquires, is living property, which does not wait the beck of rulers, or mobs, or revolutions, or fire, or storm, or bankruptcies, but perpetually renews itself wherever the man breathes. "Thy lot or portion of life," said the Caliph Ali, "is seeking after thee; therefore be at rest from seeking after it." Our dependence on these foreign goods leads us to our slavish respect for numbers. The political parties meet in numerous conventions; the greater the concourse and with each new uproar of announcement, The delegation from Essex! The Democrats from New Hampshire! The Whigs of Maine! the young patriot feels himself stronger than before by a new thousand of eyes and arms. In like manner the reformers summon conventions and vote and resolve in multitude. Not so O friends! will the God deign to enter and inhabit you, but by a method precisely the reverse. It is only as a man puts off all foreign support and stands alone that I see him to be strong and to prevail. He is weaker by every recruit to his banner. Is not a man better than a town? Ask nothing of men, and, in the endless mutation, thou only firm column must presently appear the upholder of all that surrounds thee. He who knows that power is inborn, that he is weak because he has looked for good out of him and elsewhere, and, so perceiving, throws himself unhesitatingly on his thought, instantly rights himself, stands in the erect position, commands his limbs, works miracles; just as a man who stands on his feet is stronger than a man who stands on his head.

So use all that is called Fortune. Most men gamble with her, and gain all, and lose all, as her wheel rolls. But do thou leave as unlawful these winnings, and deal with Cause and Effect, the chancellors of God. In the Will work and acquire, and thou hast chained the wheel of Chance, and shalt sit hereafter out of fear from her rotations. A political victory, a rise of rents, the recovery of your sick or the return of your absent friend, or some other favorable event raises your spirits, and you think good days are preparing for you. Do not believe it. Nothing can bring you peace but yourself. Nothing can bring you peace but the triumph of principles.

OLIVER WENDELL HOLMES

ON OLD AGE [1]

My friend, the Professor, began talking with me one day in a
dreary sort of way.   I couldn't get at the difficulty for a good
while, but at last it turned out that somebody had been calling
him an old man. — He didn't mind his students calling him *the*
old man, he said.   That was a technical expression, and he
thought that he remembered hearing it applied to himself
when he was about twenty-five.   It may be considered as
a familiar and sometimes endearing appellation.   An Irish-
woman calls her husband "the old man," and he returns the
caressing expression by speaking of her as "the old woman."
But now, said he, just suppose a case like one of these.   A
young stranger is overheard talking of you as a very nice old
gentleman.   A friendly and genial critic speaks of your green
old age as illustrating the truth of some axiom you had uttered
with reference to that period of life.   What *I* call an old man
is a person with a smooth, shining crown and a fringe of scattered white hairs, seen in the streets on sunshiny days, stooping
as he walks, bearing a cane, moving cautiously and slowly;
telling old stories, smiling at present follies, living in a narrow
world of dry habits; one that remains waking when others
have dropped asleep, and keeps a little night-lamp-flame of life
burning year after year, if the lamp is not upset, and there is
only a careful hand held round it to prevent the puffs of wind
from blowing the flame out.   That's what I call an old man.

Now, said the Professor, you don't mean to tell me that I
have got to that yet?   Why, bless you, I am several years short
of the time when — [I knew what was coming, and could hardly
keep from laughing; twenty years ago he used to quote it as one
of those absurd speeches men of genius will make, and now he
is going to argue from it] — several years short of the time
when Balzac says that men are — most — you know — dangerous to — the hearts of — in short, most to be dreaded by

[1] From *The Autocrat of the Breakfast Table* (1858).

duennas that have charge of susceptible females. — What age is that? said I, statistically. — Fifty-two years, answered the Professor. — Balzac ought to know, said I, if it is true that Goethe said of him that each of his stories must have been dug out of a woman's heart. But fifty-two is a high figure.

Stand in the light of the window, Professor, said I. — The Professor took up the desired position. — You have white hairs, I said. — Had 'em any time these twenty years, said the Professor. — And the crow's-foot, — *pes anserinus*, rather. — The Professor smiled, as I wanted him to, and the folds radiated like the ridges of a half-opened fan, from the outer corner of the eyes to the temples. — And the calipers, said I. — What are the *calipers?* he asked, curiously. — Why, the parenthesis, said I. — *Parenthesis?* said the Professor; what's that? — Why, look in the glass when you are disposed to laugh, and see if your mouth isn't framed in a couple of crescent lines, — so, my boy (   ). — It's all nonsense, said the Professor; just look at my *biceps;* — and he began pulling off his coat to show me his arm. Be careful, said I; you can't bear exposure to the air, at your time of life, as you could once. — I will box with you, said the Professor, row with you, walk with you, ride with you, swim with you, or sit at table with you, for fifty dollars a side. — Pluck survives stamina, I answered.

The Professor went off a little out of humor. A few weeks afterwards he came in, looking very good-natured, and brought me a paper, which I have here, and from which I shall read you some portions, if you don't object. He had been thinking the matter over, he said, — had read Cicero *De Senectute*, and made up his mind to meet old age half way. These were some of his reflections that he had written down; so here you have

THE PROFESSOR'S PAPER.

There is no doubt when old age begins. The human body is a furnace which keeps in blast three-score years and ten, more or less. It burns about three hundred pounds of carbon a year (besides other fuel), when in fair working order, according to a great chemist's estimate. When the fire slackens, life declines; when it goes out, we are dead.

It has been shown by some noted French experimenters,

that the amount of combustion increases up to about the thirtieth year, remains stationary to about forty-five, and then diminishes. This last is the point where old age starts from. The great fact of physical life is the perpetual commerce with the elements, and the fire is the measure of it.

About this time of life, if food is plenty where you live, — for that, you know, regulates matrimony, — you may be expecting to find yourself a grandfather some fine morning; a kind of domestic felicity that gives one a cool shiver of delight to think of, as among the not remotely possible events.

I don't mind much those slipshod lines Dr. Johnson wrote to Thrale, telling her about life's declining from *thirty-five;* the furnace is in full blast for ten years longer, as I have said. The Romans came very near the mark; their age of enlistment reached from seventeen to forty-six years.

What is the use of fighting against the seasons, or the tides, or the movements of the planetary bodies, or this ebb in the wave of life that flows through us? We are old fellows from the moment the fire begins to go out. Let us always behave like gentlemen when we are introduced to new acquaintance.

Incipit Allegoria Senectutis.

Old Age, this is Mr. Professor; Mr. Professor, this is Old Age.

Old Age. — Mr. Professor, I hope to see you well. I have known you for some time, though I think you did not know me. Shall we walk down the street together?

Professor (drawing back a little). — We can talk more quietly, perhaps, in my study. Will you tell me how it is you seem to be acquainted with everybody you are introduced to, though he evidently considers you an entire stranger?

Old Age. — I make it a rule never to force myself upon a person's recognition until I have known him at least *five years.*

Professor. — Do you mean to say that you have known me so long as that?

Old Age. — I do. I left my card on you longer ago than that, but I am afraid you never read it; yet I see you have it with you.

Professor. — Where?

Old Age. — There, between your eyebrows, — three straight lines running up and down; all the probate courts know that token, — "Old Age, his mark." Put your forefinger on the inner end of one eyebrow, and your middle finger on the inner end of the other eyebrow; now separate the fingers, and you will smooth out my sign-manual; that's the way you used to look before I left my card on you.

Professor. — What message do people generally send back when you first call on them?

Old Age. — *Not at home.* Then I leave a card and go. Next year I call; get the same answer; leave another card. So for five or six, — sometimes ten years or more. At last, if they don't let me in, I break in through the front door or the windows.

We talked together in this way some time. Then Old Age said again, — Come, let us walk down the street together, — and offered me a cane, an eyeglass, a tippet, and a pair of overshoes. — No, much obliged to you, said I. I don't want those things, and I had a little rather talk with you here, privately, in my study. So I dressed myself up in a jaunty way and walked out alone; — got a fall, caught a cold, was laid up with a lumbago, and had time to think over this whole matter.

Explicit Allegoria Senectutis.

We have settled when old age begins. Like all Nature's processes, it is gentle and gradual in its approaches, strewed with illusions, and all its little griefs soothed by natural sedatives. But the iron hand is not less irresistible because it wears the velvet glove. The button-wood throws off its bark in large flakes, which one may find lying at its foot, pushed out, and at last pushed off, by that tranquil movement from beneath, which is too slow to be seen, but too powerful to be arrested. One finds them always, but one rarely sees them fall. So it is our youth drops from us, — scales off, sapless and lifeless, and lays bare the tender and immature fresh growth of old age. Looked at collectively, the changes of old age appear as a series of personal insults and indignities, terminating at last in death, which Sir Thomas Browne has called "the very disgrace and ignominy of our natures."

My lady's cheek can boast no more
The cranberry white and pink it wore;
And where her shining locks divide,
The parting line is all too wide ——

No, no, — this will never do. Talk about men, if you will,
but spare the poor women.

We have a brief description of seven stages of life by a remarkably good observer. It is very presumptuous to attempt
to add to it, yet I have been struck with the fact that life admits of a natural analysis into no less than fifteen distinct periods. Taking the five primary divisions, infancy, childhood,
youth, manhood, old age, each of these has its own three periods
of immaturity, complete development, and decline. I recognize an *old* baby at once, — with its "pipe and mug," (a
stick of candy and a porringer,) — so does everybody; and an
old child shedding its milk-teeth is only a little prototype of the
old man shedding his permanent ones. Fifty or thereabouts is
only the childhood, as it were, of old age; the graybeard youngster must be weaned from his late suppers now. So you will
see that you have to make fifteen stages at any rate, and that
it would not be hard to make twenty-five; five primary, each
with five secondary divisions.

The infancy and childhood of commencing old age have the
same ingenuous simplicity and delightful unconsciousness
about them as the first stage of the earlier periods of life shows.
The great delusion of mankind is in supposing that to be individual and exceptional which is universal and according to
law. A person is always startled when he hears himself seriously called an old man for the first time.

Nature gets us out of youth into manhood, as sailors are
hurried on board of vessels, — in a state of intoxication. We
are hustled into maturity reeling with our passions and imaginations, and we have drifted far away from port before we
awake out of our illusions. But to carry us out of maturity
into old age, without our knowing where we are going, she
drugs us with strong opiates, and so we stagger along with wide
open eyes that see nothing until snow enough has fallen on our
heads to rouse our comatose brains out of their stupid trances.

There is one mark of age that strikes me more than any of

the physical ones; — I mean the formation of *Habits*. An old man who shrinks into himself falls into ways that become as positive and as much beyond the reach of outside influences as if they were governed by clock-work. The *animal* functions, as the physiologists call them, in distinction from the *organic*, tend, in the process of deterioration to which age and neglect united gradually lead them, to assume the periodical or rhythmical type of movement. Every man's *heart* (this organ belongs, you know, to the organic system) has a regular mode of action; but I know a great many men whose *brains*, and all their voluntary existence flowing from their brains, have a *systole* and *diastole* as regular as that of the heart itself. Habit is the approximation of the animal system to the organic. It is a confession of failure in the highest function of being, which involves a perpetual self-determination, in full view of all existing circumstances. But habit, you see, is an action in present circumstances from past motives. It is substituting a *vis a tergo* for the evolution of living force.

When a man, instead of burning up three hundred pounds of carbon a year, has got down to two hundred and fifty, it is plain enough he must economize force somewhere. Now habit is a labor-saving invention which enables a man to get along with less fuel, — that is all; for fuel is force, you know, just as much in the page I am writing for you as in the locomotive or the legs that carry it to you. Carbon is the same thing, whether you call it wood, or coal, or bread and cheese. A reverend gentleman demurred to this statement, — as if, because combustion is asserted to be the *sine qua non* of thought, therefore thought is alleged to be a purely chemical process. Facts of chemistry are one thing, I told him, and facts of consciousness another. It can be proved to him, by a very simple analysis of some of his spare elements, that every Sunday, when he does his duty faithfully, he uses up more phosphorus out of his brain and nerves than on ordinary days. But then he had his choice whether to do his duty, or to neglect it, and save his phosphorus and other combustibles.

It follows from all this that *the formation of habits* ought naturally to be, as it is, the special characteristic of age. As for the muscular powers, they pass their maximum long before the time when the true decline of life begins, if we may judge by the experience of the ring. A man is "stale," I think, in their language, soon after thirty, — often, no doubt, much earlier, as gentlemen of the pugilistic profession are exceedingly apt to keep their vital fire burning *with the blower up*.

——So far without Tully. But in the mean time I have been reading the treatise, *De Senectute*. It is not long, but a leisurely performance. The old gentleman was sixty-three years of age when he addressed it to his friend T. Pomponius Atticus, Eq., a person of distinction, some two or three years older. We read it when we are schoolboys, forget all about it for thirty years, and then take it up again by a natural instinct, — provided always that we read Latin as we drink water, without stopping to taste it, as all of us who ever learned it at school or college ought to do.

Cato is the chief speaker in the dialogue. A good deal of it is what would be called in vulgar phrase "slow." It unpacks and unfolds incidental illustrations which a modern writer would look at the back of, and toss each to its pigeon-hole. I think ancient classics and ancient people are alike in the tendency to this kind of expansion.

An old doctor came to me once (this is literal fact) with some contrivance or other for people with broken kneepans. As the patient would be confined for a good while, he might find it dull work to sit with his hands in his lap. Reading, the ingenious inventor suggested, would be an agreeable mode of passing the time. He mentioned, in his written account of his contrivance, various works that might amuse the weary hour. I remember only three, — *Don Quixote*, *Tom Jones*, and *Watts on the Mind*.

It is not generally understood that Cicero's essay was delivered as a lyceum lecture, (*concio popularis*,) at the Temple of Mercury. The journals (*papyri*) of the day ("Tempora Quotidiana," — "Tribunus Quirinalis," — "Praeco Romanus," and the rest) gave abstracts of it, one of which I have translated and modernized, as being a substitute for the analysis I intended to make.

IV. Kal. Mart. . . .

The lecture at the Temple of Mercury, last evening, was well attended by the *élite* of our great city. Two hundred thousand sestertia were thought to have been represented in the house. The doors were besieged by a mob of shabby fellows, (*illotum vulgus,*) who were at length quieted after two or three had been somewhat roughly handled (*gladio jugulati*). The speaker was the well-known Mark Tully, Eq., — the subject Old Age. Mr. T. has a lean and scraggy person, with a very unpleasant excrescence upon his nasal feature, from which his nickname of *chick-pea* (Cicero) is said by some to be derived. As a lecturer is public property, we may remark, that his outer garment (*toga*) was of cheap stuff and somewhat worn, and that his general style and appearance of dress and manner (*habitus, vestitusque*) were somewhat provincial.

The lecture consisted of an imaginary dialogue between Cato and Laelius. We found the first portion rather heavy, and retired a few moments for refreshment (*pocula quaedam vini*). — All want to reach old age, says Cato, and grumble when they get it; therefore they are donkeys. — The lecturer will allow us to say that he is the donkey; we know we shall grumble at old age, but we want to live through youth and manhood, *in spite* of the troubles we shall groan over. — There was considerable prosing as to what old age can do and can't. — True, but not new. Certainly, old folks can't jump, — break the necks of their thigh-bones, (*femorum cervices,*) if they do; can't crack nuts with their teeth; can't climb a greased pole (*malum inunctum scandere non possunt*); but they can tell old stories and give you good advice; if they know what you have made up your mind to do when you ask them. — All this is well enough, but won't set the Tiber on fire (*Tiberim accendere nequaquam potest*).

There were some clever things enough, (*dicta haud inepta,*) a few of which are worth reporting. — Old people are accused of being forgetful; but they never forget where they have put their money. — Nobody is so old he doesn't think he can live a year. — The lecturer quoted an ancient maxim, — Grow old early, if you would be old long, — but disputed it. — Authority, he thought, was the chief privilege of age. — It is not great to have money, but fine to govern those that have it. — Old age begins at *forty-six* years, according to the common opinion.

— It is not every kind of old age or of wine that grows sour with time. — Some excellent remarks were made on immortality, but mainly borrowed from and credited to Plato. — Several pleasing anecdotes were told. — Old Milo, champion of the heavy weights in his day, looked at his arms and whimpered, "They are dead." Not so dead as you, you old fool, — says Cato; — you never were good for anything but for your shoulders and flanks. — Pisistratus asked Solon what made him dare to be so obstinate. Old age, said Solon.

The lecture was on the whole acceptable, and a credit to our culture and civilization. — The reporter goes on to state that there will be no lecture next week, on account of the expected combat between the bear and the barbarian. Betting (*sponsio*) two to one (*duo ad unum*) on the bear.

—— After all, the most encouraging things I find in the treatise, *De Senectute*, are the stories of men who have found new occupations when growing old, or kept up their common pursuits in the extreme period of life. Cato learned Greek when he was old, and speaks of wishing to learn the fiddle, or some such instrument, (*fidibus*,) after the example of Socrates. Solon learned something new, every day, in his old age, as he gloried to proclaim. Cyrus pointed out with pride and pleasure the trees he had planted with his own hand. [I remember a pillar on the Duke of Northumberland's estate at Alnwick, with an inscription in similar words, if not the same. That, like other country pleasures, never wears out. None is too rich, none too poor, none too young, none too old to enjoy it.] There is a New England story I have heard more to the point, however, than any of Cicero's. A young farmer was urged to set out some apple-trees. — No, said he, they are too long growing, and I don't want to plant for other people. The young farmer's father was spoken to about it, but he, with better reason, alleged that apple-trees were slow and life was fleeting. At last some one mentioned it to the old grandfather of the young farmer. He had nothing else to do, — so he stuck in some trees. He lived long enough to drink barrels of cider made from the apples that grew on those trees.

As for myself, after visiting a friend lately, — [Do remember all the time that this is the Professor's paper.] — I satisfied myself that I had better concede the fact that — my contemporaries are not so young as they have been, — and that, — awkward as it is, — science and history agree in telling me that I can claim the immunities and must own the humiliations of the early stage of senility. Ah! but we have all gone down the hill together. The dandies of my time have split their waistbands and taken to high-low shoes. The beauties of my recollections — where are they? They have run the gantlet of the years as well as I. First the years pelted them with red roses till their cheeks were all on fire. By and by they began throwing white roses, and that morning flush passed away. At last one of the years threw a snow-ball, and after that no year let the poor girls pass without throwing snow-balls. And then came rougher missiles, — ice and stones; and from time to time an arrow whistled, and down went one of the poor girls. So there are but few left; and we don't call those few *girls*, but ——

Ah, me! here am I groaning just as the old Greek sighed *Aï, aï!* and the old Roman, *Eheu!* I have no doubt we should die of shame and grief at the indignities offered us by age, if it were not that we see so many others as badly or worse off than ourselves. We always compare ourselves with our contemporaries.

WILLIAM MAKEPEACE THACKERAY

OGRES[1]

I DARE say the reader has remarked that the upright and independent vowel, which stands in the vowel-list between E and O, has formed the subject of the main part of these essays. How does that vowel feel this morning? — fresh, good-humoured, and lively? The Roundabout lines, which fall from this pen, are correspondingly brisk and cheerful. Has anything, on the contrary, disagreed with the vowel? Has its rest been disturbed, or was yesterday's dinner too good, or yesterday's wine not good enough? Under such circumstances, a darkling misanthropic tinge, no doubt, is cast upon the paper. The jokes, if attempted, are elaborate and dreary. The bitter temper breaks out. That sneering manner is adopted, which you know, and which exhibits itself so especially when the writer is speaking about women. A moody carelessness comes over him. He sees no good in anybody or thing: and treats gentlemen, ladies, history, and things in general, with a like gloomy flippancy. Agreed, when the vowel in question is in that mood, if you like airy gaiety and tender gushing benevolence — if you want to be satisfied with yourself and the rest of your fellow-beings; I recommend you, my dear creature, to go to some other shop in Cornhill, or turn to some other article. There are moods in the mind of the vowel of which we are speaking when it is ill-conditioned and captious. Who always keeps good health and good humor? Do not philosophers grumble? Are not sages sometimes out of temper? And do not angel-women go off in tantrums? To-day my mood is dark. I scowl as I dip my pen in the inkstand.

Here is the day come round — for everything here is done with the utmost regularity: — intellectual labour, sixteen hours; meals, thirty-two minutes; exercise, a hundred and forty-eight minutes; conversation with the family, chiefly

[1] From *Roundabout Papers* (1863). Originally published in *Cornhill Magazine*, August, 1861.

literary, and about the housekeeping, one hour and four minutes; sleep, three hours and fifteen minutes (at the end of the
month, when the Magazine is complete, I own I take eight
minutes more); and the rest for the toilette and the world.
Well, I say, the *Roundabout Paper Day* being come, and the
subject long since settled in my mind, an excellent subject — a
most telling, lively, and popular subject — I go to breakfast determined to finish the meal in 9¾ minutes, as usual, and then
retire to my desk and work, when oh, — provoking! — here in
the paper is the very subject treated on which I was going to
write! Yesterday another paper which I saw treated it — and
of course, as I need not tell you, spoiled it. Last Saturday,
another paper had an article on the subject; perhaps you may
guess what it was — but I won't tell you. Only this is true, my
favourite subject, which was about to make the best paper we
have had for a long time; my bird, my game that I was going to
shoot and serve up with such a delicate sauce, has been found
by other sportsmen; and pop, pop, pop, a half-dozen of guns
have banged at it, mangled it, and brought it down.

"And can't you take some other text?" say you. All this is
mighty well. But if you have set your heart on a certain dish
for dinner, be it cold boiled veal, or what you will, and they
bring you turtle and venison, don't you feel disappointed!
During your walk you have been making up your mind that
that cold meat, with moderation and a pickle, will be a very
sufficient dinner: you have accustomed your thoughts to it; and
here, in place of it, is a turkey, surrounded by coarse sausages,
or a reeking pigeon-pie, or a fulsome roast pig. I have known
many a good and kind man made furiously angry by such a
contretemps. I have known him lose his temper, call his wife
and servants names, and a whole household made miserable.
If, then, as is notoriously the case, it is too dangerous to balk a
man about his dinner, how much more about his article! I
came to my meal with an ogre-like appetite and gusto. Fee,
faw, fum! Wife, where is that tender little princekin? Have
you trussed him, and did you stuff him nicely, and have you
taken care to baste him, and do him, not too brown, as I told
you? Quick! I am hungry! I begin to whet my knife, to roll
my eyes about, and roar and clap my huge chest like a gorilla;

and then my poor Ogrina has to tell me that the little princes have all run away, whilst she was in the kitchen, making the paste to bake them in? I pause in the description. I won't condescend to report the bad language, which you know must ensue, when an ogre, whose mind is ill-regulated, and whose habits of self-indulgence are notorious, finds himself disappointed of his greedy hopes. What treatment of his wife, what abuse and brutal behaviour to his children, who, though ogrillons, are children! My dears, you may fancy, and need not ask my delicate pen to describe, the language and behaviour of a vulgar, coarse, greedy, large man with an immense mouth and teeth, which are too frequently employed in the gobbling and crunching of raw man's meat.

And in this circuitous way you see I have reached my present subject, which is, Ogres. You fancy they are dead or only fictitious characters — mythical representatives of strength, cruelty, stupidity, and lust for blood? Though they had seven-leagued boots, you remember all sorts of little whipping-snapping Tom Thumbs used to elude and outrun them. They were so stupid that they gave in to the most shallow ambuscades and artifices: witness that well-known ogre, who, because Jack cut open the hasty-pudding, instantly ripped open his own stupid waistcoat and interior. They were cruel, brutal, disgusting, with their sharpened teeth, immense knives, and roaring voices! but they always ended by being overcome by little Tom Thumbkins, or some other smart little champion.

Yes; they were conquered in the end there is no doubt. They plunged headlong (and uttering the most frightful bad language) into some pit where Jack came with his smart *couteau de chasse*, and whipped their brutal heads off. They would be going to devour maidens,

> "But ever when it seemed
>   Their need was at the sorest,
>   A knight, in armour bright,
>   Came riding through the forest."

And down, after a combat, would go the brutal persecutor, with a lance through his midriff. Yes, I say, this is very true and well. But you remember that round the ogre's cave the ground was covered, for hundreds and hundreds of yards, *with the bones of the victims* whom he had lured into the castle. Many knights and maids came to him and perished under his knife and teeth. Were dragons the same as ogres? monsters dwelling in caverns, whence they rushed, attired in plate armour, wielding pikes and torches, and destroying stray passengers who passed by their lair? Monsters, brutes, rapacious tyrants, ruffians, as they were, doubtless they ended by being overcome. But, before they were destroyed, they did a deal of mischief. The bones round their caves were countless. They had sent many brave souls to Hades, before their own fled, howling out of their rascal carcasses, to the same place of gloom.

There is no greater mistake than to suppose that fairies, champions, distressed damsels, and by consequence ogres, have ceased to exist. It may not be *ogreable* to them (pardon the horrible pleasantry, but as I am writing in the solitude of my chamber, I am grinding my teeth — yelling, roaring, and cursing — brandishing my scissors and paper-cutter and as it were have become an ogre). I say there is no greater mistake than to suppose that ogres have ceased to exist. We all *know* ogres. Their caverns are round us, and about us. There are the castles of several ogres within a mile of the spot where I write. I think some of them suspect I am an ogre myself. I am not, but I know they are. I visit them. I don't mean to say that they take a cold roast prince out of the cupboard, and have a cannibal feast before *me*. But I see the bones lying about the roads to their houses, and in the areas and gardens. Politeness, of course, prevents me from making any remarks: but I know them well enough. One of the ways to know 'em is to watch the scared looks of the ogres' wives and children. They lead an awful life. They are present at dreadful cruelties. In their excesses those ogres will stab about and kill not only strangers who happen to call in and ask a night's lodging, but they will outrage, murder, and chop up their own kin. We all know ogres, I say, and have been in their dens often. It is not necessary that ogres who ask you to dine should offer their guests the *peculiar dish* which they like. They cannot always get a Tom Thumb family. They eat mutton and beef too; and I dare say even go out to tea, and invite you to drink it. But I

tell you there are numbers of them going about in the world.
And now you have my word for it, and this little hint, it is quite
curious what an interest society may be made to have for you
by your determining to find out the ogres you meet there.

What does the man mean? says Mrs. Downright, to whom
a joke is a very grave thing. I mean, madam, that in the company assembled in your genteel drawing-room, who bow here
and there, and smirk in white neckcloths, you receive men who
elbow through life successfully enough, but who are ogres in
private: men wicked, false, rapacious, flattering; cruel hectors
at home, smiling courtiers abroad; causing wives, children,
servants, parents, to tremble before them, and smiling and
bowing, as they bid strangers welcome into their castles. I say,
there are men who have crunched the bones of victim after
victim; in whose closets lie skeletons picked frightfully clean.
When these ogres come out into the world, you don't suppose
they show their knives, and their great teeth? A neat simple
white neckcloth, a merry rather obsequious manner, a cadaver-
ous look, perhaps, now and again, and a rather dreadful grin;
but I know ogres very considerably respected: and when you
hint to such and such a man, "My dear sir, Mr. Sharpus, whom
you appear to like, is, I assure you, a most dreadful cannibal;"
the gentleman cries, "Oh, psha, nonsense! Dare say not so
black as he is painted. Dare say not worse than his neighbours." We condone everything in this country — private
treason, falsehood, flattery, cruelty at home, roguery, and
double-dealing. What! Do you mean to say in your acquaintance you don't know ogres guilty of countless crimes of
fraud and force, and that knowing them you don't shake hands
with them; dine with them at your table; and meet them at
their own? Depend upon it in the time when they were real
live ogres, in real caverns or castles, gobbling up real knights
and virgins, when they went into the world — the neighbouring
market-town, let us say, or earl's castle — though their nature
and reputation were pretty well known, their notorious foibles
were never alluded to. You would say, "What, Blunderbore,
my boy! How do you do? How well and fresh you look!
What's the receipt you have for keeping so young and rosy?"
And your wife would softly ask after Mrs. Blunderbore and the

dear children. Or it would be, "My dear Humguffin! try that pork. It is home-bred, home-fed, and, I promise you, tender. Tell me if you think it is as good as yours? John, a glass of burgundy to Colonel Humguffin!" You don't suppose there would be any unpleasant allusions to disagreeable home-reports regarding Humguffin's manner of furnishing his larder? I say we all of us know ogres. We shake hands and dine with ogres. And if inconvenient moralists tell us we are cowards for our pains, we turn round with a *tu quoque*, or say that we don't meddle with other folk's affairs; that people are much less black than they are painted, and so on. What! Won't half the county go to Ogreham Castle? Won't some of the clergy say grace at dinner? Won't the mothers bring their daughters to dance with the young Rawheads? And if Lady Ogreham happens to die — I won't say to go the way of all flesh, that is too revolting — I say if Ogreham is a widower, do you aver, on your conscience and honour, that mothers will not be found to offer their young girls to supply the lamented lady's place? How stale this misanthropy is! Something must have disagreed with this cynic. Yes, my good woman. I dare say you would like to call another subject. Yes, my fine fellow; ogre at home, supple as a dancing-master abroad, and shaking in thy pumps, and wearing a horrible grin of sham gaiety to conceal thy terror, lest I should point thee out:— thou art prosperous and honoured, art thou? I say thou hast been a tyrant and a robber. Thou hast plundered the poor. Thou hast bullied the weak. Thou hast laid violent hands on the goods of the innocent and confiding. Thou hast made a prey of the meek and gentle who asked for thy protection. Thou hast been hard to thy kinsfolk, and cruel to thy family. Go, monster! Ah, when shall little Jack come and drill daylight through thy wicked cannibal carcass? I see the ogre pass on, bowing right and left to the company; and he gives a dreadful sidelong glance of suspicion as he is talking to my Lord Bishop in the corner there.

Ogres in our days need not be giants at all. In former times, and in children's books, where it is necessary to paint your moral in such large letters that there can be no mistake about it, ogres are made with that enormous mouth and *ratelier* [1]

---

[1] set of teeth.

which you know of, and with which they can swallow down a baby, almost without using that great knife which they always carry. They are too cunning nowadays. They go about in society, slim, small, quietly dressed, and showing no especially great appetite. In my own young days there used to be play ogres — men who would devour a young fellow in one sitting, and leave him without a bit of flesh on his bones. They were quiet gentlemanlike-looking people. They got the young fellow into their cave. Champagne, pâté-de-foie-gras, and numberless good things, were handed about; and then, having eaten, the young man was devoured in his turn. I believe these card and dice ogres have died away almost as entirely as the hasty-pudding giants whom Tom Thumb overcame. Now, there are ogres in City courts who lure you into their dens. About our Cornish mines I am told there are many most plausible ogres, who tempt you into their caverns and pick your bones there. In a certain newspaper there used to be lately a whole column of advertisments from ogres who would put on the most plausible, nay, piteous appearance, in order to inveigle their victims. You would read, "A tradesman, established for seventy years in the City, and known and much respected by Messrs. N. M. Rothschild and Baring Brothers, has pressing need for three pounds until next Saturday. He can give security for half a million, and forty thousand pounds will be given for the use of the loan," and so on; or, "An influential body of capitalists are about to establish a company, of which the business will be enormous and the profits proportionately prodigious. They will require a SECRETARY, of good address and appearance, at a salary of two thousand per annum. He need not be able to write, but address and manners are absolutely necessary. As a mark of confidence in the company, he will have to deposit," &c.; or, "A young widow (of pleasing manners and appearance) who has a pressing necessity for four pounds ten for three weeks, offers her Erard's grand piano valued at three hundred guineas; a diamond cross of eight hundred pounds; and board and lodging in her elegant villa near Banbury Cross, with the best references and society, in return for the loan." I suspect these people are ogres. There are ogres and ogres. Polyphemus was a great, tall, one-eyed, notorious ogre, fetching his victims out of a hole, and gobbling them one after another. There could be no mistake about him. But so were the Sirens ogres — pretty blue-eyed things, peeping at you coaxingly from out of the water, and singing their melodious wheedles. And the bones round their caves were more numerous than the ribs, skulls, and thigh-bones round the cavern of hulking Polypheme.

To the castle-gates of some of these monsters up rides the dapper champion of the pen; puffs boldly upon the horn which hangs by the chain; enters the hall resolutely, and challenges the big tyrant sulking within. We defy him to combat, the enormous roaring ruffian! We give him a meeting on the green plain before his castle. Green? No wonder it should be green: it is manured with human bones. After a few graceful wheels and curvets, we take our ground. We stoop over our saddle. 'Tis but to kiss the locket of our lady-love's hair. And now the vizor is up: the lance is in rest (Gillott's iron is the point for me). A touch of the spur in the gallant sides of Pegasus, and we gallop at the great brute.

"Cut off his ugly head, Flibbertigibbet, my squire!" And who are these who pour out of the castle? the imprisoned maidens, the maltreated widows, the poor old hoary grandfathers, who have been locked up in the dungeons these scores and scores of years, writhing under the tyranny of that ruffian! Ah, ye knights of the pen! May honour be your shield, and truth tip your lances! Be gentle to all gentle people. Be modest to women. Be tender to children. And as for the Ogre Humbug, out sword and have at him.

HENRY DAVID THOREAU

SOLITUDE [1]

THIS is a delicious evening, when the whole body is one sense, and imbibes delight through every pore. I go and come with a strange liberty in Nature, a part of herself. As I walk along the stony shore of the pond in my shirt sleeves, though it is cool as well as cloudy and windy, and I see nothing special to attract me, all the elements are unusually congenial to me. The bull-frogs trump to usher in the night, and the note of the whip-poorwill is borne on the rippling wind from over the water. Sympathy with the fluttering alder and poplar leaves almost takes away my breath; yet, like the lake, my serenity is rippled but not ruffled. These small waves raised by the evening wind are as remote from storm as the smooth reflecting surface. Though it is now dark, the wind still blows and roars in the wood, the waves still dash, and some creatures lull the rest with their notes. The repose is never complete. The wildest animals do not repose, but seek their prey now; the fox, and skunk, and rabbit, now roam the fields and woods without fear. They are Nature's watchmen, — links which connect the days of animated life.

When I return to my house I find that visitors have been there and left their cards, either a bunch of flowers, or a wreath of evergreen, or a name in pencil on a yellow walnut leaf or a chip. They who come rarely to the woods take some little piece of the forest into their hands to play with by the way, which they leave, either intentionally or accidentally. One has peeled a willow wand, woven it into a ring, and dropped it on my table. I could always tell if visitors had called in my absence, either by the bended twigs or grass, or the print of their shoes, and generally of what sex or age or quality they were by some slight trace left, as a flower dropped, or a bunch of grass plucked and thrown away, even as far off as the railroad, half a mile distant, or by the lingering odor of a cigar or pipe.

[1] From *Walden* (1854).

Nay, I was frequently notified of the passage of a traveller along the highway sixty rods off by the scent of his pipe.

There is commonly sufficient space about us. Our horizon is never quite at our elbows. The thick wood is not just at our door, nor the pond, but somewhat is always clearing, familiar and worn by us, appropriated and fenced in some way, and re-claimed from Nature. For what reason have I this vast range and circuit, some square miles of unfrequented forest, for my privacy, abandoned to me by men? My nearest neighbor is a mile distant, and no house is visible from any place but the hill-tops within half a mile of my own. I have my horizon bounded by woods all to myself; a distant view of the railroad where it touches the pond on the one hand, and of the fence which skirts the woodland road on the other. But for the most part it is as solitary where I live as on the prairies. It is as much Asia or Africa as New England. I have, as it were, my own sun and moon and stars, and a little world all to myself. At night there was never a traveller passed my house, or knocked at my door, more than if I were the first or last man; unless it were in the spring, when at long intervals some came from the village to fish for pouts, — they plainly fished much more in the Walden Pond of their own natures, and baited their hooks with darkness, — but they soon retreated, usually with light baskets, and left "the world to darkness and to me," and the black kernel of the night was never profaned by any human neighborhood. I believe that men are generally still a little afraid of the dark, though the witches are all hung, and Christianity and candles have been introduced.

Yet I experienced sometimes that the most sweet and tender, the most innocent and encouraging society may be found in any natural object, even for the poor misanthrope and most melancholy man. There can be no very black melancholy to him who lives in the midst of Nature and has his senses still. There was never yet such a storm but it was Æolian music to a healthy and innocent ear. Nothing can rightly compel a simple and brave man to a vulgar sadness. While I enjoy the friendship of the seasons I trust that nothing can make life a burden to me. The gentle rain which waters my beans and keeps me in the house to-day is not drear and melancholy, but good for me too.

Though it prevents my hoeing them, it is of far more worth than my hoeing. If it should continue so long as to cause the seeds to rot in the ground and destroy the potatoes in the low lands, it would still be good for the grass on the uplands, and, being good for the grass, it would be good for me. Sometimes, when I compare myself with other men, it seems as if I were more favored by the gods than they, beyond any deserts that I am conscious of; as if I had a warrant and surety at their hands which my fellows have not, and were especially guided and guarded. I do not flatter myself, but if it be possible they flatter me. I have never felt lonesome, or in the least oppressed by a sense of solitude, but once, and that was a few weeks after I came to the woods, when, for an hour, I doubted if the near neighborhood of man was not essential to a serene and healthy life. To be alone was something unpleasant. But I was at the same time conscious of a slight insanity in my mood, and seemed to foresee my recovery. In the midst of a gentle rain while these thoughts prevailed, I was suddenly sensible of such sweet and beneficent society in Nature, in the very pattering of the drops, and in every sound and sight around my house, an infinite and unaccountable friendliness all at once like an atmosphere sustaining me, as made the fancied advantages of human neighborhood insignificant, and I have never thought of them since. Every little pine needle expanded and swelled with sympathy and befriended me. I was so distinctly made aware of the presence of something kindred to me, even in scenes which we are accustomed to call wild and dreary, and also that the nearest of blood to me and humanest was not a person nor a villager, that I thought no place could ever be strange to me again. —

> "Mourning untimely consumes the sad;
> Few are their days in the land of the living,
> Beautiful daughter of Toscar."

Some of my pleasantest hours were during the long rain storms in the spring or fall, which confined me to the house for the afternoon as well as the forenoon, soothed by their ceaseless roar and pelting; when an early twilight ushered in a long evening in which many thoughts had time to take root and unfold themselves. In those driving north-east rains which tried the village houses so, when the maids stood ready with mop and pail in front entries to keep the deluge out, I sat behind my door in my little house, which was all entry, and thoroughly enjoyed its protection. In one heavy thunder shower the lightning struck a large pitch-pine across the pond, making a very conspicuous and perfectly regular spiral groove from top to bottom, an inch or more deep, and four or five inches wide, as you would groove a walking-stick. I passed it again the other day, and was struck with awe on looking up and beholding that mark, now more distinct than ever, where a terrific and resistless bolt came down out of the harmless sky eight years ago. Men frequently say to me, "I should think you would feel lonesome down there, and want to be nearer to folks, rainy and snowy days and nights especially." I am tempted to reply to such, — This whole earth which we inhabit is but a point in space. How far apart, think you, dwell the two most distant inhabitants of yonder star, the breadth of whose disk cannot be appreciated by our instruments? Why should I feel lonely? is not our planet in the Milky Way? This which you put seems to me not to be the most important question. What sort of space is that which separates a man from his fellows and makes him solitary? I have found that no exertion of the legs can bring two minds much nearer to one another. What do we want most to dwell near to? Not to many men surely, the depot, the post-office, the bar-room, the meeting-house, the school-house, the grocery, Beacon Hill, or the Five Points, where men most congregate, but to the perennial source of our life, whence in all our experience we have found that to issue, as the willow stands near the water and sends out its roots in that direction. This will vary with different natures, but this is the place where a wise man will dig his cellar. . . . I one evening overtook one of my townsmen, who has accumulated what is called "a handsome property," — though I never got a *fair* view of it, — on the Walden road, driving a pair of cattle to market, who inquired of me how I could bring my mind to give up so many of the comforts of life. I answered that I was very sure I liked it passably well; I was not joking. And so I went home to my bed, and left him to pick his way through the darkness and the mud to Brighton,

— or Brighttown, — which place he would reach some time in the morning.

Any prospect of awakening or coming to life to a dead man makes indifferent all times and places. The place where that may occur is always the same, and indescribably pleasant to all our senses. For the most part we allow only outlying and transient circumstances to make our occasions. They are, in fact, the cause of our distraction. Nearest to all things is that power which fashions their being. *Next* to us the grandest laws are continually being executed. *Next* to us is not the workman whom we have hired, with whom we love so well to talk, but the workman whose work we are.

"How vast and profound is the influence of the subtile powers of Heaven and of Earth!"

"We seek to perceive them, and we do not see them; we seek to hear them, and we do not hear them; identified with the substance of things, they cannot be separated from them."

"They cause that in all the universe men purify and sanctify their hearts, and clothe themselves in their holiday garments to offer sacrifices and oblations to their ancestors. It is an ocean of subtile intelligences. They are everywhere, above us, on our left, on our right; they environ us on all sides."

We are the subjects of an experiment which is not a little interesting to me. Can we not do without the society of our gossips a little while under these circumstances, — have our own thoughts to cheer us? Confucius says truly, "Virtue does not remain as an abandoned orphan; it must of necessity have neighbors."

With thinking we may be beside ourselves in a sane sense. By a conscious effort of the mind we can stand aloof from actions and their consequences; and all things, good and bad, go by us like a torrent. We are not wholly involved in Nature. I may be either the drift-wood in the stream, or Indra in the sky looking down on it. I *may* be affected by a theatrical exhibition; on the other hand, I *may not* be affected by an actual event which appears to concern me much more. I only know myself as a human entity; the scene, so to speak, of thoughts and affections; and am sensible of a certain doubleness by which I can stand as remote from myself as from another. However intense my experience, I am conscious of the presence and criticism of a part of me, which, as it were, is not a part of me, but spectator, sharing no experience, but taking note of it; and that is no more I than it is you. When the play, it may be the tragedy, of life is over, the spectator goes his way. It was a kind of fiction, a work of the imagination only, so far as he was concerned. This doubleness may easily make us poor neighbors and friends sometimes.

I find it wholesome to be alone the greater part of the time. To be in company, even with the best, is soon wearisome and dissipating. I love to be alone. I never found the companion that was so companionable as solitude. We are for the most part more lonely when we go abroad among men than when we stay in our chambers. A man thinking or working is always alone, let him be where he will. Solitude is not measured by the miles of space that intervene between a man and his fellows. The really diligent student in one of the crowded hives of Cambridge College is as solitary as a dervis in the desert. The farmer can work alone in the field or the woods all day, hoeing or chopping, and not feel lonesome, because he is employed; but when he comes home at night he cannot sit down in a room alone, at the mercy of his thoughts, but must be where he can "see the folks," and recreate, and as he thinks remunerate, himself for his day's solitude; and hence he wonders how the student can sit alone in the house all night and most of the day without ennui and "the blues"; but he does not realize that the student, though in the house, is still at work in *his* field, and chopping in *his* woods, as the farmer in his, and in turn seeks the same recreation and society that the latter does, though it may be a more condensed form of it.

Society is commonly too cheap. We meet at very short intervals, not having had time to acquire any new value for each other. We meet at meals three times a day, and give each other a new taste of that old musty cheese that we are. We have had to agree on a certain set of rules, called etiquette and politeness, to make this frequent meeting tolerable and that we need not come to open war. We meet at the post-office, and at the sociable, and about the fireside every night; we live thick and are in each other's way, and stumble over one another, and

I think that we thus lose some respect for one another. Certainly less frequency would suffice for all important and hearty communications. Consider the girls in a factory, — never alone, hardly in their dreams. It would be better if there were but one inhabitant to a square mile, as where I live. The value of a man is not in his skin, that we should touch him.

I have heard of a man lost in the woods and dying of famine and exhaustion at the foot of a tree, whose loneliness was relieved by the grotesque visions with which, owing to bodily weakness, his diseased imagination surrounded him, and which he believed to be real. So also, owing to bodily and mental health and strength, we may be continually cheered by a like but more normal and natural society, and come to know that we are never alone.

I have a great deal of company in my house; especially in the morning, when nobody calls. Let me suggest a few comparisons, that some one may convey an idea of my situation. I am no more lonely than the loon in the pond that laughs so loud, or than Walden Pond itself. What company has that lonely lake, I pray? And yet it has not the blue devils, but the blue angels in it, in the azure tint of its waters. The sun is alone, except in thick weather, when there sometimes appear to be two, but one is a mock sun. God is alone, — but the devil, he is far from being alone; he sees a great deal of company; he is legion. I am no more lonely than a single mullein or dandelion in a pasture, or a bean leaf, or sorrel, or a horse-fly, or a humble-bee. I am no more lonely than the Mill Brook, or a weathercock, or the north star, or the south wind, or an April shower, or a January thaw, or the first spider in a new house.

I have occasional visits in the long winter evenings, when the snow falls fast and the wind howls in the wood, from an old settler and original proprietor, who is reported to have dug Walden Pond, and stoned it, and fringed it with pine woods; who tells me stories of old time and of new eternity; and between us we manage to pass a cheerful evening with social mirth and pleasant views of things, even without apples or cider, — a most wise and humorous friend, whom I love much, who keeps himself more secret than ever did Goffe or Whalley; and though he is thought to be dead, none can show where he is buried. An elderly dame, too, dwells in my neighborhood, invisible to most persons, in whose odorous herb garden I love to stroll sometimes, gathering simples and listening to her fables; for she has a genius of unequalled fertility, and her memory runs back farther than mythology, and she can tell me the original of every fable, and on what fact every one is founded, for the incidents occurred when she was young.   A ruddy and lusty old dame, who delights in all weathers and seasons, and is likely to outlive all her children yet.

The indescribable innocence and beneficence of Nature, — of sun and wind and rain, of summer and winter, — such health, such cheer, they afford forever! and such sympathy have they ever with our race, that all Nature would be affected, and the sun's brightness fade, and the winds would sigh humanely, and the clouds rain tears, and the woods shed their leaves and put on mourning in midsummer, if any man should ever for a just cause grieve.   Shall I not have intelligence with the earth? Am I not partly leaves and vegetable mould myself?

What is the pill which will keep us well, serene, contented? Not my or thy great-grandfather's, but our great-grandmother Nature's universal, vegetable, botanic medicines, by which she has kept herself young always, outlived so many old Parrs in her day, and fed her health with their decaying fatness.   For my panacea, instead of one of those quack vials of a mixture dipped from Acheron and the Dead Sea, which come out of those long shallow black-schooner looking wagons which we sometimes see made to carry bottles, let me have a draught of undiluted morning air.   Morning air!   If men will not drink of this at the fountain-head of the day, why, then, we must even bottle up some and sell it in the shops, for the benefit of those who have lost their subscription ticket to morning time in this world.   But remember, it will not keep quite till noonday even in the coolest cellar, but drive out the stopples long ere that and follow westward the steps of Aurora.   I am no worshipper of Hygeia, who was the daughter of that old herb-doctor Æsculapius, and who is represented on monuments holding a serpent in one hand, and in the other a cup out of which the serpent sometimes drinks; but rather of Hebe, cup-bearer to Jupiter, who was the daughter of Juno and wild lettuce, and who had the power of restoring gods and men to the vigor of youth. She was probably the only thoroughly sound-conditioned, healthy, and robust young lady that ever walked the globe, and wherever she came it was spring.

JAMES RUSSELL LOWELL

AT SEA[1]

THE sea was meant to be looked at from shore, as mountains are from the plain. Lucretius made this discovery long ago, and was blunt enough to blurt it forth, romance and sentiment — in other words, the pretence of feeling what we do not feel — being inventions of a later day. To be sure, Cicero used to twaddle about Greek literature and philosophy, much as people do about ancient art nowadays; but I rather sympathize with those stout old Romans who despised both, and believed that to found an empire was as grand an achievement as to build an epic or to carve a statue. But though there might have been twaddle, (as why not, since there was a Senate?) I rather think Petrarch was the first choragus of that sentimental dance which so long led young folks away from the realities of life like the piper of Hamelin, and whose succession ended, let us hope, with Chateaubriand. But for them, Byron, whose real strength lay in his sincerity, would never have talked about the "sea bounding beneath him like a steed that knows his rider," and all that sort of thing. Even if it had been true, steam has been as fatal to that part of the romance of the sea as to hand-loom weaving. But what say you to a twelve days' calm such as we dozed through in mid-Atlantic and in mid-August? I know nothing so tedious at once and exasperating as that regular slap of the wilted sails when the ship rises and falls with the slow breathing of the sleeping sea, one greasy, brassy swell following another, slow, smooth, immitigable as the series of Wordsworth's Ecclesiastical Sonnets. Even at his best, Neptune, in a *tête-à-tête*, has a way of repeating himself, an obtuseness to the *ne quid nimis*, that is stupefying. It reminds me of organ-music and my good friend Sebastian Bach. A fugue or two will do very

[1] From *Leaves from My Journal*, in *Literary Essays*, vol. I, Riverside Edition, 1890. Originally published in *Fireside Travels* (1864), though in the collected edition the group of essays bears the date 1854, and three of them were published in *Graham's Magazine* in that year.

well; but a concert made up of nothing else is altogether too epic for me.   There is nothing so desperately monotonous as the sea, and I no longer wonder at the cruelty of pirates.   Fancy an existence in which the coming up of a clumsy finback whale, who says *Pooh!* to you solemnly as you lean over the taffrail, is an event as exciting as an election on shore!   The dampness seems to strike into the wits as into the lucifer-matches, so that one may scratch a thought half a dozen times and get nothing at last but a faint sputter, the forlorn hope of fire, which only goes far enough to leave a sense of suffocation behind it.   Even smoking becomes an employment instead of a solace.   Who less likely to come to their wit's end than W. M. T. and A. H. C.? Yet I have seen them driven to five meals a day for mental occupation.   I sometimes sit and pity Noah; but even he had this advantage over all succeeding navigators, that, wherever he landed, he was sure to get no ill news from home.   He should be canonized as the patron-saint of newspaper correspondents, being the only man who ever had the very last authentic intelligence from everywhere.

The finback whale recorded just above has much the look of a brown-paper parcel, — the whitish stripes that run across him answering for the pack-thread.   He has a kind of accidental hole in the top of his head, through which he *pooh-poohs* the rest of creation, and which looks as if it had been made by the chance thrust of a chestnut rail.   He was our first event.   Our second was harpooning a sunfish, which basked dozing on the lap of the sea, looking so much like the giant turtle of an alderman's dream, that I am persuaded he would have let himself be made into mock-turtle soup rather than acknowledge his imposture.   But he broke away just as they were hauling him over the side, and sank placidly through the clear water, leaving behind him a crimson trail that wavered a moment and was gone.

The sea, though, has better sights than these.   When we were up with the Azores, we began to meet flying-fish and Portuguese men-of-war beautiful as the galley of Cleopatra, tiny craft that dared these seas before Columbus.   I have seen one of the former rise from the crest of a wave, and, glancing from another some two hundred feet beyond, take a fresh flight of perhaps as far. How Calderon would have similized this pretty creature had he ever seen it! How would he have run him up and down the gamut of simile! If a fish, then a fish with wings; if a bird, then a bird with fins; and so on, keeping up the light shuttle-cock of a conceit as is his wont. Indeed, the poor thing is the most killing bait for a comparison, and I assure you I have three or four in my inkstand; — but be calm, they shall stay there. Moore, who looked on all nature as a kind of *Gradus ad Parnassum*, a *thesaurus* of similitude, and spent his life in a game of What is my thought like? with himself, *did* the flying-fish on his way to Bermuda. So I leave him in peace.

The most beautiful thing I have seen at sea, all the more so that I had never heard of it, is the trail of a shoal of fish through the phosphorescent water. It is like a flight of silver rockets, or the streaming of northern lights through that silent nether heaven. I thought nothing could go beyond that rustling star-foam which was churned up by our ship's bows, or those eddies and disks of dreamy flame that rose and wandered out of sight behind us.

> 'Twas fire our ship was plunging through,
> Cold fire that o'er the quarter flew;
> And wandering moons of idle flame
> Grew full and waned, and went and came,
> Dappling with light the huge sea-snake
> That slid behind us in the wake.

But there was something even more delicately rare in the apparition of the fish, as they turned up in gleaming furrows the latent moonshine which the ocean seemed to have hoarded against these vacant interlunar nights. In the Mediterranean one day, as we were lying becalmed, I observed the water freckled with dingy specks, which at last gathered to a pinkish scum on the surface. The sea had been so phosphorescent for some nights, that when the Captain gave me my bath, by dousing me with buckets from the house on deck, the spray flew off my head and shoulders in sparks. It occurred to me that this dirty-looking scum might be the luminous matter, and I had a pailful dipped up to keep till after dark. When I went to look at it after nightfall, it seemed at first perfectly dead; but when I shook it, the whole broke out into what I can only liken to milky flames, whose lambent silence was strangely beautiful, and startled me almost as actual projection might an alchemist. I could not bear to be the death of so much beauty; so I poured it all overboard again.

Another sight worth taking a voyage for is that of the sails by moonlight. Our course was "south and by east, half south," so that we seemed bound for the full moon as she rolled up over our wavering horizon. Then I used to go forward to the bowsprit and look back. Our ship was a clipper, with every rag set, stunsails, sky-scrapers, and all; nor was it easy to believe that such a wonder could be built of canvas as that white many-storied pile of cloud that stooped over me or drew back as we rose and fell with the waves.

These are all the wonders I can recall of my five weeks at sea, except the sun. Were you ever alone with the sun? You think it a very simple question; but I never was, in the full sense of the word, till I was held up to him one cloudless day on the broad buckler of the ocean. I suppose one might have the same feeling in the desert. I remember getting something like it years ago, when I climbed alone to the top of a mountain, and lay face up on the hot gray moss, striving to get a notion of how an Arab might feel. It was my American commentary of the Koran, and not a bad one. In a New England winter, too, when everything is gagged with snow, as if some gigantic physical geographer were taking a cast of the earth's face in plaster, the bare knob of a hill will introduce you to the sun as a comparative stranger. But at sea you may be alone with him day after day, and almost all day long. I never understood before that nothing short of full daylight can give the supremest sense of solitude. Darkness will not do so, for the imagination peoples it with more shapes than ever were poured from the frozen loins of the populous North. The sun, I sometimes think, is a little *grouty* at sea, especially at high noon, feeling that he wastes his beams on those fruitless furrows. It is otherwise with the moon. She "comforts the night," as Chapman finely says, and I always found her a companionable creature.

In the ocean-horizon I took untiring delight. It is the true magic-circle of expectation and conjecture, — almost as good as a wishing-ring.   What will rise over that edge we sail towards daily and never overtake?   A sail? an island? the new shore of the Old World?   Something rose every day, which I need not have gone so far to see, but at whose levee I was a much more faithful courtier than on shore.   A cloudless sunrise in mid-ocean is beyond comparison for simple grandeur.   It is like Dante's style, bare and perfect.   Naked sun meets naked sea, the true classic of nature.   There may be more sentiment in morning on shore, — the shivering fairy-jewelry of dew, the silver point-lace of sparkling hoar-frost, — but there is also more complexity, more of the romantic.   The one savors of the elder Edda, the other of the Minnesingers.

> And I thus floating, lonely elf,
> A kind of planet by myself,
> The mists draw up and furl away,
> And in the east a warming gray,
> Faint as the tint of oaken woods
> When o'er their buds May breathes and broods,
> Tells that the golden sunrise-tide
> Is lapsing up earth's thirsty side,
> Each moment purpling on the crest
> Of some stark billow farther west:
> And as the sea-moss droops and hears
> The gurgling flood that nears and nears,
> And then with tremulous content
> Floats out each thankful filament,
> So waited I until it came,
> God's daily miracle, — O shame
> That I had seen so many days
> Unthankful, without wondering praise,
> Not recking more this bliss of earth
> Than the cheap fire that lights my hearth!
> But now glad thoughts and holy pour
> Into my heart, as once a year
> To San Miniato's open door,
> In long procession, chanting clear,
> Through slopes of sun, through shadows hoar,
> The coupled monks slow-climbing sing,
> And like a golden censer swing
> From rear to front, from front to rear
> Their alternating bursts of praise,

Till the roof's fading seraphs gaze
Down through an odorous mist, that crawls
Lingeringly up the darkened walls,
And the dim arches, silent long,
Are startled with triumphant song.

I wrote yesterday that the sea still rimmed our prosy lives
with mystery and conjecture. But one is shut up on shipboard
like Montaigne in his tower, with nothing to do but to review
his own thoughts and contradict himself. *Dire, redire, et me
contredire*, will be the staple of my journal till I see land. I say
nothing of such matters as the *montagna bruna* on which Ulysses
wrecked; but since the sixteenth century could any man reasonably hope to stumble on one of those wonders which were cheap
as dirt in the days of St. Saga? Faustus, Don Juan, and Tann-
häuser are the last ghosts of legend, that lingered almost till the
Gallic cock-crow of universal enlightenment and disillusion.
The Public School had done for Imagination. What shall I see
in Outre-Mer, or on the way thither, but what can be seen with
eyes? To be sure, I stick by the sea-serpent, and would fain believe that science has scotched, not killed him. Nor is he to
be lightly given up, for, like the old Scandinavian snake, he
binds together for us the two hemispheres of Past and Present,
of Belief and Science. He is the link which knits us seaboard
Yankees with our Norse progenitors, interpreting between the
age of the dragon and that of the railroad-train. We have
made ducks and drakes of that large estate of wonder and delight bequeathed to us by ancestral vikings, and this alone remains to us unthrift Heirs of Linn.

I feel an undefined respect for a man who has seen the sea-
serpent. He is to his brother-fishers what the poet is to his
fellow-men. Where they have seen nothing better than a
school of horse-mackerel, or the idle coils of ocean round Half-
way Rock, he has caught authentic glimpses of the withdrawing
mantle-hem of the Edda age. I care not for the monster himself. It is not the thing, but the belief in the thing, that is dear
to me. May it be long before Professor Owen is comforted
with the sight of his unfleshed vertebræ, long before they
stretch many a rood behind Kimball's or Barnum's glass, reflected in the shallow orbs of Mr. and Mrs. Public, which stare,

but see not! I speak of him in the singular number, for I insist on believing that there is but one left, without chance of duplicate. When we read that Captain Spalding, of the pink-stern *Three Pollies*, has beheld him rushing through the brine like an infinite series of bewitched mackerel-casks, we feel that the mystery of old Ocean, at least, has not yet been sounded, — that Faith and Awe survive there unevaporate. I once ventured the horse-mackerel theory to an old fisherman, browner than a tomcod. "Hos-mackril!" he exclaimed indignantly, "hos-mackril be —" (here he used a phrase commonly indicated in laical literature by the same sign which serves for Doctorate in Divinity,) "don't yer spose *I* know a hos-mackril?" The intonation of that "*I*" would have silenced Professor Monkbarns Owen with his provoking *phoca* forever. What if one should ask *him* if he knew a trilobite?

The fault of modern travellers is, that they see nothing out of sight. They talk of eocene periods and tertiary formations, and tell us how the world looked to the plesiosaur. They take science (or nescience) with them, instead of that soul of generous trust their elders had. All their senses are sceptics and doubters, materialists reporting things for other sceptics to doubt still further upon. Nature becomes a reluctant witness upon the stand, badgered with geologist hammers and phials of acid. There have been no travellers since those included in Hakluyt and Purchas, except Martin, perhaps, who saw an inch or two into the invisible at the Western Islands. We have peripatetic lecturers, but no more travellers. Travellers' stories are no longer proverbial. We have picked nearly every apple (wormy or otherwise) from the world's tree of knowledge, and that without an Eve to tempt us. Two or three have hitherto hung luckily beyond reach on a lofty bough shadowing the interior of Africa, but there is a German Doctor at this very moment pelting at them with sticks and stones. It may be only next week, and these too, bitten by geographers and geologists, will be thrown away.

Analysis is carried into everything. Even Deity is subjected to chemic tests. We must have exact knowledge, a cabinet stuck full of facts pressed, dried, or preserved in spirits, instead of the large, vague world our fathers had. With them science was poetry; with us, poetry is science. Our modern Eden is a *hortus siccus*. Tourists defraud rather than enrich us. They have not that sense of æsthetic proportion which characterized the elder traveller. Earth is no longer the fine work of art it was, for nothing is left to the imagination. Job Hortop, arrived at the height of the Bermudas, thinks it full time to indulge us in a merman. Nay, there is a story told by Webster, in his Witchcraft, of a merman with a mitre, who, on being sent back to his watery diocese of finland, made what advances he could toward an episcopal benediction by bowing his head thrice. Doubtless he had been consecrated by St. Antony of Padua. A dumb bishop would be sometimes no unpleasant phenomenon, by the way. Sir John Hawkins is not satisfied with telling us about the merely sensual Canaries, but is generous enough to throw us in a handful of "certain flitting islands" to boot. Henry Hawkes describes the visible Mexican cities, and then is not so frugal but that he can give us a few invisible ones. Thus do these generous ancient mariners make children of us again. Their successors show us an earth effete and in a double sense past bearing, tracing out with the eyes of industrious fleas every wrinkle and crowfoot.

The journals of the elder navigators are prose Odysseys. The geographies of our ancestors were works of fancy and imagination. They read poems where we yawn over items. Their world was a huge wonder-horn, exhaustless as that which Thor strove to drain. Ours would scarce quench the small thirst of a bee. No modern voyager brings back the magical foundation-stones of a *Tempest*. No Marco Polo, traversing the desert beyond the city of Lok, would tell of things able to inspire the mind of Milton with

> "Calling shapes and beckoning shadows dire,
>   And airy tongues that syllable men's names
>   On sands and shores and desert wildernesses."

It was easy enough to believe the story of Dante, when two thirds of even the upper-world were yet untraversed and unmapped. With every step of the recent traveller our inheritance of the wonderful is diminished. Those beautifully pictured notes of the Possible are redeemed at a ruinous discount in the hard and cumbrous coin of the Actual. How are we not defrauded and impoverished? Does California vie with El Dorado? or are Bruce's Abyssinian kings a set-off for Prester John? A bird in the bush is worth two in the hand. And if the philosophers have not even yet been able to agree whether the world has any existence independent of ourselves, how do we not gain a loss in every addition to the catalogue of Vulgar Errors? Where are the fishes which nidificated in trees? Where the monopodes sheltering themselves from the sun beneath their single umbrella-like foot, — umbrella-like in everything but the fatal necessity of being borrowed? Where the Acephali, with whom Herodotus, in a kind of ecstasy, wound up his climax of men with abnormal top-pieces? Where the Roc whose eggs are possibly boulders, needing no far-fetched theory of glacier or iceberg to account for them? Where the tails of the men of Kent? Where the no legs of the bird of paradise? Where the Unicorn, with that single horn of his, sovereign against all manner of poisons? Where that Thessalian spring, which, without cost to the country, convicted and punished perjurers? Where the Amazons of Orellana? Where, in short, the Fountain of Youth? All these, and a thousand other varieties, we have lost, and have got nothing instead of them. And those who have robbed us of them have stolen that which not enriches themselves. It is so much wealth cast into the sea beyond all approach of diving-bells. We owe no thanks to Mr. J. E. Worcester, whose Geography we studied enforcedly at school. Yet even he had his relentings, and in some softer moment vouchsafed us a fine, inspiring print of the Maelstrom, answerable to the twenty-four mile diameter of its suction. Year by year, more and more of the world gets disenchanted. Even the icy privacy of the arctic and antarctic circles is invaded. Our youth are no longer ingenuous, as indeed no ingenuity is demanded of them. Everything is accounted for, everything cut and dried, and the world may be put together as easily as the fragments of a dissected map. The Mysterious bounds nothing now on the North, South, East, or West. We have played Jack Horner with our earth, till there is never a plum left in it.

JOHN RUSKIN

THE TWO BOYHOODS[1]

BORN half-way between the mountains and the sea — that young George of Castelfranco — of the Brave Castle: — Stout George they called him, George of Georges, so goodly a boy he was — Giorgione.

Have you ever thought what a world his eyes opened on — fair, searching eyes of youth? What a world of mighty life, from those mountain roots to the shore; — of loveliest life, when he went down, yet so young, to the marble city — and became himself as a fiery heart to it?

A city of marble, did I say? nay, rather a golden city, paved with emerald. For truly, every pinnacle and turret glanced or glowed, overlaid with gold, or bossed with jasper. Beneath, the unsullied sea drew in deep breathing, to and fro, its eddies of green wave. Deep-hearted, majestic, terrible as the sea, — the men of Venice moved in sway of power and war; pure as her pillars of alabaster, stood her mothers and maidens; from foot to brow, all noble, walked her knights; the low bronzed gleaming of sea-rusted armor shot angrily under their blood-red mantle-folds. Fearless, faithful, patient, impenetrable, implacable, — every word a fate — sate her senate. In hope and honor, lulled by flowing of wave around their isles of sacred sand, each with his name written and the cross graved at his side, lay her dead. A wonderful piece of world. Rather, itself a world. It lay along the face of the waters, no larger, as its captains saw it from their masts at evening, than a bar of sunset that could not pass away; but, for its power, it must have seemed to them as if they were sailing in the expanse of heaven, and this a great planet, whose orient edge widened through ether. A world from which all ignoble care and petty thoughts were banished, with all the common and poor elements of life. No foulness, nor tumult, in those tremulous streets, that filled, or fell, beneath the moon; but rippled music

[1] From *Modern Painters*, Vol. 5 (1860).

of majestic change, or thrilling silence. No weak walls could rise above them; no low-roofed cottage, nor straw-built shed. Only the strength as of rock, and the finished setting of stones most precious. And around them, far as the eye could reach, still the soft moving of stainless waters, proudly pure; as not the flower, so neither the thorn nor the thistle, could grow in the glancing fields. Ethereal strength of Alps, dream-like, vanishing in high procession beyond the Torcellan shore; blue islands of Paduan hills, poised in the golden west. Above, free winds and fiery clouds ranging at their will; — brightness out of the north, and balm from the south, and the stars of the evening and morning clear in the limitless light of arched heaven and circling sea.

Such was Giorgione's school — such Titian's home.

Near the south-west corner of Covent Garden, a square brick pit or well is formed by a close-set block of houses, to the back windows of which it admits a few rays of light. Access to the bottom of it is obtained out of Maiden Lane, through a low archway and an iron gate; and if you stand long enough under the archway to accustom your eyes to the darkness, you may see on the left hand a narrow door, which formerly gave quiet access to a respectable barber's shop, of which the front window, looking into Maiden Lane, is still extant, filled in this year (1860), with a row of bottles, connected, in some defunct manner, with a brewer's business. A more fashionable neighborhood, it is said, eighty years ago than now — never certainly a cheerful one — wherein a boy being born on St. George's day, 1775, began soon after to take interest in the world of Covent Garden, and put to service such spectacles of life as it afforded.

No knights to be seen there, nor, I imagine, many beautiful ladies; their costume at least disadvantageous, depending much on incumbency of hat and feather, and short waists; the majesty of men founded similarly on shoebuckles and wigs; — impressive enough when Reynolds will do his best for it; but not suggestive of much ideal delight to a boy.

"Bello ovile dov' io dormii agnello":[1] of things beautiful, besides men and women, dusty sunbeams up or down the street on summer mornings; deep furrowed cabbage leaves at the

---

[1] "Beautiful sheepfold where as a lamb I slumbered."

greengrocer's; magnificence of oranges in wheelbarrows round the corner; and Thames' shore within three minutes' race.

None of these things very glorious; the best, however, that England, it seems, was then able to provide for a boy of gift: who, such as they are, loves them — never, indeed, forgets them. The short waists modify to the last his visions of Greek ideal. His foregrounds had always a succulent cluster or two of greengrocery at the corners. Enchanted oranges gleam in Covent Gardens of the Hesperides; and great ships go to pieces in order to scatter chests of them on the waves. That mist of early sunbeams in the London dawn crosses, many and many a time, the clearness of Italian air; and by Thames' shore, with its stranded barges and glidings of red sail, dearer to us than Lucerne lake or Venetian lagoon, — by Thames' shore we will die.

With such circumstance round him in youth, let us note what necessary effects followed upon the boy. I assume him to have had Giorgione's sensibility (and more than Giorgione's, if that be possible) to color and form. I tell you farther, and this fact you may receive trustfully, that his sensibility to human affection and distress was no less keen than even his sense for natural beauty — heart-sight deep as eye-sight.

Consequently, he attaches himself with the faithfullest child-love to everything that bears an image of the place he was born in. No matter how ugly it is, — has it anything about it like Maiden Lane, or like Thames' shore? If so, it shall be painted for their sake. Hence, to the very close of life, Turner could endure ugliness which no one else, of the same sensibility, would have borne with for an instant. Dead brick walls, blank square windows, old clothes, market-womanly types of humanity — anything fishy and muddy, like Billings-gate or Hungerford Market, had great attraction for him; black barges, patched sails, and every possible condition of fog.

You will find these tolerations and affections guiding or sustaining him to the last hour of his life; the notablest of all such endurances being that of dirt. No Venetian ever draws anything foul; but Turner devoted picture after picture to the illustration of effects of dinginess, smoke, soot, dust, and dusty texture; old sides of boats, weedy roadside vegetation, dunghills, straw-yards, and all the soilings and stains of every common labor.

And more than this, he not only could endure, but enjoyed and looked for *litter*, like Covent Garden wreck after the market. His pictures are often full of it, from side to side; their foregrounds differ from all others in the natural way that things have of lying about in them. Even his richest vegetation, in ideal work, is confused; and he delights in shingle, débris, and heaps of fallen stones. The last words he ever spoke to me about a picture were in gentle exaltation about his St. Gothard: "that *litter* of stones which I endeavored to represent."

The second great result of this Covent Garden training was, understanding of and regard for the poor, whom the Venetians, we saw, despised; whom, contrarily, Turner loved, and more than loved — understood. He got no romantic sight of them, but an infallible one, as he prowled about the end of his lane, watching night effects in the wintry streets; nor sight of the poor alone, but of the poor in direct relations with the rich. He knew, in good and evil, what both classes thought of, and how they dwelt with, each other.

Reynolds and Gainsborough, bred in country villages, learned there the country boy's reverential theory of "the squire," and kept it. They painted the squire and the squire's lady as centres of the movements of the universe, to the end of their lives. But Turner perceived the younger squire in other aspects about his lane, occurring prominently in its night scenery, as a dark figure, or one of two, against the moonlight. He also the working of city commerce, from endless warehouse, towering over Thames, to the back shop in the lane, with its stale herrings — highly interesting these last; one of his father's best friends, whom he often afterwards visited affectionately at Bristol, being a fishmonger and glueboiler; which gives us a friendly turn of mind towards herring-fishing, whaling, Calais poissardes, and many other of our choicest subjects in after life; all this being connected with that mysterious forest below London Bridge on one side; — and, on the other, with these masses of human power and national wealth which weigh upon us, at Covent Garden here, with strange compression, and crush us into narrow Hand Court.

"That mysterious forest below London Bridge" — better for the boy than wood of pine, or grove of myrtle. How he must have tormented the watermen, beseeching them to let him crouch anywhere in the bows, quiet as a log, so only that he might get floated down there among the ships, and round and round the ships, and with the ships, and by the ships, and under the ships, staring and clambering; — these the only quite beautiful things he can see in all the world, except the sky; but these, when the sun is on their sails, filling or falling, endlessly disordered by sway of tide and stress of anchorage, beautiful unspeakably; which ships also are inhabited by glorious creatures — red-faced sailors, with pipes, appearing over the gunwales, true knights, over their castle parapets — the most angelic beings in the whole compass of London world. And Trafalgar happening long before we can draw ships, we, nevertheless, coax all current stories out of the wounded sailors, do our best at present to show Nelson's funeral streaming up the Thames; and vow that Trafalgar shall have its tribute of memory some day. Which, accordingly, is accomplished — once, with all our might, for its death; twice, with all our might, for its victory; thrice, in pensive farewell to the old Temeraire, and, with it, to that order of things.

Now this fond companying with sailors must have divided his time, it appears to me, pretty equally between Covent Garden and Wapping (allowing for incidental excursions to Chelsea on one side, and Greenwich on the other), which time he would spend pleasantly, but not magnificently, being limited in pocket-money, and leading a kind of "Poor-Jack" life on the river.

In some respects, no life could be better for a lad. But it was not calculated to make his ear fine to the niceties of language, nor form his moralities on an entirely regular standard. Picking up his first scraps of vigorous English chiefly at Deptford and in the markets, and his first ideas of female tenderness and beauty among nymphs of the barge and the barrow, — another boy might, perhaps, have become what people usually term "vulgar." But the original make and frame of Turner's mind being not vulgar, but as nearly as possible a combination of the minds of Keats and Dante, joining capricious waywardness, and intense openness to every fine pleasure of sense, and hot defiance of formal precedent, with a quite infinite tenderness, generosity, and desire of justice and truth — this kind of mind did not become vulgar, but very tolerant of vulgarity, even fond of it in some forms; and, on the outside, visibly infected by it, deeply enough; the curious result, in its combination of elements, being to most people wholly incomprehensible. It was as if a cable had been woven of blood-crimson silk, and then tarred on the outside. People handled it, and the tar came off on their hands; red gleams were seen through the black, underneath, at the places where it had been strained. Was it ochre? — said the world — or red lead?

Schooled thus in manners, literature, and general moral principles at Chelsea and Wapping, we have finally to inquire concerning the most important point of all. We have seen the principal differences between this boy and Giorgione, as respects sight of the beautiful, understanding of poverty, of commerce, and of order of battle; then follows another cause of difference in our training — not slight, — the aspect of religion, namely, in the neighborhood of Covent Garden. I say the aspect; for that was all the lad could judge by. Disposed, for the most part, to learn chiefly by his eyes, in this special matter he finds there is really no other way of learning. His father taught him "to lay one penny upon another." Of mother's teaching, we hear of none; of parish pastoral teaching, the reader may guess how much.

I chose Giorgione rather than Veronese to help me in carrying out this parallel; because I do not find in Giorgione's work any of the early Venetian monachist element. He seems to me to have belonged more to an abstract contemplative school. I may be wrong in this; it is no matter; — suppose it were so, and that he came down to Venice somewhat recusant, or insentient, concerning the usual priestly doctrines of his day, — how would the Venetian religion, from an outer intellectual standing-point, have *looked* to him?

He would have seen it to be a religion indisputably powerful in human affairs; often very harmfully so; sometimes devouring widows' houses, and consuming the strongest and fairest from among the young; freezing into merciless bigotry the policy of the old: also, on the other hand, animating national courage, and raising souls, otherwise sordid, into heroism: on the whole, always a real and great power; served with daily sacrifice of gold, time, and thought; putting forth its claims, if hypocritically, at least in bold hypocrisy, not waiving any atom of them in doubt or fear; and, assuredly, in large measure, sincere, believing in itself, and believed: a goodly system, moreover, in aspect; gorgeous, harmonious, mysterious; — a thing which had either to be obeyed or combated, but could not be scorned. A religion towering over all the city — many buttressed — luminous in marble stateliness, as the dome of our Lady of Safety shines over the sea; many-voiced also, giving, over all the eastern seas, to the sentinel his watchword, to the soldier his war-cry; and, on the lips of all who died for Venice, shaping the whisper of death.

I suppose the boy Turner to have regarded the religion of his city also from an external intellectual standing-point.

What did he see in Maiden Lane?

Let not the reader be offended with me; I am willing to let him describe, at his own pleasure, what Turner saw there; but to me, it seems to have been this. A religion maintained occasionally, even the whole length of the lane, at point of constable's staff; but, at other times, placed under the custody of the beadle, within certain black and unstately iron railings of St. Paul's, Covent Garden. Among the wheelbarrows and over the vegetables, no perceptible dominance of religion; in the narrow, disquieted streets, none; in the tongues, deeds, daily ways of Maiden Lane, little. Some honesty, indeed, and English industry, and kindness of heart, and general idea of justice; but faith, of any national kind, shut up from one Sunday to the next, not artistically beautiful even in those Sabbatical exhibitions; its paraphernalia being chiefly of high pews, heavy elocution, and cold grimness of behavior.

What chiaroscuro belongs to it — (dependent mostly on candlelight), — we will, however, draw, considerately; no goodliness of escutcheon, nor other respectability being omitted, and the best of their results confessed, a meek old woman and a child being let into a pew, for whom the reading by candlelight will be beneficial.[1]

For the rest, this religion seems to him discreditable — discredited — not believing in itself, putting forth its authority in a cowardly way, watching how far it might be tolerated, continually shrinking, disclaiming, fencing, finessing; divided against itself, not by stormy rents, but by thin fissures, and splittings of plaster from the walls. Not to be either obeyed, or combated, by an ignorant, yet clear-sighted youth; only to be scorned. And scorned not one whit the less, though also the dome dedicated to *it* looms high over distant winding of the Thames; as St. Mark's campanile rose, for goodly landmark, over mirage of lagoon. For St. Mark ruled over life; the Saint of London over death; St. Mark over St. Mark's Place, but St. Paul over St. Paul's Churchyard.

Under these influences pass away the first reflective hours of life, with such conclusion as they can reach. In consequence of a fit of illness, he was taken — I cannot ascertain in what year — to live with an aunt, at Brentford; and here, I believe, received some schooling, which he seems to have snatched vigorously; getting knowledge, at least by translation, of the more picturesque classical authors, which he turned presently to use, as we shall see. Hence also, walks about Putney and Twickenham in the summer time acquainted him with the look of English meadow-ground in its restricted states of paddock and park; and with some round-headed appearances of trees, and stately entrances to houses of mark: the avenue at Bushy, and the iron gates and carved pillars of Hampton, impressing him apparently with great awe and admiration; so that in after life his little country house is, — of all places in the world, — at Twickenham! Of swans and reedy shores he now learns the soft motion and the green mystery, in a way not to be forgotten.

And at last fortune wills that the lad's true life shall begin; and one summer's evening, after various wonderful stage-

---

[1] Liber Studiorum. "Interior of a church." It is worthy of remark that Giorgione and Titian are always delighted to have an opportunity of drawing priests. The English church may, perhaps, accept it as matter of congratulation that this is the only instance in which Turner drew a clergyman.

coach experiences on the north road, which gave him a love of stage-coaches ever after, he finds himself sitting alone among the Yorkshire hills.[1] For the first time, the silence of Nature round him, her freedom sealed to him, her glory opened to him. Peace at last; no roll of cart-wheel, nor mutter of sullen voices in the back shop; but curlew-cry in space of heaven, and welling of bell-toned streamlet by its shadowy rock. Freedom at last. Dead-wall, dark railing, fenced field, gated garden, all passed away like the dream of a prisoner; and behold, far as foot or eye can race or range, the moor, and cloud. Loveliness at last. It is here then, among these deserted vales! Not among men. Those pale, poverty-struck, or cruel faces; — that multitudinous, marred humanity — are not the only things that God has made. Here is something He has made which no one has marred. Pride of purple rocks, and river pools of blue, and tender wilderness of glittering trees, and misty lights of evening on immeasurable hills.

Beauty, and freedom, and peace; and yet another teacher, graver than these. Sound preaching at last here, in Kirkstall crypt, concerning fate and life. Here, where the dark pool reflects the chancel pillars, and the cattle lie in unhindered rest, the soft sunshine on their dappled bodies, instead of priests' vestments; their white furry hair ruffled a little, fitfully, by the evening wind, deep-scented from the meadow thyme.

Consider deeply the import to him of this, his first sight of ruin, and compare it with the effect of the architecture that was around Giorgione. There were indeed aged buildings, at Venice, in his time, but none in decay. All ruin was removed, and its place filled as quickly as in our London; but filled always by architecture loftier and more wonderful than that whose place it took, the boy himself happy to work upon the walls of it; so that the idea of the passing away of the strength of men and beauty of their works never could occur to him sternly. Brighter and brighter the cities of Italy had been

[1] I do not mean that this is his first acquaintance with the country, but the first impressive and touching one, after his mind was formed. The earliest sketches I found in the National collection are at Clifton and Bristol; the next, at Oxford.

rising and broadening on hill and plain, for three hundred years. He saw only strength and immortality, could not but paint both; conceived the form of man as deathless, calm with power, and fiery with life.

Turner saw the exact reverse of this. In the present work of men, meanness, aimlessness, unsightliness: thin-walled, lath-divided, narrow-garreted houses of clay; booths of a darksome Vanity Fair, busily base.

But on Whitby Hill, and by Bolton Brook, remained traces of other handiwork. Men who could build had been there; and who also had wrought, not merely for their own days. But to what purpose? Strong faith, and steady hands, and patient souls — can this, then, be all you have left! this the sum of your doing on the earth! — a nest whence the night-owl may whimper to the brook, and a ribbed skeleton of consumed arches, looming above the bleak banks of mist, from its cliff to the sea?

As the strength of men to Giorgione, to Turner their weakness and vileness, were alone visible. They themselves, unworthy or ephemeral; their work, despicable, or decayed. In the Venetian's eyes, all beauty depended on man's presence and pride; in Turner's, on the solitude he had left, and the humiliation he had suffered.

And thus the fate and issue of all his work were determined at once. He must be a painter of the strength of nature, there was no beauty elsewhere than in that; he must paint also the labor and sorrow and passing away of men; this was the great human truth visible to him.

Their labor, their sorrow, and their death. Mark the three. Labor; by sea and land, in field and city, at forge and furnace, helm and plough. No pastoral indolence nor classic pride shall stand between him and the troubling of the world; still less between him and the toil of his country, — blind, tormented, unwearied, marvellous England.

Also their Sorrow; Ruin of all their glorious work, passing away of their thoughts and their honor, mirage of pleasure, FALLACY OF HOPE; gathering of weed on temple step; gaining of wave on deserted strand; weeping of the mother for the children, desolate by her breathless first-born in the streets of the city,[1] desolate by her last sons slain, among the beasts of the field.[2]

And their Death. That old Greek question again; — yet unanswered. The unconquerable spectre still flitting among the forest trees at twilight; rising ribbed out of the sea-sand; — white, a strange Aphrodite, — out of the sea-foam; stretching its gray, cloven wings among the clouds; turning the light of their sunsets into blood. This has to be looked upon, and in a more terrible shape than ever Salvator or Durer saw it. The wreck of one guilty country does not infer the ruin of all countries, and need not cause general terror respecting the laws of the universe. Neither did the orderly and narrow succession of domestic joy and sorrow in a small German community bring the question in its breadth, or in any unresolvable shape, before the mind of Durer. But the English death — the European death of the nineteenth century — was of another range and power; more terrible a thousand-fold in its merely physical grasp and grief; more terrible, incalculably, in its mystery and shame. What were the robber's casual pang, or the rage of the flying skirmish, compared to the work of the axe, and the sword, and the famine, which was done during this man's youth on all the hills and plains of the Christian earth, from Moscow to Gibraltar. He was eighteen years old when Napoleon came down on Arcola. Look on the map of Europe, and count the blood-stains on it, between Arcola and Waterloo.

Not alone those blood-stains on the Alpine snow, and the blue of the Lombard plain. The English death was before his eyes also. No decent, calculable, consoled dying; no passing to rest like that of the aged burghers of Nuremberg town. No gentle processions to churchyards among the fields, the bronze crests bossed deep on the memorial tablets, and the skylark singing above them from among the corn. But the life trampled out in the slime of the street, crushed to dust amidst the roaring of the wheel, tossed countlessly away into howling winter wind along five hundred leagues of rock-fanged shore. Or, worst of all, rotted down to forgotten graves through years of ignorant patience, and vain seeking for help from man, for hope in God — infirm, imperfect yearning, as of motherless

---

[1] "The Tenth Plague of Egypt."   [2] "Rizpah, the Daughter of Aiah."

infants starving at the dawn; oppressed royalties of captive thought, vague ague-fits of bleak, amazed despair.

A goodly landscape this, for the lad to paint, and under a goodly light. Wide enough the light was, and clear; no more Salvator's lurid chasm on jagged horizon, nor Durer's spotted rest of sunny gleam on hedgerow and field; but light over all the world. Full shone now its awful globe, one pallid charnel-house, — a ball strewn bright with human ashes, glaring in poised sway beneath the sun, all blinding-white with death from pole to pole, — death, not of myriads of poor bodies only, but of will, and mercy, and conscience; death, not once inflicted on the flesh, but daily, fastening on the spirit; death, not silent or patient, waiting his appointed hour, but voiceful, venomous; death with the taunting word, and burning grasp, and infixed sting.

"Put ye in the sickle, for the harvest is ripe." The word is spoken in our ears continually to other reapers than the angels — to the busy skeletons that never tire for stooping. When the measure of iniquity is full, and it seems that another day might bring repentance and redemption, — "Put ye in the sickle." When the young life has been wasted all away, and the eyes are just opening upon the tracks of ruin, and faint resolution rising in the heart for nobler things, — "Put ye in the sickle." When the roughest blows of fortune have been borne long and bravely, and the hand is just stretched to grasp its goal, — "Put ye in the sickle." And when there are but a few in the midst of a nation, to save it, or to teach, or to cherish; and all its life is bound up in those few golden ears, — "Put ye in the sickle, pale reapers, and pour hemlock for your feast of harvest home."

This was the sight which opened on the young eyes, this the watchword sounding within the heart of Turner in his youth.

So taught, and prepared for his life's labor, sate the boy at last alone among his fair English hills; and began to paint, with cautious toil, the rocks, and fields, and trickling brooks, and soft, white clouds of heaven.

MATTHEW ARNOLD

MILTON [1]

THE most eloquent voice of our century uttered, shortly before leaving the world, a warning cry against "the Anglo-Saxon contagion." The tendencies and aims, the view of life and the social economy of the ever-multiplying and spreading Anglo-Saxon race, would be found congenial, this prophet feared, by all the prose, all the vulgarity amongst mankind, and would invade and overpower all nations. The true ideal would be lost, a general sterility of mind and heart would set in.

The prophet had in view, no doubt, in the warning thus given, us and our colonies, but the United States still more. There the Anglo-Saxon race is already most numerous, there it increases fastest; there material interests are most absorbing and pursued with most energy; there the ideal, the saving ideal, of a high and rare excellence, seems perhaps to suffer most danger of being obscured and lost. Whatever one may think of the general danger to the world from the Anglo-Saxon contagion, it appears to me difficult to deny that the growing greatness and influence of the United States does bring with it some danger to the ideal of a high and rare excellence. The *average man* is too much a religion there; his performance is unduly magnified, his shortcomings are not duly seen and admitted. A lady in the State of Ohio sent to me only the other day a volume on American authors; the praise given throughout was of such high pitch that in thanking her I could not forbear saying that for only one or two of the authors' names was such a strain of praise admissible, and that we lost all real standard of excellence by praising so uniformly and immoderately. She answered me with charming good temper, that very likely I was quite right, but it was pleasant to her to

[1] From *Essays in Criticism, Second Series* (1888). An address delivered in St. Margaret's Church, Westminster, on the 13th of February, 1888, at the unveiling of a Memorial Window presented by Mr. George W. Childs of Philadelphia.

think that excellence was common and abundant. But excellence is not common and abundant; on the contrary, as the Greek poet long ago said, excellence dwells among rocks hardly accessible, and a man must almost wear his heart out before he can reach her. Whoever talks of excellence as common and abundant, is on the way to lose all right standard of excellence. And when the right standard of excellence is lost, it is not likely that much which is excellent will be produced.

To habituate ourselves, therefore, to approve, as the Bible says, things that are really excellent, is of the highest importance. And some apprehension may justly be caused by a tendency in Americans to take, or, at any rate, attempt to take, profess to take, the average man and his performances too seriously, to over-rate and over-praise what is not really superior.

But we have met here to-day to witness the unveiling of a gift in Milton's honour, and a gift bestowed by an American, Mr. Childs of Philadelphia; whose cordial hospitality so many Englishmen, I myself among the number, have experienced in America. It was only last autumn that Stratford-upon-Avon celebrated the reception of a gift from the same generous donor in honour of Shakespeare. Shakespeare and Milton — he who wishes to keep his standard of excellence high, cannot choose two better objects of regard and honour. And it is an American who has chosen them, and whose beautiful gift in honour of one of them, Milton, with Mr. Whittier's simple and true lines inscribed upon it, is unveiled to-day. Perhaps this gift in honour of Milton, of which I am asked to speak, is, even more than the gift in honour of Shakespeare, one to suggest edifying reflections to us.

Like Mr. Whittier, I treat the gift of Mr. Childs as a gift in honour of Milton, although the window given is in memory of his second wife, Catherine Woodcock, the "late espoused saint" of the famous sonnet, who died in child-bed at the end of the first year of her marriage with Milton, and who lies buried here with her infant. Milton is buried in Cripplegate, but he lived for a good while in this parish of St. Margaret's, Westminster, and here he composed part of *Paradise Lost*, and the whole of *Paradise Regained* and *Samson Agonistes*. When death deprived him of the Catherine whom the new window commemorates, Milton had still some eighteen years to live, and Cromwell, his "chief of men," was yet ruling England. But the Restoration, with its "Sons of Belial," was not far off; and in the meantime Milton's heavy affliction had laid fast hold upon him, his eyesight had failed totally, he was blind. In what remained to him of life he had the consolation of producing the *Paradise Lost* and the *Samson Agonistes*, and such a consolation we may indeed count as no slight one. But the daily life of happiness in common things and in domestic affections — a life of which, to Milton as to Dante, too small a share was given — he seems to have known most, if not only, in his one married year with the wife who is here buried. Her form "vested all in white," as in his sonnet he relates that after her death she appeared to him, her face veiled, but with "love, sweetness, and goodness" shining in her person, — this fair and gentle daughter of the rigid sectarist of Hackney, this lovable companion with whom Milton had rest and happiness one year, is a part of Milton indeed, and in calling up her memory, we call up his.

And in calling up Milton's memory we call up, let me say, a memory upon which, in prospect of the Anglo-Saxon contagion and of its dangers supposed and real, it may be well to lay stress even more than upon Shakespeare's. If to our English race an inadequate sense for perfection of work is a real danger, if the discipline of respect for a high and flawless excellence is peculiarly needed by us, Milton is of all our gifted men the best lesson, the most salutary influence. In the sure and flawless perfection of his rhythm and diction he is as admirable as Virgil or Dante, and in this respect he is unique amongst us. No one else in English literature and art possesses the like distinction.

Thomson, Cowper, Wordsworth, all of them good poets who have studied Milton, followed Milton, adopted his form, fail in their diction and rhythm if we try them by that high standard of excellence maintained by Milton constantly. From style really high and pure Milton never departs; their departures from it are frequent.

Shakespeare is divinely strong, rich, and attractive. But

sureness of perfect style Shakespeare himself does not possess. I have heard a politician express wonder at the treasures of political wisdom in a certain celebrated scene of *Troilus and Cressida*; for my part I am at least equally moved to wonder at the fantastic and false diction in which Shakespeare has in that scene clothed them. Milton, from one end of *Paradise Lost* to the other, is in his diction and rhythm constantly a great artist in the great style. Whatever may be said as to the subject of his poem, as to the conditions under which he received his subject and treated it, that praise, at any rate, is assured to him.

For the rest, justice is not at present done, in my opinion, to Milton's management of the inevitable matter of a Puritan epic, a matter full of difficulties, for a poet. Justice is not done to the *architectonics*, as Goethe would have called them, of *Paradise Lost*; in these, too, the power of Milton's art is remarkable. But this may be a proposition which requires discussion and development for establishing it, and they are impossible on an occasion like the present.

That Milton, of all our English race, is by his diction and rhythm the one artist of the highest rank in the great style whom we have; this I take as requiring no discussion, this I take as certain.

The mighty power of poetry and art is generally admitted. But where the soul of this power, of this power at its best, chiefly resides, very many of us fail to see. It resides chiefly in the refining and elevation wrought in us by the high and rare excellence of the great style. We may feel the effect without being able to give ourselves clear account of its cause, but the thing is so. Now, no race needs the influences mentioned, the influences of refining and elevation, more than ours; and in poetry and art our grand source for them is Milton.

To what does he owe this supreme distinction? To nature first and foremost, to that bent of nature for inequality which to the worshippers of the average man is so unacceptable; to a gift, a divine favour. "The older one grows," says Goethe, "the more one prizes natural gifts, because by no possibility can they be procured and stuck on." Nature formed Milton to be a great poet. But what other poet has shown so sincere a sense of the grandeur of his vocation, and a moral effort so constant and sublime to make and keep himself worthy of it? The Milton of religious and political controversy, and perhaps of domestic life also, is not seldom disfigured by want of amenity, by acerbity. The Milton of poetry, on the other hand, is one of those great men "who are modest" — to quote a fine remark of Leopardi, that gifted and stricken young Italian, who in his sense for poetic style is worthy to be named with Dante and Milton — "who are modest, because they continually compare themselves, not with other men, but with that idea of the perfect which they have before their mind." The Milton of poetry is the man, in his own magnificent phrase, of "devout prayer to that Eternal Spirit that can enrich with all utterance and knowledge, and sends out his Seraphim with the hallowed fire of his altar, to touch and purify the lips of whom he pleases." And finally, the Milton of poetry is, in his own words again, the man of "industrious and select reading." Continually he lived in companionship with high and rare excellence, with the great Hebrew poets and prophets, with the great poets of Greece and Rome. The Hebrew compositions were not in verse, and can be not inadequately represented by the grand, measured prose of our English Bible. The verse of the poets of Greece and Rome no translation can adequately reproduce. Prose cannot have the power of verse; verse-translation may give whatever of charm is in the soul and talent of the translator himself, but never the specific charm of the verse and poet translated. In our race are thousands of readers, presently there will be millions, who know not a word of Greek and Latin, and will never learn those languages. If this host of readers are ever to gain any sense of the power and charm of the great poets of antiquity, their way to gain it is not through translations of the ancients, but through the original poetry of Milton, who has the like power and charm, because he has the like great style.

Through Milton they may gain it, for, in conclusion, Milton is English; this master in the great style of the ancients is English. Virgil, whom Milton loved and honoured, has at the end of the *Æneid* a noble passage, where Juno, seeing the defeat of Turnus and the Italians imminent, the victory of the

Trojan invaders assured, entreats Jupiter that Italy may nevertheless survive and be herself still, may retain her own mind, manners, and language, and not adopt those of the conqueror.

"Sit Latium, sint Albani per secula reges!"[1]

Jupiter grants the prayer; he promises perpetuity and the future to Italy — Italy reinforced by whatever virtue the Trojan race has, but Italy, not Troy. This we may take as a sort of parable suiting ourselves. All the Anglo-Saxon contagion, all the flood of Anglo-Saxon commonness, beats vainly against the great style but cannot shake it, and has to accept its triumph. But it triumphs in Milton, in one of our own race, tongue, faith, and morals. Milton has made the great style no longer an exotic here; he has made it an inmate amongst us, a leaven, and a power. Nevertheless he, and his hearers on both sides of the Atlantic, are English, and will remain English —

"Sermonem Ausonii patrium moresque tenebunt."[2]

The English race overspreads the world, and at the same time the ideal of an excellence the most high and the most rare abides a possession with it for ever.

[1] "Let there be Latium still: let there be centuries of Alban kings." (Conington.)

[2] "The Ausonians shall keep their native tongue, their native customs." (Conington.)

WILLIAM DEAN HOWELLS

TOLSTOY [1]

I COME now, though not quite in the order of time, to the noblest of all these enthusiasms—namely, my devotion for the writings of Lyof Tolstoy. I should wish to speak of him with his own incomparable truth, yet I do not know how to give a notion of his influence without the effect of exaggeration. As much as one merely human being can help another I believe that he has helped me; he has not influenced me in æsthetics only, but in ethics, too, so that I can never again see life in the way I saw it before I knew him. Tolstoy awakens in his reader the will to be a man; not effectively, not spectacularly, but simply, really. He leads you back to the only true ideal, away from that false standard of the gentleman, to the Man who sought not to be distinguished from other men, but identified with them, to that Presence in which the finest gentleman shows his alloy of vanity, and the greatest genius shrinks to the measure of his miserable egotism. I learned from Tolstoy to try character and motive by no other test, and though I am perpetually false to that sublime ideal myself, still the ideal remains with me, to make me ashamed that I am not true to it. Tolstoy gave me heart to hope that the world may yet be made over in the image of Him who died for it, when all Cæsar's things shall be finally rendered unto Cæsar, and men shall come into their own, into the right to labor and the right to enjoy the fruits of their labor, each one master of himself and servant to every other. He taught me to see life not as a chase of a forever impossible personal happiness, but as a field for endeavor towards the happiness of the whole human family; and I can never lose this vision, however I close my eyes, and strive to see my own interest as the highest good. He gave me new criterions, new principles, which, after all, were those that are taught us in our earliest childhood, before we have come to the

---

[1] From *My Literary Passions*. Copyright, 1895, by Harper and Brothers; copyright, 1922, by Mildred Howells and John Mead Howells. By permission.

evil wisdom of the world. As I read his different ethical books, *What to Do, My Confession,* and *My Religion,* I recognized their truth with a rapture such as I have known in no other reading, and I rendered them my allegiance, heart and soul, with whatever sickness of the one and despair of the other. They have it yet, and I believe they will have it while I live. It is with inexpressible astonishment that I hear them attainted of pessimism, as if the teaching of a man whose ideal was simple goodness must mean the prevalence of evil. The way he showed me seemed indeed impossible to my will, but to my conscience it was and is the only possible way. If there is any point on which he has not convinced my reason it is that of our ability to walk this narrow way alone. Even there he is logical, but as Zola subtly distinguishes in speaking of Tolstoy's essay on "Money," he is not reasonable. Solitude enfeebles and palsies, and it is as comrades and brothers that men must save the world from itself, rather than themselves from the world. It was so the earliest Christians, who had all things common, understood the life of Christ, and I believe that the latest will understand it so.

I have spoken first of the ethical works of Tolstoy, because they are of the first importance to me, but I think that his æsthetical works are as perfect. To my thinking they transcend in truth, which is the highest beauty, all other works of fiction that have been written, and I believe that they do this because they obey the law of the author's own life. His conscience is one ethically and one æsthetically; with his will to be true to himself he cannot be false to his knowledge of others. I thought the last word in literary art had been said to me by the novels of Tourguenief, but it seemed like the first, merely, when I began to acquaint myself with the simpler method of Tolstoy. I came to it by accident, and without any manner of preoccupation in *The Cossacks,* one of his early books, which had been on my shelves unread for five or six years. I did not know even Tolstoy's name when I opened it, and it was with a kind of amaze that I read it, and felt word by word, and line by line, the truth of a new art in it.

I do not know how it is that the great Russians have the secret of simplicity. Some say it is because they have not a long literary past and are not conventionalized by the usage of many generations of other writers, but this will hardly account for the brotherly directness of their dealing with human nature; the absence of experience elsewhere characterizes the artist with crudeness, and simplicity is the last effect of knowledge. Tolstoy is, of course, the first of them in this supreme grace. He has not only Tourguenief's transparency of style, unclouded by any mist of the personality which we mistakenly value in style, and which ought no more to be there than the artist's personality should be in a portrait; but he has a method which not only seems without artifice, but is so. I can get at the manner of most writers, and tell what it is, but I should be baffled to tell what Tolstoy's manner is; perhaps he has no manner. This appears to me true of his novels, which, with their vast variety of character and incident, are alike in their single endeavor to get the persons living before you, both in their action and in the peculiarly dramatic interpretation of their emotion and cogitation. There are plenty of novelists to tell you that their characters felt and thought so and so, but you have to take it on trust; Tolstoy alone makes you know how and why it was so with them and not otherwise. If there is anything in him which can be copied or burlesqued it is this ability of his to show men inwardly as well as outwardly; it is the only trait of his which I can put my hand on.

After *The Cossacks* I read *Anna Karenina* with a deepening sense of the author's unrivalled greatness. I thought that I saw through his eyes a human affair of that most sorrowful sort as it must appear to the Infinite Compassion; the book is a sort of revelation of human nature in circumstances that have been so perpetually lied about that we have almost lost the faculty of perceiving the truth concerning an illicit love. When you have once read *Anna Karenina* you know how fatally miserable and essentially unhappy such a love must be. But the character of Karenin himself is quite as important as the intrigue of Anna and Vronsky. It is wonderful how such a man, cold, Philistine and even mean in certain ways, towers into a sublimity unknown (to me, at least), in fiction when he forgives, and yet knows that he cannot forgive with dignity. There is something crucial, and something triumphant, not beyond the power, but hitherto beyond the imagination of men in this effect, which is not solicited, not forced, not in the least romantic, but comes naturally, almost inevitably, from the make of man.

The vast prospects, the far-reaching perspectives of *War and Peace* made it as great a surprise for me in the historical novel as *Anna Karenina* had been in the study of contemporary life; and its people and interests did not seem more remote, since they are of a civilization always as strange and of a humanity always as known.

I read some shorter stories of Tolstoy's before I came to this greatest work of his: I read *Scenes of the Siege of Sebastopol*, which is so much of the same quality as *War and Peace*; and I read *Policoushka* and most of his short stories with a sense of my unity with their people such as I had never felt with the people of other fiction.

His didactic stories, like all stories of the sort, dwindle into allegories; perhaps they do their work the better for this, with the simple intelligences they address; but I think that where Tolstoy becomes impatient of his office of artist, and prefers to be directly a teacher, he robs himself of more than half his strength with those he can move only through the realization of themselves in others. The simple pathos, and the apparent indirectness of such a tale as that of *Policoushka*, the peasant conscript, is of vastly more value to the world at large than all his parables; and *The Death of Ivan Ilyitch*, the Philistine worldling, will turn the hearts of many more from the love of the world than such pale fables of the early Christian life as "Work while ye have the light." A man's gifts are not given him for nothing, and the man who has the great gift of dramatic fiction has no right to cast it away or to let it rust out in disuse.

Terrible as the *Kreutzer Sonata* was, it had a moral effect dramatically which it lost altogether when the author descended to exegesis, and applied to marriage the lesson of one evil marriage. In fine, Tolstoy is certainly not to be held up as infallible. He is very distinctly fallible, but I think his life is not less instructive because in certain things it seems a failure. There was but one life ever lived upon the earth which was without failure, and that was Christ's, whose erring and stumbling follower Tolstoy is. There is no other example, no other ideal, and the chief use of Tolstoy is to enforce this fact in our age, after nineteen centuries of hopeless endeavor to substitute ceremony for character, and the creed for the life. I recognize the truth of this without pretending to have been changed in anything but my point of view of it. What I feel sure is that I can never look at life in the mean and sordid way that I did before I read Tolstoy.

Artistically, he has shown me a greatness that he can never teach me. I am long past the age when I could wish to form myself upon another writer, and I do not think I could now insensibly take on the likeness of another; but his work has been a revelation and a delight to me, such as I am sure I can never know again. I do not believe that in the whole course of my reading, and not even in the early moment of my literary enthusiasms, I have known such utter satisfaction in any writer, and this supreme joy has come to me at a time of life when new friendships, not to say new passions, are rare and reluctant. It is as if the best wine at this high feast where I have sat so long had been kept for the last, and I need not deny a miracle in it in order to attest my skill in judging vintages. In fact, I prefer to believe that my life has been full of miracles, and that the good has always come to me at the right time, so that I could profit most by it. I believe if I had not turned the corner of my fiftieth year, when I first knew Tolstoy, I should not have been able to know him as fully as I did. He has been to me that final consciousness, which he speaks of so wisely in his essay on "Life." I came in it to the knowledge of myself in ways I had not dreamt of before, and began at least to discern my relations to the race, without which we are each nothing. The supreme art in literature had its highest effect in making me set art forever below humanity, and it is with the wish to offer the greatest homage to his heart and mind, which any man can pay another, that I close this record with the name of Lyof Tolstoy.

WALTER PATER

CONCLUSION[1]

Λέγει που Ἡράκλειτος ὅτι πάντα χωρεῖ καὶ οὐδὲν μὲν μένει [2]

To regard all things and principles of things as inconstant
modes or fashions has more and more become the tendency of
modern thought. Let us begin with that which is without —
our physical life. Fix upon it in one of its more exquisite
intervals, the moment, for instance, of delicious recoil from the
flood of water in summer heat. What is the whole physical
life in that moment but a combination of natural elements to
which science gives their names? But these elements, phosphorus and lime and delicate fibres, are present not in the
human body alone: we detect them in places most remote from
it. Our physical life is a perpetual motion of them — the
passage of the blood, the wasting and repairing of the lenses
of the eye, the modification of the tissues of the brain by every
ray of light and sound — processes which science reduces to
simpler and more elementary forces. Like the elements of
which we are composed, the action of these forces extends beyond us; it rusts iron and ripens corn. Far out on every side
of us those elements are broadcast, driven by many forces; and
birth and gesture and death and the springing of violets from
the grave are but a few out of ten thousand resultant combinations. That clear, perpetual outline of face and limb is but an
image of ours, under which we group them — a design in a
web, the actual threads of which pass out beyond it. This at
least of flame-like our life has, that it is but the concurrence,
renewed from moment to moment, of forces parting sooner or
later on their ways.

Or if we begin with the inward world of thought and feeling,
the whirlpool is still more rapid, the flame more eager and
devouring. There it is no longer the gradual darkening of the

[1] From *The Renaissance* (1873); essay dated 1868.

[2] Heracleitus says somewhere that everything flows on and nothing rests.

eye and fading of colour from the wall, — the movement of the shore-side, where the water flows down indeed, though in apparent rest, — but the race of the mid-stream, a drift of momentary acts of sight and passion and thought. At first sight experience seems to bury us under a flood of external objects, pressing upon us with a sharp and importunate reality, calling us out of ourselves in a thousand forms of action. But when reflexion begins to act upon those objects they are dissipated under its influence; the cohesive force seems suspended like a trick of magic; each object is loosed into a group of impressions — colour, odour, texture — in the mind of the observer. And if we continue to dwell in thought on this world, not of objects in the solidity with which language invests them, but of impressions unstable, flickering, inconsistent, which burn and are extinguished with our consciousness of them, it contracts still further; the whole scope of observation is dwarfed to the narrow chamber of the individual mind. Experience, already reduced to a swarm of impressions, is ringed round for each one of us by that thick wall of personality through which no real voice has ever pierced on its way to us, or from us to that which we can only conjecture to be without. Every one of those impressions is the impression of the individual in his isolation, each mind keeping as a solitary prisoner its own dream of a world. Analysis goes a step farther still, and assures us that those impressions of the individual mind to which, for each one of us, experience dwindles down, are in perpetual flight; that each of them is limited by time, and that as time is infinitely divisible, each of them is infinitely divisible also; all that is actual in it being a single moment, gone while we try to apprehend it, of which it may ever be more truly said that it has ceased to be than that it is. To such a tremulous wisp constantly reforming itself on the stream, to a single sharp impression, with a sense in it, a relic more or less fleeting, of such moments gone by, what is real in our life fines itself down. It is with this movement, with the passage and dissolution of impressions, images, sensations, that analysis leaves off — that continual vanishing away, that strange, perpetual weaving and unweaving of ourselves.

Philosophiren, says Novalis, *ist dephlegmatisiren vivificiren.*

The service of philosophy, of speculative culture, towards the human spirit is to rouse, to startle it into sharp and eager observation. Every moment some form grows perfect in hand or face; some tone on the hills or the sea is choicer than the rest; some mood of passion or insight or intellectual excitement is irresistibly real and attractive for us, — for that moment only. Not the fruit of experience, but experience itself, is the end. A counted number of pulses only is given to us of a variegated, dramatic life. How may we see in them all that is to be seen in them by the finest senses? How shall we pass most swiftly from point to point, and be present always at the focus where the greatest number of vital forces unite in their purest energy?

To burn always with this hard, gemlike flame, to maintain this ecstasy, is success in life. In a sense it might even be said that our failure is to form habits: for, after all, habit is relative to a stereotyped world, and meantime it is only the roughness of the eye that makes any two persons, things, situations, seem alike. While all melts under our feet, we may well catch at any exquisite passion, or any contribution to knowledge that seems by a lifted horizon to set the spirit free for a moment, or any stirring of the senses, strange dyes, strange colours, and curious odours, or work of the artist's hands, or the face of one's friend. Not to discriminate every moment some passionate attitude in those about us, and in the brilliancy of their gifts some tragic dividing of forces on their ways, is, on this short day of frost and sun, to sleep before evening. With this sense of the splendour of our experience and of its awful brevity, gathering all we are into one desperate effort to see and touch, we shall hardly have time to make theories about the things we see and touch. What we have to do is to be for ever curiously testing new opinions and courting new impressions, never acquiescing in a facile orthodoxy of Comte, or of Hegel, or of our own. Philosophical theories or ideas, as points of view, instruments of criticism, may help us to gather up what might otherwise pass unregarded by us. "Philosophy is the microscope of thought." The theory or idea or system which requires of us the sacrifice of any part of this experience, in consideration of some interest into which we cannot enter, or some abstract theory we have not identified with ourselves, or what is only conventional, has no real claim upon us.

One of the most beautiful passages in the writings of Rousseau is that in the sixth book of the *Confessions*, where he describes the awakening in him of the literary sense. An undefinable taint of death had always clung about him, and now in early manhood he believed himself smitten by mortal disease. He asked himself how he might make as much as possible of the interval that remained; and he was not biassed by anything in his previous life when he decided that it must be by intellectual excitement, which he found just then in the clear, fresh writings of Voltaire. Well! we are all *condamnés*, as Victor Hugo says: we are all under sentence of death but with a sort of indefinite reprieve — *les hommes sont tous condamnés à mort avec des sursis indéfinis*: we have an interval, and then our place knows us no more. Some spend this interval in listlessness, some in high passions, the wisest, at least among "the children of this world," in art and song. For our one chance lies in expanding that interval, in getting as many pulsations as possible into the given time. Great passions may give us this quickened sense of life, ecstasy and sorrow of love, the various forms of enthusiastic activity, disinterested or otherwise, which come naturally to many of us. Only be sure it is passion — that it does yield you this fruit of a quickened, multiplied consciousness. Of this wisdom, the poetic passion, the desire of beauty, the love of art for art's sake, has most; for art comes to you professing frankly to give nothing but the highest quality to your moments as they pass, and simply for those moments' sake.

WILLIAM HENRY HUDSON

ROMAN CALLEVA [1]

AN afternoon in the late November of 1903. Frost, gales, and
abundant rains have more than half stripped the oaks of their
yellow leaves. But the rain is over now, the sky once more a
pure lucid blue above me — all around me, in fact, since I am
standing high on the top of the ancient stupendous earthwork,
grown over with oak wood and underwood of holly and thorn
and hazel with tangle of ivy and bramble and briar. It is
marvellously still; no sound from the village reaches me; I only
hear the faint rustle of the dead leaves as they fall, and the
robin, for one spied me here and has come to keep me company.
At intervals he spurts out his brilliant little fountain of sound;
and that sudden bright melody and the bright colour of the
sunlit translucent leaves seem like one thing. Nature is still,
and I am still, standing concealed among trees, or moving cautiously through the dead russet bracken. Not that I am expecting to get a glimpse of the badger who has his hermitage in
this solitary place, but I am on forbidden ground, in the heart
of a sacred pheasant preserve, where one must do one's prowl-
ing warily. Hard by, almost within a stone's throw of the
wood-grown earthwork on which I stand, are the ruinous walls
of Roman Calleva — the Silchester which the antiquarians
have been occupied in uncovering these dozen years or longer.
The stone walls, too, like the more ancient earthwork, are
overgrown with trees and brambles and ivy. The trees have
grown upon the wall, sending roots deep down between the
stones, through the crumbling cement; and so fast are they
anchored that never a tree falls but it brings down huge masses
of masonry with it. This slow levelling process has been going
on for centuries, and it was doubtless in this way that the buildings within the walls were pulled down long ages ago. Then the
action of the earth-worms began, and floors and foundations,
with fallen stones and tiles, were gradually buried in the soil,

[1] From *Afoot in England*, 1909. By permission of J. M. Dent and Sons., Ltd.

and what was once a city was a dense thicket of oak and holly and thorn. Finally the wood was cleared, and the city was a walled wheat field — so far as we know, the ground has been cultivated since the days of King John. But the entire history of this green walled space before me — less than twenty centuries in duration — does not seem so very long compared with that of the huge earthen wall I am standing on, which dates back to prehistoric times.

Standing here, knee-deep in the dead ruddy bracken, in the "coloured shade" of the oaks, idly watching the leaves fall fluttering to the ground, thinking in an aimless way of the remains of the two ancient cities before me, the British and the Roman, and of their comparative antiquity, I am struck with the thought that the sweet sensations produced in me by the scene differ in character from the feeling I have had in other solitary places. The peculiar sense of satisfaction, of restfulness, of peace, experienced here is very perfect; but in the wilderness, where man has never been, or has at all events left no trace of his former presence, there is ever a mysterious sense of loneliness, of desolation, underlying our pleasure in nature. Here it seems good to know, or to imagine, that the men I occasionally meet in my solitary rambles, and those I see in the scattered rustic village hard by, are of the same race, and possibly the descendants, of the people who occupied this spot in the remote past — Iberian and Celt, and Roman and Saxon and Dane. If that hard-featured and sour-visaged old gamekeeper, with the cold blue unfriendly eyes, should come upon me here in my hiding-place, and scowl as he is accustomed to do, standing silent before me, gun in hand, to hear my excuses for trespassing in his preserves, I should say (mentally): This man is distinctly English, and his far-off progenitors, somewhere about sixteen hundred years ago, probably assisted at the massacre of the inhabitants of the pleasant little city at my feet. By and by, leaving the ruins, I may meet with other villagers of different features and different colour in hair, skin, and eyes, and of a pleasanter expression; and in them I may see the remote descendants of other older races of men, some who were lords here before the Romans came, and of others before them, even back to Neolithic times.

This, I take it, is a satisfaction, a sweetness and peace to the soul in nature, because it carries with it a sense of the continuity of the human race, its undying vigour, its everlastingness. After all the tempests that have overcome it, through all mutations in such immense stretches of time, how stable it is!

I recall the time when I lived on a vast vacant level green plain, an earth which to the eye, and to the mind which sees .with the eye, appeared illimitable, like the ocean; where the house I was born in was the oldest in the district — a century old, it was said; where the people were the children's children of emigrants from Europe who had conquered and colonized the country, and had enjoyed but half a century of national life. But the people who had possessed the land before these emigrants — what of them? They were but a memory, a tradition, a story told in books and hardly more to us than a fable; perhaps they had dwelt there for long centuries, or for thousands of years; perhaps they had come, a wandering horde, to pass quickly away like a flight of migrating locusts; for no memorial existed, no work of their hands, not the faintest trace of their occupancy.

Walking one day at the side of a ditch, which had been newly cut through a meadow at the end of our plantation, I caught sight of a small black object protruding from the side of the cutting, which turned out to be a fragment of Indian pottery made of coarse clay, very black, and rudely ornamented on one side. On searching further a few more pieces were found. I took them home and preserved them carefully, experiencing a novel and keen sense of pleasure in their possession; for though worthless, they were man's handiwork, the only real evidence I had come upon of that vanished people who had been before us; and it was as if those bits of baked clay, with a pattern incised on them by a man's finger-nail, had in them some magical property which enabled me to realize the past, and to see that vacant plain repeopled with long dead and forgotten men.

Doubtless we all possess the feeling in some degree — the sense of loneliness and desolation and dismay at the thought of an uninhabited world, and of long periods when man was not. Is it not the absence of human life or remains rather than the illimitable wastes of thick-ribbed ice and snow which daunts us at the thought of Arctic and Antarctic regions? Again, in the story of the earth, as told by geology, do we not also experience the same sense of dismay, and the soul shrinking back on itself, when we come in imagination to those deserts desolate in time when the continuity of the race was broken and the world dispeopled? The doctrine of evolution has made us tolerant of the thought of human animals — our progenitors as we must believe — who were of brutish aspect, and whose period on this planet was so long that, compared with it, the historic and prehistoric periods are but as the life of an individual. A quarter of a million years has perhaps elapsed since the beginning of that cold period which, at all events in this part of the earth, killed Palæolithic man; yet how small a part of his racial life even that time would seem if, as some believe, his remains may be traced as far back as the Eocene! But after this rude man of the Quaternary and Tertiary epochs had passed away there is a void, a period which to the imagination seems measureless, when sun and moon and stars looked on a waste and mindless world. When man once more reappears he seems to have been re-created on somewhat different lines.

It is this break in the history of the human race which amazes and daunts us, which "shadows forth the heartless voids and immensities of the universe, *and thus stabs us from behind with the thought of annihilation.*"

Here, in these words of Hermann Melville, we are let all at once into the true meaning of those disquieting and seemingly indefinable emotions so often experienced, even by the most ardent lovers of nature and of solitude, in uninhabited deserts, on great mountains, and on the sea. We find here the origin of that horror of mountains which was so common until recent times. A friend once confessed to me that he was always profoundly unhappy at sea during long voyages, and the reason was that his sustaining belief in a superintending Power and in immortality left him when he was on that waste of waters which have no human associations. The feeling, so intense in his case, is known to most if not all of us; but we feel it faintly as a disquieting element in nature of which we may be but vaguely conscious.

Most travelled Englishmen who have seen much of the world and resided for long or short periods in many widely separated countries would probably agree that there is a vast difference in the feeling of strangeness, or want of harmony with our surroundings, experienced in old and in new countries. It is a compound feeling and some of its elements are the same in both cases; but in one there is a disquieting element which the other is without. Thus, in Southern Europe, Egypt, Syria, and in many countries of Asia, and some portions of Africa, the wanderer from home might experience dissatisfaction and be ill at ease and wish for old familiar sights and sounds; but in a colony like Tasmania, and in any new country where there were no remains of antiquity, no links with the past, the feeling would be very much more poignant, and in some scenes and moods would be like that sense of desolation which assails us at the thought of the heartless voids and immensities of the universe.

He recognizes that he is in a world on which we have but recently entered, and in which our position is not yet assured.

Here, standing on this mound, as on other occasions past counting, I recognize and appreciate the enormous difference which human associations make in the effect produced on us by visible nature. In this silent solitary place, with the walled field which was once Calleva Atrebatum at my feet, I yet have a sense of satisfaction, of security, never felt in a land that had no historic past. The knowledge that my individual life is but a span, a breath; that in a little while I too must wither and mingle like one of those fallen yellow leaves with the mould, does not grieve me. I know it and yet disbelieve it; for am I not here alive, where men have inhabited for thousands of years, feeling what I now feel — their oneness with everlasting nature and the undying human family? The very soil and wet carpet of moss on which their feet were set, the standing trees and leaves, green or yellow, the rain-drops, the air they breathed, the sunshine in their eyes and hearts, was part of them, not a garment, but of their very substance and spirit. Feeling this, death becomes an illusion; and the illusion that the continuous life of the species (its immortality) and the individual life are one and the same is the reality and truth. An illusion, but, as Mill says, deprive us of our illusions and life would be intolerable. Happily we are not easily deprived of them, since they are of the nature of instincts and ineradicable. And this very one which our reason can prove to be the most childish, the absurdest of all, is yet the greatest, the most fruitful of good for the race. To those who have discarded supernatural religion, it may be a religion, or at all events the foundation to build one on. For there is no comfort to the healthy natural man in being told that the good he does will not be interred with his bones, since he does not wish to think, and in fact refuses to think, that his bones will ever be interred. Joy in the "choir invisible" is to him a mere poetic fancy, or at best a rarefied transcendentalism, which fails to sustain him. If altruism, or the religion of humanity, is a living vigorous plant, and as some believe flourishes more with the progress of the centuries, it must, like other "soul-growths," have a deeper, tougher woodier root in our soil.

Central idea —

HENRY JAMES

AN EXCURSION [1]

... THERE seemed ... a general consensus of opinion as to its being a great pity that a stranger in England should miss the Derby day. Every one assured me that this was the great festival of the English people, and the most characteristic of national holidays. So much, since it had to do with horse-flesh, I could readily believe. Had not the newspapers been filled for weeks with recurrent dissertations upon the animals concerned in the ceremony? and was not the event, to the nation at large, only imperceptibly less momentous than the other great question of the day — the fate of empires and the reapportionment of the East? The space allotted to sporting intelligence in a compact, eclectic, "intellectual" journal like the *Pall Mall Gazette*, had seemed to me for some time past a measure of the hold of such questions upon the British mind. These things, however, are very natural in a country in which in "society" you are liable to make the acquaintance of some such syllogism as the following. You are seated at dinner next a foreign lady, who has on her other hand a native gentleman, by whom she is being instructed in the art of getting the right point-of-view for looking at English life. I profit by their conversation, and I learn that this point-of-view is apparently the saddle. "You see, English life," says the gentleman, "is really English country life. It's the country that is the basis of English society. And you see, country life is — well, it's the *hunting*. It's the hunting that is at the bottom of it all." In other words, "the hunting" is the basis of English society. Duly initiated into this interpretation of things, the American observer is prepared for the colossal proportions of the annual pilgrimage to Epsom. This pilgrimage, however, I was as-

---

[1] From *Portraits of Places* (1884), where it appears as the first of "Two Excursions," the second describing an Oxford "Commemoration." Originally published as *Three Excursions* (including the account of a visit to Hatfield House), in *The Galaxy*, September, 1877.

sured, though still well worth taking part in, is by no means so characteristic as in former days. It is now performed in a large measure by rail, and the spectacle on the road has lost its ancient brilliancy. The road has been given up more and more to the populace and the strangers, and has ceased to be graced by the presence of ladies. Nevertheless, as a man and a stranger, I was strongly recommended to take it; for the return from the Derby is still, with all its abatements, a classic spectacle.

I mounted upon a four-horse coach, a charming coach, with a yellow body, and handsome, clean-flanked leaders; placing myself beside the coachman, as I had been told this was the point of vantage. The coach was one of the vehicles of the new fashion — the fashion of public conveyances driven, for the entertainment of themselves and of the public, by gentlemen of leisure. On the Derby day all the coaches that start from the classic head-quarters — the "White Horse," in Piccadilly — and stretch away from London toward a dozen different and well-selected goals, had been dedicated to the Epsom road. The body of the vehicle is empty, as no one thinks of occupying any but one of the thirteen places on the top. On the Derby day, however, a properly laden coach carries a company of hampers and champagne-baskets in its inside places. I must add that on this occasion my companion was by exception a professional whip, who proved an entertaining cicerone. Other companions there were, perched in the twelve places behind me, whose social quality I made less of a point of testing — though in the course of the expedition their various characteristics, under the influence of champagne, expanded so freely as greatly to facilitate the operation. We were a society of exotics — Spaniards, Frenchmen, Germans. There were only two Britons, and these, according to my theory, were Australians — an antipodal bride and groom, on a centripetal wedding-tour.

The drive to Epsom, when you get well out of London, is sufficiently pretty; but the part of it which most took my fancy was a suburban district — the classic neighbourhood of Clapham. The vision of Clapham had been a part of the furniture of my imagination — the vision of its respectable common, its evangelical society, and its goodly brick mansions of the

Georgian era. I now beheld these objects for the first time, and I thought them very charming. This epithet, indeed, scarcely applies to the evangelical society, which naturally, on the morning of the Derby day, and during the desecrating progress of the Epsom revellers, was not much in the foreground. But all around the verdant, if cockneyfied common, are ranged commodious houses of a sober red complexion, from under whose neoclassic pediments you expect to see a mild-faced lady emerge — a lady in a cottage-bonnet and mittens, distributing tracts from a little satchel. It would take an energetic piety, however, to stem the current of heterogeneous vehicles which at about this point takes up its metropolitan affluents and bears them in its rumbling, rattling tide. The concourse of wheeled conveyances of every possible order here becomes dense, and the spectacle from the top of the coach proportionately absorbing. You begin to perceive that the brilliancy of the road has in truth departed, and that well-appointed elegance is not the prevailing characteristic. But when once you have grasped this fact your entertainment is continuous. You perceive that you are "in," as the phrase is, for something vulgar, something colossally, unimaginably, heroically vulgar; all that is necessary is to accept this situation and look out for illustrations. Beside you, before you, behind you, is the mighty London populace, taking its *ébats*. You get for the first time a notion of the London population at large. It has piled itself into carts, into omnibuses, into every possible and impossible species of "trap." A large proportion of it is of course on foot, trudging along the perilous margin of the middle way, in such comfort as may be gathered from fifteen miles' dodging of broken shins. The smaller the vehicle, the more rat-like the animal that drags it, the more numerous and ponderous its human freight; and as every one is nursing in his lap a parcel of provender as big as himself, wrapped in ragged newspapers, it is not surprising that roadside halts are frequent, and that the taverns all the way to Epsom (it is wonderful how many there are) are encompassed by dense groups of dusty pilgrims, indulging liberally in refreshment for man and beast. And when I say man I must by no means be understood to exclude woman. The female contingent on the Derby day is not the least remarkable part of

the London multitude.   Every one is prepared for an "outing,"
but the women are even more brilliantly and resolutely prepared than the men; it is the best possible chance to observe the
various types of the British female of the lower orders.   The
lady in question is usually not ornamental.   She is useful,
robust, prolific, excellently fitted to play the somewhat arduous
part allotted to her in the great scheme of English civilisation.
But she has not those graces which enable her to become easily
and harmoniously festal.   On smaller holidays — or on simple
working-days — in London crowds, I have often thought her
handsome; thought, that is, that she has handsome points, and
that it was not impossible to see how it is that she helps to
make the English race, on the whole, the comeliest in the
world.   But at Epsom she is too stout, too hot, too red, too
thirsty, too boisterous, too strangely accoutred.   And yet I
wish to do her justice; so I must add that if there is something
to which an American cannot refuse a tribute of admiration in
the gross plebeian jollity of the Derby day, it is not evident
why these lusty she-revellers should not get part of the credit
of it.   The striking thing, the interesting thing, both on the
outward drive and on the return, was that the holiday was so
frankly, heartily, good-humouredly taken.   The people that of
all peoples is habitually the most governed by decencies, pro-
prieties, rigidities of conduct, was, for one happy day, unbuttoning its respectable straight-jacket and letting its powerful,
carnal, healthy temperament take the air.   In such a spectacle
there was inevitably much that was unlucky and unprofitable;
these things came uppermost chiefly on the return, when demoralisation was supreme, when the temperament in question
had quite taken what the French call the key of the fields, and
seemed in no mood to come back and give an account of itself.
For the rest, to be dressed with a kind of brutal gaudiness, to be
very thirsty and violently flushed, to laugh perpetually at
everything and at nothing, thoroughly to enjoy, in short, a
momentous occasion — all this is not, in simple persons of the
more susceptible sex, an unpardonable crime.

The course at Epsom is in itself very pretty, and disposed by
nature herself in sympathetic prevision of the sporting passion.
It is something like the crater of a volcano, without the moun-

tain. The outer rim is the course proper; the space within it is
a vast, shallow, grassy concavity in which vehicles are drawn
up and beasts tethered, and in which the greater part of the
multitude — the mountebanks, the betting-men, and the myr-
iad hangers-on of the scene — are congregated. The outer
margin of the uplifted rim in question is occupied by the grand
stand, the small stands, the paddock. The day was exception-
ally beautiful; the charming sky was spotted over with little
idle-looking, loafing, irresponsible clouds; the Epsom Downs
went swelling away as greenly as in a coloured sporting-print,
and the wooded uplands, in the middle distance, looked as innocent and pastoral as if they had never seen a policeman or a
rowdy. The crowd that spread itself over this immense expanse was the richest representation of human life that I have
ever looked upon. One's first fate after arriving, if one is
perched upon a coach, is to see the coach guided, by means best
known to the coachman himself, through the tremendous press
of vehicles and pedestrians, introduced into a precinct roped off
and guarded from intrusion save under payment of a fee, and
then drawn up alongside of the course, as nearly as possible opposite the grand stand and the winning post. Here you have
only to stand up in your place — on tiptoe, it is true, and with
a good deal of stretching — to see the race fairly well. But I
hasten to add that seeing the race is indifferent entertainment.
If I might be Irish on the occasion of a frolic, I would say that
in the first place you do not see it at all, and in the second place
you perceive it to be not much worth the seeing. It may be
very fine in quality, but in quantity it is inappreciable. The
horses and their jockeys first go dandling and cantering along
the course to the starting-point, looking as insubstantial as
sifted sunbeams. Then there is a long wait, during which, of
the sixty thousand people present (my figures are imaginary)
thirty thousand affirm positively that they have started, and
thirty thousand as positively deny it. Then the whole sixty
thousand are suddenly resolved into unanimity by the sight of
a dozen small jockey-heads whizzing along a very distant sky-
line. In a shorter space of time than it takes me to write it, the
whole thing is before you, and for the instant it is anything but
beautiful. A dozen furiously revolving arms — pink, green,

orange, scarlet, white — whacking the flanks of as many straining steeds; a glimpse of this, and the spectacle is over. The spectacle, however, is of course an infinitesimally small part of the purpose of Epsom and the interest of the Derby. The interest is in having money in the affair, and doubtless those most interested do not trouble themselves particularly to watch the race. They learn soon enough whether they are, in the English phrase, to the good or to the bad.

When the Derby stakes had been carried off by a horse of which I confess I am barbarous enough to have forgotten the name, I turned my back to the running, for all the world as if I too were largely "interested," and sought entertainment in looking at the crowd. The crowd was very animated; that is the most succinct description I can give of it. The horses of course had been removed from the vehicles, so that the pedestrians were free to surge against the wheels and even to a certain extent to scale and overrun the carriages. This tendency became most pronounced when, as the mid-period of the day was reached, the process of lunching began to unfold itself and every coach-top to become the scene of a picnic. From this moment, at the Derby, demoralisation begins. I was in a position to observe it, all around me, in the most characteristic forms. The whole affair, as regards the conventional rigidities I spoke of a while since, becomes a real _dégringolade._ The shabbier pedestrians bustle about the vehicles, staring up at the lucky mortals who are perched in a kind of tormentingly near empyrean — a region in which dishes of lobster-salad are passed about and champagne-corks cleave the air like celestial meteors. There are nigger-minstrels and beggars and mountebanks and spangled persons on stilts, and gipsy matrons, as genuine as possible, with glowing Oriental eyes and dropping their _h_'s; these last offer you for sixpence the promise of everything genteel in life except the aspirate. On a coach drawn up beside the one on which I had a place, a party of opulent young men were passing from one stage of exhilaration to another with a punctuality which excited my admiration. They were accompanied by two or three young ladies of the kind that usually shares the choicest pleasures of youthful British opulence — young ladies in whom nothing has been neglected that can make a complexion Titianesque. The whole party had been drinking deep, and one of the young men, a pretty lad of twenty, had in an indiscreet moment staggered down as best he could to the ground. Here his cups proved too many for him, and he collapsed and rolled over. In plain English, he was beastly drunk. It was the scene that followed that arrested my observation. His companions on the top of the coach called down to the people herding under the wheels to pick him up and put him away inside. These people were the grimiest of the rabble, and a couple of men who looked like coal-heavers out of work undertook to handle this hapless youth. But their task was difficult; it was impossible to imagine a young man more drunk. He was a mere bag of liquor — at once too ponderous and too flaccid to be lifted. He lay in a helpless heap under the feet of the crowd — the best intoxicated young man in England. His extemporised chamberlains took him first in one way and then in another; but he was like water in a sieve. The crowd hustled over him; every one wanted to see; he was pulled and shoved and fumbled. The spectacle had a grotesque side, and this it was that seemed to strike the fancy of the young man's comrades. They had not done lunching, so they were unable to bestow upon the incident the whole of that consideration which its high comicality deserved. But they did what they could. They looked down very often, glass in hand, during the half-hour that it went on, and they stinted neither their generous, joyous laughter, nor their appreciative comments. Women are said to have no sense of humour; but the Titianesque young ladies did liberal justice to the pleasantry of the scene. Toward the last, indeed, their attention rather flagged; for even the best joke suffers by reiteration, and when you have seen a stupefied young man, infinitely bedusted, slip out of the embrace of a couple of clumsy paupers for the twentieth time, you may very properly suppose that you have arrived at the farthest limits of the ludicrous.

After the great race had been run I quitted my perch and spent the rest of the afternoon in wandering about that grassy concave I have mentioned. It was amusing and picturesque; it was like a huge Bohemian encampment. Here also a great number of carriages were stationed, freighted in like manner with free-handed youths and young ladies with gilded tresses. These young ladies were almost the only representatives of their sex with pretensions to elegance; they were often pretty and always exhilarated. Gentlemen in pairs, mounted on stools, habited in fantastic sporting garments, and offering bets to whomsoever listed, were a conspicuous feature of the scene. It was equally striking that they were not preaching in the desert and that they found plenty of patrons among the baser sort. I returned to my place in time to assist at the rather complicated operation of starting for the drive back to London. Putting in horses and getting vehicles into line seemed in the midst of the general crush and entanglement a process not to be facilitated even by the most liberal swearing on the part of those engaged in it. But little by little we came to the end of it; and as by this time a kind of mellow cheerfulness pervaded the upper atmosphere — the region of the perpendicular whip — even those interruptions most trying to patience were somehow made to minister to jollity. It was for people below to not get trampled to death or crunched between opposing wheel-hubs, if they could manage it. Above, the carnival of "chaff" had set in, and it deepened as the lock of vehicles grew denser. As they were all locked together (with a comfortable padding of pedestrians at points of acutest contact), they contrived somehow to move together; so that we gradually got away and into the road. The four or five hours consumed on the road were simply as I say, a carnival of "chaff," the profusely good-humoured savour of which, on the whole, was certainly striking. The chaff was not brilliant nor subtle nor especially graceful; and here and there it was quite too tipsy to be even articulate. But as an expression of that unbuttoning of the popular straight-jacket of which I spoke awhile since, it had its wholesome and even innocent side. It took, indeed, frequently an importunate physical form; it sought emphasis in the use of pea-shooters and water-squirts. At its best, too, it was extremely low and rowdyish. But a stranger even of the most refined tastes might be glad to have a glimpse of this popular revel, for it would make him feel that he was learning something more about the English people. It would give a meaning to the old words "merry England." It would remind him that the natives of that country are subject to some of the most frolicsome of the human passions, and that the decent, dusky vistas of the London residential streets — those discreet creations of which Thackeray's "Baker Street" is the type — are not a complete symbol of the complicated race that erected them.

ROBERT LOUIS STEVENSON

PAN'S PIPES[1]

THE world in which we live has been variously said and sung by the most ingenious poets and philosophers: these reducing it to formulæ and chemical ingredients, those striking the lyre in high-sounding measures for the handiwork of God.   What experience supplies is of a mingled tissue, and the choosing mind has much to reject before it can get together the materials of a theory.   Dew and thunder, destroying Attila and the Spring lambkins, belong to an order of contrasts which no repetition can assimilate.   There is an uncouth, outlandish strain throughout the web of the world, as from a vexatious planet in the house of life.   Things are not congruous and wear strange disguises: the consummate flower is fostered out of dung, and after nourishing itself awhile with heaven's delicate distillations, decays again into indistinguishable soil; and with Cæsar's ashes, Hamlet tells us, the urchins make dirt pies and filthily besmear their countenance.   Nay, the kindly shine of summer, when tracked home with the scientific spyglass, is found to issue from the most portentous nightmare of the universe — the great, conflagrant sun: a world of hell's squibs, tumultuary, roaring aloud, inimical to life.   The sun itself is enough to disgust a human being of the scene which he inhabits; and you would not fancy there was a green or habitable spot in a universe thus awfully lighted up.   And yet it is by the blaze of such a conflagration, to which the fire of Rome was but a spark, that we do all our fiddling, and hold domestic tea-parties at the arbour door.

The Greeks figured Pan, the god of Nature, now terribly stamping his foot, so that armies were dispersed; now by the woodside on a summer noon trolling on his pipe until he charmed the hearts of upland ploughmen.   And the Greeks, in so figuring, uttered the last word of human experience.   To cer-

---

[1] From *Virginibus Puerisque* (1881).   Originally published in *London Magazine*, May 4, 1878.

tain smoke-dried spirits, matter and motion and elastic æthers, and the hypothesis of this or that other spectacled professor, tell a speaking story; but for youth and all ductile and congenial minds, Pan is not dead, but of all the classic hierarchy alone survives in triumph; goat-footed, with a gleeful and an angry look, the type of the shaggy world: and in every wood, if you go with a spirit properly prepared, you shall hear the note of his pipe.

For it is a shaggy world, and yet studded with gardens; where the salt and tumbling sea receives clear rivers running from among reeds and lilies; fruitful and austere; a rustic world; sunshiny, lewd, and cruel. What is it the birds sing among the trees in pairing-time? What means the sound of the rain falling far and wide upon the leafy forest? To what tune does the fisherman whistle, as he hauls in his net at morning, and the bright fish are heaped inside the boat? These are all airs upon Pan's pipe; he it was who gave them breath in the exultation of his heart, and gleefully modulated their outflow with his lips and fingers. The coarse mirth of herdsmen, shaking the dells with laughter and striking out high echoes from the rock; the tune of moving feet in the lamplit city, or on the smooth ball-room floor; the hooves of many horses, beating the wide pastures in alarm; the song of hurrying rivers; the colour of clear skies; and smiles and the live touch of hands; and the voice of things, and their significant look, and the renovating influence they breathe forth — these are his joyful measures, to which the whole earth treads in choral harmony. To this music the young lambs bound as to a tabor, and the London shop-girl skips rudely in the dance. For it puts a spirit of gladness in all hearts; and to look on the happy side of nature is common, in their hours, to all created things. Some are vocal under a good influence, are pleasing whenever they are pleased, and hand on their happiness to others, as a child who, looking upon lovely things, looks lovely. Some leap to the strains with unapt foot, and make a halting figure in the universal dance. And some, like sour spectators at the play, receive the music into their hearts with an unmoved countenance, and walk like strangers through the general rejoicing. But let him feign never so carefully, there is not a man but has his pulses shaken when Pan trolls out a stave of ecstasy and sets the world a-singing.

Alas, if that were all! But oftentimes the air is changed; and in the screech of the night wind, chasing navies, subverting the tall ships and the rooted cedar of the hills; in the random deadly levin or the fury of headlong floods, we recognize the "dread foundation" of life and the anger in Pan's heart. Earth wages open war against her children, and under her softest touch hides treacherous claws. The cool waters invite us in to drown; the domestic hearth burns up in the hour of sleep, and makes an end of all. Everything is good or bad, helpful or deadly; not in itself, but by its circumstances. For a few bright days in England the hurricane must break forth and the North Sea pay a toll of populous ships. And when the universal music has led lovers into the paths of dalliance, confident of Nature's sympathy, suddenly the air shifts into a minor, and death makes a clutch from his ambuscade below the bed of marriage. For death is given in a kiss; the dearest kindnesses are fatal; and into this life, where one thing preys upon another, the child too often makes its entrance from the mother's corpse. It is no wonder, with so traitorous a scheme of things, if the wise people who created for us the idea of Pan thought that of all fears the fear of him was the most terrible, since it embraces all. And still we preserve the phrase: a panic terror. To reckon dangers too curiously, to hearken too intently for the threat that runs through all the winning music of the world, to hold back the hand from the rose because of the thorn, and from life because of death: this it is to be afraid of Pan. Highly respectable citizens who flee life's pleasures and responsibilities and keep, with upright hat, upon the midway of custom, avoiding the right hand and the left, the ecstasies and the agonies, how surprised they would be if they could hear their attitude mythologically expressed, and knew themselves as tooth-chattering ones, who flee from Nature because they fear the hand of Nature's God! Shrilly sound Pan's pipes; and behold the banker instantly concealed in the bank parlour! For to distrust one's impulses is to be recreant to Pan.

There are moments when the mind refuses to be satisfied with evolution, and demands a ruddier presentation of the sum of man's experience. Sometimes the mood is brought about by laughter at the humorous side of life, as when, abstracting ourselves from earth, we imagine people plodding on foot, or seated in ships and speedy trains, with the planet all the while whirling in the opposite direction, so that, for all their hurry, they travel back-foremost through the universe of space. Sometimes it comes by the spirit of delight, and sometimes by the spirit of terror. At least, there will always be hours when we refuse to be put off by the feint of explanation, nicknamed science; and demand instead some palpitating image of our estate, that shall represent the troubled and uncertain element in which we dwell, and satisfy reason by the means of art. Science writes of the world as if with the cold finger of a starfish; it is all true; but what is it when compared to the reality of which it discourses? where hearts beat high in April, and death strikes, and hills totter in the earthquake, and there is a glamour over all the objects of sight, and a thrill in all noises for the ear, and Romance herself has made her dwelling among men? So we come back to the old myth, and hear the goat-footed piper making the music which is itself the charm and terror of things; and when a glen invites our visiting footsteps, fancy that Pan leads us thither with a gracious tremolo; or when our hearts quail at the thunder of the cataract, tell ourselves that he has stamped his hoof in the nigh thicket.

EDMUND GOSSE

A VISIT TO WHITTIER [1]

WHEN I was in Boston in 1884, my brilliant and hospitable friend Mr. W. D. Howells received a letter from the poet Whittier, expressing a most kind wish that I should visit him. It would have been a great satisfaction to me to have seen him in summer, and in his own beautiful home at Amesbury, where he settled in 1836, and where he resided until his death in 1892, although at the moment of his demise he happened to be visiting a friend at Horton Falls. It would have been delightful to carry away an impression of that noble, calm figure in the midst of its household gods. But, if I remember rightly, the mansion at Amesbury was at that time being altered in some way; at all events, Mr. Whittier was staying with female relations at a house, called Oak Knoll, near the town of Danvers. It was, moreover, in the depth of the hard New England winter; all the landscape was choked with snow. Certainly, the visitor's attention would be the more exclusively concentrated on the appearance and conversation of his celebrated host. Accordingly, an appointment was made, and on December 6 I set forth on quite an arctic expedition to discover the author of "Snow Bound."

I have a superstition that all very agreeable adventures begin with a slight mishap. I was not prepared to believe Mr. Whittier so difficult to reach as I found him. We arrived early at the dismal railway station of Danvers, and a hack was persuaded to drive us to the entrance of Oak Knoll. All this Massachusetts landscape, doubtless enchanting at other times of the year, is of a most forbidding bleakness in midwinter. The carriage deposited us and drove off, leaving us to struggle up to the homestead, and we arrived with relief under the great pillars of an ample piazza. Perhaps, in leafy seasons, Oak Knoll may have its charms, but it was distinctly sinister that December morning.

[1] From *Portraits and Sketches* (1912). By permission of the publishers, William Heinemann, Limited, and Charles Scribner's Sons.

We rang, and after a long pause the front door opened slightly, and a very unprepossessing dog emerged, and shut the door (if I may say so) behind him. We were face to face with this animal, which presented none of the features identified in one's mind with the idea of Mr. Whittier. It sniffed unpleasantly, but we spoke to it most blandly, and it became assured that we were not tramps. The dog sat down and looked at us; we had nowhere to sit down, but we looked at the dog. Then, after many blandishments, but feeling very uncomfortable, I ventured to hold the dog in conversation, while I rang again. After another pause, the door was very slightly opened, and a voice of no agreeable timbre asked what we wanted. We explained, across the dog, that we had come by appointment to see Mr. Whittier. The door was closed a second time, and, if our carriage had still been waiting, we should certainly have driven back to Danvers. But at length a hard-featured woman grudgingly admitted us, and showed us, growling as she did it, into a parlour.

Our troubles were then over, for Mr. Whittier himself appeared, with all that report had ever told of gentle sweetness and dignified, cordial courtesy. He was then seventy-seven years old, and, although he spoke of age and feebleness, he showed few signs of either; he was, in fact, to live eight years more. Perhaps because the room was low, he seemed surprisingly tall; he must, in fact, have been a little less than six feet high. The peculiarity of his face rested in the extraordinarily large and luminous black eyes, set in black eyebrows, and fringed with thick black eyelashes curiously curved inwards. This bar of vivid black across the countenance was startlingly contrasted with the bushy snow-white beard and hair, offering a sort of contradiction which was surprising and presently pleasing. He was careful to keep on my right side, I noticed, being presumably deaf in the right ear; even if this were the case, which he concealed, his hearing continued to be markedly quick in a man of his years.

His generosity to those much younger and less gifted than himself is well known, and I shall not dwell on the good-natured things which he proceeded to say to his English visitor. He made no profession at any time of being a critic, and his formula was that such and such verse or prose had given him pleasure — "I am grateful to thee for all that enjoyment," was his charming way of being kind. But I will mention what he said about one book, the "Life of Gray," because I do not remember that Gray is mentioned in any of the published works of Whittier. He said that he had delighted in that narrative of a life so quiet and so sequestered that, as he put it, it was almost more "Quakerly" than that of any famous member of the Society; and he added that he had been greatly moved by the fullness and the significance of a career which to the outside world might have seemed absolutely without movement. "Thee were very fortunate," he went on, "to have that beautiful, restful story left to tell after almost all the histories of great men had been made so fully known to readers."

He asked me what and whom I had seen. Had I yet visited Concord? I responded that I was immediately about to do so, and then he said quickly, "Ah! thee should have come a little sooner, when we were still united. There were four of us a little while ago, but two are gone, and what is Concord without Emerson?" He spoke with great emotion of Emerson — "the noblest human being I have known" — and of Longfellow — "perhaps the sweetest. But you will see Holmes," he added. I replied it was my great privilege to be seeing Dr. Holmes every day, and that the night before he had sent all sorts of affectionate messages by me to Mr. Whittier. The latter expressed great curiosity to see Holmes's short "Life of Emerson," which, in fact, was published five or six days later. With reminiscences of the past, and especially of the great group of the poets his contemporaries, my venerable host kept me long entertained.

He presently said that he would leave me that he might search for a portrait of himself, which he was so kind as to offer to me as a memorial of my visit. I proposed to take my leave, but he insisted that I must not go; he was absent about twenty minutes, resting, as I gathered, from the exertion of speaking, which had caused a noticeable hoarseness. He returned, entirely refreshed, and was once more delightfully communicative. I know not how he was induced to go back to the early anti-slavery days, but this subject having been started, he pursued it with the greatest vivacity. I was left with the impression that on his sedentary and noiseless existence the troubles of 1835 had left an indelible impression — that these formed, indeed, the most exciting pivot for his reminiscences. He told the story of the Concord riots eagerly and merrily, no doubt in almost the same words as he had often told it before. His eyes flashed, he slapped his knees, he may almost be said to have gesticulated, and there was something less than Quakerly quietism in his gusto at the exciting incidents of the narrative. He told how he was met in the street of Concord by the rioters, who were looking for George Thompson, the abolitionist lecturer. Thompson was a man of about his own age, and the mob, supposing Whittier to be he, pelted the poet with rotten eggs and, worse than that, with stones. Their aim was bad, for they scarcely touched Whittier with the more serious missiles, which rattled instead on the wooden fence behind him. He said it made him feel like the Apostle Paul. Another abolitionist, a Mr. Kent, at this moment providentially opened his street-door, and Whittier was pulled in out of the angry crowd. I forget exactly what happened next, but there was a great deal of shouting and firing, and in the process of time George Thompson seems to have joined the other anti-slavery men in their refuge. At all events, Mr. Whittier described, with immense animation and spirit, how it became necessary at length to make a dash, and how Thompson and he were brought in a carriage to a side-door, and the horse suddenly whipped through the unexpectant crowds out of the town and far away before any one thought of pursuing them. At this final recital the old gentleman could remain seated no longer, but started from his chair and fought his battle o'er again. No doubt it was all recorded history, and could be reconstructed with closer accuracy from the books, but it was a delightful and quite sufficing experience to hear it thus told by the most distinguished person engaged, after an interim of nearly fifty years.

If it is not too trifling, I must mention, in connection with his magnificent, lustrous eyes, that, the conversation turning upon the hues of things, Mr. Whittier greatly surprised me by confessing that he was quite colour-blind. He exemplified his

condition by saying that if I came to Amesbury I should be
scandalised by one of his carpets.   It appeared that he was
never permitted by the guardian goddesses of his hearth to
go "shopping" for himself, but that once, being in Boston, and
remembering that he needed a carpet, he had ventured to go to
a store and buy what he thought to be a very nice, quiet article, precisely suited to adorn a Quaker home.   When it arrived
at Amesbury there was a universal shout of horror, for what
had struck Mr. Whittier as a particularly soft combination of
browns and greys proved to normal eyes to be a loud pattern
of bright red roses on a field of the crudest cabbage-green.
When he had told me this, it was then easy to observe that the
fullness and brilliancy of his wonderful eyes had something
which was not entirely normal about them.

He struck me as very gay and cheerful, in spite of his occasional references to the passage of time and the vanishing of
beloved faces.   He even laughed, frequently and with a childlike suddenness, but without a sound.   His face had none of
the immobility so frequent with very aged persons; on the
contrary, waves of mood were always sparkling across his features and leaving nothing stationary there except the narrow,
high, and strangely receding forehead.   His language, very
fluid and easy, had an agreeable touch of the soil, an occasional
rustic note in its elegant colloquialism, that seemed very pleasant and appropriate, as if it linked him naturally with the long
line of sturdy ancestors of whom he was the final blossoming.
In connection with his poetry, I think it would be difficult to
form in the imagination a figure more appropriate to Whittier's
writings than Whittier himself proved to be in the flesh.

Two days later I received from Mr. Whittier a very kind
letter and the gift of his latest volume of poems, "The Bay of
Seven Islands."   It was far from being his last, for it was to be
followed by two more in his lifetime and by a gleaning of posthumous verses.   But it was the book of an old man, and in
reading it one was reminded that fifty-three years had passed
since "Legends of New England" had first given the name of
Whittier to the lovers of poetry.   In saying that "The Bay of
Seven Islands" is an old man's book, however, I do not mean
that it shows marks of senile failure, but only that the eye of

the writer is constantly on the past, counting the sheaves, watching the red colour in the western sky. In verses not less sincere because they are a little rough, he offers his own apologia. He desires, he says, that it shall be said of him when he is gone:

> *Hater of din and riot*
> *He lived in days unquiet;*
> *And, lover of all beauty,*
> *Trod the hard ways of duty.*
>
> *To all who dumbly suffered,*
> *His tongue and pen he offered;*
> *His life was not his own,*
> *Nor lived for self alone.*

This we can clearly assert must always be said of Whittier. But what will impartial criticism, which is deaf to all the virtues if their expression be not enshrined and kept fresh in really fine literature, decide about the poetry of this good and graceful man?

Mr. Whittier was composing verses all his life, and the difference of quality between those he wrote at twenty and at eighty is remarkably small. He was a poet in the lifetime of Gifford and Crabbe, and he was still a poet when Mr. Rudyard Kipling was already famous. During this vast period of time his style changed very little; it had its ups and downs, its laxities and then its felicities, but it bore very little relation to passing conditions. There rose up beside it Tennyson and Browning, Rossetti and Swinburne, but none of these affected Whittier. His genius, or talent, or knack — whichever we choose to call it — was an absolutely local and native thing. It was like the Indian waters of strange name of which it sang, Winnepesaukee and Merrimac and Katahdin; it streamed forth, untouched by Europe, from among the butternuts and maples of the hard New England landscape. The art in Whittier's verse was primitive. Those who love his poetry most will wish that he had possessed a better ear, that he could have felt that "mateless" does not rhyme with "greatness." In all his books there is a tendency to excess, to redundancy; he babbles on, even when he has nothing very inspired to say.

But when all this is acknowledged, none but a very hasty reader will fail to recognise Whittier's lasting place in the history of literature. He is not rich, nor sonorous, nor a splendid artist; he is even rather rarely exquisite, but he has an individuality of his own that is of durable importance. He is filled with moral enthusiasm, as a trumpet is filled with the breath of him who blows it. His Quaker quietism concentrates itself till it breaks in a real passion-storm of humanity, and when Whittier is roused he sings with the thrilling sweetness of a wood-thrush. By dint of simplicity and earnestness, he frequently hits upon the most charming phrases, instinct with life and truth; so that the English poet with whom it seems most natural to compare him in the lyrical order is the epic and didactic Crabbe. If the author of "The Borough" had been dowered with the gift of writing in octosyllabics and short stanzaic measures, and had been born of stern Puritan stock in Massachusetts, and had been roused by the sight of a public iniquity, such as slavery, recognised and applauded in society, he might have presented to the world a talent very much resembling that of Whittier. But, as it is, we look around in vain for an English or American poet of anything like the same merit who shares the place of Whittier.

The grave of the admirable Quaker poet at Amesbury is hemmed in by a hedge of vigorous arbor vitæ. His memory in like manner, depends for its protection, not on the praise of exotic communities which can never, though they admire, rightly comprehend it, but on the conscience of New England, shy, tenacious, intrepid, to which, more than any other poet has done, Whittier made a direct and constant appeal.

ALICE MEYNELL

PRUE [1]

THROUGH the long history of human relations, which is the history of the life of our race, there sounds at intervals the clamour of a single voice which has not the tone of oratory, but asks, answers, interrupts itself, interrupts — what else? Whatever else it interrupts is silence; there are pauses, but no answers. There is the jest without the laugh, and again the laugh without the jest. And this is because the letters written by Madame de Sévigné were all saved, and not many written to her; because Swift burnt the letters that were the dearest things in life to him, while "MD" both made a treasury of his; and because Prue kept all the letters which Steele wrote to her from their marriage-day onwards, and Steele kept none of hers.

In Swift's case the silence is full of echoes; that is to say, his letters repeat the phrases of Stella's and Dingley's, to play with them, flout them, and toss them back against the two silenced voices. He never lets the word of these two women fall to the ground; and when they have but blundered with it, and aimed it wide, and sent it weakly, he will catch it, and play you twenty delicate and expert juggling pranks with it as he sends it back into their innocent faces. So we have something of MD's letters in the "Journal," and this in the only form in which we desire them, to tell the truth; for when Swift gravely saves us some specimens of Stella's wit, after her death, as she spoke them, and not as he mimicked them, they make a sorry show.

In many correspondences, where one voice remains and the other is gone, the retort is enough for two. It is as when, the other day, the half of a pretty quarrel between nurse and child came down from an upper floor to the ears of a mother who decided that she need not interfere. The voice of the undaunted child it was that was audible alone, and it replied,

[1] From *Essays* (1914). By permission of Mr. Wilfrid Meynell.

"I'm not; *you* are;" and anon, "I'll tell *yours*." Nothing was
really missing there.

But Steele's letters to Prue, his wife, are no such simple
matter. The turn we shall give them depends upon the un-
heard tone whereto they reply. And there is room for conjecture. It has pleased the more modern of the many spirits
of banter to supply Prue's eternal silence with the voice of a
scold. It is painful to me to complain of Thackeray; but see
what a figure he makes of Prue in "Esmond." It is, says the
nineteenth-century humourist, in defence against the pursuit
of a jealous, exacting, neglected, or evaded wife that poor Dick
Steele sends those little notes of excuse: "Dearest Being on
earth, pardon me if you do not see me till eleven o'clock, having met a schoolfellow from India"; "My dear, dear wife, I
write to let you know I do not come home to dinner, being
obliged to attend some business abroad, of which I shall give
you an account (when I see you in the evening), as becomes
your dutiful and obedient husband"; "Dear Prue, I cannot
come home to dinner. I languish for your welfare"; "I stay
here in order to get Tonson to discount a bill for me, and shall
dine with him to that end"; and so forth. Once only does
Steele really afford the recent humourist the suggestion that is
apparently always so welcome. It is when he writes that he is
invited to supper to Mr. Boyle's, and adds: "Dear Prue, do not
send after me, for I shall be ridiculous." But even this is to
be read not ungracefully by a well-graced reader. Prue was
young and unused to the world. Her husband, by the way,
had been already married; and his greater age makes his constant deference all the more charming.

But with this one exception, Steele's little notes, kept by
his wife while she lived, and treasured after her death by her
daughter and his, are no record of the watchings and dodgings
of a London farce. It is worth while to remember that Steele's
dinner, which it was so often difficult to eat at home, was a
thing of midday, and therefore of mid-business. But that is
a detail. What is desirable is that a reasonable degree of
sweetness should be attributed to Prue; for it was no more
than just. To her Steele wrote in a dedication: "How often
has your tenderness removed pain from my aching head, how

often anguish from my afflicted heart. If there are such beings as guardian angels, they are thus employed. I cannot believe one of them to be more good in inclination, or more charming in form, than my wife."

True, this was for the public; but not so were these daily notes; and these carry to her his assurance that she is "the beautifullest object in the world. I know no happiness in this life in any degree comparable to the pleasure I have in your person and society." "But indeed, though you have every perfection, you have an extravagant fault, which almost frustrates the good in you to me; and that is, that you do not love to dress, to appear, to shine out, even at my request, and to make me proud of you, or rather to indulge the pride I have that you are mine." The correction of the phrase is finely considerate.

Prue cannot have been a dull wife, for this last compliment is a reply, full of polite alacrity, to a letter from her asking for a little flattery. How assiduously, and with what a civilized absence of uncouthness, of shamefacedness, and of slang of the mind, with what simplicity, alertness, and finish, does he step out at her invitation, and perform! She wanted a compliment, though they had been long married then, and he immediately turned it. This was no dowdy Prue.

Her request, by the way, which he repeats in obeying it, is one of the few instances of the other side of the correspondence — one of the few direct echoes of that one of the two voices which is silent.

The ceremony of the letters and the deferent method of address and signature are never dropped in this most intimate of letter-writing. It is not a little depressing to think that in this very form and state is supposed, by the modern reader, to lurk the stealthiness of the husband of farce, the "rogue." One does not like the word. Is it not clownish to apply it with intention to the husband of Prue? He did not pay, he was always in difficulties, he hid from bailiffs, he did many other things that tarnish honour, more or less, and things for which he had to beg Prue's special pardon; but yet he is not a fit subject for the unhandsome incredulity which is proud to be always at hand with an ironic commentary on such letters as his.

I have no wish to bowdlerize Sir Richard Steele, his ways and words. He wrote to Prue at night when the burgundy had been too much for him, and in the morning after. He announces that he is coming to her "within a pint of wine." One of his gayest letters — a love-letter before the marriage, addressed to "dear lovely Mrs. Scurlock" — confesses candidly that he had been pledging her too well: "I have been in very good company, where your health, under the character of the woman I loved best, has been often drunk; so that I may say that I am dead drunk for your sake, which is more than *I die for you.*"

Steele obviously drank burgundy wildly, as did his "good company"; as did also the admirable Addison, who was so solitary in character and so serene in temperament. But no one has, for this fault, the right to put a railing accusation into the mouth of Prue. Every woman has a right to her own silence, whether her silence be hers of set purpose or by accident. And every creature has a right to security from the banterings peculiar to the humourists of a succeeding age. To every century its own ironies, to every century its own vulgarities. In Steele's time they had theirs. They might have rallied Prue more coarsely, but it would have been with a different rallying. Writers of the nineteenth century went about to rob her of her grace.

She kept some four hundred of these little letters of her lord's. It was a loyal keeping. But what does Thackeray call it? His word is "thrifty." He says: "There are four hundred letters of Dick Steele's to his wife, which that thrifty woman preserved accurately."

"Thrifty" is a hard word to apply to her whom Steele styled, in the year before her death, his "charming little insolent." She was ill in Wales, and he, at home, wept upon her pillow, and "took it to be a sin to go to sleep." Thrifty they may call her, and accurate if they will; but she lies in Westminster Abbey, and Steele called her "your Prueship."

JOSEPH CONRAD

INITIATION [1]

"Ships!" exclaimed an elderly seaman in clean, shore togs. "Ships!" — and his keen glance, turning away from my face, ran along the vista of magnificent figure-heads that in the late seventies used to overhang in a serried rank the muddy pavement by the side of the New South Dock — "ships are all right; it's the men in 'em. . . ."

Fifty hulls, at least, moulded on lines of beauty and speed — hulls of wood, of iron, expressing in their forms the highest achievement of modern ship-building — lay moored all in a row, stem to quay, as if assembled there for an exhibition, not of a great industry, but of a great art. Their colors were grey, black, dark green, with a narrow strip of yellow moulding defining their sheer, or with a row of painted ports decking in warlike decoration their robust flanks of cargo-carriers that would know no triumph but of speed in carrying a burden, no glory other than of a long service, no victory but that of an endless, obscure contest with the sea. The great empty hulls with swept holds, just out of dry-dock, with their paint glistening freshly, sat high-sided with ponderous dignity alongside the wooden jetties, looking more like unmovable buildings than things meant to go afloat; others, half loaded, far on the way to recover the true sea-physiognomy of a ship brought down to her load-line, looked more accessible. Their less steeply slanting gangways seemed to invite the strolling sailors in search of a berth to walk on board and try "for a chance" with the chief mate, the guardian of a ship's efficiency. As if anxious to remain unperceived amongst their overtopping sisters, two or three "finished" ships floated low, with an air of straining at the leash of their level headfasts, exposing to view their cleared decks and covered hatches, prepared to drop stern first out of the labouring ranks, displaying the true comeliness of form

[1] From *The Mirror of the Sea* (1906), incorporating the phrasal revisions of 1919. By permission of James B. Pinker and Sons and of the publishers, Doubleday, Doran and Company, Inc.

which only her proper sea-trim gives to a ship. And for a good quarter of a mile, from the dockyard-gate to the farthest corner, where the old housed-in hulk, the *President* (drill-ship, then, of the Naval Reserve), used to lie with her frigate side rubbing against the stone of the quay, above all these hulls, ready and unready, a hundred and fifty lofty masts, more or less, held out the web of their rigging like an immense net, in whose close mesh, black against the sky, the heavy yards seemed to be entangled and suspended.

It was a sight. The humblest craft that floats makes its appeal to a seaman by the faithfulness of her life; and this was the place where one beheld the aristocracy of ships. It was a noble gathering of the fairest and swiftest, each bearing at the bow the carved emblem of her name, as in a gallery of plaster-casts, figures of women with mural crowns, women with flowing robes, with gold fillets on their hair or blue scarves round their waists, stretching out rounded arms as if to point the way; heads of men helmeted or bare; full lengths of warriors, of kings, of statesmen, of lords and princesses, all white from top to toe; with here and there a dusky, turbaned figure, bedizened in many colours, of some Eastern sultan or hero, all inclined forward under the slant of mighty bowsprits as if eager to begin another run of eleven thousand miles in their leaning attitudes. These were the fine figure-heads of the finest ships afloat. But why, unless for the love of the life those effigies shared with us in their wandering impassivity, should one try to reproduce in words an impression of whose fidelity there can be no critic and no judge, since such an exhibition of the art of ship-building and the art of figure-head carving as was seen from year's end to year's end in the open-air gallery of the New South Dock no man's eye shall behold again? All that patient, pale company of queens and princesses, of kings and warriors, of allegorical women, of heroines and statesmen and heathen gods, crowned, helmeted, bare-headed, has run for good off the sea, stretching to the last above the tumbling foam their fair, rounded arms, holding out their spears, swords, shields, tridents in the same unwearied, striving-forward pose. And nothing remains but lingering perhaps in the memory of a few men, the sound of their names, vanished a long time ago from the first page of the great London dailies; from big posters in railway stations and the doors of shipping-offices; from the minds of sailors, dock-masters, pilots, and tugmen; from the hail of gruff voices and the flutter of signal-flags exchanged between ships closing upon each other and drawing apart in the open immensity of the sea.

The elderly, respectable seaman, withdrawing his gaze from that multitude of spars, gave me a glance to make sure of our fellowship in the craft and mystery of the sea. We had met casually, and had got into contact as I had stopped near him, my attention being caught by the same peculiarity he was looking at in the rigging of an obviously new ship, a ship with her reputation all to make yet in the talk of the seamen who were to share their life with her. Her name was already on their lips. I had heard it uttered between two thick, red-necked fellows of the semi-nautical type at the Fenchurch Street railway station, where, in those days, the everyday male crowd was attired in jerseys and pilot-cloth mostly, and had the air of being more conversant with the times of high-water than with the times of the trains. I had noticed that new ship's name on the first page of my morning paper. I had stared at the unfamiliar grouping of its letters, blue on white ground, on the advertisement boards, whenever the train came to a standstill alongside one of the shabby, wooden, wharf-like platforms of the dock railway line. She had been named, with proper observances, on the day she came off the stocks, no doubt, but she was very far yet from "having a name." Untried, ignorant of the ways of the sea, she had been thrust amongst that renowned company of ships to load for her maiden voyage. There was nothing to vouch for her soundness and the worth of her character but the reputation of the building-yard whence she was launched headlong into the world of waters. She looked modest to me. I imagined her diffident, lying very quiet, with her side nestling shyly against the wharf to which she was made fast with very new lines, intimidated by the company of her tried and experienced sisters already familiar with all the violences of the ocean and the exacting love of men. They had had more long voyages to make their names in than she had known weeks of carefully tended life, for a new ship receives as much attention as if she were a young bride. Even crabbed old dock-masters look at her with benevolent eyes. In her shyness at the threshold of a laborious and uncertain life, where so much is expected of a ship, she could not have been better heartened and comforted, had she only been able to hear and understand, than by the tone of deep conviction in which my elderly, respectable seaman repeated the first part of his saying, "Ships are all right. . . ."

His civility prevented him from repeating the other, the bitter part. It had occurred to him that it was perhaps indelicate to insist. He had recognized in me a ship's officer, very possibly looking for a berth like himself, and so far a comrade, but still a man belonging to that sparsely peopled after-end of a ship, where a great part of her reputation as a "good ship," in seaman's parlance, is made or marred.

"Can you say that of all ships without exception?" I asked, being in an idle mood, because, if an obvious ship's officer, I was not, as a matter of fact, down at the docks to "look for a berth," an occupation as engrossing as gambling, and as little favourable to the free exchange of ideas, besides being destructive of the kindly temper needed for casual intercourse with one's fellow-creatures.

"You can always put up with 'em," opined the respectable seaman judicially.

He was not averse from talking, either. If he had come down to the dock to look for a berth, he did not seem oppressed by anxiety as to his chances. He had the serenity of a man whose estimable character is fortunately expressed by his personal appearance in an unobtrusive yet convincing manner which no chief officer in want of hands could resist. And, true enough, I learned presently that the mate of the *Hyperion* had "taken down" his name for quartermaster. "We sign on Friday, and join next day for the morning tide," he remarked, in a deliberate, careless tone, which contrasted strongly with his evident readiness to stand there yarning for an hour or so with an utter stranger.

"*Hyperion*," I said. "I don't remember ever seeing that ship anywhere. What sort of a name has she got?"

It appeared from his discursive answer that she had not

much of a name one way or another. She was not very fast. It took no fool, though, to steer her straight, he believed. Some years ago he had seen her in Calcutta, and he remembered being told by somebody then that on her passage up the river she had carried away both her hawse-pipes. But that might have been the pilot's fault. Just now, yarning with the apprentices on board, he had heard that this very voyage, brought up in the Downs, outward bound, she broke her sheer, struck adrift, and lost an anchor and chain. But that might have occurred through want of careful tending in a tideway. All the same, this looked as though she were pretty hard on her ground-tackle. Didn't it? She seemed a heavy ship to handle, anyway. For the rest, as she had a new captain and a new mate this voyage, he understood, one couldn't say how she would turn out. . . .

In such marine shore-talk as this is the name of a ship slowly established, her fame made for her, the tale of her qualities and of her defects kept, her idiosyncrasies commented upon with the zest of personal gossip, her achievements made much of, her faults glossed over as things that, being without remedy in our imperfect world, should not be dwelt upon too much by men who, with the help of ships, wrest out a bitter living from the rough grasp of the sea. All that talk makes up her "name," which is handed over from one crew to another without bitterness, without animosity, with the indulgence of mutual dependence, and with the feeling of close association in the exercise of her perfections and in the danger of her defects.

This feeling explains men's pride in ships. "Ships are all right," as my middle-aged, respectable quartermaster said with much conviction and some irony; but they are not exactly what men make them. They have their own nature; they can of themselves minister to our self-esteem by the demand their qualities make upon our skill and their shortcomings upon our hardiness and endurance. Which is the more flattering exaction it is hard to say; but there is the fact that in listening for upwards of twenty years to the sea-talk that goes on afloat and ashore I have never detected the true note of animosity. I won't deny that at sea, sometimes, the note of profanity was audible enough in those chiding interpellations a wet, cold, weary seaman addresses to his ship, and in moments of exasperation is disposed to extend to all ships that ever were launched — to the whole everlastingly exacting brood that swims in deep waters. And I have heard curses launched at the unstable element itself, whose fascination, outlasting the accumulated experience of ages, had captured him as it had captured the generations of his forbears.

For all that has been said of the love that certain natures (on shore) have professed to feel for it, for all the celebrations it has been the object of in prose and song, the sea has never been friendly to man. At most it has been the accomplice of human restlessness, and playing the part of dangerous abettor of world-wide ambitions. Faithful to no race after the manner of the kindly earth, receiving no impress from valour and toil and self-sacrifice, recognizing no finality of dominion, the sea has never adopted the cause of its masters like those lands where the victorious nations of mankind have taken root, rocking their cradles and setting up their gravestones. He — man or people — who, putting his trust in the friendship of the sea, neglects the strength and cunning of his right hand, is a fool! As if it were too great, too mighty for common virtues, the ocean has no compassion, no faith, no law, no memory. Its fickleness is to be held true to men's purposes only by an undaunted resolution, and by a sleepless, armed, jealous vigilance, in which, perhaps, there has always been more hate than love. *Odi et amo* may well be the confession of those who consciously or blindly have surrendered their existence to the fascination of the sea. All the tempestuous passions of mankind's young days, the love of loot and the love of glory, the love of adventure and the love of danger, with the great love of the unknown and vast dreams of dominion and power, have passed like images reflected from a mirror, leaving no record upon the mysterious face of the sea. Impenetrable and heartless, the sea has given nothing of itself to the suitors for its precarious favours. Unlike the earth, it cannot be subjugated at any cost of patience and toil. For all its fascination that has lured so many to a violent death, its immensity has never been loved as the mountains, the plains, the desert itself, have been loved. Indeed, I suspect that, leaving aside the protestations and tributes of writers who, one is safe in saying, care for little else in the world than the rhythm of their lines and the cadence of their phrase, the love of the sea, to which some men and nations confess so readily, is a complex sentiment wherein pride enters for much, necessity for not a little, and the love of ships — the untiring servants of our hopes and our self-esteem — for the best and most genuine part. For the hundreds who have reviled the sea, beginning with Shakespeare in the line —

"More fell than hunger, anguish, or the sea,"

down to the last obscure sea-dog of the "old model," having but few words and still fewer thoughts, there could not be found, I believe, one sailor who has ever coupled a curse with the good or bad name of a ship. If ever his profanity, provoked by the hardships of the sea, went so far as to touch his ship, it would be lightly, as a hand may, without sin, be laid in the way of kindness on a woman.

The love that is given to ships is profoundly different from the love men feel for every other work of their hands — the love they bear to their houses, for instance — because it is untainted by the pride of possession. The pride of skill, the pride of responsibility, the pride of endurance there may be, but otherwise it is disinterested sentiment. No seaman ever cherished a ship, even if she belonged to him, merely because of the profit she put in his pocket. No one, I think, ever did; for a ship-owner, even of the best, has always been outside the pale of that sentiment embracing in a feeling of intimate, equal fellowship the ship and the man, backing each other against the implacable, if sometimes dissembled, hostility of their world of waters. The sea — this truth must be confessed — has no generosity. No display of manly qualities — courage, hardihood, endurance, faithfulness — has ever been known to touch its irresponsible consciousness of power. The ocean has the conscienceless temper of a savage autocrat spoiled by much adulation. He cannot brook the slightest appearance of defiance, and has remained the irreconcilable enemy of ships and men ever since ships and men had the unheard-of audacity to go afloat together in the face of his frown. From that day he has gone on swallowing up fleets and men without his resentment being glutted by the number of victims — by so many wrecked ships and wrecked lives. To-day, as ever, he is ready to beguile and betray, to smash and to drown the incorrigible optimism of men who, backed by the fidelity of ships, are trying to wrest from him the fortune of their house, the dominion of their world, or only a dole of food for their hunger. If not always in the hot mood to smash, he is always stealthily ready for a drowning. The most amazing wonder of the deep is its unfathomable cruelty.

I felt its dread for the first time in mid-Atlantic one day, many years ago, when we took off the crew of a Danish brig homeward-bound from the West Indies. A thin, silvery mist softened the calm and majestic splendour of light without shadows — seemed to render the sky less remote and the ocean less immense. It was one of the days when the might of the sea appears indeed lovable, like the nature of a strong man in moments of quiet intimacy. At sunrise we had made out a black speck to the westward, apparently suspended high up in the void behind a stirring, shimmering veil of silvery blue gauze that seemed at times to stir and float in the breeze which fanned us slowly along. The peace of that enchanting forenoon was so profound, so untroubled, that it seemed that every word pronounced loudly on our deck would penetrate to the very heart of that infinite mystery born from the conjunction of water and sky. We did not raise our voices. "A waterlogged derelict, I think, sir," said the second officer, quietly, coming down from aloft with the binoculars in their case slung across his shoulders; and our captain, without a word, signed to the helmsman to steer for the black speck. Presently we made out a low, jagged stump sticking up forward — all that remained of her departed masts.

The captain was expatiating in a low, conversational tone to the chief mate upon the danger of these derelicts, and upon his dread of coming upon them at night, when suddenly a man forward screamed out, "There's people on board of her, sir! I see them!" in a most extraordinary voice — a voice never heard before in our ship; the amazing voice of a stranger. It gave the signal for a sudden tumult of shouts. The watch below ran up the forecastle head in a body, the cook dashed out of the galley. Everybody saw the poor fellows now. They were there! And all at once our ship, which had the well-earned name of being without a rival for speed in light winds, seemed to us to have lost the power of motion, as if the sea, becoming viscous, had clung to her sides. And yet she moved. Immensity, the inseparable companion of a ship's life, chose that day to breathe upon her as gently as a sleeping child. The clamour of our excitement had died out, and our living ship, famous for never losing steerage way as long as there was air enough to float a feather, stole, without a ripple, silent and white as a ghost, towards her mutilated and wounded sister, come upon at the point of death in the sunlit haze of a calm day at sea.

With the binoculars glued to his eyes, the captain said in a quavering tone: "They are waving to us with something aft there." He put down the glasses on the skylight brusquely, and began to walk about the poop. "A shirt or a flag," he ejaculated, irritably. "Can't make it out.... Some damn rag or other!" He took a few more turns on the poop, glancing down over the rail now and then to see how fast we were moving. His nervous footsteps rang sharply in the quiet of the ship, where the other men, all looking the same way, had forgotten themselves in a staring immobility. "This will never do!" he cried out, suddenly. "Lower the boats at once! Down with them!"

Before I jumped into mine he took me aside, as being an inexperienced junior, for a word of warning.

"You look out as you come alongside that she doesn't take you down with her. You understand?"

He murmured this confidentially, so that none of the men at the falls should overhear, and I was shocked. "Heavens! as if in such an emergency one stopped to think of danger!" I exclaimed to myself mentally, in scorn of such cold-blooded caution.

It takes many lessons to make a real seaman, and I got my rebuke at once. My experienced commander seemed in one searching glance to read my thoughts on my ingenuous face.

"What you're going for is to save life, not to drown your boat's crew for nothing," he growled severely in my ear. But

as we shoved off he leaned over and cried out: "It all rests on
the power of your arms, men.   Give way for life!"

We made a race of it, and I would never have believed that
a common boat's crew of a merchantman could keep up so
much determined fierceness in the regular swing of their stroke.
What our captain had clearly perceived before we left had become plain to all of us since.   The issue of our enterprise hung
on a hair above that abyss of waters which will not give up its
dead till the Day of Judgment.   It was a race of two ship's
boats matched against Death for a prize of nine men's lives,
and Death had a long start.   We saw the crew of the brig from
afar working at the pumps — still pumping on that wreck,
which already had settled so far down that the gentle, low swell,
over which our boats rose and fell easily without a check to
their speed, welling up almost level with her head-rails, plucked
at the ends of broken gear swinging desolately under her naked
bowsprit.

We could not, in all conscience, have picked out a better day
for our regatta had we had the free choice of all the days that
ever dawned upon the lonely struggles and solitary agonies of
ships since the Norse rovers first steered to the westward
against the run of Atlantic waves.   It was a very good race.
At the finish there was not an oar's-length between the first
and second boat, with Death coming in a good third on the top
of the very next smooth swell, for all one knew to the contrary.
The scuppers of the brig gurgled softly all together when the
water rising against her sides subsided sleepily with a low
wash, as if playing about an immovable rock.   Her bulwarks
were gone fore and aft, and one saw her bare deck low-lying
like a raft and swept clean of boats, spars, houses — of everything except the ringbolts and the heads of the pumps.   I had
one dismal glimpse of it as I braced myself up to receive upon
my breast the last man to leave her, the captain, who literally
let himself fall into my arms.

It had been a weirdly silent rescue — a rescue without a
hail, without a single uttered word, without a gesture or a sign,
without a conscious exchange of glances.   Up to the very last
moment those on board stuck to their pumps, which spouted
two clear streams of water upon their bare feet.   Their brown

skin showed through the rents of their shirts; and the two small bunches of half-naked, tattered men went on bowing from the waist to each other in their back-breaking labour, up and down, absorbed, with no time for a glance over the shoulder at the help that was coming to them. As we dashed, unregarded, alongside, a voice let out one, only one hoarse howl of command, and then, just as they stood, without caps, with the salt drying grey in the wrinkles and folds of their hairy, haggard faces, blinking stupidly at us their red eyelids, they made a bolt away from the handles, tottering and justling against each other, and positively flung themselves over upon our very heads. The clatter they made tumbling into the boats had an extraordinarily destructive effect upon the illusion of tragic dignity our self-esteem had thrown over the contests of mankind with the sea. On that exquisite day of gentle breathing peace and veiled sunshine perished my romantic love to what men's imagination had proclaimed the most august aspect of Nature. The cynical indifference of the sea to the merits of human suffering and courage, laid bare in this ridiculous, panic-tainted performance extorted from the dire extremity of nine good and honourable seamen, revolted me. I saw the duplicity of the sea's most tender mood. It was so because it could not help itself, but the awed respect of the early days was gone. I felt ready to smile bitterly at its enchanting charm and glare viciously at its furies. In a moment, before we shoved off, I had looked coolly at the life of my choice. Its illusions were gone, but its fascination remained. I had become a seaman at last.

We pulled hard for a quarter of an hour, then laid on our oars waiting for our ship. She was coming down on us with swelling sails, looking delicately tall and exquisitely noble through the mist. The captain of the brig, who sat in the stern-sheets by my side with his face in his hands, raised his head and began to speak with a sort of sombre volubility. They had lost their masts and sprung a leak in a hurricane; drifted for weeks, always at the pumps, met more bad weather; the ships they sighted failed to make them out, the leak gained upon them slowly, and the seas had left them nothing to make a raft of. It was very hard to see ship after ship pass by at a distance, "as if everybody had agreed that we must be left to drown," he added. But they went on trying to keep the brig afloat as long as possible, and working the pumps constantly on insufficient food, mostly raw, till "yesterday evening," he continued, monotonously, "just as the sun went down, the men's hearts broke."

He made an almost imperceptible pause here, and went on again with exactly the same intonation:

"They told me the brig could not be saved, and they thought they had done enough for themselves. I said nothing to that. It was true. It was no mutiny. I had nothing to say to them. They lay about aft all night, as still as so many dead men. I did not lie down. I kept a lookout. When the first light came I saw your ship at once. I waited for more light; the breeze began to fail on my face. Then I shouted out as loud as I was able, "Look at that ship!" but only two men got up very slowly and came to me. At first only we three stood alone, for a long time, watching you coming down to us, and feeling the breeze drop to a calm almost; but afterwards others, too, rose, one after another, and by and by I had all my crew behind me. I turned round and said to them that they could see the ship was coming our way, but in this small breeze she might come too late after all, unless we turned to and tried to keep the brig afloat long enough to give you time to save us all. I spoke like that to them, and then I gave the command to man the pumps."

He gave the command, and gave the example, too, by going himself to the handles, but it seems that these men did actually hang back for a moment, looking at each other dubiously before they followed him. "He! he! he!" He broke out into a most unexpected, imbecile, pathetic, nervous little giggle. "Their hearts were broken so! They had been played with too long," he explained apologetically, lowering his eyes, and became silent.

Twenty-five years is a long time — a quarter of a century is a dim and distant past; but to this day I remember the dark-brown feet, hands, and faces of two of these men whose hearts had been broken by the sea. They were lying very still on their sides on the bottom boards between the thwarts, curled up like dogs. My boat's crew, leaning over the looms of their oars, stared and listened as if at the play. The master of the brig looked up suddenly to ask me what day it was.

They had lost the date. When I told him it was Sunday, the 22d, he frowned, making some mental calculation, then nodded twice sadly to himself, staring at nothing.

His aspect was miserably unkempt and wildly sorrowful. Had it not been for the unquenchable candour of his blue eyes, whose unhappy, tired glance every moment sought his abandoned, sinking brig, as if it could find rest nowhere else, he would have appeared mad. But he was too simple to go mad, too simple with that manly simplicity which alone can bear men unscathed in mind and body through an encounter with the deadly playfulness of the sea or with its less abominable fury.

Neither angry nor playful nor smiling, it enveloped our distant ship growing bigger as she neared us, our boats with the rescued men and the dismantled hull of the brig we were leaving behind, in the large and placid embrace of its quietness, half lost in the fair haze, as if in a dream of infinite and tender clemency. There was no frown, no wrinkle on its face, not a ripple. And the run of the slight swell was so smooth that it resembled the graceful undulation of a piece of shimmering grey silk shot with gleams of green. We pulled an easy stroke; but when the master of the brig, after a glance over his shoulder, stood up with a low exclamation, my men feathered their oars instinctively, without an order, and the boat lost her way.

He was steadying himself on my shoulder with a strong grip, while his other arm, flung up rigidly, pointed a denunciatory finger at the immense tranquillity of the ocean. After his first exclamation, which stopped the swing of our oars, he made no sound, but his whole attitude seemed to cry out an indignant "Behold!" ... I could not imagine what vision of evil had come to him. I was startled, and the amazing energy of his immobilized gesture made my heart beat faster with the anticipation of something monstrous and unsuspected. The stillness around us became crushing.

For a moment the succession of silky undulations ran on innocently. I saw each of them swell up the misty line of the horizon, far, far away beyond the derelict brig, and the next moment, with a slight, friendly toss of our boat, it had passed under us and was gone. The lulling cadence of the rise and fall, the invariable gentleness of this irresistible force, the great charm of the deep waters, warmed my breast deliciously, like the subtle poison of a love-potion. But all this lasted only a few soothing seconds before I jumped up, too, making the boat roll like the veriest landlubber.

Something startling, mysterious, hastily confused, was taking place. I watched it with incredulous and fascinated awe, as one watches the confused, swift movements of some deed of violence done in the dark. As if at a given signal, the run of the smooth undulations seemed checked suddenly around the brig. By a strange optical delusion the whole sea appeared to rise upon her in one overwhelming heave of its silky surface, where in one spot a smother of foam broke out ferociously. And then the effort subsided. It was all over, and the smooth swell ran on as before from the horizon in uninterrupted cadence of motion, passing under us with a slight, friendly toss of our boat. Far away, where the brig had been, an angry white stain undulating on the surface of steely-grey waters, shot with gleams of green, diminished swiftly, without a hiss, like a patch of pure snow melting in the sun. And the great stillness after this initiation into the sea's implacable hate seemed full of dread thoughts and shadows of disaster.

"Gone!" ejaculated from the depths of his chest my bowman in a final tone. He spat in his hands, and took a better grip on his oar. The captain of the brig lowered his rigid arm slowly, and looked at our faces in a solemnly conscious silence, which called upon us to share in his simple-minded, marvelling awe. All at once he sat down by my side, and leaned forward earnestly at my boat's crew, who, swinging together in a long, easy stroke, kept their eyes fixed upon him faithfully.

"No ship could have done so well," he addressed them firmly, after a moment of strained silence, during which he seemed with trembling lips to seek for words fit to bear such high testimony. "She was small, but she was good. I had no anxiety. She was strong. Last voyage I had my wife and two children in her. No other ship could have stood so long the weather she had to live through for days and days before we got dismasted a fortnight ago. She was fairly worn out, and that's all. You may believe me. She lasted under us for days and days, but she could not last forever. It was long enough. I am glad it is over. No better ship was ever left to sink at sea on such a day as this."

He was competent to pronounce the funereal oration of a ship, this son of ancient sea-folk, whose national existence, so little stained by the excesses of manly virtues, had demanded nothing but the merest foothold from the earth. By the merits of his sea-wise forefathers and by the artlessness of his heart, he was made fit to deliver this excellent discourse. There was nothing wanting in its orderly arrangement — neither piety nor faith, nor the tribute of praise due to the worthy dead, with the edifying recital of their achievement. She had lived, he had loved her; she had suffered, and he was glad she was at rest. It was an excellent discourse. And it was orthodox, too, in its fidelity to the cardinal article of a sea-man's faith, of which it was a single-minded confession. "Ships are all right." They are. They who live with the sea have got to hold by that creed first and last; and it came to me, as I glanced at him sideways, that some men were not altogether unworthy in honour and conscience to pronounce the funereal eulogium of a ship's constancy in life and death.

After this, sitting by my side with his loosely clasped hands hanging between his knees, he uttered no word, made no movement till the shadow of our ship's sails fell on the boat, when, at the loud cheer greeting the return of the victors with their prize, he lifted up his troubled face with a faint smile of pathetic indulgence. This smile of the worthy descendant of the most ancient sea-folk whose audacity and hardihood had left no trace of greatness and glory upon the waters, completed the cycle of my initiation. There was an infinite depth of hereditary wisdom in its pitying sadness. It made the hearty bursts of cheering sound like a childish noise of triumph. Our crew shouted with immense confidence — honest souls! As if anybody could ever make sure of having prevailed against the sea, which has betrayed so many ships of great "name," so many proud men, so many towering ambitions of fame, power, wealth, greatness!

As I brought the boat under the falls my captain, in high good-humour, leaned over, spreading his red and freckled elbows on the rail, and called down to me sarcastically, out of the depths of his cynic philosopher's beard:

"So you have brought the boat back after all, have you?"

Sarcasm was "his way," and the most that can be said for it is that it was natural. This did not make it lovable. But it is decorous and expedient to fall in with one's commander's way. "Yes. I brought the boat back all right, sir," I answered. And the good man believed me. It was not for him to discern upon me the marks of my recent initiation. And yet I was not exactly the same youngster who had taken the boat away — all impatience for a race against Death, with the prize of nine men's lives at the end.

Already I looked with other eyes upon the sea. I knew it capable of betraying the generous ardour of youth as implacably as, indifferent to evil and good, it would have betrayed the basest greed or the noblest heroism. My conception of its magnanimous greatness was gone. And I looked upon the true sea — the sea that plays with men till their hearts are broken, and wears stout ships to death. Nothing can touch the brooding bitterness of its soul. Open to all and faithful to none, it exercises its fascination for the undoing of the best. To love it is not well. It knows no bond of plighted troth, no fidelity to misfortune, to long companionship, to long devotion. The promise it holds out perpetually is very great; but the only secret of its possession is strength, strength — the jealous, sleepless strength of a man guarding a coveted treasure within his gates.

SAMUEL McCHORD CROTHERS
LEISURE WHILE YOU WAIT [1]

MUCH has been written in praise of leisure. Leisurely writing and leisurely reading have been commended as good for the soul's health. The mind should not always be on the stretch, but there should be intervals in which we should do no manner of work; at least any that is imposed upon us. The intellect should have leisure to refresh itself at the fountain head. It should not be made a wheezy pump to lift water from a half-filled cistern. There should be a sense of effortless abundance.

To all this we agree, but there is one consideration that causes pain. The cultivation of leisure seems to take a great deal of time.

"The wisdom of the learned man," says the son of Sirach, "cometh by the opportunity of leisure, and he that hath little business shall be wise." He then turns to those who do not belong to the leisure class, and quenches their aspirations after wisdom. It is a luxury that is beyond their station in life.

"How can he get wisdom that holdeth the plough and glorieth in the goad, that driveth oxen and is occupied in their labors, and whose talk is bullocks? So is every carpenter and work master that laboreth day and night. The smith also sitting by the anvil and considering the iron work and fighting with the heat of the furnace." In no better plight is "the potter sitting at his work, and turning the wheel with his feet, and his eyes look still upon the pattern of the thing that he maketh."

All these busy people, he says, are necessary. Without them the city cannot be inhabited. "They maintain the state of the world and their desire is in the work of their hands." They are very useful, very indispensable, but they have not leisure to grow wise. Their minds cannot ripen properly.

[1] From *The Cheerful Giver* (1923). By permission of the publishers, Houghton Mifflin Company.

"They cannot declare justice and judgment, and they shall not be found where parables are spoken."

This is so, but it is not the whole story. Skilled artisans are not the only persons who suffer from the lack of the opportunities of leisure. The intellectual classes, as their interests become highly specialized, find it difficult to give their minds free play. One who aims at what is called "productive scholarship" has not the time to sit at ease "where parables are spoken." The parable must be cut short. If only he who has little business shall be wise, then there is small hope for the University Professor. Wherein does the potter, turning the wheel with his foot while his eyes look still upon the pattern of the thing that he maketh, differ from the harassed candidate for a Ph.D. degree, as he looks at the pattern of the thesis that he maketh? Wherein does a society of scholars whose tasks are set by an efficiency expert differ from any other well-organized body of industrialists? It is hard to evade the consequences of all work and no play.

It is our habit to think of everything in terms of big business, and yet there are times when we rebel against the creed that the whole duty of man is to keep busy. Surely we were not born to spend our lives in involuntary servitude. It must be right now and then to do as we please. But how can we find time for such laudable truancies? That is what causes anxious thought.

There is a letter of Cornelius Fronto to his pupil, Marcus Aurelius Antoninus, which takes up this matter from the standpoint of health. The young Emperor's conscience was a taskmaster demanding continual toil. Fronto reminds him that it is possible for one with the best intentions to destroy his own powers for usefulness by overstrain.

"What do circumstances demand of you? Not study, not toil, not duties. What bow is forever strung?"

He suggests to him that the very best service he could render to the Roman Empire would be that he should get into such a state of mind that after each day's work he would be sure of a good night's sleep. He urges him not to look upon his duties with a prolonged stare. "Learn to wink." It was good advice for the serious Stoic. "Remember your father, that god-like man who excelled others in continence and righteousness, yet he knew how to relax. He baited a hook and laughed at buffoons."

Then Fronto put his good advice in the form of an apologue. In the beginning, Father Jove divided man's life into two parts and gave equal value to both. The day he assigned to work, the night to rest. But he did not think of creating sleep, for he took it for granted that every one would be wise enough to rest while awake.

But little by little business began to encroach on the time allotted to rest, and both gods and men fell into the bad habit of turning night into day. First Neptune complained of fatigue. The waves, he said, were so restless that he was kept busy all the time in the attempt to control them and to keep them from encroaching on the shore.

Pluto reported that Hades was so crowded and disturbed that he had no leisure for his own meditations. "He had a watchdog to terrify any shades that tried to escape. It had three throats for barking, three gaping jaws, and three sets of terrible teeth; still he was so anxious over what might happen that he could get no rest."

"Then Jupiter questioned the other gods and found that they were turning night into day. So Jupiter created Sleep, and set him in charge of the night." There must be a time when men might "forget the whirling of chariots and the thunder of steeds." Fronto advises Marcus to learn to sleep till such time as he can learn to rest during his waking hours.

The reply of Marcus Aurelius to this advice is written in the tone of the tired business man:

"*To my master Fronto, greeting.*

"I have just received your letter, which I will enjoy presently. But for the moment I have duties hanging over me that cannot be begged off. Meanwhile, I am very busy."

Then by way of postscript he adds: "After dictating the above, I read the letter while the others were dining. I shall read it often, that I may know how to rest. But you know how exacting duty is."

That notion that leisure is a luxury forbidden to people who work with their hands or brains, is denied by those who hold that it is a state of mind, not dependent on particular circumstances. It is possible to cultivate this state of mind, and it doesn't take so much time as some people suppose. Saint Paul, writing to the Thessalonians, says, "Study to be quiet." This is a mental exercise much to be commended to Americans. But Paul looked upon it as quite compatible with one's ordinary activities. His exhortation to restfulness is followed by a commendation of the industrial virtues. "Study to be quiet, and to do your own business, and to work with your own hands."

People who complain of the high cost of leisure at the present time are apt to look back with futile regret to some golden age which has forever passed. How restful to have lived in the days of Charles Lamb, when one could browse among old books and enjoy his own thoughts without looking at the clock!

But one has doubts as he reads a letter of Lamb to his friend Wordsworth. It would indicate that leisure was not always had for the asking, even by one so capable of appreciating it:

"*My dear W.*: I have scarce time or quiet to explain my present situation, how unquiet and distracted it is, owing to the absence of some of my compeers, and to the deficient state of payments in the E.I.H. owing to bad peace speculations in the calico market!"

He is compelled to work nights in order to catch up with the accumulation of business. "The nature of my work, too, puzzling and hurrying, has so shaken my spirits that my sleep is nothing but a succession of dreams of business I cannot do, of assistants that give me no assistance, of terrible responsibilities. . . . I see no prospect of a quiet day, or hour even, till this week and the next are past."

That sounds very familiar. But in parentheses Lamb lets us into a secret that relieves the situation. He says, "(I write this to W. W. Esq., Collector of Stamp Duties for the conjoint Northern Counties, not W. W. Poet.)" While the clerk at India House and the collector of stamps for the "conjoint Northern Counties" were complaining of being overworked, the author of the "Excursion" and the author of the "Essays of Elia" were not greatly affected. They were prepared to enjoy bits of time which were not devoted to business purposes. Wordsworth, indeed, succeeded in getting a good deal of time for his own uses, but Lamb had to do his meditating on London streets. So one may see a beauty-loving railway section hand cultivating his little flower garden on "the right of way." The company doesn't mind, and it gives him a real pleasure.

Speaking of the "right of way" reminds me that the word "leisure" is derived from the Latin, *licere*, to be permitted, and is connected with our word "license." It implies that we are permitted to do something for our own pleasure in time not needed for strictly utilitarian uses. We are allowed to cultivate the right of way, so long as these adornments do not interfere with the passage of the trains. So Sir Thomas Browne found time in hours not taken up by his medical practice to jot down some thoughts that had pleased him. He says of his book that it was something that "I had at leisurable hours composed." These leisurable hours do not always come in large pieces. Leisure is often more highly valued when it must be taken in installments.

The number of these leisurable hours that any one has at his disposal is limited, and their distribution throughout a lifetime is often beyond the control of the individual. William Penn's "Fruits of Solitude" was the result of a season of forced retirement. But Penn was a very wealthy man, and, besides, was a Quaker. He may be looked upon as a plutocrat in the way of leisure. Most of us must get our solitude in broken lots.

Yet it is remarkable how many opportunities for leisure one can find if he is on the lookout for them. We are told that even an atom is more roomy than one would imagine. An electron moves about in its vast spaces like a lonely planet. And one can get a good deal of aloneness in a minute. Our thoughts need not be hurried or crowded if each is allowed to take its moment when it comes. There are fragments of time that come from broken engagements. These are periods of salutary waiting; waiting for street cars, and dentists, and committees whose chairmen have been delayed by other committees. There are moments in the busiest day when through no fault of our own we are left accidentally alone. There may not be time in these chance intervals for the choicer fruits of solitude to ripen, but there is at least time for some mushroom growths. The punctual man has many such moments for solitary musing while he is waiting for the unpunctual man.

The mind is its own place and in itself can create a driven feeling in the Vale of Arcady. And where is there more calm repose than in the mind of the officer at Fifth Avenue and Forty-Second Street, as he deliberately moves his hands, like Moses at the Red Sea, dividing the waves of traffic that the hurried people may pass in safety?

To take advantage of these fleeting opportunities, one must have a quick control over his own mind. He must not only be able to start his mental machinery, but he must be able to stop it when it is moving to no purpose. This is the more difficult matter. Many persons keep their minds revolving ceaselessly on one subject for the same reason that the driver of a temperamental automobile lets his engine run while the car stops. He is afraid that if it gets cool he can't crank it again. A reliable self-starter would save a great deal of wear and tear.

I cannot include under the pleasant name of "leisure" those activities that are carried on systematically after business hours. Very soon they become things that *must* be done. There are misers of time who clutch at each spare moment and put it to usury. They expect some definite return from their investment. All mental activities which are closely articulated and planned in advance should be classed under the head of "overtime work." In our moments of true leisure the unexpected happens, or, if nothing happens, we do not care. We do that which is unprofitable because it pleases us. We read a book because it happens to be near us and it looks inviting. It is a case where propinquity is everything. The latchstring of the mind is out. We entertain random thoughts and are occasionally surprised to find that we have entertained wisdom unawares. Our attitude is like that of Elizabeth's great minister, Lord Burleigh, who at the end of a day's work would fling his robe of office on the floor and say, "Lie there, my Lord Treasurer, till I call for you in the morning." In a healthy mind there is an interim between one duty and another. This prevents them from wearing each other out. These intervals of soothing carelessness, if not unduly prolonged, are very restorative. Lord Burleigh in the morning resumed his robe of office with zest, because he had been able to throw it off so lightly.

That leisure is compatible with a good deal of work I learned as a child from my Aunt Frances. She was the wife of the village physician. She had twelve children and lived in a large, rambling house which was not planned for saving steps. Yet she was never in a hurry. A peculiar institution of Aunt Frances's house was the *as-you*. It saved no end of worry. When anything was lost, my aunt would say placidly, "You'll probably find it on the as-you"; and so we usually did.

The as-you was a broad landing on the stairs that led from the basement kitchen to the living-room. Usually the members of the family had their hands full when they went upstairs. In such cases they were apt to leave something in the landing with the full assurance that it would be there for them when they made the next trip. The remark that you would find a household article "as you go up," or "as you go down," had been, at last, contracted into a place-name.

I think that every well-ordered mind ought to have an as-you. It is not like an attic where you put decrepit pieces of furniture which you think you will use again, but which you never do.

There are duties which you lay down temporarily because you have your hands too full. You don't want to put them aside where you will forget them. You want to put them where you can pick them up again without too much trouble. There they lie in plain view. You have a feeling that you have carried them as far as you are able to-day. As you come that way to-morrow it will be a pleasure to take them up again. In the meantime they are quite safe on the as-you.

AGNES REPPLIER

THE VIRTUOUS VICTORIAN [1]

WHEN Miss Amy Lowell, in her essay on Émile Verhaeren, says that the influence of Zola on the younger writers of France and Belgium was necessary "to down the long set of sentimental hypocrisies known in England as 'Victorian,'" she repeats a formula which has been in popular use for many years, and to which we attach no very exact significance. "Early-Victorian," "mid-Victorian," we use the phrases glibly, and without being aware that the mental attitude to which we refer is sometimes not Victorian at all, but Georgian. Take, for example, that fairly famous sentiment about the British navy being "if possible, more distinguished in its domestic virtues than in its national importance." Nothing more oppressively smug was ever uttered in the reign of the virtuous Queen; yet it was written by the most humorous and most pitiless of Georgian novelists, and it expressed the conviction of her soul.

When we permit ourselves to sneer at Victorian hypocrisies, we allude, as a rule, to the superficial observance of religious practices, and to the artificial reticence concerning illicit sexual relations. The former affected life more than it did literature; the latter affected literature more than it did life. A resolute silence is apt to imply or involve an equally resolute denial; and there came a time when certain plain truths were denied because there was no other way of keeping them out of sight. Novelists and poets conformed to a standard which was set by the taste of their day. So profoundly was the great Victorian laureate influenced by this taste that he grew reluctant to accept those simple old English stories, those charming old English traditions, the propriety or impropriety of which had never been a matter for concern. His "fair Rosamond" believes herself a wedded wife, and so escapes culpability. His "Maid Marian" wanders through Sherwood Forest under the re-

---

[1] From *Points of Friction* (1920). By permission of the publishers, Houghton Mifflin Company.

spectable chaperonage of her father, and will not permit to
Robin Hood the harmless liberties common among betrothed
lovers.

> "Robin, I will not kiss thee,
> For that belongs to marriage; but I hold thee
> The husband of my heart; the noblest light
> That ever flashed across my life, and I
> Embrace thee with the kisses of the soul.
> *Robin:* I thank thee."

It is a bit frigid and a bit stilted for the merry outlaws. "If
love were all," we might admit that conventionalism had
chilled the laureate's pen; but, happily for the great adventures
we call life and death, love is not all. The world swings on its
way, peopled by other men than lovers; and it is to Tennyson
we owe the most splendid denial of domesticity — and duty —
that was ever made deathless by verse. With what unequalled
ardour his Ulysses abandons home and country, the faithful,
but ageing, Penelope, the devoted, but dull, Telemachus, and
the troublesome business of law-making! He does not covet
safety. He does not enjoy the tranquil reward of his labours,
nor the tranquil discharge of his obligations. He will drink life
to the lees. He will seek the still untravelled world, and take
what buffets fortune sends him.

> "For my purpose holds
> To sail beyond the sunset, and the baths
> Of all the western stars, until I die.
> It may be that the gulfs will wash us down;
> It may be we shall touch the Happy Isles,
> And see the great Achilles whom we knew."

Poor Penelope! What chance has she against such glad decision, such golden dreams! It is plain that the Ithacan navy
was less distinguished than the British navy for the development of domestic virtues. Until such time as Germany fulfils
her threat, and drives the "bastard tongue of canting island
pirates" from its hold on the civilized world, Tennyson's
Ulysses will survive as the embodiment of the adventurous
spirit which brooks no restraint, and heeds no liability.

The great Victorian novelists were well aware that, albeit

the average man does his share of love-making, he neither lives nor dies for love. Mr. Edmund Gosse, reared in the strictest sect of Plymouth Brethren, and professing religion at ten, was nevertheless permitted by his father to read the novels of Dickens, because they dealt with the passion of love in a humorous manner. More often they deal with it in a purely perfunctory manner, recognizing it as a prelude to marriage, and as something to which the novelist must not forget to make an occasional reference. Nicholas Nickleby is a young man and a hero. Consequently an assortment of female virtues and of female charms is labelled, docketed, provided with ringlets and a capacity for appropriate swooning, — and behold, Nicholas has a wife. Kate Nickleby's husband is even more sketchily outlined. He has a name, and — we are told — an impetuous and generous disposition. He makes his appearance when a suitor is needed, stands up to be married when a husband is called for, and that is all there is of him. But what do these puppets matter in a book which gives us Mrs. Nickleby, Vincent Crummles, Fanny Squeers, and the ever-beloved Kenwigses. It took a great genius to enliven the hideous picture of Dotheboys Hall with the appropriate and immortal Fanny, whom we could never have borne to lose. It took a great genius to evolve from nothingness the name "Morleena Kenwigs." So perfect a result, achieved from a mere combination of letters, confers distinction on the English alphabet.

The charge of conventionalism brought against Thackeray and Trollope has more substance, because these novelists essayed to portray life soberly and veraciously. "Trollope," says Sir Leslie Stephen, "was in the awkward position of a realist, bound to ignore realities." Thackeray was restrained, partly by the sensitive propriety of British readers who winced at the frank admission of sexual infirmities, and partly by the quality of his own taste. In deference to the public, he forbore to make Arthur Pendennis the lover of Fanny Bolton; and when we remember the gallant part that Fanny plays when safely settled at Clavering, her loyalty to her old friend, Bows, and her dexterity in serving him, we are glad she went unsmirched into that sheltered port.

The restrictions so cheerfully accepted by Thackeray, and his reticence — which is merely the reticence observed by every gentleman of his day — leave him an uncrippled spectator and analyst of the complicated business of living. The world is not nearly so simple a place as the sexualists seem to consider it. To the author of " Vanity Fair " it was not simple at all. Acting and reacting upon one another, his characters crowd the canvas, their desires and ambitions, their successes and failures, inextricably interwoven into one vast social scheme. It is not the decency of Thackeray's novels which affronts us (we are seldom unduly aware that they are decent), but the severity with which he judges his own creations, and his rank and shameless favouritism. What business has he to coddle Rawdon Crawley ("honest Rawdon," forsooth!), to lay siege to our hearts with all the skill of a great artificer, and compel our liking for this fool and reprobate? What business has he to pursue Becky Sharp like a prosecuting attorney, to trip her up at every step, to betray, to our discomfiture, his cold hostility? He treats Blanche Amory in the same merciless fashion, and no one cares. But Becky! Becky, that peerless adventuress who, as Mr. Brownell reminds us, ran her memorable career before psychology was thought of as an essential element of fiction. Becky whose scheming has beguiled our weary hours, and recompensed us for the labour of learning to read. How shall we fathom the mental attitude of a novelist who could create such a character, control her fluctuating fortunes, lift her to dizzy heights, topple her to ruin, extricate her from the dust and débris of her downfall, — and hate her!

Trollope, working on a lower level, observant rather than creative, was less stern a moralist than Thackeray, but infinitely more cautious of his footsteps. He kept soberly in the appointed path, and never once in thirty years trod on the grass or flower-beds. Lady Glencora Palliser thinks, indeed, of leaving her husband; but she does not do it, and her continency is rewarded after a fashion which is very satisfactory to the reader. Mr. Palliser aspires somewhat stiffly to be the lover of Lady Dumbello; but that wise worldling, ranking love the least of assets, declines to make any sacrifice at its shrine. Trollope unhesitatingly and proudly claimed for himself the quality of harmlessness. "I do believe," he said, "that no girl has risen from the reading of my pages less modest than she was before, and that some girls may have learned from them that modesty is a charm worth possessing."

This is one of the admirable sentiments which should have been left unspoken. It is a true word as far as it goes, but more suggestive of "Little Women," or "A Summer in Leslie Goldthwaite's Life," than of those virile, varied and animated novels which make no appeal to immaturity. In Trollope's teeming world, as in the teeming world about us, a few young people fall in love and are married, but this is an infrequent episode. Most of his men and women, like the men and women whom we know, are engrossed in other activities. Once, indeed, Bishop Proudie wooed and won Mrs. Proudie. Once Archdeacon Grantly wooed and won Mrs. Grantly. But neither of these gentlemen could possibly have belonged to "the great cruising brotherhood of the Pilgrims of Love." "Le culte de la femme" has never been a popular pastime in Britain, and Trollope was the last man on the island to have appreciated its significance. He preferred politics, the hunting-field, and the church.

Yet surely Archdeacon Grantly is worth a brace of lovers. With what sincerity he is drawn, and with what consummate care! A churchman who, as Sir Leslie Stephen somewhat petulantly observes, "gives no indication of having any religious views whatever, beyond a dislike to dissenters." A solidly respectable member of provincial clerical society, ambitious, worldly, prizing wealth, honouring rank, unspiritual, unprogressive, — but none the less a man who would have proved his worth in the hour of England's trial.

It is a testimony to the power of fiction that, having read with breathless concern and through countless pages Mr. Britling's reflections on the war, my soul suddenly cried out within me for the reflections of Archdeacon Grantly. Mr. Britling is an acute and sensitive thinker. The archdeacon's mental processes are of the simplest. Mr. Britling has winged his triumphant flight from "the clumsy, crawling, snobbish, comfort-loving caterpillar of Victorian England." The archdeacon is still confessedly a grub. Mr. Britling has "truckled to no domesticated god." The archdeacon's deity is open to such grievous innuendoes. Yet I wish I could have stood on the smooth lawn of Plumstead, and have heard what the archdeacon had to say when he learned that an English scholar and gentleman had smuggled out of England, by the help of a female "confidential agent," a treacherous appeal to the President of the United States, asking that pressure should be brought upon fighting Englishmen in the interests of peace. I wish I could have heard the cawing rooks of Plumstead echo his mighty wrath. For there is that in the heart of a man, even a Victorian churchman with a love of preferment and a distaste for dissenters, which holds scatheless the sacred thing called honour.

Trollope is as frank about the archdeacon's frailties as Mr. Wells is frank about Mr. Britling's frailties. In piping days of peace, the archdeacon's contempt for Mr. Britling would have been as sincere and hearty as Mr. Britling's contempt for the archdeacon. But under the hard, heroic discipline of war there would have come to the archdeacon, as to Mr. Britling, a white dawn of revelation. Both men have the liberating qualities of manhood.

It is always hard to make an elastic phrase fit with precision. We know what we mean by Victorian conventions and hypocrisies, but the perpetual intrusion of blinding truths disturbs our point of view. The new Reform bill and the extension of the suffrage were hardy denials of convention. "The Origin of Species" and "Zoölogical Evidences as to Man's Place in Nature" were not published in the interests of hypocrisy. There was nothing oppressively respectable about "The Ring and the Book"; and Swinburne can hardly be said to have needed correction at Zola's hands. These mid-Victorian products have a savour of freedom about them, and so has "The Ordeal of Richard Feverel." Even the Homeric eloquence of Ruskin was essentially the eloquence of the free. The two lessons he sought to drive home to his reluctant readers were, first, that Englishmen were not living on an illuminated earth spot, under the especial patronage of the Almighty; and, second, that no one was called by Providence to the enjoyment of wealth and security. If such unpleasant and reiterated truths — as applicable to the United States to-day as

they were to Victoria's England — are "smug," then Jeremiah
is sugar-coated, and the Baptist an apostle of ease.

The English have at all times lacked the courage of their
emotions, but not the emotions themselves.   Their reticence
has stood for strength as well as for stiffness.   The pre-
Raphaelites, indeed, surrendered their souls with docility to
every wavelet of feeling, and produced something iridescent,
like the shining of wet sand.   Love, according to their canon,
was expressed with transparent ease.   It was "a great but
rather sloppy passion," says Mr. Ford Madox Hueffer, "which
you swooned about on broad general lines."   A pre-Raphaelite
corsair languished as visibly as a pre-Raphaelite seraph.   He
could be bowled over by a worsted ball; but he was at least
more vigorous and more ruddy than a cubist nude.   One
doubted his seared conscience and his thousand crimes; but not
his ability to walk unassisted downstairs.

The Victorian giants were of mighty girth.   They trod the
earth with proud and heavy steps, and with a strength of conviction which was as vast and tranquil as the plains.   We have
parted with their convictions and with their tranquillity.   We
have parted also with their binding prejudices and with their
standards of taste.   Freedom has come to us, not broadening
down

"from precedent to precedent,"

but swiftly and comprehensively.   There are no more taboos,
no more silent or sentimental hypocrisies.   We should now
know a great many interesting details concerning the Marquis
of Steyne and the Duke of Omnium, if these two imposing
figures had not passed forever from our ken.   We should have
search-lights thrown upon Becky Sharp, if Becky had not escaped into the gloom.   Her successors sin exhaustively, and
with a lamentable lack of *esprit*.   We are bidden to scrutinize
their transgressions, but Becky's least peccadillo is more en-
gaging than all their broken commandments.   The possibility
of profound tediousness accompanying perfect candour dawns
slowly on the truth-tellers of fiction.   It takes a great artist,
like Edith Wharton, to recognize and deplore "the freedom of
speech which never arrives at wit, and the freedom of act which
never makes for romance."

MAURICE HEWLETT

MONTAIGNE [1]

WE owe the Press many things, not all of them gladly; but for one thing at least we may be its thankful debtors, and that is that it has allowed, if not engaged, the Essay to survive. From the days of Addison the essayist has been journalist too, and that which cost Montaigne a lifetime has thereafter been compassed within the year, if not to its advantage, then to its perennity. That is an accident of public economy, however, which is beside the matter, for both Montaigne and Bacon were very capable of journalism for all their leisurely habit. One was deeply versed in affairs, the other kept a wary eye for them and knew, as we put it, the time of day with the best. But politics was not Montaigne's business, who if he had been living to-day would be one of our best "middle" practitioners, a writer deliberately desultory, occasional; "fluctuating and various," as he said; a man not always, and never purposely, didactic, but, as he went on, not far from the vein of Polonius; a full man, however, bursting with anecdote, and one of a singularly detached, dry, not to say frosty, judgement. I could name the weekly which he would adorn, and those which would have none of him. And the daily also. There is but one. I think he would be welcomed there.

The Essay may be *décousu* if the essayist pleases, and as Montaigne certainly did — that is, if himself is so. It is better thus, for the general, than that it should be crabbed, though personally I like close writing. It may, indeed, be both crabbed and desultory; and that was Montaigne's way; for however much he might meander he had a serried mind and massed himself upon his points as they turned up. That was by no means in any orderly sequence, as he proves abundantly by thrusting his tenderest reminiscences of his father into his Es-

[1] From *Extemporary Essays* (1922). By permission of the publisher, Mr. Humphrey Milford, and of Mr. Robin Richards, executor of the estate of Maurice Hewlett.

say "De l' Yvrongnerie,"[1] with which the worthy man had nothing at all to do. He slips into them by exclaiming, "C'est merveille des contes que j'ay ouy faire à mon père de la chasteté de son siècle," and breaks them off abruptly with, "Revenons à nos bouteilles." That is so desultory as to be casual; yet the simplicity of handling rids it of offence. He adored his father. The occasion of his writing Essays may account for the form which they took. He began by making extracts from the Classics into a commonplace book. Thereafter, when a subject occurred to him, he looked through his notes, picked his quotations, and there, practically, you were. He picked too many, and used them all. Some of his early essays merely strung them together like beads. But he set the fashion which did not forsake us till the other day (and then for a very good reason) and became a quarry for his disciples, as Burton of the *Anatomy* also became. Men went to Montaigne, not to follow out his vagaries but to stimulate their own. As he grew more into the work he was doing he improved vastly upon his first attempts. He kept closer to life, dealt less in general ideas. His citations then had point, by ceasing to be the only point. He is at his highest in his Third Book, as in "Sur des Vers de Virgile," and "Du Repentir," and very nearly as good in the twelfth essay of the Second Book: "Apologie de Raimond de Sebonde." In each of those three he has a subject close to his heart — Love, Himself, Mankind. There, having something better to do, he makes the Classics fetch and carry for him. Nobody who desires to know to what point detachment can be carried without ceasing to be human can afford to neglect the "Apologie." It is the best alterative conceivable for what ills an excessive use of *Gulliver's Travels* may have induced in the reader. "J'ay veu en mon temps cent artisans, cent laboureurs, plus sages et plus heureux que des Recteurs de l'Université." And again, "La peste de l'homme c'est l'opinion de sçavoir." And once more, "Notre bien-estre, ce n'est que la privation d'estre mal. Voylà pourquoy la secte de philosophie qui a le plus faict valoir la volupté encore a-elle rangée à la seule indolence." The last is a paradox which I don't admit, except as a masterly reduction of facts to an ab-

[1] "On Drunkenness."

surdity. As you read you can see the frosty old eyelids glimmering over it.

With those and certain other exceptions, I don't pretend to idolatrous admiration of Montaigne. I will play with anybody at anything up and down the world, but must know what game it is we are playing. Montaigne does not. There never was a man who cared less for sum-m-ject and om-m-ject. Though he prefers to handle general notions, he takes them by the handful at a time; and I don't believe you will find a core of idea in an essay of his. Sometimes he will intend for one and never reach it. There is an essay of good length in the Second Book called "Coustume de l'Isle de Cea," in which there is not a word either of the island or the custom, whatever it was. He had not reached them, I suppose, by the time he was tired. One in the Third Book, "Des Coches," opens with a discussion of the habit of blessing the sneezer — a pretty oblique attack. But one does not go to Montaigne to find a theme stated, or disquisition festooned about a peg. He is one to be opened at hazard; a good man for the *sortes*. You will find wisdom on every page: "Le prix de l'âme ne consiste pas à aller haut, mais ordonnément. Sa grandeur ne s'exerce par de la grandeur, c'est en la médiocrité;" many a sharp sentence: "Nos folies ne me font pas rire; c'est nos sapiences"; a pungency, a salt; but you will seldom be touched either to laughter or tears; and for a kindly old man, as he surely was, he is curiously without charm. He had friends — he tells us so; but they were few, and in general he held men at arm's length. "La froideur de ma conversation m'a desrobé avec raison la bienvaillance de plusieurs." How many friends has he made since his death? Think of him beside Burton, Sir Thomas Browne, Charles Lamb. If the whole of his book had been as the last half of it we might have had a different feeling towards him. If his heart had gone in, ours might have gone out. His writing mellows as it goes on, as no doubt he did himself. Whether it tells us anything is another matter.

> With this key
> Shakespeare unlocked his heart . . .

that is, with the sonnet. Can that be said of Montaigne and

the Essay? If the essayist is not personal he is nought, and
may as well class himself pamphleteer at once. Personal
they have been, one and all, importing their egos into any
argument whatsoever, allowing no other staple, considering no
appeals. Except lyric poetry, I suppose there is no such fun
in the world, given the knack, as essay-writing. You write of
what you know best and love best. "Son plus laborieux et
principal estude c'est s'estudier soy," Montaigne reported of
his own wit. That is by no means to say that he publishes all
his discoveries. Other things besides interest go into the study.
Vanity goes in; prejudice is never out. Humility may be
under the table, and modesty have her back to the wall. When
you read Montaigne upon *le Repentir* you may think he has
told you everything, so much has he the air of having dis-
charged his bosom. Analyse the essay and you will find that
he has indeed been frank about his tower, chamber, library, and
basse-cour, but singularly discreet about himself and his own
plenishings. A word or two of his habits — eating, drinking,
sleeping: nothing else, and nothing that matters. After
studying the subject for forty years, that is not all he had
learned. It is what he has thought fit to tell, and I don't
think that either modesty or humility held his hand.

For that apparent candour and real secretiveness, I conclude,
and not because he was perfectly calm about the St. Bartholo-
mew and the like of that, Michelet could not find a good word
to say for him. Certainly, if a man is writing the History of
France he may be pardoned for losing patience with a man or
with mankind. Man as he ought not to be was good enough
for Montaigne, whose historical researches went no further
than the fall of the Roman Empire, and could not have discovered him much about the French one even if he had been
concerned about it. No doubt also that he took more interest
in Man than in men. He was ever a solitary. He mentions
the Wars of Religion rarely, and mostly as a bore. He reports
that he has seen men burnt for religion's sake — "ces pauvres
gens" — and has remarked their wild devotions in the midst of
the fire. By such exercises, he deems, they kept the faith, or
rather they gave it new direction; which, he goes on, says much
for their piety, little for their constancy. He is woundily

right, as usual, but it is a hard saying. There are not many more references to passing events: the Execution of Mary Stuart is one, and no reprobation for it. He calls François II, her first husband, the greatest king in Christendom, which is a compliment probably to the realm rather than to the little monarch. As for his own beliefs, he professed himself a Catholic, and purposed to live and die in that persuasion — as in fact he did. For all that appears he was what we call a deist. The *Paternoster* was enough prayer for him; but there is as little about the Saviour in the *Essais* as there is in *Lycidas*, nothing of the Madonna, nothing of the hierarchies except a good story of an old woman who was found with two tapers alight before the altar of St. Michael, one for him and one for the dragon. I think Montaigne burnt his candles in duplicate too. He was, and professed to be, the man of common sense, the average concupiscent male who had contrived to temper appetite by maintaining an accurate view of the consequences of indulgence. He positively declined to regret anything he had done. "Si j'avois à revivre, je revivrais comme j'ay vescu." That is the saying of a very sincere or very foolish man. Myself, I believe him.

I have been led away from the *Essais* to consider the Essayist, a vain exercise if I am right in thinking that he purposely spun himself out of sight in them. No matter for that: he has done his work, done it so well that from his day to our own the form has persisted without any material change. If one had to define the Essay it would be as the written, after-dinner monologue of a well-read, well-satisfied man of, at least, five-and-forty. Years don't matter: the spirit of years matters very much. You must be mature enough to pontificate and wise enough to do it tactfully. You must not be long, you should not be difficult; you may be discursive, but not abrupt. You may eschew eloquence and outrageous fun; you should subserve the chuckle. You may bedew the eyes, not drown them. You may not take sides, nor improve the occasion. Your teaching must be by the way. "Je n'enseigne point," Montaigne says, "je raconte." You will be allusive, of course — all full men are so; and you will quote freely, often inaccurately. Anecdote should be your salt, but I don't think quotation should be your pepper.

It was Montaigne's undoubtedly, and, like his anecdotes, almost entirely of one people and language. It was very well for his auditory of the moment which, with him, spoke Latin at least as well as French — he himself spoke it better. But that implacable people, the Romans, have receded far from us. Neither Troy nor Rome stands where it did. Our essayists have since discovered other nations. First it was Israel, and you had Abishai and Aholibah, Hophni and Phineas walking familiarly in the page; next it was Shakespeare; and now we have more Keats than we really need. But certainly we are more temperate, or more ignorant, than our fathers; and at least we are short. So had I better be.

PAUL ELMER MORE

DECADENT WIT [1]

MR. HOLBROOK JACKSON [2] has done a good service, though perhaps not quite in the manner he intended, by giving us a history of the spasmodic irruption of decadent wit into English art and literature in the closing years of the nineteenth century. His quotations are so apt and abundant, his characterizations so clear and well-instructed, that one would scarcely need to go outside of his pages to form an independent judgement of the men; while the confusion of his own ideas when he tries to moralize the facts, is an added document in evidence of the condition which he expounds as apologist. Nor was the movement, however abruptly its peculiar manifestation may seem to have begun and ended, without deep roots in the past and strong influence on the present.

The naughty decade, to give it a name in its own taste, may be said to have opened with the publication of Oscar Wilde's *Decay of Lying* and *Picture of Dorian Gray* in 1890, and to have closed with his pitiful death in 1900. By the little band who were working so feverishly in the midst of the surrounding British philistinism it was thought to be the dawn of a new era for art — "a great creative period is at hand," wrote William Sharp. While at the same time it was felt to be the end of all things, and the phrase *fin de siècle* was whispered as a kind of magic formula. "It's *fang-de-seeaycle* that does it," says one of John Davidson's burlesque characters, "and education, and reading French." As one goes back to the productions of these men now, and particularly as one turns over the effusions in the early volumes of the *Yellow Book*, one is likely to be impressed mainly by a note of amateurishness running through their work. In comparison with the decadents of the Continent

[1] From *With the Wits: Shelburne Essays, Tenth Series* (1919). By permission of the author and of the publishers, Houghton Mifflin Company.

[2] *The Eighteen Nineties*. By Holbrook Jackson. New York: Mitchell Kennerley. 1913.

whom they attempted to imitate, they appear rather like truant
boys who need to be spanked and sent again to their lessons.
In the first issue of the *Yellow Book*, the "incomparable" Max
Beerbohm prints *A Defence of Cosmetics*, wherein he observes
sententiously that "the Victorian era comes to its end and the
day of sancta simplicitas is quite ended." The essay seems to
us to-day, with the reek of Broadway in our nostrils, as childlike a piece of extravagance as could well be imagined; yet it
succeeded in rousing a little storm of protest, and one solemn
critic wrote it down as "the rankest and most nauseous thing in
all literature." Another contributor, Lionel Johnson, asks, in
surprise at his own naughtiness: "What would the moral
philosophers, those puzzled sages, think of me? An harmless
hedonist? An amateur in morals, who means well, though
meaning very little?" And one is inclined to answer: "My
dear sir, be comforted; the puzzled sages would not have
thought of you at all."

Yet however we may, and do, pass by these books as largely
factitious imitations, there is an aspect of the revolt that is
serious enough in all conscience. The disease from which it
sprung was no jest, and beneath the antic contortions of their
wit these men were suffering the very real pangs of physical
disorganization. It is in fact like a nightmare to read their
lives. The hectic decay of Aubrey Beardsley is almost health in
comparison with the state of most of those who gave to the
movement its tone. Of the living we speak not: but there is
Lionel Johnson, the best artist of them all when he grew serious,
a victim of absinthe, found in the gutter with his skull crushed;
there is John Davidson, with his vision of a new universe ended
in mad suicide; there are Ernest Dowson and Francis Thompson, mingling their religion with the fumes of alcohol and opium;
there are others whose tainted lives and early deaths need not
be examined; and, above all, is the hideous tragedy in Reading
Jail. These men, who appeared to be treading so fantastically
in "the variant bypaths of the uncertain heart," knew also in
the flesh the certain terrors of organic decay.

No, we shall do these men less than justice if we merely smile
at their mopping and mowing as at the gestures borrowed of a
jackanapes. They are worthy of condemnation. They had

a real driving motive in the flesh, and they had their ideal philosophy. Through all their works, now in the form of direct argument, now implied in the symbol of verse or picture, you will find running the ambitious design of making life itself into a fine art, of welding life and art into one indistinguishable creation. As Oscar Wilde says of his hero in the book which is the completest manifesto of the school, "There were many, especially among the very young men, who saw, or fancied that they saw, in Dorian Gray the true realization of a type of which they had often dreamed in Eton or Oxford days — a type that was to combine something of the real culture of the scholar with all the grace and distinction and perfect manner of a citizen of the world. To them he seemed to be of the company whom Dante describes as having sought to 'make themselves perfect by the worship of beauty.'" And with this coalescence of art and life, as its very source and purpose, was to be joined the garnering of sensations, in a manner which these young enthusiasts caught up from Rossetti and Walter Pater and the other virtuosos of the vibrating nerve. Thus, to the confusion of the Philistine, the Puritan, and the votary of common-sense, they were to create for the world a new Hedonism: "It was to have its service of the intellect, certainly; yet it was never to accept any theory or system that would involve the sacrifice of any mode of passionate experience. Its aim, indeed, was to be experience itself, and not the fruits of experience, sweet or bitter as they might be."

In this longing after the fulness of experience, without consideration of the lessons of experience, we come close to the heart of the movement, and we also see how it was no vagary of a few isolated youths, but was the product of the most characteristic evolution of the age. "It was," as our present guide rightly observes, "the mortal ripening of that flower which blossomed upon the ruins of the French Revolution, heralding not only the rights of man, which was an abstraction savouring more of the classical ideal, but the rights of personality, of unique, varied, and varying men." Personality was to assert itself in the direction of unlimited and unquestioned expansiveness, in the claim of the individual to be purely and intensely himself, in the free pursuit of those emotions and sensations which are the root of division among mankind, while denying those rights of man, in the classical sense, which mean the subordination of the individualizing desires to the commonalty of the law of reason.   And, as life and art were to proceed hand in hand, personality was to manifest itself in a symbolism which should endeavour, in the words of Arthur Symons, "to fix the last fine shade, the quintessence of things; to fix it fleetingly; to be a disembodied voice, and yet the voice of a human soul."   The final marriage of life and art was to be in the swooning ecstasy of music.   There was nothing discordant between the toil of the artist to fix the quintessence of things in fleeting form and the insatiable curiosity of a chaotic egotism.   Nietzsche had said it: "Unless you have chaos within, you cannot give birth to a dancing star" — an idea which Mr. Jackson has developed at hazardous length, thus:

Indeed, when wrought into the metal of a soul impelled to adventure at whatever personal hazard, for sheer love of expanding the boundaries of human experience and knowledge and power, they [this egotism and curiosity] become, as it were, the senses by which such a soul tests the flavour and determines the quality of its progress.   In that light they are not decadent, they are at one with all great endeavour since the dawn of human consciousness.   What, after all, is human consciousness when compared with Nature but a perversity — the self turning from Nature to contemplate itself? . . . Not even a child has curiosity until it has experienced something; all inquisitiveness is in the nature of life asking for more, and all so-called decadence is civilization rejecting, through certain specialized persons, the accumulated experiences and sensations of the race.

There is no need to illustrate this philosophy by examples. Any one who has read Oscar Wilde's *Picture of Dorian Gray* may waive the pleasure or pain of going through the other productions of the school.   Most of these writers, in fact, had a perfectly clear knowledge of what they desired to be and to accomplish.   And not seldom they knew the fruits of their philosophy and experience, as any one may discover by turning over the pages of Mr. Jackson's book.   The root of the whole matter lay in a febrile satiety of the flesh, in a certain physical lesion, which the sufferers, having no philosophy of moral resistance to oppose to it, translated into a moral fatigue.   "It was as though they had grown tired of being good, in the old accepted way; they wanted to experience the piquancy of being good after a debauch." In this mood the literature of exquisite curiosity, whether veiled under the English cant of Epicurean austerity or announced more boldly from across the Channel, fell upon the dryness of their souls like a spark of fire upon parched grass. The consequence is set forth in Dorian Gray's discovery of *A Rebours:*

It was the strangest book that he had ever read. It seemed to him that in exquisite raiment, and to the delicate sound of flutes, the sins of the world were passing in dumb show before him. . . . There were in it metaphors as monstrous as orchids, and as subtle in colour. The life of the senses was described in the terms of mystical philosophy. One hardly knew at times whether one was reading the spiritual ecstasies of some mediæval saint or the morbid confessions of a modern sinner. It was a poisonous book. The heavy odor of incense seemed to cling about its pages and to trouble the brain. The mere cadence of the sentences, the subtle monotony of their music, so full as it was of complex refrains and movements elaborately repeated, produced in the mind of the lad, as he passed from chapter to chapter, a form of reverie, a malady of dreaming.

There could not be a better description of the way in which art revealed itself to all the men of the group as a kind of narcotic for the torture of tired nerves, evoking under brush or pen the images of artificial dreaming, whether these displayed "the wan and saintly amorousness" of Burne-Jones's figures for *The Romaunt of the Rose*, or waxed "fat with luxury" in the illustrations of Aubrey Beardsley, or flaunted the ghastly cosmetic rictus of Arthur Symons's creatures of the stage. Almost always behind the veil, and too often stalking wantonly into view, is the horror of an impotent sex-inquisitiveness and perversion. The subject is not agreeable to touch on, but any one who thinks such a statement too strong may satisfy himself by the frank confessions of their apologist. Beardsley, for instance, "loved the abnormal, and he invented a sort of phallic symbolism to express his interest in passionate perversities. His prose work, *Under the Hill*, is an uncompleted study in the art of aberration." The spectacular disaster of Reading Jail has so impressed our imagination that we are apt to regard its victim as a monster among his fellows, whereas in his heart of hearts he was probably less perverted than were many of those who went through life unscathed by public opinion. But if the author of Dorian Gray carried the outer brand, the wages of an evil mind fell upon them all. It is said of Aubrey Beardsley that he "introduced into art the desolation of experience, the *ennui* of sin." That is to take him, perhaps, a trifle too gravely, but there is something in the conduct of his later years that may at least remind us of Poe's decrepit *Man of the Crowd.* "His restlessness," observes his friend, Max Beerbohm, "was, I suppose, one of the symptoms of his malady. He was always most content where there was the greatest noise and bustle, the largest number of people, and the most brilliant light." And that, adds Mr. Jackson, "is a picture of the age, as well as of its epitome, Aubrey Beardsley." The right of personality to reject "the accumulated experience" of the race, and to expand indefinitely in the search of sensations, turns out in reality to be in no wise "at one with all great endeavour," but to be in the main the unfruitful restlessness of satiety and impotence.

I would not have it inferred that the votaries of the Yellow Nineties produced nothing of pure beauty and intrinsic value. One of them, indeed, Ernest Dowson, who died just as the decade came to an end, left a modest body of verse, which possesses a singular fascination, and which, though Mr. Jackson quotes, I believe, not a line of it, may still be prized when many of its more assertive contemporaries are all but forgotten. The little collection opens with a variation on the old Horatian theme, *Vitae summa brevis:*

> They are not long, the weeping and the laughter,
>   Love and desire and hate:
> I think they have no portion in us after
>   We pass the gate.
>
> They are not long, the days of wine and roses:
>   Out of a misty dream
> Our path emerges for a while, then closes
>   Within a dream.

That is all: two light stanzas, with no mark of originality, unless it be in the sighing melody of the words. Yet you will not read them without saying to yourself: This is poetry, the ancient wonderful heritage, though held in feeble hands. And in the whole collection, amid a good deal that flutters ineffectually, you will find some ten or twelve other poems that carry the same note of indefinable charm. Such a product is not to be reckoned with the great and grave things of literature. If you wish to feel this distinction, read the last of the lisping lines at the head of which Dowson has written the majestic Latin phrases: *O mors! quam amara est memoria tua homini pacem habenti in substantiis suis;* and then, having read these, turn to No. 120 of the *Adventurer*, in which Dr. Johnson has unrolled his solemn meditations on the same text:

Affliction is inseparable from our present state; it adheres to all the inhabitants of this world, in different proportions indeed, but with an allotment which seems very little regulated by our own conduct. It has been the boast of some swelling moralists, that every man's fortune was in his own power, that prudence supplied the place of all other divinities, and that happiness is the unfailing consequence of virtue. But, surely, the quiver of Omnipotence is stored with arrows, against which the shield of human virtue, however adamantine it has been boasted, is held up in vain: we do not always suffer by our crimes; we are not always protected by our innocence. . . .

Nothing confers so much ability to resist the temptations that perpetually surround us, as an habitual consideration of the shortness of life, and the uncertainty of those pleasures that solicit our pursuit; and this consideration can be inculcated only by affliction. "O death! how bitter is the remembrance of thee, to a man that lives at ease in his possessions!"

Dowson's is the poetry of weakness, but of weakness that veils itself in subtle reticences and in the praise of silence — his favourite word — and, above all, that wears the loveliness of purity. Strange as it may sound, in connection with his life and his associations, there is something of almost virginal innocence in his muse. To read his *Pierrot of the Minute* after hearing others of the decadent band, is as if a silence had suddenly fallen upon a place of unclean revelry, and out of the silence there rose the thin sweet voice of a child singing of pathetic things it scarcely understood. I may be peculiar in

my taste, but in my ears he bears comparison well even with
the religious poet whose reputation has been growing so por-
tentously these latter days.   His *Amor Umbratilis*, simple and
unsuggestive as it is, arrests me with a touch that I somehow
miss in the more complicated stanzas of Francis Thompson on
the same theme of love's renunciation; and in all the gorgeous,
stirring pomp of Thompson's odes there is still lacking — to
me at least, though his best admirers will judge otherwise —
some mark of the divine submissiveness which I find, or almost
find, in such a poem as Dowson's *Nuns of the Perpetual Adoration:*

> Calm, sad, secure; behind high convent walls,
>   These watch the sacred lamp, these watch and pray:
> And it is one with them when evening falls,
>   And one with them the cold return of day.
>   .   .   .   .
>
> They saw the glory of the world displayed;
>   They saw the bitter of it, and the sweet;
> They knew the roses of the world should fade,
>   And be trod under by the hurrying feet.
>
> Therefore they rather put away desire,
>   And crossed their hands and came to sanctuary;
> And veiled their heads and put on coarse attire:
>   Because their comeliness was vanity.
>
> And there they rest; they have serene insight
>   Of the illuminating dawn to be:
> Mary's sweet Star dispels for them the night,
>   The proper darkness of humanity.
>
> Calm, sad, serene; with faces worn and mild:
>   Surely their choice of vigil is the best?
> Yea! for our roses fade, the world is wild;
>   But there, beside the altar, there, is rest.

The strange thing, as I have said, yet not so strange perhaps,
when we reflect on it, is that this sweetness and purity should
be found in one who was so thoroughly corrupt in body and
habit.   There was the weariness of the devastation in his soul,
as expressed in the refrain of the poem by which he is best
known:

Last night, ah, yesternight, betwixt her lips and mine
There fell thy shadow, Cynara! thy breath was shed
Upon my soul between the kisses and the wine;
And I was desolate and sick of an old passion,
Yea, I was desolate and bowed my head:
I have been faithful to thee, Cynara! in my fashion.

But it was not the hardening desolation of the inner lie, and decadence kept him, as it were, in a state of fragile immaturity. His face, as we see it in the photograph or in the sketch by Mr. Rothenstein, with its unclean lips and furtive eyes, has the look with which we are too familiar in the degenerate types of our city streets, and from which we turn away with physical revulsion; but it half conceals also something of the expression of Keats, a Keats ruined. He was, as Mr. Symons says of him so finely, "a soul 'unspotted from the world,' in a body which one sees visibly soiling under one's eyes; . . . there never was a simpler or more attaching charm, because there never was a sweeter or more honest nature." [1] He suffered the penalties of physical decay without corrosion of the soul.

I would not say that Dowson was altogether peculiar in this respect, but it is true, nevertheless, that the malady of the flesh, with rare exceptions, carried its contagion into the very stronghold of the mind, creating thus what may be called the decadent or, in its wider application, the romantic Illusion. The nature and extent of this illusion may be inferred from the quotations and illustrations already given; but we need not rest in inference alone. It is, in fact, hard for a man to admit that he is simply futile or vile, and so, when the decadent is not flaunting his ill deeds wantonly in the face of the world in the vanity of excess, you are likely to find him posing as a martyr of the higher life. With the composure of a saint he will tell you that physical disease is a cause of the soul's health, that nastiness of the mind itself is the price of mental expansion, that, in a word,

---

[1] Mr. Symons has written nothing better than the brief biographical sketch attached to the volume of Dowson's *Poems*. It has something of the quality (only finer) of Miss Louise Imogen Guiney's *Study* prefixed to the *Selected Poems of James Clarence Mangan*. Much may be forgiven Dowson for the "most exquisite and appropriate impossibility" of his love for the refugee's daughter, as the story is told by Mr. Symons.

any morbid symptom is the indication of spirituality. He believes, as Swift said of certain men of an earlier day, that "the corruption of the senses is the generation of the spirit." This ancient, ineradicable error is implicit in the aphorism of John Davidson: "Decadence in any art is always the manure and root of a higher manifestation of that art." It is more clearly stated in Mr. Jackson's apology: "All the cynicisms and petulances and flippancies of the decadence, the febrile self-assertion, the voluptuousness, the perversity, were, consciously or unconsciously, efforts towards the rehabilitation of spiritual power." And it is expanded with Celtic fluency by Mr. Yeats:

I see, indeed, in the arts of every country those faint lights and faint colours and faint outlines and faint energies which many call "the decadence," and which I, because I believe that the arts lie dreaming of things to come, prefer to call the autumn of the body. An Irish poet, whose rhythms are like the cry of a sea-bird in autumn twilight, has told its meaning in the line, "the very sunlight's weary, and it's time to quit the plough." Its importance is great because it comes to us at the moment when we are beginning to be interested in many things which positive science, the interpreter of exterior law, has always denied: communion of mind with mind in thought and without words, foreknowledge in dreams and in visions, and the coming among us of the dead, and of much else. We are, it may be, at a crowning crisis of the world, at the moment when man is about to ascend, with the wealth he has been so long gathering upon his shoulders, the stairway he has been descending from the first days.

That is very pretty and sweet, and no doubt our wings are growing, but it is not easy to associate these flattering prognostics with such a movement as that which was represented in the Nineties by the particular band of rebels and revellers of whom Mr. Yeats was the leading mind, as he is the most distinguished survivor. The little *Book of the Rhymers' Club*, published in 1892, lies before me now, and as I turn its pages I discover nothing very wicked or startling, but of notable promise equally nothing. Should we, indeed, expect new life from young men to whom "the sunlight's weary"? Mr. Yeats himself, in his more candid moments, is not always so hopeful. I have heard him complain whimsically that the "Rhymers" had the morals of brigands and the manners of bishops, whereas the youngsters who are carrying the torch to-day have the morals of bishops and the manners of brigands — a sad derogation from the faith.

It may be unkind to say it, but one cannot study the lives of these men without feeling that the conversion of so many of them, including Aubrey Beardsley, to Catholicism was only another manifestation of the same illusion of the decadent as that which speaks in his theories of art. There is an unpleasant savour of truth, though not at all as Mr. Jackson meant it, in his saying of Francis Thompson, that "he took to poverty as he took to opium, as a sedative for the malady of spirit." Religion was not altogether for Thompson an opiate for *malady of spirit*, but with some of his contemporaries the two were as closely connected as their art was dependent on opium and alcohol. Too often conversion was merely the fruit of perversion.

This is rather the personal aspect of the decadent paradox, but it wore a social aspect which is more dangerous, as it is more deceptive. "It will seem, then," observes Mr. Jackson, "that the two paths of the modern art movement resolved themselves into two very definite and very different aims: the communal and the individual, the public and the private." There is nothing unusual in this, but we enter into the region of paradox when we find that many of the votaries of the modern art saw no incompatibility at all in these different aims. "All really great works of art are public works — monumental, collective, generic — expressing the ideas of a race, a community, a united people; not the ideas of a class," says Mr. Walter Crane, speaking for himself and William Morris and other temperamental socialists. Now, again, in a sense, that is true: art does spring naturally from a convention and a certain higher community of feeling; but it is at least questionable, in the face of the records, to define this convention as contrary to the ideas of class, for hitherto "great art," as contrasted with popular art, whether in Greece or Italy or France or China or Japan, has been aristocratic in its purpose and support. And, certainly, to suppose, as so many of the artists of the *fin de siècle* did suppose, that there was any bond of sound communism in their search for the last refinements of personality and in their theory of untrammelled expansiveness — certainly, there is in this something almost grotesquely absurd. Here, too, Oscar Wilde is a type and exponent of his fellows. He was not jesting, but rather stating their sober practice, when he boasted of "the beautiful sterile emotions" of art as hateful in the eyes of society: nor was it altogether a piece of idle persiflage when he took as his hero of the artistic temperament that master of "pen, pencil, and poison," Thomas Griffiths Wainewright, who, being reproached for the murder of Helen Abercrombie, merely shrugged his shoulders and said, "Yes, it was a dreadful thing to do, but she had very thick ankles." Were not the story too repulsive for print, I could parallel that seemingly childish effrontery with what I heard told only yesterday here in New York in perfect seriousness. But what shall we think of the sincerity of the author of *Salome* when he begins to indulge in humanitarian dreams, and what shall we say of this citizen of a Utopia for dandies when he undertakes to write solemnly of *The Soul of Man Under Socialism?* As a matter of fact, he was as sincere in this as in any other of his attitudes, and his inability to see anything incongruous in a humanitarian communism of totally undisciplined individualists was only one phase of the extraordinary illusion which held most of his comrades. As physical degeneration and morbid restlessness seemed to these men, looking at themselves, the marks of superiority in things spiritual, so, looking at the State, they dreamed of creating a gentle concert of souls out of lawless individualism. Wit for wit, there is better art and there is a sounder view of life in the avowed cynicism and social hatred of Swift and his friends than in this modern dream of social sympathy without the discipline of character.

The particular movement of Mr. Jackson's eulogy has come to its end, and most of the boastful voices of rebellion have fallen into one or the other silence; they were never a great force in English society. But the twin illusion which formed the real creed of the decadents has by no means disappeared with them, as it by no means began with them. It had its source in one of the great guiding movements of the nineteenth century, was caught up in self-justification and noisily bruited about by a band of men who were really and physically diseased, and now it is becoming the common property of innumerable good citizens of England and America who would shudder at its practical application.

It is scarcely necessary to observe that the fountain-head of the stream is in the Germany of the later decades of the eighteenth century. One of its earliest manifestations was Heinse's tale of *Ardinghello*, in which "the evangel of art went hand in hand with naked, unveiled sensuality," and which announced with sufficient frankness that "the decency of our common prosaic life is not permitted in art." Add to this such maxims of Wackenroder's as that "art is a seductive, forbidden fruit, and he who has once tasted its inmost sweetest sap is forever lost for the practical living world," and that "the fairest stream of life springs from the coming together of the streams of art and religion"; illustrate them with the identification in Novalis of beauty and sickliness, and crown them with Schleiermacher's glorification in the pulpit of the man who, "in the caprice of liberty, makes his personal view of the universe the centre of all religion" — combine these variously with a thousand other similar sentiments, develop them into a vast literature of prose and verse, and you will know whence the Continental artists of the nineteenth century learnt their creed of uncontrolled personal expansion, with the illusions that follow in its wake. Nor has the source dried up. Quite recently one of our distinguished German professors lent his name to the propagandist publication in English of the morbid obscenities of Friedrich Schlegel's *Lucinde*, and another well-known teacher of German has made himself the public defender of a group of unwholesome moderns who still believe that "decency is not permitted to art."

But the more immediate literary source of this perversion in the Nineties was rather French than German. To-day it is to be found in the group of powerful Russian writers, with their congeners in Scandinavia and the other northern countries, whose works for some time past have been flooding the world in French and English translations. How deeply this literature is tainted could be shown by innumerable examples; one must suffice. If there is any book thoroughly typical of the Russian and Scandinavian ideal it is *Crime and Punishment,* and if there is a single passage in which the moral of that book is typified it is the scene selected by its latest editor in English, Mr. Laurence Irving, as the epitome of "the animating spirit of Dostoieffsky":

His eyes gleamed, his lips trembled, and, resting his two hands on her shoulders, he cast an angry look on this face bathed in tears. In a moment, he bent downwards, kissing the girl's feet. She started back frightened, as she would have done from a madman. For Rashkolnikoff's face at this moment was that of one.

"What are you doing? And to me?" stammered Sonia, growing pale with sorrow-smitten heart.

Upon this he rose. "I did not bow down to you, personally, but to suffering humanity in your person."

Not long since, at a dinner with a philosopher and two professors of French and English literature, respectively, I observed casually that my summer had been darkened by dwelling in the nightmare of *Crime and Punishment* and other books of its class. At this my friends, better read in this literature than I, no doubt, admitted the nightmare, but clamorously rebuked me for not feeling uplifted by its spiritual implications. There it is. Somehow we are to be lifted up by sympathizing with a madman worshipping humanity in the person of a girl of the street. Filth, disease, morbid dreams, bestiality, insanity, sodden crime, these are the natural pathway to the emancipation of the spirit; these in some mysterious way are spirituality. And the same lesson runs through Tolstoy and Strindberg and a dozen other moralists who are, as it were, the Prophets of our young. In subdued form, befitting what remains of the reticence of the English temperament, it lurks among the present-day inheritors in London of the Yellow Nineties. It will be found hidden in some of the writings of Mr. Galsworthy, who is perhaps at this moment the most notable of the group — scarcely concealed at all in his latest novel, *The Dark Flower*, with its sickly analysis of illicit emotion, its satirical desiccation of the intellectual life, its presentation of virtue as a kind of impotence, its constant insinuation that the only escape of the spirit from stolid defeat is through "the passionate obsessions that cannot decently be satisfied." One is reminded again of the old scornful saying of Swift: "The corruption of the senses is the generation of the spirit."

What else is the meaning of the outburst of filth on the stage under the pretext of "social uplift"? Would any sane man, in the name of virtue, defend the representation before young men and maidens of the inner nastiness of the stews (made nastier by the dramatist's imagination), or the exhibition of the revolting details of physical corruption, if his understanding had not been obscured by the insidious theory that associates art and spirituality with licence and disease? Alas, it is still true that the human heart is deceitful above all things. Some time ago a friend of mine was present at the Boston opera when a certain morbid piece was sung. He was amused, and, being somewhat old-fashioned, was a little shocked, at seeing the dowagers of the town, in their conspicuous circle, clapping their hands at the exhibition of a theme of perverted sexuality. The next day he was less amused, and more shocked, to read the names of the same dowagers among those who had met together to hear the horrors of "white slavery" discussed and to concert means for its repression.

Even more pervasive is the illusion that through the very licence of personality men are to be brought into the bond of social communism, and the kinship of this illusion with the other and their source are clearly implied in the typical scene from Dostoieffsky already quoted. Or, if a stronger illustration of this theme in Russian is desired, it may be found in a tale of Leonid Andreyeff's which was the occasion of comment some ten or twelve years ago. In decency — shall I say, unfortunately? — I can do no more than hint at the narration. We are to suppose, then, that a proper young man is walking through a lonely country with his betrothed. They are attacked by a party of tramps, and the girl is killed. After the departure of the tramps the young man, by yielding to his bestial instincts, comes to realize that he is essentially of the same stuff as the outcasts of society, and that in the lowest depths of the heart is the common meeting-place of humanity. It used to be held that the peculiar bond and unity of mankind was to be sought in the higher plane of reason, with its law of self-restraint, whereas by the passions we were united with the unreasoning beasts; it has remained for certain doctors of modern literature to teach us otherwise.

There may seem to be a great gulf between such a writer as Andreyeff and the socialistic wits now entertaining London. There is, indeed, a gulf — and yet! Strip off the rags of decorum which Bernard Shaw, despite his protests, still wears as an Englishman; look at the real meaning of the thing, and you will find that the moral of *Fanny's First Play*, for example, which our kindly good folk enjoy so innocently, is not very different from that of the more barbarously logical Russians. What else does Bernard Shaw's laughter mean, when he represents a girl of modest upbringing as awakened to the hypocrisy of convention and the solidarity of mankind by getting arrested at night in the streets of London for disorderly conduct? It is the comedian's way of saying that spirituality is the product of vice, and that the uniting bond of society is the revolt against restraint. Mr. Shaw is a delightful humorist. Some one should suggest to him, as a subject amazingly suited to his genius, the state of life in a communistic society made up of such effronteries of egotism as himself. Perhaps I am myself eccentric in this, but, after all, I can read with less insult to my reason the rather childishly flaunted paradoxes of the naughty decade, and am inclined to think their perversion less insidiously dangerous, than the smug prurience of Mr. Galsworthy and the other bourgeois wits who are to-day taken with a certain seriousness as critics of our social conventions.

I write "to-day," and to-morrow the thunder of these men may be rolling as dimly about the horizon as is now the revolutionary noise of the "Rhymers," and these happenings I record may seem as ancient as the wickedness of Nineveh. But other men, and this is the whole charge against decadent wit, will be forgetting that art, so long as it is human, must concern itself with the portrayal of character — triumphant or defeated, still character — just as surely as religion is concerned with the creation of character. The truth of it is summed up in the sentence of Whichcote, one of the great divines who were preaching when Milton was writing his poems: "For we all say, that which doth not proceed from the judgement of the mind, and the choice of the will, is not an *human act*, though the act of a man."

JOHN GALSWORTHY

ABOUT CENSORSHIP [1]

SINCE, time and again, it has been proved, in this country of
free institutions, that the great majority of our fellow-countrymen consider the only Censorship that now obtains amongst
us, namely the Censorship of Plays, a bulwark for the preservation of their comfort and sensibility against the spiritual researches and speculations of bolder and too active spirits — it
has become time to consider whether we should not seriously
extend a principle, so grateful to the majority, to all our institutions.

For no one can deny that in practice the Censorship of
Drama works with a smooth swiftness — a lack of delay and
friction unexampled in any public office. No troublesome
publicity and tedious postponement for the purpose of appeal
mar its efficiency. It is neither hampered by the Law nor by
the slow process of popular election. Welcomed by the overwhelming majority of the public; objected to only by such
persons as suffer from it, and a negligible faction, who, wedded
pedantically to liberty of the subject, are resentful of summary
powers vested in a single person responsible only to his own
conscience — it is amazingly, triumphantly, successful.

Why, then, in a democratic State, is so valuable a protector
of the will, the interests, and pleasure of the majority not bestowed on other branches of the public being? Opponents of
the Censorship of Plays have been led by the absence of such
other Censorships to conclude that this Office is an archaic
survival, persisting into times that have outgrown it. They
have been known to allege that the reason of its survival is
simply the fact that Dramatic Authors, whose reputation and
means of livelihood it threatens, have ever been few in number
and poorly organised — that the reason, in short, is the help-
lessness and weakness of the interests concerned. We must all

[1] From *The Inn of Tranquillity.* Copyright, 1912, by Charles Scribner's Sons.
By permission of the publishers.

combat with force such an aspersion on our Legislature. Can it even for a second be supposed that a State which gives trial by Jury to the meanest, poorest, most helpless of its citizens, and concedes to the greatest criminals the right of appeal, could have debarred a body of reputable men from the ordinary rights of citizenship for so cynical a reason as that their numbers were small, their interests unjoined, their protests feeble? Such a supposition were intolerable! We do not in this country deprive a class of citizens of their ordinary rights, we do not place their produce under the irresponsible control of one not amenable to Law, by any sort of political accident! That would indeed be to laugh at Justice in this Kingdom! That would indeed be cynical and unsound! We must never admit that there is no basic Justice controlling the edifice of our Civic Rights. We do, we must, conclude that a just and well-considered principle underlies this despotic Institution; for surely, else, it would not be suffered to survive for a single moment! Pom! Pom!

If, then, the Censorship of Plays be just, beneficent, and based on a well-considered principle, we must rightly inquire what good and logical reason there is for the absence of Censorship in other departments of the national life. If Censorship of the Drama be in the real interests of the people, or at all events in what the Censor for the time being conceives to be their interest — then Censorships of Art, Literature, Religion, Science, and Politics are in the interests of the people, unless it can be proved that there exists essential difference between the Drama and these other branches of the public being. Let us consider whether there is any such essential difference.

It is fact, beyond dispute, that every year numbers of books appear which strain the average reader's intelligence and sensibilities to an unendurable extent; books whose speculations are totally unsuited to normal thinking powers; books which contain views of morality divergent from the customary, and discussions of themes unsuited to the young person; books which, in fine, provide the greater Public with no pleasure whatsoever, and, either by harrowing their feelings or offending their good taste, cause them real pain.

It is true that, precisely as in the case of Plays, the Public are protected by a vigilant and critical Press from works of this description; that, further, they are protected by the commercial instinct of the Libraries, who will not stock an article which may offend their customers — just as, in the case of Plays, the Public are protected by the common-sense of theatrical Managers; that, finally, they are protected by the Police and the Common Law of the land. But despite all these protections, it is no uncommon thing for an average citizen to purchase one of these disturbing or dubious books. Has he, on discovering its true nature, the right to call on the bookseller to refund its value? He has not. And thus he runs a danger obviated in the case of the Drama which has the protection of a prudential Censorship. For this reason alone, how much better, then, that there should exist a paternal authority (some, no doubt, will call it grand-maternal — but sneers must not be confounded with argument) to suppress these books before appearance, and safeguard us from the danger of buying and possibly reading undesirable or painful literature!

A specious reason, however, is advanced for exempting Literature from the Censorship accorded to Plays. He — it is said — who attends the performance of a play, attends it in public, where his feelings may be harrowed and his taste offended, cheek by jowl with boys, or women of all ages; it may even chance that he has taken to this entertainment his wife, or the young persons of his household. He — on the other hand — who reads a book, reads it in privacy. True; but the wielder of this argument has clasped his fingers round a two-edged blade. The very fact that the book has no mixed audience removes from Literature an element which is ever the greatest cheek on licentiousness in Drama. No manager of a theatre, — a man of the world engaged in the acquisition of his livelihood, — unless guaranteed by the license of the Censor, dare risk the presentment before a mixed audience of that which might cause an *émeute* among his clients. It has, indeed, always been observed that the theatrical manager, almost without exception, thoughtfully recoils from the responsibility that would be thrust on him by the abolition of the Censorship. The fear of the mixed audience is ever suspended above his head. No such fear threatens the publisher, who displays his wares to one man at a time. And for this very reason of the mixed audience, perpetually and perversely cited to the contrary by such as have no firm grasp of this matter, there is a greater necessity for a Censorship on Literature than for one on Plays.

Further, if there were but a Censorship of Literature, no matter how dubious the books that were allowed to pass, the conscience of no reader need ever be troubled. For, that the perfect rest of the public conscience is the first result of Censorship, is proved to certainty by the protected Drama, since many dubious plays are yearly put before the play-going Public without tending in any way to disturb a complacency engendered by the security from harm guaranteed by this beneficent, if despotic, Institution. Pundits who, to the discomfort of the populace, foster this exemption of Literature from discipline, cling to the old-fashioned notion that ulcers should be encouraged to discharge themselves upon the surface, instead of being quietly and decently driven into the system and allowed to fester there.

The remaining plea for exempting Literature from Censorship, put forward by unreflecting persons: That it would require too many Censors — besides being unworthy, is, on the face of it, erroneous. Special tests have never been thought necessary in appointing Examiners of Plays. They would, indeed, not only be unnecessary, but positively dangerous, seeing that the essential function of Censorship is protection of the ordinary prejudices and forms of thought. There would, then, be no difficulty in securing to-morrow as many Censors of Literature as might be necessary (say twenty or thirty); since all that would be required of each one of them would be that he should secretly exercise, in his uncontrolled discretion, his individual taste. In a word, this Free Literature of ours protects advancing thought and speculation; and those who believe in civic freedom subject only to Common Law, and espouse the cause of free literature, are championing a system which is essentially undemocratic, essentially inimical to the will of the majority, who have certainly no desire for any such things as advancing thought and speculation. Such persons, indeed, merely hold the faith that the *People, as a whole, unprotected by the despotic judgments of single persons, have enough strength and wisdom to know what is and what is not harmful to themselves. They put their trust in a Public Press and a Common Law, which deriving from the Conscience of the Country, is openly administered and within the reach of all.* How absurd, how inadequate this all is we see from the existence of the Censorship on Drama.

Having observed that there is no reason whatever for the exemption of Literature, let us now turn to the case of Art. Every picture hung in a gallery, every statue placed on a pedestal, is exposed to the public stare of a mixed company. Why, then, have we no Censorship to protect us from the possibility of encountering works that bring blushes to the cheek of the young person? The reason cannot be that the proprietors of Galleries are more worthy of trust than the managers of Theatres; this would be to make an odious distinction which those very Managers who uphold the Censorship of Plays would be the first to resent. It is true that Societies of artists and the proprietors of Galleries are subject to the prosecution of the Law if they offend against the ordinary standards of public decency; but precisely the same liability attaches to theatrical managers and proprietors of Theatres, in whose case it has been found necessary and beneficial to add the Censorship. And in this connection let it once more be noted how much more easily the ordinary standards of public decency can be assessed by a single person responsible to no one, than by the clumsy (if more open) process of public protest.

What, then, in the light of the proved justice and efficiency of the Censorship of Drama, *is* the reason for the absence of the Censorship of Art? The more closely the matter is regarded, the more plain it is, that *there is none!* At any moment we may have to look upon some painting, or contemplate some statue, as tragic, heart-rending, and dubiously delicate in theme as that censured play "The Cenci," by one Shelley; as dangerous to prejudice, and suggestive of new thought as the censured "Ghosts," by one Ibsen. Let us protest against this peril suspended over our heads, and demand the immediate appointment of a single person not selected for any pretentiously artistic feelings, but endowed with summary powers of prohibiting the exhibition, in public galleries or places, of such

works as he shall deem, in his uncontrolled discretion, unsuited
to average intelligence or sensibility. Let us demand it in the
interest, not only of the young person, but of those whole sections of the community which cannot be expected to take an
interest in Art, and to whom the purpose, speculations, and
achievements of great artists, working not only for to-day but
for to-morrow, must naturally be dark riddles. Let us even
require that this official should be empowered to order the
destruction of the works which he has deemed unsuited to
average intelligence and sensibility, lest their creators should,
by private sale, make a profit out of them, such as, in the nature
of the case, Dramatic Authors are debarred from making out of
plays which, having been censured, cannot be played for money.
Let us ask this with confidence; for it is not compatible with
common justice that there should be any favouring of Painter
over Playwright. They are both artists — let them both be
measured by the same last!

But let us now consider the case of Science. It will not, indeed cannot, be contended that the investigations of scientific
men, whether committed to writing or to speech, are always
suited to the taste and capacities of our general public. There
was, for example, the well-known doctrine of Evolution, the
teachings of Charles Darwin and Alfred Russel Wallace, who
gathered up certain facts, hitherto but vaguely known, into
presentments, irreverent and startling, which, at the time, profoundly disturbed every normal mind. Not only did religion,
as then accepted, suffer in this cataclysm, but our taste and
feeling were inexpressibly shocked by the discovery, so em-
phasised by Thomas Henry Huxley, of Man's descent from
Apes. It was felt, and is felt by many to this day, that the
advancement of that theory grossly and dangerously violated
every canon of decency. What pain, then, might have been
averted, what far-reaching consequences and incalculable sub-
version of primitive faiths checked, if some judicious Censor of
scientific thought had existed in those days to demand, in ac-
cordance with his private estimate of the will and temper of the
majority, the suppression of the doctrine of Evolution.

Innumerable investigations of scientists on subjects such as
the date of the world's creation, have from time to time been

summarised and inconsiderately sprung on a Public shocked and startled by the revelation that facts which they were accustomed to revere were conspicuously at fault. So, too, in the range of medicine, it would be difficult to cite any radical discovery (such as the preventive power of vaccination), whose unchecked publication has not violated the prejudices and disturbed the immediate comfort of the common mind. Had these discoveries been judiciously suppressed, or pared away to suit what a Censorship conceived to be the popular palate of the time, all this disturbance and discomfort might have been avoided.

It will doubtless be contended (for there are no such violent opponents of Censorship as those who are threatened with the same) that to compare a momentous disclosure, such as the doctrine of Evolution, to a mere drama, were unprofitable. The answer to this ungenerous contention is fortunately plain. Had a judicious Censorship existed over our scientific matters, such as for two hundred years has existed over our Drama, scientific discoveries *would have been no more disturbing and momentous than those which we are accustomed to see made on our nicely pruned and tutored stage.* For not only would the more dangerous and penetrating scientific truths have been carefully destroyed at birth, but scientists, aware that the results of investigations offensive to accepted notions would be suppressed, would long have ceased to waste their time in search of a knowledge repugnant to average intelligence, and thus foredoomed, and have occupied themselves with services more agreeable to the public taste, such as the rediscovery of truths already known and published.

Indissolubly connected with the desirability of a Censorship of Science, is the need for Religious Censorship. For in this, assuredly not the least important department of the nation's life, we are witnessing week by week and year by year, what in the light of the security guaranteed by the Censorship of Drama, we are justified in terming an alarming spectacle. Thousands of men are licensed to proclaim from their pulpits, Sunday after Sunday, their individual beliefs, quite regardless of the settled convictions of the masses of their congregations. It is true, indeed, that the vast majority of sermons (like the vast majority of plays) are, and will always be, harmonious with the feelings of the average citizen; for neither priest nor playwright have customarily any such peculiar gift of spiritual daring as might render them unsafe mentors of their fellows; and there is not wanting the deterrent of common-sense to keep them in bounds. Yet it can hardly be denied that there spring up at times men — like John Wesley or General Booth — of such incurable temperament as to be capable of abusing their freedom by the promulgation of doctrine or procedure, divergent from the current traditions of religion. Nor must it be forgotten that sermons, like plays, are addressed to a mixed audience of families, and that the spiritual teachings of a lifetime may be destroyed by ten minutes of uncensured pronouncement from a pulpit, the while parents are sitting, not, as in a theatre vested with the right of protest, but dumb and excoriated to the soul, watching their children, perhaps of tender age, eagerly drinking in words at variance with that which they themselves have been at such pains to instil.

If a set of Censors — for it would, as in the case of Literature, indubitably require more than one (perhaps one hundred and eighty, but, for reasons already given, there should be no difficulty whatever in procuring them) endowed with the swift powers conferred by freedom from the dull tedium of responsibility, and not remarkable for religious temperament, were appointed, to whom all sermons and public addresses on religious subjects must be submitted before delivery, and whose duty after perusal should be to excise all portions not conformable to their private ideas of what was at the moment suitable to the Public's ears, we should be far on the road toward that proper preservation of the *status quo* so desirable if the faiths and ethical standards of the less exuberantly spiritual masses are to be maintained in their full bloom. As things now stand, the nation has absolutely nothing to safeguard it against religious progress.

We have seen, then, that Censorship is at least as necessary over Literature, Art, Science, and Religion as it is over our Drama. We have now to call attention to the crowning need — the want of a Censorship in Politics.

If Censorship be based on justice, if it be proved to serve the

Public and to be successful in its lonely vigil over Drama, it should, *and logically must be,* extended to all parallel cases; it cannot, it dare not, stop short at Politics. For, precisely in this supreme branch of the public life are we most menaced by the rule and license of the leading spirit. To appreciate this fact, we need only examine the Constitution of the House of Commons. Six hundred and seventy persons chosen from a population numbering four and forty millions, must necessarily, whatever their individual defects, be citizens of *more than average* enterprise, resource, and resolution. They are elected for a period that may last five years. Many of them are ambitious; some uncompromising; not a few enthusiastically eager to do something for their country; filled with designs and aspirations for national or social betterment, with which the masses, sunk in the immediate pursuits of life, can in the nature of things have little sympathy. And yet we find these men licensed to pour forth at pleasure, before mixed audiences, checked only by Common Law and Common-Sense political utterances which may have the gravest, the most terrific consequences; utterances which may at any moment let loose revolution, or plunge the country into war; which often, as a fact, excite an utter detestation, terror, and mistrust; or shock the most sacred domestic and proprietary convictions in the breasts of vast majorities of their fellow-countrymen! And we incur this appalling risk for the want of a single, or at the most, a handful of Censors, invested with a simple but limitless discretion to excise or to suppress entirely such political utterances as may seem to their private judgments calculated to cause pain or moral disturbance in the average man. The masses, it is true, have their protection and remedy against injudicious or inflammatory politicians in the Law and the so-called democratic process of election; but we have seen that theatre audiences have also the protection of the Law, and the remedy of boycott, and that in their case this protection and this remedy are not deemed enough. What, then, shall we say of the case of Politics, where the dangers attending inflammatory or subversive utterance are greater a million fold, and the remedy a thousand times less expeditious?

Our Legislators have laid down Censorship as the basic

principle of Justice underlying the civic rights of dramatists. Then, let "Censorship for all" be their motto, and this country no longer be ridden and destroyed by free Institutions! Let them not only establish forthwith Censorships of Literature, Art, Science, and Religion, but also *place themselves* beneath the regimen with which they have calmly fettered Dramatic Authors. They cannot deem it becoming to their regard for justice, to their honour, to their sense of humour, to recoil from a restriction which, in a parallel case they have imposed on others. It is an old and homely saying that good officers never place their men in positions they would not themselves be willing to fill. And we are not entitled to believe that our Legislators, having set Dramatic Authors where they have been set, will — now that their duty is made plain — for a moment hesitate to step down and stand alongside.

But if by any chance they should recoil, and thus make answer: "We are ready at all times to submit to the Law and the People's will, and to bow to their demands, but we cannot and must not be asked to place our calling, our duty, and our honour beneath the irresponsible rule of an arbitrary autocrat, however sympathetic with the generality he may chance to be!" Then, we would ask: "Sirs, did you ever hear of that great saying: 'Do unto others as ye would they should do unto you!'" For it is but fair presumption that the Dramatists, whom our Legislators have placed in bondage to a despot, are, no less than those Legislators, proud of their calling, conscious of their duty, and jealous of their honour.

HILAIRE BELLOC

A LITTLE CONVERSATION IN HEREFORDSHIRE [1]

THERE is a country house (as the English phrase goes) in the County of Hereford, at a little distance from the River Wye; the people who live in this house are very rich. They are not rich precariously, nor with doubts here and there, nor for the time, but in a solid manner; that is, they believe their riches to be eternal. Their income springs from very many places, of which they have not an idea; it is spent in a straightforward manner, which they fully comprehend. It is spent in relieving the incompetence — the economic incompetence — of all those about them; in causing wine to come into England from Ay, Vosne, Barsac, and (though they do not know it) from the rougher soil of Algiers. It also causes (does the way in which they exercise what only pedants call their Potential Demand) tea to be grown in Ceylon for their servants and in China for themselves, horses to be bred in Ireland, and wheat to be sown and most laboriously garnered in Western Canada, Ohio, India, South Russia, the Argentine, and other places. Also, were you to seek out every economic cause and effect, you would find missionaries living where no man can live, save by artifice, and living upon artificial supply in a strange climate by the strength of this Potential Demand rooted in the meadows of the Welsh March.

Then, also, if you were to follow the places whence their wealth is derived, it would interest you very much. You would see one man earning so much in the docks and handing on a Saturday evening so much of his wages into their fund. You would see another clipping off cloth in Manchester and offering it to them, and another plucking cotton in Egypt and exchanging it, at their order, against something which they, not he, needed. Altogether you would see the whole world paying tithe, and a stream flowing into Hereford as into a reservoir, and a stream flowing out again by many channels.

[1] Taken by permission from Hilaire Belloc's *On Everything* (1909), published and copyrighted by E. P. Dutton and Company, Inc., New York. By permission also of the author and of the English publishers, Messrs. Methuen and Company.

These good people were at dinner; upon the 5th of October, to be accurate. Parliament had not yet met, but football had begun, and there was shooting, also a little riding upon horses, though this is not to-day a popular amusement, and few will practise it. As for the women, one wrote and the other read — which was a fair division of labour; but the woman who wrote was not read by the woman who read, for the woman who wrote (and she was the daughter) preferred to write upon problems. But her mother, who did the reading, preferred what is called fiction, and Mr. Meredith was a favourite author of hers; but, indeed, she would read all fiction so only that it was in her native tongue.

Now the men of the family were very different from this, and the things they liked were hunting of a particular kind (which I shall not here describe), shooting of a similar kind, their country, and politics, which last interest it would have been abominable to deny them, for the two men, both father and son, were actively engaged in the making of laws, each in a different place; the laws they made (it is true in the company of, and with the advice of, others) are to be found in what is called the Statute Book, which neither you nor I have ever seen.

All these four, the father, the son, the mother, and the daughter, in different ways intelligent, but all four very kind and good, were at dinner upon this day of which I speak, the 5th of October, but they were not alone. They had to meet them several people who were staying in the house. The one was a satirist who had been born in Lithuania. He was poor and proud and had learnt the English tongue, and he wrote books upon the pride of race and upon battling with the sea. He was an envious sort of man, but as he never had nor ever would have any home or lineage, England was much the same to him as any other place. He hated all our nations with an equal hatred.

Another guest was a little man called Copp. He was a lord; his title was not Copp. Only his name was Copp, and even this name he hid, for old father Copp, who had married a Miss Billings in the eighteenth century, had had a son John Billings, since the Billings were richer than the Copps. And John Billings had married Mary Steyning, who was the Squire's daughter, and they had had a son John Steyning, since John was by this time the hereditary name. Now John Steyning was in the Parliament that worked for the Regent, and a short one it was, and he became plain Lord Steyning, and then he and his son and his grandson married in all sorts of ways, and the title now was Bramber, but the family name was Steyning, and the real name was Copp. So much for Copp. He was as lively as a grig, he had travelled everywhere, and he knew about ten languages. He was peculiarly brave, and as a boy he had stoutly refused to go to the University.

Then also there was the Doctor, who was absurdly nervous and could ill afford to dine out, and there was a young man who was in Parliament with the son of the family; this young man had been to Oxford with him also, not at Cambridge; he was a lawyer, and he was making three thousand pounds a year, but he said he was making six when he talked to his wife and mother, and most serious men believed that he was making ten. The women of these were also present with them, saving always that Copp, who was called Steyning, and whose title was Bramber, was not married.

These then, sitting round the table, came to talk of something after all not remote from the interest of their lives. They talked of Socialists, and it all began by Copp (who called himself Steyning, while his title was Bramber) saying that his uncle Gwilliam had just missed being a Socialist because he was too stupid.

The Head of the Family, who had most imperfectly caught the pronouncement of Copp as to his relative, said, "Yes, Bramber; got to be pretty stupid to be that!" By which the Head of the House meant that one had to be pretty stupid to be a Socialist, whereas what Copp had said was that his uncle had been too stupid to be a Socialist. But it was all one.

The Son of the House said that there were lots of Socialists going about, and the young lawyer friend said there were a lot of people who said they were Socialists but who were not Socialists.

The Daughter of the House said that it was very interesting the way in which Socialism went up and down. She said: "Look at the Fabians!" The Mother of the House looked all round, smiling genially, for she thought that her daughter was speaking of the name of a book.

The Doctor said: "It's all a pose, those sort of people." But which sort he did not say, so the Daughter of the House said sharply: "Which sort of people?" For she loved to cross-examine struggling professional men, and the Doctor got quite red, and said; "Oh, all that sort of people!"

The young lawyer, who was quick to see a difficulty, helped him out by saying, "He means people like Bensington!"

The Doctor, who had never heard of Bensington, nodded eagerly, and the Head of the House frowning a healthy frown, said, "What, not John Bensington, old William Bensington's son?"

"Yes," said the young lawyer. "That's the kind of man he means," and the Doctor nodded again.

His enemy was dropping farther and farther behind him with every stride, but she made a brilliant rally. "Do you mean John Bensington?" she said. The Doctor, in some alarm, and with his mouth full, nodded vigorously for the third time. The Head of the House, still frowning, broke into all this with a solid roar: "I don't believe a word of it." He sat leaning back again, not relaxing his frown and trying to connect the son of his old friend with a gang of treasonable robbers. He remembered Jock's marriage — for it was a bad one — and a silly book of verses he had written, and how keen he had been against his father's selling the bit of land along the coast, because it was bound to go up. He could fit Jock in with many unpleasant things, but he couldn't fit him in with the very definite picture that rose in his mind whenever he heard the word "Socialist." There was something adventurous and violent and lean about the word — something like a wolf. There was nothing of all that in Jock. So much thought matured at last into living words, and the Head of the House said, "Why, he's on the County Council."

The Daughter of the House turned to the lawyer and said, "How would you define a Socialist, Mr. Layton?"

Mr. Layton defined a Socialist, and his silent wife, who was sitting opposite, looked at him happily on account of the power of his mind. The Lithuanian, who had said nothing all this while, but had been glancing with eyes as bright as a bird's, now at one speaker, now at another, nerved himself to intervene. Then there passed over his little soul the vivid pictures of things he had seen and known; the dens in Riga, the pain, the flight upon a Danish ship, the assumption first of German, then of English nationality, the easy gullibility of the large-hearted wealthy people of this land. He remembered his own confidence, his own unwavering talent, and his contempt of, and hatred for, other men. He could have trusted himself to speak, for he was in full command of his little soul, and there was not a trace of anything in his accent definitely foreign. But the virtue and the folly of these happy luxurious people about him pleased him too much and pleased him wickedly.

He went on tasting them in silence, until the Daughter of the House, who felt awe for him alone of all those present — much more awe than she did for her strong and good father — said to him, almost with reverence, that he should take to writing now of the meadows of England, since he had so wonderfully described her battles at sea. And the Lithuanian was ready to turn the talk upon letters, his bright eyes darting all the while. The old man, the Head of the House, sighed and muttered: "Jock was no Socialist." That was the one thing that he retained; . . . and meanwhile wealth continued to pour in from all corners of the world into his house, and to pour out again over the four seas, doing his will, and no one in the world, not even the chief victims of that wealth, hated it as the little Lithuanian did, and no one in the world — not even of them who had seen most of that wealth — hungered bestially for it as did he.

MAX BEERBOHM

"A CLERGYMAN"[1]

FRAGMENTARY, pale, momentary; almost nothing; glimpsed and gone; as it were, a faint human hand thrust up, never to reappear, from beneath the rolling waters of Time, he forever haunts my memory and solicits my weak imagination. Nothing is told of him but that once, abruptly, he asked a question, and received an answer.

This was on the afternoon of April 7th, 1778, at Streatham, in the well-appointed house of Mr. Thrale. Johnson, on the morning of that day, had entertained Boswell at breakfast in Bolt Court and invited him to dine at Thrale Hall. The two took coach and arrived early. It seems that Sir John Pringle had asked Boswell to ask Johnson "what were the best English sermons for style." In the interval before dinner, accordingly, Boswell reeled off the names of several divines whose prose might or might not win commendation. "Atterbury?" he suggested. "JOHNSON: Yes, Sir, one of the best. BOSWELL: Tillotson? JOHNSON: Why, not now. I should not advise any one to imitate Tillotson's style; though I don't know; I should be cautious of censuring anything that has been applauded by so many suffrages. — South is one of the best, if you except his peculiarities, and his violence, and sometimes coarseness of language. — Seed has a very fine style; but he is not very theological. — Jortin's sermons are very elegant. — Sherlock's style, too, is very elegant, though he has not made it his principal study. — And you may add Smalridge. BOSWELL: I like Ogden's Sermons on Prayer very much, both for neatness of style and subtilty of reasoning. JOHNSON: I should like to read all that Ogden has written. BOSWELL: What I want to know is, what sermons afford the best specimen of English pulpit eloquence. JOHNSON: We have no sermons addressed to the passions, that are good for anything; if you mean that kind of elo-

[1] Taken by permission from *And Even Now* (1920), published and copyrighted by E. P. Dutton and Company, Inc., New York. Also by permission of the author. Written in 1918.

quence. A CLERGYMAN, whose name I do not recollect: Were not Dodd's sermons addressed to the passions? JOHNSON: They were nothing, Sir, be they addressed to what they may."

The suddenness of it! Bang! — and the rabbit that had popped from its burrow was no more.

I know not which is the more startling — the début of the unfortunate clergyman, or the instantaneousness of his end. Why hadn't Boswell told us there was a clergyman present? Well, we may be sure that so careful and acute an artist had some good reason. And I suppose the clergyman was left to take us unawares because just so did he take the company. Had we been told he was there, we might have expected that sooner or later he would join in the conversation. He would have had a place in our minds. We may assume that in the minds of the company around Johnson he had no place. He sat forgotten, overlooked; so that his self-assertion startled every one just as on Boswell's page it startles us. In Johnson's massive and magnetic presence only some very remarkable man, such as Mr. Burke, was sharply distinguishable from the rest. Others might, if they had something in them, stand out slightly. This unfortunate clergyman may have had something in him, but I judge that he lacked the gift of seeming as if he had. That deficiency, however, does not account for the horrid fate that befell him. One of Johnson's strongest and most inveterate feelings was his veneration for the Cloth. To any one in Holy Orders he habitually listened with a grave and charming deference. To-day, moreover, he was in excellent good humour. He was at the Thrales', where he so loved to be; the day was fine; a fine dinner was in close prospect; and he had had what he always declared to be the sum of human felicity — a ride in a coach. Nor was there in the question put by the clergyman anything likely to enrage him. Dodd was one whom Johnson had befriended in adversity; and it had always been agreed that Dodd in his pulpit was very emotional. What drew the blasting flash must have been not the question itself, but the manner in which it was asked. And I think we can guess what that manner was.

Say the words aloud: "Were not Dodd's sermons addressed to the passions?" They are words which, if you have any dramatic and histrionic sense, *cannot* be said except in a high, thin voice.

You may, from sheer perversity, utter them in a rich and sonorous baritone or bass. But if you do so, they sound utterly unnatural. To make them carry the conviction of human utterance, you have no choice: you must pipe them.

Remember, now, Johnson was very deaf. Even the people whom he knew well, the people to whose voices he was accustomed, had to address him very loudly. It is probable that this unregarded, young, shy clergyman, when at length he suddenly mustered courage to "cut in," let his high, thin voice soar *too* high, insomuch that it was a kind of scream. On no other hypothesis can we account for the ferocity with which Johnson turned and rended him. Johnson didn't, we may be sure, mean to be cruel. The old lion, startled, just struck out blindly. But the force of paw and claws was not the less lethal. We have endless testimony to the strength of Johnson's voice; and the very cadence of those words, "They were nothing, Sir, be they addressed to what they may," convinces me that the old lion's jaws never gave forth a louder roar. Boswell does not record that there was any further conversation before the announcement of dinner. Perhaps the whole company had been temporarily deafened. But I am not bothering about *them*. My heart goes out to the poor dear clergyman exclusively.

I said a moment ago that he was young and shy; and I admit that I slipped those epithets in without having justified them to you by due process of induction. Your quick mind will have already supplied what I omitted. A man with a high, thin voice, and without power to impress any one with a sense of his importance, a man so null in effect that even the retentive mind of Boswell did not retain his very name, would assuredly not be a self-confident man. Even if he were not naturally shy, social courage would soon have been sapped in him, and would in time have been destroyed, by experience. That he had not yet given himself up as a bad job, that he still had faint wild hopes, is proved by the fact that he did snatch the opportunity for asking that question. He must, accordingly, have been young. Was he the curate of the neighbouring church? I

think so. It would account for his having been invited. I see
him as he sits there listening to the great Doctor's pronouncement on Atterbury and those others. He sits on the edge of a
chair in the background. He has colourless eyes, fixed earnestly, and a face almost as pale as the clerical bands beneath
his somewhat receding chin. His forehead is high and narrow,
his hair mouse-coloured. His hands are clasped tight before
him, the knuckles standing out sharply. This constriction
does not mean that he is steeling himself to speak. He has no
positive intention of speaking. Very much, nevertheless, is he
wishing in the back of his mind that he *could* say something —
something whereat the great Doctor would turn on him and
say, after a pause for thought, "Why yes, Sir. That is most
justly observed" or "Sir, this has never occurred to me. I
thank you" — thereby fixing the observer forever high in the
esteem of all. And now in a flash the chance presents itself.
"We have," shouts Johnson, "no sermons addressed to the
passions, that are good for anything." I see the curate's
frame quiver with sudden impulse, and his mouth fly open,
and — no, I can't bear it, I shut my eyes and ears. But audible, even so, is something shrill, followed by something thun-
derous.

Presently I re-open my eyes. The crimson has not yet faded
from that young face yonder, and slowly down either cheek
falls a glistening tear. Shades of Atterbury and Tillotson!
Such weakness shames the Established Church. What would
Jortin and Smalridge have said? — what Seed and South?
And, by the way, who *were* they, these worthies? It is a
solemn thought that so little is conveyed to us by names which
to the palæo-Georgians conveyed so much. We discern a
dim, composite picture of a big man in a big wig and a billowing
black gown, with a big congregation beneath him. But we
are not anxious to hear what he is saying. We know it is all
very elegant. We know it will be printed and be bound in
finely tooled full calf, and no palæo-Georgian gentleman's
library will be complete without it. Literate people in those
days were comparatively few; but, bating that, one may say
that sermons were as much in request as novels are to-day.
I wonder, will mankind continue to be capricious? It is a very

solemn thought indeed that no more than a hundred-and-
fifty years hence the novelists of our time, with all their moral
and political and sociological outlook and influence, will perhaps shine as indistinctly as do those old preachers, with all
their elegance, now. "Yes, Sir," some great pundit may be
telling a disciple at this moment, "Wells is one of the best.
Galsworthy is one of the best, if you except his concern for
delicacy of style. Mrs. Ward has a very firm grasp of problems, but is not very creational. — Caine's books are very
edifying. I should like to read all that Caine has written.
Miss Corelli, too, is very edifying. — And you may add Upton
Sinclair." "What I want to know," says the disciple, "is,
what English novels may be selected as specially enthralling."
The pundit answers: "We have no novels addressed to the
passions that are good for anything, if you mean that kind of
enthralment." And here some poor wretch (whose name the
disciple will not remember) inquires: "Are not Mrs. Glyn's
novels addressed to the passions?" and is in due form annihi-
lated. Can it be that a time will come when readers of this
passage in our pundit's life will take more interest in the poor
nameless wretch than in all the bearers of those great names
put together, being no more able or anxious to discriminate
between (say) Mrs. Ward and Mr. Sinclair than we are to set
Ogden above Sherlock, or Sherlock above Ogden? It seems
impossible. But we must remember that things are not always what they seem.

Every man illustrious in his day, however much he may be
gratified by his fame, looks with an eager eye to posterity for a
continuance of past favours, and would even live the remainder of his life in obscurity if by so doing he could insure that
future generations would preserve a correct attitude towards
him forever. This is very natural and human, but, like so
many very natural and human things, very silly. Tillotson and
the rest need not, after all, be pitied for our neglect of them.
They either know nothing about it, or are above such terrene
trifles. Let us keep our pity for the great seething mass of
divines who were *not* elegantly verbose, and had no fun or
glory while they lasted. And let us keep a specially large
portion for one whose lot was so much worse than merely un-

distinguished. If that nameless curate had not been at the Thrales' that day, or, being there, had kept the silence that so well became him, his life would have been drab enough in all conscience. But at any rate an unpromising career would not have been nipped in the bud. And that is what in fact happened, I'm sure of it. A robust man might have rallied under the blow. Not so our friend. Those who knew him in infancy had not expected that he would be reared. Better for him had they been right. It is well to grow up and be ordained, but not if you are delicate and very sensitive, and shall happen to annoy the greatest, the most stentorian and roughest of contemporary personages. "A Clergyman" never held up his head or smiled again after the brief encounter recorded for us by Boswell. He sank into a rapid decline. Before the next blossoming of Thrale Hall's almond trees he was no more. I like to think that he died forgiving Dr. Johnson.

Satirical repetition - parody.

BERTRAND RUSSELL

THE FREE MAN'S WORSHIP [1]

To Dr. Faustus in his study Mephistopheles told the history
of the Creation, saying:

"The endless praises of the choirs of angels had begun to
grow wearisome; for, after all, did he not deserve their praise?
Had he not given them endless joy? Would it not be more
amusing to obtain undeserved praise, to be worshipped by
beings whom he tortured? He smiled inwardly, and resolved
that the great drama should be performed.

"For countless ages the hot nebula whirled aimlessly through
space. At length it began to take shape, the central mass
threw off planets, the planets cooled, boiling seas and burning
mountains heaved and tossed, from black masses of cloud hot
sheets of rain deluged the barely solid crust. And now the
first germ of life grew in the depths of the ocean, and developed
rapidly in the fructifying warmth into vast forest trees, huge
ferns springing from the damp mould, sea monsters breeding,
fighting, devouring, and passing away. And from the monsters,
as the play unfolded itself, Man was born, with the power of
thought, the knowledge of good and evil, and the cruel thirst
for worship. And Man saw that all is passing in this mad,
monstrous world, that all is struggling to snatch, at any cost, a
few brief moments of life before Death's inexorable decree.
And Man said: 'There is a hidden purpose, could we but
fathom it, and the purpose is good; for we must reverence
something, and in the visible world there is nothing worthy of
reverence.' And Man stood aside from the struggle, resolving
that God intended harmony to come out of chaos by human
efforts. And when he followed the instincts which God had
transmitted to him from his ancestry of beasts of prey, he called
it Sin, and asked God to forgive him. But he doubted whether

[1] From *Philosophical Essays* (1910). Originally published in *The Independent
Review* in 1902. By permission of the publishers, Longmans, Green and Company.

he could be justly forgiven, until he invented a divine Plan by which God's wrath was to have been appeased. And seeing the present was bad, he made it yet worse, that thereby the future might be better. And he gave God thanks for the strength that enabled him to forego even the joys that were possible. And God smiled; and when he saw that Man had become perfect in renunciation and worship, he sent another sun through the sky, which crashed into Man's sun; and all returned again to nebula.

"'Yes,' he murmured, 'it was a good play; I will have it performed again.'"

Such, in outline, but even more purposeless, more void of meaning, is the world which Science presents for our belief. Amid such a world, if anywhere, our ideals henceforward must find a home. That Man is the product of causes which had no prevision of the end they were achieving; that his origin, his growth, his hopes and fears, his loves and his beliefs, are but the outcome of accidental collocations of atoms; that no fire, no heroism, no intensity of thought and feeling, can preserve an individual life beyond the grave; that all the labours of the ages, all the devotion, all the inspiration, all the noonday brightness of human genius, are destined to extinction in the vast death of the solar system, and that the whole temple of Man's achievement must inevitably be buried beneath the débris of a universe in ruins — all these things, if not quite beyond dispute, are yet so nearly certain, that no philosophy which rejects them can hope to stand. Only within the scaffolding of these truths, only on the firm foundation of unyielding despair, can the soul's habitation henceforth be safely built.

How, in such an alien and inhuman world, can so powerless a creature as Man preserve his aspirations untarnished? A strange mystery it is that Nature, omnipotent but blind, in the revolutions of her secular hurryings through the abysses of space, has brought forth at last a child, subject still to her power, but gifted with sight, with knowledge of good and evil, with the capacity of judging all the works of his unthinking Mother. In spite of Death, the mark and seal of the parental control, Man is yet free, during his brief years, to examine, to criticise, to know, and in imagination to create. To him alone, in the world with which he is acquainted, this freedom belongs; and in this lies his superiority to the resistless forces that control his outward life.

The savage, like ourselves, feels the oppression of his impotence before the powers of Nature; but having in himself nothing that he respects more than Power, he is willing to prostrate himself before his gods, without inquiring whether they are worthy of his worship. Pathetic and very terrible is the long history of cruelty and torture, of degradation and human sacrifice, endured in the hope of placating the jealous gods: surely, the trembling believer thinks, when what is most precious has been freely given, their lust for blood must be appeased, and more will not be required. The religion of Moloch — as such creeds may be generically called — is in essence the cringing submission of the slave, who dares not, even in his heart, allow the thought that his master deserves no adulation. Since the independence of ideals is not yet acknowledged, Power may be freely worshipped, and receive an unlimited respect, despite its wanton infliction of pain.

But gradually, as morality grows bolder, the claim of the ideal world begins to be felt; and worship, if it is not to cease, must be given to gods of another kind than those created by the savage. Some, though they feel the demands of the ideal, will still consciously reject them, still urging that naked Power is worthy of worship. Such is the attitude inculcated in God's answer to Job out of the whirlwind: the divine power and knowledge are paraded, but of the divine goodness there is no hint. Such also is the attitude of those who, in our own day, base their morality upon the struggle for survival, maintaining that the survivors are necessarily the fittest. But others, not content with an answer so repugnant to the moral sense, will adopt the position which we have become accustomed to regard as specially religious, maintaining that, in some hidden manner, the world of fact is really harmonious with the world of ideals. Thus Man creates God, all-powerful and all-good, the mystic unity of what is and what should be.

But the world of fact, after all, is not good; and, in submitting our judgment to it, there is an element of slavishness from which our thoughts must be purged. For in all things it is well to exalt the dignity of Man, by freeing him, as far as possible, from the tyranny of non-human Power. When we have realised that Power is largely bad, that man, with his knowledge of good and evil, is but a helpless atom in a world which has no such knowledge, the choice is again presented to us: Shall we worship Force, or shall we worship Goodness? Shall our God exist and be evil, or shall he be recognised as the creation of our own conscience?

The answer to this question is very momentous, and affects profoundly our whole morality. The worship of Force, to which Carlyle and Nietzsche and the creed of Militarism have accustomed us, is the result of failure to maintain our own ideals against a hostile universe: it is itself a prostrate submission to evil, a sacrifice of our best to Moloch. If strength indeed is to be respected, let us respect rather the strength of those who refuse that false "recognition of facts" which fails to recognise that facts are often bad. Let us admit that, in the world we know, there are many things that would be better otherwise, and that the ideals to which we do and must adhere are not realised in the realm of matter. Let us preserve our respect for truth, for beauty, for the ideal of perfection which life does not permit us to attain, though none of these things meet with the approval of the unconscious universe. If Power is bad, as it seems to be, let us reject it from our hearts. In this lies Man's true freedom: in determination to worship only the God created by our own love of the good, to respect only the heaven which inspires the insight of our best moments. In action, in desire, we must submit perpetually to the tyranny of outside forces; but in thought, in aspiration, we are free, free from our fellow-men, free from the petty planet on which our bodies impotently crawl, free even, while we live, from the tyranny of death. Let us learn, then, that energy of faith which enables us to live constantly in the vision of the good; and let us descend, in action, into the world of fact, with that vision always before us.

When first the opposition of fact and ideal grows fully visible, a spirit of fiery revolt, of fierce hatred of the gods, seems necessary to the assertion of freedom. To defy with

Promethean constancy a hostile universe, to keep its evil always in view, always actively hated, to refuse no pain that the malice of Power can invent, appears to be the duty of all who will not bow before the inevitable. But indignation is still a bondage, for it compels our thoughts to be occupied with an evil world; and in the fierceness of desire from which rebellion springs there is a kind of self-assertion which it is necessary for the wise to overcome. Indignation is a submission of our thoughts, but not of our desires; the Stoic freedom in which wisdom consists is found in the submission of our desires, but not of our thoughts. From the submission of our desires springs the virtue of resignation; from the freedom of our thoughts springs the whole world of art and philosophy, and the vision of beauty by which, at last, we half reconquer the reluctant world. But the vision of beauty is possible only to unfettered contemplation, to thoughts not weighted by the load of eager wishes; and thus Freedom comes only to those who no longer ask of life that it shall yield them any of those personal goods that are subject to the mutations of Time.

Although the necessity of renunciation is evidence of the existence of evil, yet Christianity, in preaching it, has shown a wisdom exceeding that of the Promethean philosophy of rebellion. It must be admitted that, of the things we desire, some, though they prove impossible, are yet real goods; others, however, as ardently longed for, do not form part of a fully purified ideal. The belief that what must be renounced is bad, though sometimes false, is far less often false than untamed passion supposes; and the creed of religion, by providing a reason for proving that it is never false, has been the means of purifying our hopes by the discovery of many austere truths.

But there is in resignation a further good element: even real goods, when they are unattainable, ought not to be fretfully desired. To every man comes, sooner or later, the great renunciation. For the young, there is nothing unattainable; a good thing desired with the whole force of a passionate will, and yet impossible, is to them not credible. Yet, by death, by illness, by poverty, or by the voice of duty, we must learn, each one of us, that the world was not made for us, and that, however beautiful may be the things we crave, Fate may nevertheless forbid them. It is the part of courage, when misfortune comes, to bear without repining the ruin of our hopes, to turn away our thoughts from vain regrets. This degree of submission to Power is not only just and right: it is the very gate of wisdom.

But passive renunciation is not the whole of wisdom; for not by renunciation alone can we build a temple for the worship of our own ideals. Haunting foreshadowings of the temple appear in the realm of imagination, in music, in architecture, in the untroubled kingdom of reason, and in the golden sunset magic of lyrics, where beauty shines and glows, remote from the touch of sorrow, remote from the fear of change, remote from the failures and disenchantments of the world of fact. In the contemplation of these things the vision of heaven will shape itself in our hearts, giving at once a touchstone to judge the world about us, and an inspiration by which to fashion to our needs whatever is not incapable of serving as a stone in the sacred temple.

Except for those rare spirits that are born without sin, there is a cavern of darkness to be traversed before that temple can be entered. The gate of the cavern is despair, and its floor is paved with the gravestones of abandoned hopes. There Self must die; there the eagerness, the greed of untamed desire must be slain, for only so can the soul be freed from the empire of Fate. But out of the cavern the Gate of Renunciation leads again to the daylight of wisdom, by whose radiance a new insight, a new joy, a new tenderness, shine forth to gladden the pilgrim's heart.

When, without the bitterness of impotent rebellion, we have learnt both to resign ourselves to the outward rule of Fate and to recognise that the non-human world is unworthy of our worship, it becomes possible at last so to transform and refashion the unconscious universe, so to transmute it in the crucible of imagination, that a new image of shining gold replaces the old idol of clay. In all the multiform facts of the world — in the visual shapes of trees and mountains and clouds, in the events of the life of man, even in the very omnipotence of Death — the insight of creative idealism can find the reflection of a beauty which its own thoughts first made.

In this way mind asserts its subtle mastery over the thoughtless forces of Nature. The more evil the material with which it deals, the more thwarting to untrained desire, the greater is its achievement in inducing the reluctant rock to yield up its hidden treasures, the prouder its victory in compelling the opposing forces to swell the pageant of its triumph. Of all the arts, Tragedy is the proudest, the most triumphant; for it builds its shining citadel in the very centre of the enemy's country, on the very summit of his highest mountain; from its impregnable watch-towers, his camps and arsenals, his columns and forts, are all revealed; within its walls the free life continues, while the legions of Death and Pain and Despair, and all the servile captains of tyrant Fate, afford the burghers of that dauntless city new spectacles of beauty. Happy those sacred ramparts, thrice happy the dwellers on that all-seeing eminence. Honour to those brave warriors who, through countless ages of warfare, have preserved for us the priceless heritage of liberty, and have kept undefiled by sacrilegious invaders the home of the unsubdued.

But the beauty of Tragedy does but make visible a quality which, in more or less obvious shapes, is present always and everywhere in life. In the spectacle of Death, in the endurance of intolerable pain, and in the irrevocableness of a vanished past, there is a sacredness, an overpowering awe, a feeling of the vastness, the depth, the inexhaustible mystery of existence, in which, as by some strange marriage of pain, the sufferer is bound to the world by bonds of sorrow. In these moments of insight, we lose all eagerness of temporary desire, all struggling and striving for petty ends, all care for the little trivial things that, to a superficial view, make up the common life of day by day; we see, surrounding the narrow raft illumined by the flickering light of human comradeship, the dark ocean on whose rolling waves we toss for a brief hour; from the great night without, a chill blast breaks in upon our refuge; all the loneliness of humanity amid hostile forces is concentrated upon the individual soul, which must struggle alone, with what of courage it can command, against the whole weight of a universe that cares nothing for its hopes and fears. Victory, in this struggle with the powers of darkness, is the true baptism into the glorious company of heroes, the true initiation into the overmastering beauty of human existence. From that awful encounter of the soul with the outer world, renunciation, wisdom, and charity are born; and with their birth a new life begins. To take into the inmost shrine of the soul the irresistible forces whose puppets we seem to be — Death and change, the irrevocableness of the past, and the powerlessness of man before the blind hurry of the universe from vanity to vanity — to feel these things and know them is to conquer them.

This is the reason why the Past has such magical power. The beauty of its motionless and silent pictures is like the enchanted purity of late autumn, when the leaves, though one breath would make them fall, still glow against the sky in golden glory. The Past does not change or strive; like Duncan, after life's fitful fever it sleeps well; what was eager and grasping, what was petty and transitory, has faded away, the things that were beautiful and eternal shine out of it like stars in the night. Its beauty, to a soul not worthy of it, is unendurable; but to a soul which has conquered Fate it is the key of religion.

The life of Man, viewed outwardly, is but a small thing in comparison with the forces of Nature. The slave is doomed to worship Time and Fate and Death, because they are greater than anything he finds in himself, and because all his thoughts are of things which they devour. But, great as they are, to think of them greatly, to feel their passionless splendour, is greater still. And such thought makes us free men; we no longer bow before the inevitable in oriental subjection, but we absorb it, and make it a part of ourselves. To abandon the struggle for private happiness, to expel all eagerness of temporary desire, to burn with passion for eternal things — this is emancipation, and this is the free man's worship. And this liberation is effected by a contemplation of Fate; for Fate itself is subdued by the mind which leaves nothing to be purged by the purifying fire of Time.

United with his fellow-men by the strongest of all ties, the tie of a common doom, the free man finds that a new vision is with him always, shedding over every daily task the light of love. The life of Man is a long march through the night, surrounded by invisible foes, tortured by weariness and pain, towards a goal that few can hope to reach, and where none may tarry long. One by one, as they march, our comrades vanish from our sight, seized by the silent orders of omnipotent Death. Very brief is the time in which we can help them, in which their happiness or misery is decided. Be it ours to shed sunshine on their path, to lighten their sorrows by the balm of sympathy, to give them the pure joy of a never-tiring affection, to strengthen failing courage, to instil faith in hours of despair. Let us not weigh in grudging scales their merits and demerits, but let us think only of their need — of the sorrows, the difficulties, perhaps the blindnesses, that make the misery of their lives; let us remember that they are fellow-sufferers in the same darkness, actors in the same tragedy with ourselves. And so, when their day is over, when their good and their evil have become eternal by the immortality of the past, be it ours to feel that, where they suffered, where they failed, no deed of ours was the cause; but wherever a spark of the divine fire kindled in their hearts, we were ready with encouragement, with sympathy, with brave words in which high courage glowed.

Brief and powerless is Man's life; on him and all his race the slow, sure doom falls pitiless and dark. Blind to good and evil, reckless of destruction, omnipotent matter rolls on its relentless way; for Man, condemned to-day to lose his dearest, to-morrow himself to pass through the gate of darkness, it remains only to cherish, ere yet the blow falls, the lofty thoughts that ennoble his little day; disdaining the coward terrors of the slave of Fate, to worship at the shrine that his own hands have built; undismayed by the empire of chance, to preserve a mind free from the wanton tyranny that rules his outward life; proudly defiant of the irresistible forces that tolerate, for a moment, his knowledge and his condemnation, to sustain alone, a weary but unyielding Atlas, the world that his own ideals have fashioned despite the trampling march of unconscious power.

GILBERT KEITH CHESTERTON

ON MR. McCABE AND A DIVINE FRIVOLITY [1]

A CRITIC once remonstrated with me, saying, with an air of indignant reasonableness, "If you must make jokes, at least you need not make them on such serious subjects." I replied with a natural simplicity and wonder, "About what other subjects can one make jokes except serious subjects?" It is quite useless to talk about profane jesting. All jesting is in its nature profane, in the sense that it must be the sudden realization that something which thinks itself solemn is not so very solemn after all. If a joke is not a joke about religion or morals, it is a joke about police-magistrates or scientific professors or undergraduates dressed up as Queen Victoria. And people joke about the police-magistrate more than they joke about the Pope, not because the police-magistrate is a more frivolous subject, but, on the contrary, because the police-magistrate is a more serious subject than the Pope. The Bishop of Rome has no jurisdiction in this realm of England; whereas the police-magistrate may bring his solemnity to bear quite suddenly upon us. Men make jokes about old scientific professors, even more than they make them about bishops — not because science is lighter than religion, but because science is always by its nature more solemn and austere than religion. It is not I; it is not even a particular class of journalists or jesters who make jokes about the matters which are of most awful import; it is the whole human race. If there is one thing more than another which any one will admit who has the smallest knowledge of the world, it is that men are always speaking gravely and earnestly and with the utmost possible care about the things that are not important, but always talking frivolously about the things that are. Men talk for hours with the faces of a college of cardinals about things like golf, or tobacco, or waistcoats, or party politics. But all the most grave and dreadful things in the world are the oldest jokes in the world — being married; being hanged.

[1] From *Heretics* (1905). Copyright by Dodd, Mead and Company, Inc.

One gentleman, however, Mr. McCabe, has in this matter made to me something that almost amounts to a personal appeal; and as he happens to be a man for whose sincerity and intellectual virtue I have a high respect, I do not feel inclined to let it pass without some attempt to satisfy my critic in the matter. Mr. McCabe devotes a considerable part of the last essay in the collection called "Christianity and Rationalism on Trial" to an objection, not to my thesis, but to my method, and a very friendly and dignified appeal to me to alter it. I am much inclined to defend myself in this matter out of mere respect for Mr. McCabe, and still more so out of mere respect for the truth which is, I think, in danger by his error, not only in this question, but in others. In order that there may be no injustice done in the matter, I will quote Mr. McCabe himself. "But before I follow Mr. Chesterton in some detail, I would make a general observation on his method. He is as serious as I am in his ultimate purpose, and I respect him for that. He knows, as I do, that humanity stands at a solemn parting of the ways. Towards some unknown goal it presses through the ages, impelled by an overmastering desire of happiness. To-day it hesitates, light-heartedly enough, but every serious thinker knows how momentous the decision may be. It is, apparently, deserting the path of religion and entering upon the path of secularism. Will it lose itself in quagmires of sensuality down this new path, and pant and toil through years of civic and industrial anarchy, only to learn it had lost the road, and must return to religion? Or will it find that at last it is leaving the mists and the quagmires behind it; that it is ascending the slope of the hill so long dimly discerned ahead, and making straight for the long-sought Utopia? This is the drama of our time, and every man and every woman should understand it.

"Mr. Chesterton understands it. Further, he gives us credit for understanding it. He has nothing of that paltry meanness or strange density of so many of his colleagues, who put us down as aimless iconoclasts or moral anarchists. He admits that we are waging a thankless war for what we take to be Truth and Progress. He is doing the same. But why, in the name of all that is reasonable, should we, when we are agreed

on the momentousness of the issue either way, forthwith desert
serious methods of conducting the controversy?   Why, when
the vital need of our time is to induce men and women to collect
their thoughts occasionally, and be men and women — nay, to
remember that they are really gods that hold the destinies of
humanity on their knees — why should we think that this
kaleidoscopic play of phrases is inopportune?   The ballets of
the Alhambra, and the fireworks of the Crystal Palace, and Mr.
Chesterton's *Daily News* articles, have their place in life.   But
how a serious social student can think of curing the thoughtlessness of our generation by strained paradoxes; of giving
people a sane grasp of social problems by literary sleight-of-
hand; of settling important questions by a reckless shower of
rocket-metaphors and inaccurate 'facts,' and the substitution
of imagination for judgment, I cannot see."

I quote this passage with a particular pleasure, because Mr.
McCabe certainly cannot put too strongly the degree to which
I give him and his school credit for their complete sincerity and
responsibility of philosophical attitude.   I am quite certain
that they mean every word they say.   I also mean every word
I say.   But why is it that Mr. McCabe has some sort of mysterious hesitation about admitting that I mean every word I
say; why is it that he is not quite as certain of my mental responsibility as I am of his mental responsibility?   If we attempt to answer the question directly and well, we shall, I
think, have come to the root of the matter by the shortest cut.

Mr. McCabe thinks that I am not serious but only funny, because Mr. McCabe thinks that funny is the opposite of serious.
Funny is the opposite of not funny, and of nothing else.   The
question of whether a man expresses himself in a grotesque or
laughable phraseology, or in a stately and restrained phraseology, is not a question of motive or of moral state, it is a question of instinctive language and self-expression.   Whether a
man chooses to tell the truth in long sentences or short jokes is
a problem analogous to whether he chooses to tell the truth in
French or German.   Whether a man preaches his gospel grotesquely or gravely is merely like the question of whether he
preaches it in prose or verse.   The question of whether Swift
was funny in his irony is quite another sort of question to the

question of whether Swift was serious in his pessimism. Surely even Mr. McCabe would not maintain that the more funny "Gulliver" is in its method the less it can be sincere in its object. The truth is, as I have said, that in this sense the two qualities of fun and seriousness have nothing whatever to do with each other; they are no more comparable than black and triangular. Mr. Bernard Shaw is funny and sincere. Mr. George Robey is funny and not sincere. Mr. McCabe is sincere and not funny. The average Cabinet Minister is not sincere and not funny.

In short, Mr. McCabe is under the influence of a primary fallacy which I have found very common in men of the clerical type. Numbers of clergymen have from time to time reproached me for making jokes about religion; and they have almost always invoked the authority of that very sensible commandment which says, "Thou shalt not take the name of the Lord thy God in vain." Of course, I pointed out that I was not in any conceivable sense taking the name in vain. To take a thing and make a joke out of it is not to take it in vain. It is, on the contrary, to take it and use it for an uncommonly good object. To use a thing in vain means to use it without use. But a joke may be exceedingly useful; it may contain the whole earthly sense, not to mention the whole heavenly sense, of a situation. And those who find in the Bible the commandment can find in the Bible any number of the jokes. In the same book in which God's name is fenced from being taken in vain, God himself overwhelms Job with a torrent of terrible levities. The same book which says that God's name must not be taken vainly, talks easily and carelessly about God laughing and God winking. Evidently it is not here that we have to look for genuine examples of what is meant by a vain use of the name. And it is not very difficult to see where we have really to look for it. The people (as I tactfully pointed out to them) who really take the name of the Lord in vain are the clergymen themselves. The thing which is fundamentally and really frivolous is not a careless joke. The thing which is fundamentally and really frivolous is a careless solemnity. If Mr. McCabe really wishes to know what sort of guarantee of reality and solidity is afforded by the mere act of what is called talking seriously, let him spend a happy Sunday in going the round of the pulpits. Or, better still, let him drop in at the House of Commons or the House of Lords. Even Mr. McCabe would admit that these men are solemn — more solemn than I am. And even Mr. McCabe, I think, would admit that these men are frivolous — more frivolous than I am. Why should Mr. McCabe be so eloquent about the danger arising from fantastic and paradoxical writers? Why should he be so ardent in desiring grave and verbose writers? There are not so very many fantastic and paradoxical writers. But there are a gigantic number of grave and verbose writers; and it is by the efforts of the grave and verbose writers that everything that Mr. Mc-Cabe detests (and everything that I detest, for that matter) is kept in existence and energy. How can it have come about that a man as intelligent as Mr. McCabe can think that paradox and jesting stop the way? It is solemnity that is stopping the way in every department of modern effort. It is his own favourite "serious methods"; it is his own favourite "momentousness"; it is his own favourite "judgment" which stops the way everywhere. Every man who has ever headed a deputation to a minister knows this. Every man who has ever written a letter to the *Times* knows it. Every rich man who wishes to stop the mouths of the poor talks about "momentousness." Every Cabinet minister who has not got an answer suddenly develops a "judgment." Every sweater who uses vile methods recommends "serious methods." I said a moment ago that sincerity had nothing to do with solemnity, but I confess that I am not so certain that I was right. In the modern world, at any rate, I am not so sure that I was right. In the modern world solemnity is the direct enemy of sincerity. In the modern world sincerity is almost always on one side, and solemnity almost always on the other. The only answer possible to the fierce and glad attack of sincerity is the miserable answer of solemnity. Let Mr. McCabe, or any one else who is much concerned that we should be grave in order to be sincere, simply imagine the scene in some government office in which Mr. Bernard Shaw should head a Socialist deputation to Mr. Austen Chamberlain. On which side would be the solemnity? And on which the sincerity?

I am, indeed, delighted to discover that Mr. McCabe reckons Mr. Shaw along with me in his system of condemnation of frivolity. He said once, I believe, that he always wanted Mr. Shaw to label his paragraphs serious or comic. I do not know which paragraphs of Mr. Shaw are paragraphs to be labelled serious; but surely there can be no doubt that this paragraph of Mr. McCabe's is one to be labelled comic. He also says, in the article I am now discussing, that Mr. Shaw has the reputation of deliberately saying everything which his hearers do not expect him to say. I need not labour the inconclusiveness and weakness of this, because it has already been dealt with in my remarks on Mr. Bernard Shaw. Suffice it to say here that the only serious reason which I can imagine inducing any one person to listen to any other is, that the first person looks to the second person with an ardent faith and a fixed attention, expecting him to say what he does not expect him to say. It may be a paradox, but that is because paradoxes are true. It may not be rational, but that is because rationalism is wrong. But clearly it is quite true that whenever we go to hear a prophet or teacher we may or may not expect wit, we may or may not expect eloquence, but we do expect what we do not expect. We may not expect the true, we may not even expect the wise, but we do expect the unexpected. If we do not expect the unexpected, why do we go there at all? If we expect the expected, why do we not sit at home and expect it by ourselves? If Mr. McCabe means merely this about Mr. Shaw, that he always has some unexpected application of his doctrine to give to those who listen to him, what he says is quite true, and to say it is only to say that Mr. Shaw is an original man. But if he means that Mr. Shaw has ever professed or preached any doctrine but one, and that his own, then what he says is not true. It is not my business to defend Mr. Shaw; as has been seen already, I disagree with him altogether. But I do not mind, on his behalf, offering in this matter a flat defiance to all his ordinary opponents, such as Mr. McCabe. I defy Mr. McCabe, or anybody else, to mention one single instance in which Mr. Shaw has, for the sake of wit or novelty, taken up any position which was not directly deducible from the body of his doctrine as elsewhere expressed. I have been, I am happy to say, a tolerably close student of Mr. Shaw's utterances, and I request Mr. McCabe, if he will not believe that I mean anything else, to believe that I mean this challenge.

All this, however, is a parenthesis. The thing with which I am here immediately concerned is Mr. McCabe's appeal to me not to be so frivolous. Let me return to the actual text of that appeal. There are, of course, a great many things that I might say about it in detail. But I may start with saying that Mr. McCabe is in error in supposing that the danger which I anticipate from the disappearance of religion is the increase of sensuality. On the contrary, I should be inclined to anticipate a decrease in sensuality, because I anticipate a decrease in life. I do not think that under modern Western materialism we should have anarchy. I doubt whether we should have enough individual valour and spirit even to have liberty. It is quite an old-fashioned fallacy to suppose that our objection to scepticism is that it removes the discipline from life. Our objection to scepticism is that it removes the motive power. Materialism is not a thing which destroys mere restraint. Materialism itself is the great restraint. The McCabe school advocates a political liberty, but it denies spiritual liberty. That is, it abolishes the laws which could be broken, and substitutes laws that cannot. And that is the real slavery.

The truth is that the scientific civilization in which Mr. McCabe believes has one rather particular defect; it is perpetually tending to destroy that democracy or power of the ordinary man in which Mr. McCabe also believes. Science means specialism, and specialism means oligarchy. If you once establish the habit of trusting particular men to produce particular results in physics or astronomy, you leave the door open for the equally natural demand that you should trust particular men to do particular things in government and the coercing of men. If you feel it to be reasonable that one beetle should be the only study of one man, and that one man the only student of that one beetle, it is surely a very harmless consequence to go on to say that politics should be the only study of one man, and that one man the only student of politics. As I have pointed out elsewhere in this book, the expert is more aristocratic than the aristocrat, because the aristocrat is only the man who lives well,

reductio ad absurdum

while the expert is the man who knows better. But if we look at the progress of our scientific civilization we see a gradual increase everywhere of the specialist over the popular function. Once men sang together round a table in chorus; now one man sings alone, for the absurd reason that he can sing better. If scientific civilization goes on (which is most improbable) only one man will laugh, because he can laugh better than the rest.

I do not know that I can express this more shortly than by taking as a text the single sentence of Mr. McCabe, which runs as follows: "The ballets of the Alhambra and the fireworks of the Crystal Palace and Mr. Chesterton's *Daily News* articles have their places in life." I wish that my articles had as noble a place as either of the other two things mentioned. But let us ask ourselves (in a spirit of love, as Mr. Chadband would say), what *are* the ballets of the Alhambra? The ballets of the Alhambra are institutions in which a particular selected row of persons in pink go through an operation known as dancing. Now, in all commonwealths dominated by a religion — in the Christian commonwealths of the Middle Ages and in many rude societies — this habit of dancing was a common habit with everybody, and was not necessarily confined to a professional class. A person could dance without being a dancer; a person could dance without being a specialist; a person could dance without being pink. And, in proportion as Mr. McCabe's scientific civilization advances — that is, in proportion as religious civilization (or real civilization) decays — the more and more "well trained," the more and more pink, become the people who do dance, and the more and more numerous become the people who don't. Mr. McCabe may recognize an example of what I mean in the gradual discrediting in society of the ancient European waltz or dance with partners, and the substitution of that horrible and degrading oriental interlude which is known as skirt-dancing. That is the whole essence of decadence, the effacement of five people who do a thing for fun by one person who does it for money. Now it follows, therefore, that when Mr. McCabe says that the ballets of the Alhambra and my articles "have their place in life," it ought to be pointed out to him that he is doing his best to create a world in which dancing, properly speaking, will have no place in life at all. He is, indeed, trying to create a world in which there will be no life for dancing to have a place in. The very fact that Mr. McCabe thinks of dancing as a thing belonging to some hired women at the Alhambra is an illustration of the same principle by which he is able to think of religion as a thing belonging to some hired men in white neckties. Both these things are things which should not be done for us, but by us. If Mr. McCabe were really religious he would be happy. If he were really happy he would dance.

Briefly, we may put the matter in this way. The main point of modern life is not that the Alhambra ballet has its place in life. The main point, the main enormous tragedy of modern life, is that Mr. McCabe has not his place in the Alhambra ballet. The joy of changing and graceful posture, the joy of suiting the swing of music to the swing of limbs, the joy of whirling drapery, the joy of standing on one leg, — all these should belong by rights to Mr. McCabe and to me; in short, to the ordinary healthy citizen. Probably we should not consent to go through these evolutions. But that is because we are miserable moderns and rationalists. We do not merely love ourselves more than we love duty; we actually love ourselves more than we love joy.

When, therefore, Mr. McCabe says that he gives the Alhambra dances (and my articles) their place in life, I think we are justified in pointing out that by the very nature of the case of his philosophy and of his favourite civilization he gives them a very inadequate place. For (if I may pursue the too flattering parallel) Mr. McCabe thinks of the Alhambra and of my articles as two very odd and absurd things, which some special people do (probably for money) in order to amuse him. But if he had ever felt himself the ancient, sublime, elemental, human instinct to dance, he would have discovered that dancing is not a frivolous thing at all, but a very serious thing. He would have discovered that it is the one grave and chaste and decent method of expressing a certain class of emotions. And similarly, if he had ever had, as Mr. Shaw and I have had, the impulse to what he calls paradox, he would have discovered that paradox again is not a frivolous thing, but a very serious thing. He would have found that paradox simply means a certain defiant joy which belongs to belief. I should regard any civilization which was without a universal habit of uproarious dancing as being, from the full human point of view, a defective civilization. And I should regard any mind which had not got the habit in one form or another of uproarious thinking as being, from the full human point of view, a defective mind. It is vain for Mr. McCabe to say that a ballet is a part of him. He should be part of a ballet, or else he is only part of a man. It is in vain for him to say that he is "not quarrelling with the importation of humour into the controversy." He ought himself to be importing humour into every controversy; for unless a man is in part a humorist, he is only in part a man. To sum up the whole matter very simply, if Mr. McCabe asks me why I import frivolity into a discussion of the nature of man, I answer, because frivolity is a part of the nature of man. If he asks me why I introduce what he calls paradoxes into a philosophical problem, I answer, because all philosophical problems tend to become paradoxical. If he objects to my treating of life riotously, I reply that life is a riot. And I say that the Universe as I see it, at any rate, is very much more like the fireworks at the Crystal Palace than it is like his own philosophy. About the whole cosmos there is a tense and secret festivity — like preparations for Guy Fawkes' day. Eternity is the eve of something. I never look up at the stars without feeling that they are the fires of a schoolboy's rocket, fixed in their everlasting fall.

HENRY LOUIS MENCKEN

THE GENEALOGY OF ETIQUETTE [1]

BARRING sociology (which is yet, of course, scarcely a science at all, but rather a monkey-shine which happens to pay, like play-acting or theology), psychology is the youngest of the sciences, and hence chiefly guesswork, empiricism, hocus-pocus, poppycock. On the one hand, there are still enormous gaps in its data, so that the determination of its simplest principles remains difficult, not to say impossible; and, on the other hand, the very hollowness and nebulosity of it, particularly around its edges, encourages a horde of quacks to invade it, sophisticate it and make nonsense of it. Worse, this state of affairs tends to such confusion of effort and direction that the quack and the honest inquirer are often found in the same man. It is, indeed, a commonplace to encounter a professor who spends his days in the laborious accumulation of psychological statistics, sticking pins into babies and platting upon a chart the ebb and flow of their yells, and his nights chasing poltergeists and other such celestial fauna over the hurdles of a spiritualist's atelier, or gazing into a crystal in the privacy of his own chamber. The Binét test and the buncombe of mesmerism are alike the children of what we roughly denominate psychology, and perhaps of equal legitimacy. Even so ingenious and competent an investigator as Prof. Dr. Sigmund Freud, who has told us a lot that is of the first importance about the materials and machinery of thought, has also told us a lot that is trivial and dubious. The essential doctrines of Freudism, no doubt, come close to the truth, but many of Freud's remoter deductions are far more scandalous than sound, and many of the professed Freudians, both American and European, have grease-paint on their noses and bladders in their hands and are otherwise quite indistinguishable from evangelists and circus clowns.

[1] Reprinted from *Prejudices: First Series* (1919) by H. L. Mencken by and with permission of and special arrangement with Alfred A. Knopf, Inc., authorized publishers.

In this condition of the science it is no wonder that we find it wasting its chief force upon problems that are petty and idle when they are not downright and palpably insoluble, and passing over problems that are of immediate concern to all of us, and that might be quite readily solved, or, at any rate, considerably illuminated, by an intelligent study of the data already available. After all, not many of us care a hoot whether Sir Oliver Lodge and the Indian chief Wok-a-wok-a-mok are happy in heaven, for not many of us have any hope or desire to meet them there. Nor are we greatly excited by the discovery that, of twenty-five freshmen who are hit with clubs, 17¾ will say "Ouch!" and 22⅕ will say "Damn!"; nor by a table showing that 38.2 per centum of all men accused of homicide confess when locked up with the carcasses of their victims, including 23.4 per centum who are innocent; nor by plans and specifications, by Cagliostro out of Lucrezia Borgia, for teaching poor, God-forsaken school children to write before they can read and to multiply before they can add; nor by endless disputes between half-witted pundits as to the precise difference between perception and cognition; nor by even longer feuds, between pundits even crazier, over free will, the subconscious, the endoneurium, the functions of the corpora quadrigemina, and the meaning of dreams in which one is pursued by hyenas, process-servers or grass-widows.

Nay; we do not bubble with rejoicing when such fruits of psychological deep-down-diving and much-mud-upbringing researches are laid before us, for after all they do not offer us any nourishment, there is nothing in them to engage our teeth, they fail to make life more comprehensible, and hence more bearable. What we yearn to know something about is the process whereby the ideas of everyday are engendered in the skulls of those about us, to the end that we may pursue a straighter and a safer course through the muddle that is life. Why do the great majority of Presbyterians (and, for that matter, of Baptists, Episcopalians, and Swedenborgians as well) regard it as unlucky to meet a black cat and lucky to find a pin? What are the logical steps behind the theory that it is indecent to eat peas with a knife? By what process does an otherwise sane man arrive at the conclusion that he will go to hell unless he is baptized by total immersion in water? What causes men to be faithful to their wives: habit, fear, poverty, lack of imagination, lack of enterprise, stupidity, religion? What is the psychological basis of commercial morality? What is the true nature of the vague pooling of desires that Rousseau called the social contract? Why does an American regard it as scandalous to wear dress clothes at a funeral, and a Frenchman regard it as equally scandalous *not* to wear them? Why is it that men trust one another so readily, and women trust one another so seldom? Why are we all so greatly affected by statements that we know are not true? — e.g. in Lincoln's Gettysburg speech, the Declaration of Independence and the CIII Psalm. What is the origin of the so-called double standard of morality? Why are women forbidden to take off their hats in church? What is happiness? Intelligence? Sin? Courage? Virtue? Beauty?

All these are questions of interest and importance to all of us, for their solution would materially improve the accuracy of our outlook upon the world, and with it our mastery of our environment, but the psychologists, busily engaged in chasing their tails, leave them unanswered, and, in most cases, even unasked. The late William James, more acute than the general, saw how precious little was known about the psychological inwardness of religion, and to the illumination of this darkness he addressed himself in his book, "The Varieties of Religious Experience." But life being short and science long, he got little beyond the statement of the problem and the marshalling of the grosser evidence — and even at this business he allowed himself to be constantly interrupted by spooks, hobgoblins, seventh sons of seventh sons and other such characteristic pets of psychologists.   In the same way one Gustav le Bon, a Frenchman, undertook a psychological study of the crowd mind — and then blew up.   Add the investigations of Freud and his school, chiefly into abnormal states of mind, and those of Lombroso and his school, chiefly quackish and for the yellow journals, and the idle romancing of such inquirers as Prof. Dr. Thorstein Veblen, and you have exhausted the list of contributions to what may be called practical and everyday psychology.   The rev. professors, I daresay, have been doing some useful plowing and planting. All of their meticulous pin-sticking and measuring and chart-making, in the course of time, will enable their successors to approach the real problems of mind with more assurance than is now possible, and perhaps help to their solution. But in the meantime the public and social utility of psychology remains very small, for it is still unable to differentiate accurately between the true and the false, or to give us any effective protection against the fallacies, superstitions, crazes and hysterias which rage in the world.

In this emergency it is not only permissible but even laudable for the amateur to sniff inquiringly through the psychological pasture, essaying modestly to uproot things that the myopic (or, perhaps more accurately, hypermetropic) professionals have overlooked. The late Friedrich Wilhelm Nietzsche did it often, and the usufructs were many curious and daring guesses, some of them probably close to accuracy, as to the genesis of this, that or the other common delusion of man — i.e., the delusion that the law of the survival of the fittest may be repealed by an act of Congress. Into the same field several very interesting expeditions have been made by Dr. Elsie Clews Parsons, a lady once celebrated by Park Row for her invention of trial marriage — an invention, by the way, in which the Nietzsche aforesaid preceded her by at least a dozen years. The records of her researches are to be found in a brief series of books: "The Family," "The Old-Fashioned Woman" and "Fear and Conventionality." Apparently they have wrung relatively little esteem from the learned, for I seldom encounter a reference to them, and Dr. Parsons herself is denied the very modest reward of mention in "Who's Who in America." Nevertheless, they are extremely instructive books, particularly "Fear and Conventionality." I know of no other work, indeed, which offers a better array of observations upon that powerful complex of assumptions, prejudices, instinctive reactions, racial emotions and unbreakable vices of mind which enters so massively into the daily thinking of all of us. The author does not concern herself, as so many psychologists fall into the habit of doing, with thinking as a purely laboratory phenomenon, a process in vacuo. What she deals with is thinking as it is done by men and women in the real world —

thinking that is only half intellectual, the other half being as automatic and unintelligent as swallowing, blinking the eye or falling in love.

The power of the complex that I have mentioned is usually very much underestimated, not only by psychologists, but also by all other persons who pretend to culture. We take pride in the fact that we are thinking animals, and like to believe that our thoughts are free, but the truth is that nine-tenths of them are rigidly conditioned by the babbling that goes on around us from birth, and that the business of considering this babbling objectively, separating the true in it from the false, is an intellectual feat of such stupendous difficulty that very few men are ever able to achieve it. The amazing slanging which went on between the English professors and the German professors in the early days of the late war showed how little even cold and academic men are really moved by the bald truth and how much by hot and unintelligible likes and dislikes. The patriotic hysteria of the war simply allowed these eminent pedagogues to say of one another openly and to loud applause what they would have been ashamed to say in times of greater amenity, and what most of them would have denied stoutly that they believed. Nevertheless, it is probably a fact that before there was a sign of war the average English professor, deep down in his heart, thought that any man who ate sauerkraut, and went to the opera in a sackcoat, and intrigued for the appellation of *Geheimrat*, and preferred German music to English poetry, and venerated Bismarck, and called his wife "Mutter," was a scoundrel. He did not say so aloud, and no doubt it would have offended him had you accused him of believing it, but he believed it all the same, and his belief in it gave a muddy, bilious color to his view of German metaphysics, German electrochemistry and the German chronology of Babylonian kings. And by the same token the average German professor, far down in the ghostly recesses of his hulk, held that any man who read the London *Times*, and ate salt fish at first breakfast, and drank tea of an afternoon, and spoke of Oxford as a university was a *Schafskopf*, a *Schuft* and possibly even a *Schweinehund*.

Nay, not one of us is a free agent. Not one of us actually thinks for himself, or in any orderly and scientific manner.

The pressure of environment, of mass ideas, of the socialized intelligence, improperly so called, is too enormous to be withstood. No American, no matter how sharp his critical sense, can ever get away from the notion that democracy is, in some subtle and mysterious way, more conducive to human progress and more pleasing to a just God than any of the systems of government which stand opposed to it. In the privacy of his study he may observe very clearly that it exalts the facile and specious man above the really competent man, and from this observation he may draw the conclusion that its abandonment would be desirable, but once he emerges from his academic seclusion and resumes the rubbing of noses with his fellow-men, he will begin to be tortured by a sneaking feeling that such ideas are heretical and unmanly, and the next time the band begins to play he will thrill with the best of them — or the worst. The actual phenomenon, in truth, was copiously on display during the war. Having myself the character among my acquaintances of one holding the democratic theory in some doubt, I was often approached by gentlemen who told me, in great confidence, that they had been seized by the same tremors. Among them were journalists employed daily in demanding that democracy be forced upon the whole world, and army officers engaged, at least theoretically, in forcing it. All these men, in reflective moments, struggled with ifs and buts. But every one of them, in his public capacity as a good citizen, quickly went back to *thinking* as a good citizen was then expected to think, and even to a certain inflammatory ranting for what, behind the door, he gravely questioned. . . .

It is the business of Dr. Parsons, in "Fear and Conventionality," to prod into certain of the ideas which thus pour into every man's mind from the circumambient air, sweeping away, like some huge cataract, the feeble resistance that his own powers of ratiocination can offer. In particular, she devotes herself to an examination of those general ideas which condition the thought and action of man as a social being — those general ideas which govern his everyday attitude toward his fellow-men and his prevailing view of himself. In one direction they lay upon us the bonds of what we call etiquette, i.e., the duty of considering the habits and feelings of those around

THE GENEALOGY OF ETIQUETTE

us — and in another direction they throttle us with what we call morality — i.e., the rules which protect the life and property of those around us.   But, as Dr. Parsons shows, the boundary between etiquette and morality is very dimly drawn, and it is often impossible to say of a given action whether it is ˙ downright immoral or merely a breach of the punctilio.   Even when the moral law is plainly running, considerations of mere amenity and politeness may still make themselves felt.   Thus, as Dr. Parsons points out, there is even an etiquette of adultery. "The *ami de la famille* vows not to kiss his mistress in her husband's house" — not in fear, but "as an expression of conjugal consideration," as a sign that he has not forgotten the thoughtfulness expected of a gentleman.   And in this delicate field, as might be expected, the differences in racial attitudes are almost diametrical.   The Englishman, surprising his wife with a lover, sues the rogue for damages and has public opinion behind him, but for an American to do it would be for him to lose caste at once and forever.   The plain and only duty of the American is to open upon the fellow with artillery, hitting him if the scene is south of the Potomac and missing him if it is above.

I confess to an endless interest in such puzzling niceties, and to much curiosity as to their origins and meaning.   Why do we Americans take off our hats when we meet a flapper on the street, and yet stand covered before a male of the highest eminence?   A Continental would regard this last as boorish to the last degree; in greeting any equal or superior, male or female, actual or merely conventional, he lifts his head-piece. Why does it strike us as ludicrous to see a man in dress clothes before 6 P.M.?   The Continental puts them on whenever he has a solemn visit to make, whether the hour be six or noon. Why do we regard it as indecent to tuck the napkin between the waistcoat buttons — or into the neck! — at meals?   The Frenchman does it without thought of crime.   So does the Italian.   So does the German.   All three are punctilious men — far more so, indeed, than we are.   Why do we snicker at the man who wears a wedding ring?   Most Continentals would stare askance at the husband who didn't.   Why is it bad manners in Europe and America to ask a stranger his or her age, and a friendly attention in China?   Why do we regard it as absurd to distinguish a woman by her husband's title — e.g., Mrs. Judge Jones, Mrs. Professor Smith? In Teutonic and Scandinavian Europe the omission of the title would be looked upon as an affront.

Such fine distinctions, so ardently supported, raise many interesting questions, but the attempt to answer them quickly gets one bogged. Several years ago I ventured to lift a sad voice against a custom common in America: that of married men, in speaking of their wives, employing the full panoply of "Mrs. Brown." It was my contention — supported, I thought, by logical considerations of the loftiest order — that a husband, in speaking of his wife to his equals, should say "my wife" — that the more formal mode of designation should be reserved for inferiors and for strangers of undetermined position. This contention, somewhat to my surprise, was vigorously combated by various volunteer experts. At first they rested their case upon the mere authority of custom, forgetting that this custom was by no means universal. But finally one of them came forward with a more analytical and cogent defense — the defense, to wit, that "my wife" connoted proprietorship and was thus offensive to a wife's *amour propre*. But what of "my sister" and "my mother"? Surely it is nowhere the custom for a man, addressing an equal, to speak of his sister as "Miss Smith." . . . The discussion, however, came to nothing. It was impossible to carry it on logically. The essence of all such inquiries lies in the discovery that there is a force within the liver and lights of man that is infinitely more potent than logic. His reflections, perhaps, may take on intellectually recognizable forms, but they seldom lead to intellectually recognizable conclusions.

Nevertheless, Dr. Parsons offers something in her book that may conceivably help to a better understanding of them, and that is the doctrine that the strange persistence of these rubber-stamp ideas, often unintelligible and sometimes plainly absurd, is due to fear, and that this fear is the product of a very real danger. The safety of human society lies in the assumption that every individual composing it, in a given situation, will act in a manner hitherto approved as seemly. That is to say, he is expected to react to his environment according to a fixed pattern, not necessarily because that pattern is the best imaginable, but simply because it is determined and understood. If he fails to do so, if he reacts in a novel manner — conducive, perhaps, to his better advantage or to what he thinks is his better advantage — then he disappoints the expectation of those around him, and forces them to meet the new situation he has created by the exercise of independent thought. Such independent thought, to a good many men, is quite impossible, and to the overwhelming majority of men, extremely painful. "To all of us," says Dr. Parsons, "to the animal, to the savage and to the civilized being, few demands are as uncomfortable, . . . disquieting or fearful, as the call to innovate. . . . Adaptations we all of us dislike or hate. We dodge or shirk them as best we may." And the man who compels us to make them against our wills we punish by withdrawing from him that understanding and friendliness which he, in turn, looks for and counts upon. In other words, we set him apart as one who is anti-social and not to be dealt with, and according as his rebellion has been small or great, we call him a boor or a criminal.

This distrust of the unknown, this fear of doing something unusual, is probably at the bottom of many ideas and institutions that are commonly credited to other motives. For example, monogamy. The orthodox explanation of monogamy is that it is a manifestation of the desire to have and to hold property — that the husband defends his solitary right to his wife, even at the cost of his own freedom, because she is the pearl among his chattels. But Dr. Parsons argues, and with a good deal of plausibility, that the real moving force, both in the husband and the wife, may be merely the force of habit, the antipathy to experiment and innovation. It is easier and safer to stick to the one wife than to risk adventures with another wife — and the immense social pressure that I have just described is all on the side of sticking. Moreover, the indulgence of a habit automatically strengthens its bonds. What we have done once or thought once, we are more apt than we were before to do and think again. Or, as the late Prof. William James put it, "the selection of a particular hole to live in, of a particular mate, . . . a particular anything, in short, out of a possible multitude ... carries with it an insensibility to *other* opportunities and occasions — an insensibility which can only be described physiologically as an inhibition of new impulses by the habit of old ones already formed. The possession of homes and wives of our own makes us strangely insensible to the charms of other people. ... The original impulse which got us homes, wives, ... seems to exhaust itself in its first achievements and to leave no surplus energy for reacting on new cases." Thus the benedict looks no more on women (at least for a while), and the post-honeymoon bride, as the late David Graham Phillips once told us, neglects the bedizenments which got her a man.

In view of the popular or general character of most of the taboos which put a brake upon personal liberty in thought and action — that is to say, in view of their enforcement by people in the mass, and not by definite specialists in conduct — it is quite natural to find that they are of extra force in democratic societies, for it is the distinguishing mark of democratic societies that they exalt the powers of the majority almost infinitely, and tend to deny the minority any rights whatever. Under a society dominated by a small caste the revolutionist in custom, despite the axiom to the contrary, has a relatively easy time of it, for the persons whose approval he seeks for his innovation are relatively few in number, and most of them are already habituated to more or less intelligible and independent thinking. But under a democracy he is opposed by a horde so vast that it is a practical impossibility for him, without complex and expensive machinery, to reach and convince all of its members, and even if he could reach them he would find most of them quite incapable of rising out of their accustomed grooves. They cannot understand innovations that are genuinely novel and they don't want to understand them; their one desire is to put them down. Even at this late day, with enlightenment raging through the republic like a pestilence, it would cost the average Southern or Middle Western Congressman his seat if he appeared among his constituents in spats, or wearing a wrist-watch. And if a Justice of the Supreme Court of the United States, however gigantic his learning and his juridic rectitude, were taken in crim. con. with the wife of a

Senator, he would be destroyed instanter. And if, suddenly revolting against the democratic idea, he were to propose, however gingerly, its abandonment, he would be destroyed with the same dispatch.

But how, then, explain the fact that the populace is constantly ravished and set aflame by fresh brigades of moral, political and sociological revolutionists — that it is forever playing the eager victim to new mountebanks? The explanation lies in the simple circumstance that these performers upon the public midriff are always careful to ladle out nothing actually new, and hence nothing incomprehensible, alarming and accursed. What they offer is always the same old panacea with an extra-gaudy label — the tried, tasted and much-loved dose, the colic cure that mother used to make. Superficially, the United States seems to suffer from an endless and astounding neophilism; actually all its thinking is done within the boundaries of a very small group of political, economic and religious ideas, most of them unsound. For example, there is the fundamental idea of democracy — the idea that all political power should remain in the hands of the populace, that its exercise by superior men is intrinsically immoral. Out of this idea spring innumerable notions and crazes that are no more, at bottom, than restatements of it in sentimental terms: rotation in office, direct elections, the initiative and referendum, the recall, the popular primary, and so on. Again, there is the primary doctrine that the possession of great wealth is a crime — a doctrine half a religious heritage and half the product of mere mob envy. Out of it have come free silver, trust-busting, government ownership, muck-raking, Populism, Bleaseism, Progressivism, the milder forms of Socialism, the whole gasconade of "reform" politics. Yet again, there is the ineradicable peasant suspicion of the man who is having a better time in the world — a suspicion grounded, like the foregoing, partly upon undisguised envy and partly upon archaic and barbaric religious taboos. Out of it have come all the glittering pearls of the uplift, from Abolition to Prohibition, and from the crusade against horse-racing to the Mann Act. The whole political history of the United States is a history of these three ideas. There has never been an issue before the people that could not be translated into one or another of them. What is more, they have also colored the fundamental philosophical (and particularly epistemological) doctrines of the American people, and their moral theory, and even their foreign relations. The late war, very unpopular at the start, was "sold" to them, as the advertising phrase has it, by representing it as a campaign for the salvation of democracy, half religious and wholly altruistic. So represented to them, they embraced it; represented as the highly obscure and complex thing it actually was, it would have been beyond their comprehension, and hence abhorrent to them.

Outside this circle of their elemental convictions they are quite incapable of rational thought. One is not surprised to hear of Bismarck, a thorough royalist, discussing democracy with calm and fairness, but it would be unimaginable for the American people, or for any other democratic people, to discuss royalism in the same manner: it would take a cataclysm to bring them to any such violation of their mental habits. When such a cataclysm occurs, they embrace the new ideas that are its fruits with the same adamantine firmness. One year before the French Revolution, disobedience to the king was unthinkable to the average Frenchman; only a few daringly immoral men cherished the notion. But one year *after* the fall of the Bastile, obedience to the king was equally unthinkable. The Russian Bolsheviki, whose doings have furnished a great deal of immensely interesting material to the student of popular psychology, put the principle into plain words. Once they were in the saddle, they decreed the abolition of the old imperial censorship and announced that speech would be free henceforth — but only so long as it kept within the bounds of the Bolshevist revelation! In other words, any citizen was free to think and speak whatever he pleased — but only so long as it did not violate certain fundamental ideas. This is precisely the sort of freedom that has prevailed in the United States since the first days. It is the only sort of freedom comprehensible to the average man. It accurately reveals his constitutional inability to shake himself free from the illogical and often quite unintelligible prejudices, instincts and mental vices that condition ninety per cent. of all his thinking. . . .

But here I wander into political speculation and no doubt stand in contumacy of some statute of Congress. Dr. Parsons avoids politics in her very interesting book. She confines herself to the purely social relations, e.g., between man and woman, parent and child, host and guest, master and servant. The facts she offers are vastly interesting, and their discovery and coördination reveal a tremendous industry, but of even greater interest are the facts that lie over the margin of her inquiry. Here is a golden opportunity for other investigators: I often wonder that the field is so little explored. Perhaps the Freudians, once they get rid of their sexual obsession, will enter it and chart it. No doubt the inferiority complex described by Prof. Dr. Alfred Adler will one day provide an intelligible explanation of many of the puzzling phenomena of mob thinking. In the work of Prof. Dr. Freud himself there is, perhaps, a clew to the origin and anatomy of Puritanism, that worst of intellectual nephritises. I live in hope that the Freudians will fall upon the business without much further delay. Why do otherwise sane men believe in spirits? What is the genesis of the American axiom that the fine arts are unmanly? What is the precise machinery of the process called falling in love? Why do people believe newspapers? ... Let there be light!

STUART PRATT SHERMAN

TRADITION [1]

To lengthen the childhood of the individual, at the same time bringing to bear upon it the influences of tradition, is the obvious way to shorten the childhood of races, nations, classes, and so to quicken the general processes of civilization. Yet in the busy hum of self-approbation which accompanies the critical activities of our young people, perhaps the dominant note is their satisfaction at having emancipated themselves from the fetters of tradition, the oppression of classical precedent, the burden of an inherited culture. By detaching the new literature from its learned past they are confident that they are assuring it a popular future. Turn to any one of half a dozen books which discuss the present movement, and you will learn that people are now discovering, for example, "often to their own surprise," that they can read and enjoy poetry. That is because poetry has been subjected to "democratization." The elder writers, such as Shakespeare, Milton, Emerson, and Longfellow, constantly gravelled them with strange and obsolete phrases, like "multitudinous seas incarnadine," and like "tumultuous privacy of storm." The ancient writers sent them to out-of-the-way reference books to look up obscure legends about Troy, not the city where collars are made, and old stuff about war in heaven, and the landing at Plymouth Rock. It is therefore a relief to countless eager young souls that Mr. Mencken has dismissed all this as "the fossil literature taught in colleges," and that Mary Austin insists that native verse rhythms must be "within the capacity of the democratically bred." It is a joy to hear from Mr. Untermeyer that modern readers of poetry may now come out from the "lifeless and literary storehouse" and use life itself for their glossary, as indeed they may — or the morning's newspaper.

Those who encourage us to hope for crops without tillage,

---

[1] From *Americans* (1922). By permission of the publishers, Charles Scribner's Sons.

learning without study, and literary birth without gestation or travail are doubtless animated by a desire to augment the sum of human felicity; but one recalls Burke's passionate ejaculation: "Oh! no, sir, no. Those things which are not practicable are not desirable." To the new mode of procuring a literary renascence there may be raised one objection, which, to minds of a certain temper, will seem rather grave: all experience is against it. Such is the thesis recently argued by an English critic, Mr. H. J. Massingham, who reviews with mingled amusement and alarm the present "self-conscious rebellion against tradition." In the eyes of our excited young "cosmopolitans," whose culture has a geographic rather than an historical extension, Mr. Massingham's opinions will of course appear to be hopelessly prejudiced by his Oxford breeding, his acquaintance with the classics, his saturation in Elizabethan literature, and his avowed passion for old books in early editions, drilled by the bibliomaniac worm, "prehistoric" things, like Nares' *Glossary* and Camden's *Remains*. But it is not merely the opinion of our critic that is formidable: "The restoration of the traditional link with the art of the past is a conservative and revolutionary necessity." It is not the supporting opinion of Sir Joshua Reynolds: "The only food and nourishment of the mind of an artist is the great works of his predecessors." Sir Joshua, too, was prejudiced by his position as a pillar of the robust English classicism of George III's time. It is not even the opinion of Henry James, whom Mr. Massingham proclaims the profoundest critic since Coleridge, and who even our own irreverent youth seem to suspect should be mentioned respectfully: "It takes an endless amount of history to make even a little tradition and an endless amount of tradition to make even a little taste and an endless amount of taste, by the same token, to make even a little tranquillity."

The formidable arguments against the radical engineers of renascence are just the notorious facts of literary history. The fact that a bit of the "fossil literature taught in colleges," the story of Arthur, written in Latin by a Welsh monk in the twelfth century, has flowered and fruited in poetry, painting, and music generation after generation pretty much over the civilized world. The fact that Chaucer and his contemporaries,

satire — making fun of follies and in this way make people change

in whom poetry had a glorious rebirth, had previously devoured everything in what Mr. Untermeyer would call the "lifeless and literary storehouse" of the Middle Ages. The fact that the Elizabethans, to quote Mr. Massingham's vigorous phrase, flung themselves on tradition "like a hungry wolf, not only upon the classics but upon all the tradition open to them." The fact that Restoration comedy is simply a revival of late Caroline in the hands of men who had studied Molière. The fact that the leaders of the new movement in the eighteenth century, when they wished to break from the stereotyped classicism, did not urge young people to slam the door on the past, but, on the contrary, harked back over the heads of Pope and Dryden to the elder and more central tradition of Milton, Shakespeare, and Spenser; and sluiced into the arid fields of common sense, grown platitudinous, the long-dammed or subterranean currents of mediæval romance. The fact that "Childe Harold," "Adonais," "The Eve of St. Agnes," "The Cotter's Saturday Night," and "The Castle of Indolence" were all written by imitators of Spenser or by imitators of his imitators. The fact, to omit the Victorians, that Mr. W. B. Yeats, the most skilful living engineer of literary renascence, set all his collaborators to digging around the roots of the ancient Celtic tree before we enjoyed the blossoming of the new spring in Ireland. The fact that John Masefield, freshest and most tuneful voice in England, is obviously steeped to the lips in the poetry of Byron, Shakespeare, Spenser, and Chaucer.

Why is it that the great poets, novelists, and critics, with few exceptions, have been, in the more liberal sense of the word, scholars — masters of several languages, students of history and philosophy, antiquarians? First of all because the great writer conceives of his vocation as the most magnificent and the most complex of crafts. He is to be his own architect, master-builder, carpenter, painter, singer, orator, poet and dramatist. His materials, his tools, his methods are, or may be, infinite. To him, then, the written tradition is a school and a museum in which, if he has a critical and inventive mind, he learns, from both the successes and the failures of his predecessors, how to set to work upon his own problems of expression. As Mr. Yeats is fond of pointing out, the young poet may

find Herbert and Vaughan more helpful to him than the work of
his own contemporaries, because the faults in the elder poets,
the purple patches that failed to hold their color, will not attract and mislead him.

But tradition is more than a school of crafts.   It is a school
of mood and manners.   The artist who is also a scholar cannot
fail to discover that what distinguishes all the golden periods of
art, what constitutes the perpetual appeal of the masters, is a
kind of innermost poise and serenity, tragic in Sophocles,
heroic in Michelangelo, skeptical in Montaigne, idyllic in
Sidney, ironic in Fielding.   This enviable tranquillity reigns
only in a mind that, looking before and after, feels itself the
representative of something outlasting time, some national
ideal, some religious faith, some permanent human experience,
some endless human quest.   Nothing begets this mood and
manner, the sovereign mark of good breeding in letters, like
habitual association with those who have it, the majority of
whom are, in the vulgar sense of the word, dead.   Izaak Walton, a minor writer in whose work there is a golden afterglow of
the great age, calls, in one of his Angler's Dialogues, for "that
smooth song which was made by Kit Marlowe, now at least
fifty years ago," and for the answer to it "which was made by
Sir Walter Raleigh in his younger days."   If some of our
modern imitators of the auctioneer and the steam calliope
would now and then, instead of reading one another, step into
the "lifeless and literary storehouse" and compare these
"fossils" conscientiously with their own recent efforts to make
verse popular!   "They were old-fashioned poetry," says
Piscator apologetically, "but choicely good, I think much better than the strong lines that are now in fashion in this critical
age."

Out of the tranquillity induced by working in a good literary
tradition develops form.   The clever theorists who insist that
form alone matters, that form is the only preservative element
in literature, forget that form is not "self-begotten" but a
product of the formative spirit.   Mr. Massingham is a bit
fastidious in his use of this word.   He denies form, for example,
to Pope and to Swinburne.   Though both have technique,
that is another matter.   "Form," he declares, "is a vision con-

tained and made manifest." He attributes the unproductive-
ness of our age in the field of satire to a vision without a traditional base, reeling and shifting in the choppy waters of contemporary opinion. His remarks on the deficiencies of Gilbert
Cannan as a satirist and novelist further elucidate his idea; and
they may serve also as a comment upon many of the younger
writers in America:

The works of Mr. Cannan seem to say, "That is what life is — a
surge of base and beautiful forces, intensified in the consciousness of
man." But that is a fallacy. Life is like that to the layman, but it
is the business of the artist to see a clue in it, to give it shape and
order, to weld its particles into congruity. Here is where his lack of
a constructive or satiric purpose growing out of and controlling the
material tells to his hurt. He knows life in the raw, but the satirist
would put it in the oven and dish it up. So he wanders in the dark,
and we blunder after him. But we want light, if it be only from a
tallow candle.

Now, many of the young writers in America are disposed to
reject the English tradition as unserviceable lumber. They
scorn equally the greater part of the American tradition as
puritanical, effeminate, or over-intellectualized. If they seek
foreign allies, it is with those who help them forget our national characteristics, our native bent and purposes, our discovered special American "genius." In what measure is the
revolt due to the conduct of the movement by writers whose
blood and breeding are as hostile to the English strain as a cat
to water? Whatever the answer, I suspect that the young people who are being congratulated right and left on their emancipation from tradition are rather open to condolence than to
felicitation. They have broken away from so much that was
formative, and they suffer so obviously in consequence of the
break. Their poets have lost a skill which Poe had: though
they paint a little, and chant a little, and speak a great deal of
faintly rhythmical prose, they have not learned how to sing.
Their novelists have lost a vision which Howells had: though
they have shaken off the "moralistic incubus" and have re-
leased their "suppressed desires," they have not learned how
to conceive or to present a coherent picture of civilized society.
Their leaders have lost a constructiveness which a critic so

laden with explosives as Emerson exhibited: though they have blown up the old highways they have not made new roads.

Am I doing the "young people" an injustice? I turn from their anthologies of verse, where I keep searching in vain for such music as the angler's milkmaid sang; and from the novels of Mr. Cabell, in whom I have not discovered that ascending sun heralded by the lookouts; to *A Modern Book of Criticism*, recently collected and put forth by Mr. Ludwig Lewisohn. The editor's desire is to show us that "a group of critics, young men or men who do not grow old, are at work upon the creation of a civilized cultural atmosphere in America." The idea resembles that, does it not? of Mr. Waldo Frank, who recently informed us that literature began in America in 1900 — or was it 1910? — at Mr. Stieglitz's place in New York. It is related also to that recent comprehensive indictment edited by Mr. Harold Stearns and ironically entitled *Civilization in the United States*. The implication is clearly that the country which developed Bradford, Franklin, Emerson, Lincoln, Thoreau, Whitman, Mark Twain, here and there in villages and backwoods, had no "civilized cultural atmosphere" worth mentioning. It does not seem quite plausible.

But let us proceed with Mr. Lewisohn. His critics: — "Like a group of shivering young Davids — slim and frail but with a glimpse of morning sunshine on their foreheads — they face an army of Goliaths." The slim and shivering young Davids turn out on investigation to be Mr. Huneker, Mr. Spingarn, Mr. Mencken, Mr. Lewisohn, Mr. Hackett, Mr. Van Wyck Brooks, and Randolph Bourne. It is not a group, taken as a whole, however it may be connected with the house of Jesse, which should be expected to hear any profound murmuring of ancestral voices or to experience any mysterious inflowing of national experience in meditating on the names of Mark Twain, Whitman, Thoreau, Lincoln, Emerson, Franklin, and Bradford. One doesn't blame our Davids for their inability to connect themselves vitally with this line of Americans, for their inability to receive its tradition or to carry it on. But one cannot help asking whether this inability does not largely account for the fact that Mr. Lewisohn's group of critics are restless impressionists, almost destitute of doctrine, and with no discoverable unifying tendency except to let themselves out into a homeless happy land where they may enjoy the "colorful" cosmic weather, untroubled by business men, or middle-class Americans, or Congressmen, or moralists, or humanists, or philosophers, or professors, or Victorians, or Puritans, or New Englanders, or Messrs. Tarkington and Churchill. A jolly lot of Goliaths to slay before we get that "civilized cultural atmosphere."

By faithfully studying the writings of Mr. Mencken, Mr. Lewisohn, and other "shivering young Davids," I have obtained a fairly clear conception of what a "civilized cultural atmosphere" is not. It consists of none of those heart-remembered things — our own revenue officers probing our old shoes for diamond necklaces, our own New York newspapers, and Maryland chicken on the Albany boat — which cause a native American returning from a year in Europe to exclaim as he sails up the tranquil bosom of the Hudson and rushes by a standard steel Pullman, back to the great warm embrace of his own land, "Thank Heaven, we are home again." No, it is none of these things. If, without going to Munich, you wish to know what a "civilized cultural atmosphere" really is, you must let Mr. Lewisohn describe it for you as it existed, till the passage of the Volstead act, in one or two odd corners of old New York: "The lamps of the tavern had orange-colored shades, the wainscoting was black with age. The place was filled with a soothing dusk and the blended odor of beer and tobacco and Wiener Schnitzel. *I was, at least, back in civilization.* That tavern is gone now, swept away by the barbarism of the Neo-Puritans."

To the book from which this quotation is made, Mr. Lewisohn's recently published autobiographical record, *Up Stream*, students of contemporary critical currents and eddies are much indebted. The author, like many of the other belligerent young writers who have shown in recent years a grave concern for the state of civilization in America, has ostensibly been directing his attack against our national culture from a very elevated position. He has professed himself one of the enlightened spirits who from time to time rise above the narrowing prejudices of nationality into the free air of the republic of letters, the grand cosmopolis of the true humanist. From his watch-tower — apparently "in the skies" — he has launched lightnings of derision at those who still weave garlands for their Lares and Penates, at the nationalist with his "selective sympathies," at the traditionalist with his sentimental fondness for folk-ways. Those who feel strongly attracted, as I do myself, to the Ciceronian and Stoic conception of a universal humanity and by the Christian and Augustinian vision of a universal City of God, may easily have mistaken Mr. Lewisohn for a "sharp-shooter" of the next age, an outpost from the land of their heart's desire. But in *Up Stream*, Mr. Lewisohn drops the mask and reveals himself, for all his Jewish radicalism,[1] as essentially a sentimental and homesick German, longing in exile for a Germany which exists only in his imagination.

Even the purified and liberated mind of a Child of Light, living according to nature and reason, is unable to rid itself wholly of "selective sympathies." It betrays under provocation a merely "traditional emotion" for a cultural atmosphere compounded of the odors of beer, tobacco, and Wiener Schnitzel, with perhaps a whiff of Kant and a strain of Hungarian music floating through it, while two or three high philosophical spirits discuss what a poet can do when his wife grows old and stringy. I do not think it necessary to remonstrate with a man merely because his effective nature responds powerfully to a vision of felicity thus composed; but I think it a bit impractical to ask "a nation of prohibitionists and Puritans" to accept this vision as the goal of cultural efforts in America. It is a help to fruitful controversy, however, when a man abandons his absurdly insincere professions of "universal sympathy" — his purring protestation that he desires "neither

---

[1] In a notably competent article on "The Case of Mr. Lewisohn," which appeared in *The Menorah Journal* of June, 1922, Professor Jacob Zeitlin writes: "Whether entirely just or strongly colored, it is evident that Mr. Lewisohn's criticism of State Universities has little relevance to his character as a Jew. It indicates nothing more than that his sensitive æsthetic organism recoiled in pain from an environment that was uncongenial. And the same observation holds concerning his reaction toward American life in general. He but adds his voice to a chorus of growing volume, reiterating the now familiar burden of the crudeness and narrowness of our political and social ideas. There is ample ground for such a protest as he makes, but it is not a protest that can be identified with any recognizably Jewish outlook."

to judge nor to condemn" — and frankly admits that he likes
the German life, what he knows of it, and that he regards
American life, what he knows of it, as "ugly and mean."

The militant hostility of alien-minded critics towards what
they conceive to be the dominant traits of the national character is, on the whole, to be welcomed as provocative of reflection
and as a corrective to national conceit. But the amendment
of that which is really ugly and mean and basely repressive in
our contemporary society is less likely to be achieved by listening to the counsels of exiled emancipators from Munich
than by harking back to our own liberative tradition, which
long antedates the efforts of these bewildered impressionists.

When we grow dull and inadventurous and slothfully content with our present conditions and our old habits, it is not
because we are "traditionalists"; it is, on the contrary, because
we have ceased to feel the formative spirit of our own traditions.
It is not much in the American vein, to be sure, to construct
private little anarchies in the haze of a smoking-room; but
practical revolt, on a large scale and sagaciously conducted, is
an American tradition, which we should continue to view with
courage and the tranquillity which is related to courage.
America was born because it revolted. It revolted because it
condemned. It condemned because its sympathies were not
universal but selective. Its sympathies were selective because
it had a vision of a better life, pressing for fulfilment. That
vision, and not a conception of life as a meaningless "surge of
base and beautiful forces" liberated its chief men of letters.
Thence their serenity, in place of that "gentle but chronic
dizziness" which a critic of Young Germany, Hugo von Hof-
mannsthal says, "vibrates among us." Thence, too, their freedom from ancestor-worship and bondage to the letter. Listen
to Emerson:

> Ask not me, as Muftis can,
> To recite the Alcoran;
> Well I love the meaning sweet;
> I tread the book beneath my feet.

Thence, too, the traditional bent of the American spirit toward modernity, toward realism. It was nearly a hundred

years ago that our then-leading critic wrote in his journal·
"You must exercise your genius in some form that has essential
life now; do something which is proper to the hour and cannot
but be done." Did he not recognize what was to be done? I
quote once more from him a finer sentence than any of our
impressionists has ever written: "A wife, a babe, a brother,
poverty, and a country, which the Greeks had, I have." The
grip and the beauty of that simple sentence are due to a union
in it of an Athenian vision with Yankee self-reliance. It is the
kind of feeling that comes to a man who has lived in a great
tradition.

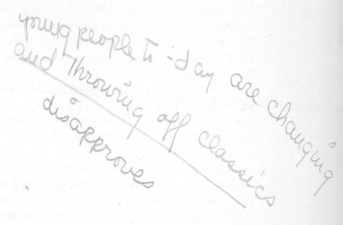

young people to-day are changing
and throwing off classics
disapproves

PHILIP GUEDALLA

THE CRITICS [1]

ONE of the most touching things about the United States (and they are rather touching — although like most people they would infinitely prefer to appear fierce or impressive or even a trifle forbidding) is their perennial interest in the state of English letters.   Over here one is a little inclined to take them for granted, to let those exquisite plants grow unconsciously — with an occasional afternoon for weeding.   But that mild, inactive attitude is not nearly enterprising enough for our friends across the sea.   They seem to us, as we sit back in a long chair and look at the sky through the leaves, to be perpetually busy about the garden, always trotting up and down the paths with an anxious eye and a basket full of the dangerous looking instruments of literary horticulture, stopping every minute to bend over a bed of young novelists or tie up a drooping reputation, prodding the subsoil with an enquiring fork, or taking a selection of promising young plants into their own charming conservatory to tell them (from the lecture platform) just how they are growing.

They are afflicted, in fact, with that nervous inability to enjoy things which Mr. Ford Madox Hueffer defined ever so many years ago as the Critical Attitude.   One knows (or, at any rate, one has always preferred to think) that no landscape is ever enjoyed by those gifted persons who know the names of all the plants in it.   They are far too busy murmuring *Celosia Jonesii* and *Ampelopis hirsuta* to notice the faint line of the river through the trees and the slow drift of the cloud-shadows across the silent hills.   One may leave such simple pleasures to the uninstructed observer who can hardly, poor fellow, see the trees for the wood.   But while he and his uncultivated friends are gesticulating on the hilltops and generalizing a little wildly about the view, the expert passes proudly by with his trained

[1] From *Masters and Men*.   Copyright, 1923, by G. P. Putnam's Sons.   By permission of the publishers.

nose kept well below the ground-level and stops every now and then to examine a moss or prod a saxifrage.

He knows about it all. *He* knows. HE knows.

And that knowledge, so patiently accumulated, is impressively communicated to the world in those little essays in criticism, those short courses in how to do it by which (if only they would read them) those who are rash enough to do it are periodically kept straight by those who are not.

America has not yet, so far as the torpid British perception is aware, reached the second (or graver) stage of the ailment. It is with her at present in the lighter, preliminary form; and there is still some hope that the complaint may pass away altogether and leave her no worse than she was before. One says this because her tendency at present is merely to appreciate and estimate and value and revalue those English writers whose work reaches her: that is an early symptom. But she rarely (perhaps too rarely) tells our young people how to write. That is the final, the most exasperating stage of criticism.

The Critical Attitude, which disables a man from enjoying a book in precisely the same way that nervous hyperæsthesia disables him from enjoying his life, passes in the normal case through two phases. In essence, of course, it is prompted by the barren spirit of enquiry which drives small children to extract all the works of a favourite clock-work bear; and it has been observed that bears (and novelists) who have been subjected to this searching analysis rarely function with the same freedom after the critical process. But one is less concerned with its effects on writers than with its broader and more disastrous influence on readers. The temper of criticism was once defined by the accomplished Mr. Hueffer in the striking exhortation to his countrymen: "Examine into the composition and the past history of your pill before you swallow it." Yet however salutary this injunction may be to those about to consume patent medicines, one somehow doubts its efficacy as a general guide to life. Besides, the normal person is not perpetually employed in taking pills. The habit of invariably pausing with the morsel half-way to one's mouth, while its composition and antecedents are critically considered, may save a few drug-takers. But it will spoil a good many dinners. Persons afflicted with the Critical Attitude suffer from an almost total inability to enjoy a book as the simple thing that it really is. In the earlier stages of the complaint (and there, unless I am profoundly in error, so many readers are to be found) the patient's mind runs, while he is reading, on Estimates and Appreciations and Tendencies and Literary Values. He is perpetually *placing* writers, like those mental sufferers whose sole occupation is to arrange things in long lines or interminable tabulated schemes. He thinks of poets in *schools* (as though they were porpoises) or of novelists in *groups* (as though they were bulky athletic gentlemen being photographed after a foot-ball match). And, above all, he never reads a book with the simple object of getting out of it just what the author put into it. But in the second (and fatal) stage the symptoms grow graver. Primary criticism is mainly a failure to enjoy things unless they are arranged in critical categories. In cases of secondary criticism the patient feels an overmastering need to tell those who do things how they should have done them. If he has relatives, they will restrain him; but since critics are recruited almost entirely from the ranks of foundlings, they are totally unrestrained. In this case the sufferer may be overheard muttering about Technique and Method. He scrawls "Flaubert" on people's doors and runs away. The inability to read becomes complete; but unfortunately it is only in rare cases accompanied by a corresponding inability to write, and the written by-products of this distressing malady are known as Criticism.

As a continent America has not reached (and one prays to heaven that it may never reach) the second stage of this dreadful and progressive ailment. But it would seem that they are tolerably well advanced in the earlier phase. They are always *placing* our established writers. They have a vast appetite for Groups of Younger Men. And the result, if one may offer a word of mild advice, is that this view of English letters is just a shade too inclusive. We have a tolerable poet or so — although they are not at the moment particularly thick on the ground. But in their determination to observe a School of .

British Poetry they have included in their serious, their kindly appreciation quite a number of industrious persons whose contribution to our verse exports would never upset the balance of trade. They have got in because American taste was set on having a British School, and one can hardly have a School of two. Errors of that type are apt to occur when one ceases to read and begins instead to criticise. And the same taste for criticism misleads them sometimes into solemn appreciation of quite negligible writers. It is such fun, when once one is bitten with the *tic* of criticism, to estimate, to appreciate, to revalue, to wield the solemn critical scales; and if no Shakespeares are about to tip the beam, one pops in Mr. X. Which is all very well as an exercise in criticism and so long as one remembers that he is only Mr. X. But once a writer has been solemnly discussed, one is so apt to think quite solemnly about him. And that is bad for one's judgment — as well as very bad indeed for Mr. X.

A distaste for criticism is as natural as a distaste for medicine; and in England we have had far too much of both lately. There has been a queer revival of the critical habit, a rise of critics in public estimation which has culminated in the past few years in the erection of a definite critical hierarchy. We are drifting gradually towards that critically perfect state in which it is felt to be more important to know (as Mr. Gosse does) what to say about a book than to write one, far higher in the intellectual scale to adjust the fine balances of criticism than to supply the *corpus vile* which they weigh. It is a strange, almost an alarming development. One had grown accustomed, since the death of Matthew Arnold, to see criticism left exclusively to the *amateur*, to the unbiased judgment of some friend of the editor who wanted to get books for nothing. There was something to be said for the method, since it arrived by a rather devious route at a general, popular judgment on the works, and it eluded the professionalism which is the British bugbear. The editor's friend was fairly representative of the great community for which he acted as taster, and his ineptitude was a very fair measure of the ineptitude of the reading public. Somewhere on the heights above him the great critics of the past paraded their lonely figures through the mist; and they, no doubt, in their dogmatism and their spiritual pride were the models of our young friends, the modern critics.   They set out with a brave determination to give their public something more than a bare verdict on the work which they criticised.   Cheese-tasters and reviewers might confine themselves to a curt, disgusted "This is bad."   But a critic, they felt, was expected to give reasons for his judgment, to lay down laws, to erect standards.   So they cultivated an exquisite sensibility and a broad, impressive range of allusion; and at their best they have a stale flavour of Matthew Arnold.   But how different the method and the medium in which their instruction is conveyed to the listening spheres. The old lonely critic ingeminating woe on English letters has been replaced by lively, active little groups.   The literary streets are crowded with earnest people, all called Diogenes, and each of them looking vainly for one just writer; and the lions are considerably outnumbered by the throng of Daniels come to judgment.   The shrill young voices ring out in chorus; and the law, in these delicate critical matters, is laid down for us by a syndicated lawgiver.   Worse still, the multitude of critics has produced schism; and we have a Pope or so at Avignon fulminating critical excommunication against the Pope of Rome.   There is an admirable confusion of voices, and counsel is exquisitely darkened.

There are, broadly speaking, in England at the present moment more critics than anything else.   They certainly outnumber the readers; and they probably outnumber the writers, too.   When a book is rash enough to appear, the writer is summoned before an overcrowded Bench; and the judgments serve to remind one by their abundance that the law is always most fully stated by Courts with not quite enough work to do.   But the situation is more serious than that: it has something of the gravity of a crop failure, when the mills are kept standing for want of raw material.   The critics of England stand hollow-eyed in their doorways, waiting for work to do.   But there has been boll weevil among the early poets; the novels are all mildewed, and there is even blight among the essayists.   In the full horror of the famine the critics have set to work to turn out raw material for their own mills. There was a desperate search among the rubbish-heaps of past literature. Backnumbers were ransacked for unsuspected treasure, and Old Masters were hastily fabricated from the rag and bone shop. It was a simple-minded quest, which deceived no one but the dithyrambic gentlemen who wrote prefaces for the Collected Remains of deceased, almost too deceased authors. But it made quite a vogue for an idiot poet or so; and it gave the critics some work to do, when work was badly needed.

A sounder method, although it involved some sacrifice of critical dignity, was the confection of masterpieces by the critics themselves. To indulge in mere composition, when one was born to the higher calling of criticism, of appraisement, of knowing how it is done, might seem a grave decline. But the sacrifice was made; the works were written; and the critics, by turning author, got something to write about. Mr. Squire laid aside the sceptre of the *London Mercury*, spent a few mornings with his Muse, and became a poet again. Mr. Middleton Murry tuned his frail instrument to the coarse notes of fiction. Miss Rebecca West hung up the flail and borrowed a pen with results which made one regret that she loses so much time in reading bad novels which she might spend in writing good ones. There was a sudden burst of books by critics, and one half expected Mr. Gosse to write a sonnet. But the crisis was averted. The critics were given something to criticise, and England resumed her sleep in the shadow of their pulpits. In their truculence and their domination they are at the moment the most conspicuous, if hardly the most hopeful, feature of English letters. There has been nothing quite like it since the critics killed Keats.

CHRISTOPHER MORLEY

ON UNANSWERING LETTERS [1]

THERE are a great many people who really believe in answering letters the day they are received, just as there are people who go to the movies at 9 o'clock in the morning; but these people are stunted and queer.

It is a great mistake. Such crass and breathless promptness takes away a great deal of the pleasure of correspondence.

The psychological didoes involved in receiving letters and making up one's mind to answer them are very complex. If the tangled process could be clearly analyzed and its component involutions isolated for inspection we might reach a clearer comprehension of that curious bag of tricks, the efficient Masculine Mind.

Take Bill F., for instance, a man so delightful that even to contemplate his existence puts us in good humor and makes us think well of a world that can exhibit an individual equally comely in mind, body and estate. Every now and then we get a letter from Bill, and immediately we pass into a kind of trance, in which our mind rapidly enunciates the ideas, thoughts, surmises and contradictions that we would like to write to him in reply. We think what fun it would be to sit right down and churn the ink-well, spreading speculation and cynicism over a number of sheets of foolscap to be wafted Billward.

Sternly we repress the impulse for we know that the shock to Bill of getting so immediate a retort would surely unhinge the well-fitted panels of his intellect.

We add his letter to the large delta of unanswered mail on our desk, taking occasion to turn the mass over once or twice and run through it in a brisk, smiling mood, thinking of all the jolly letters we shall write some day.

After Bill's letter has lain on the pile for a fortnight or so it has been gently silted over by about twenty other pleasantly

[1] From *Mince Pie.* Copyright, 1919, by Doubleday, Page and Company.

postponed manuscripts. Coming upon it by chance, we reflect that any specific problems raised by Bill in that manifesto will by this time have settled themselves. And his random speculations upon household management and human destiny will probably have taken a new slant by now, so that to answer his letter in its own tune will not be congruent with his present fevers. We had better bide a wee until we really have something of circumstance to impart.

We wait a week.

By this time a certain sense of shame has begun to invade the privacy of our brain. We feel that to answer that letter now would be an indelicacy. Better to pretend that we never got it. By and by Bill will write again and then we will answer promptly. We put the letter back in the middle of the heap and think what a fine chap Bill is. But he knows we love him, so it doesn't really matter whether we write or not.

Another week passes by, and no further communication from Bill. We wonder whether he does love us as much as we thought. Still — we are too proud to write and ask.

A few days later a new thought strikes us. Perhaps Bill thinks we have died and he is annoyed because he wasn't invited to the funeral. Ought we to wire him? No, because after all we are not dead, and even if he thinks we are, his subsequent relief at hearing the good news of our survival will outweigh his bitterness during the interval. One of these days we will write him a letter that will really express our heart, filled with all the grindings and gear-work of our mind, rich in affection and fallacy. But we had better let it ripen and mellow for a while. Letters, like wines, accumulate bright fumes and bubblings if kept under cork.

Presently we turn over that pile of letters again. We find in the lees of the heap two or three that have gone for six months and can safely be destroyed. Bill is still on our mind, but in a pleasant, dreamy kind of way. He does not ache or twinge us as he did a month ago. It is fine to have old friends like that and keep in touch with them. We wonder how he is and whether he has two children or three. Splendid old Bill!

By this time we have written Bill several letters in imagination and enjoyed doing so, but the matter of sending him an actual letter has begun to pall. The thought no longer has the savor and vivid sparkle it had once. When one feels like that it is unwise to write. Letters should be spontaneous out-pourings: they should never be undertaken merely from a sense of duty. We know that Bill wouldn't want to get a letter that was dictated by a feeling of obligation.

Another fortnight or so elapsing, it occurs to us that we have entirely forgotten what Bill said to us in that letter. We take it out and con it over. Delightful fellow! It is full of his own felicitous kinks of whim, though some of it sounds a little old-fashioned by now. It seems a bit stale, has lost some of its freshness and surprise. Better not answer it just yet, for Christmas will soon be here and we shall have to write then anyway. We wonder, can Bill hold out until Christmas with-out a letter?

We have been rereading some of those imaginary letters to Bill that have been dancing in our head. They are full of all sorts of fine stuff. If Bill ever gets them he will know how we love him. To use O. Henry's immortal joke, we have days of Damon and Knights of Pythias writing those uninked letters to Bill. A curious thought has come to us. Perhaps it would be better if we never saw Bill again. It is very difficult to talk to a man when you like him so much. It is much easier to write in the sweet fantastic strain. We are so inarticulate when face to face. If Bill comes to town we will leave word that we have gone away. Good old Bill! He will always be a precious memory.

A few days later a sudden frenzy sweeps over us, and though we have many pressing matters on hand, we mobilize pen and paper and literary shock troops and prepare to hurl several battalions at Bill. But, strangely enough, our utterance seems stilted and stiff. We have nothing to say. *My dear Bill*, we begin, *it seems a long time since we heard from you. Why don't you write? We still love you, in spite of all your shortcomings*.

That doesn't seem very cordial. We muse over the pen and nothing comes. Bursting with affection, we are unable to say a word.

Just then the phone rings. "Hello?" we say.

It is Bill, come to town unexpectedly.

"Good old fish!" we cry, ecstatic. "Meet you at the corner of Tenth and Chestnut in five minutes."

We tear up the unfinished letter. Bill will never know how much we love him. Perhaps it is just as well. It is very embarrassing to have your friends know how you feel about them. When we meet him we will be a little bit on our guard. It would not be well to be betrayed into any extravagance of cordiality.

And perhaps a not altogether false little story could be written about a man who never visited those most dear to him, because it panged him so to say good-bye when he had to leave.

APPENDIX

BIOGRAPHICAL AND BIBLIOGRAPHICAL NOTES

I. NOTES ON INDIVIDUAL ESSAYISTS

Montaigne, Michel Eyquem de (1533–92).

I. Born in family château at Périgord, February 28, 1533; educated at Collège de Guienne at Bordeaux; studied law, probably at Toulouse, 1546–48. Counsellor in the Bordeaux Parlement, 1554; at court and with French army, 1558–63; married Françoise de la Chassaigne, 1565. Returned to château, 1571; given Order of St. Michel, 1571; Gentleman-in-ordinary to Henry III, 1576; to Henry of Navarre, 1576; traveled to Italy; Mayor of Bordeaux, 1581–85. Died September 13, 1592.

II. *Essays*: first two books, 1580; third book, with additions, 1588; collected edition, 1595.

Translation: Florio, John, 1603; Cotton, C., 1685; revised Hazlitt, W. C., 1892; Ives, G. B., with Introduction by Grace Norton, 4 v., 1925.

III. *a.* Dowden, E.: *Michel de Montaigne*, 1905; Robertson, J. M.: *Montaigne and Shakespeare*, 1909; St. John, B.: *Montaigne the Essayist*, 1858; Sichel, Edith: *Michel de Montaigne*, 1911.

b. Essays by R. W. Emerson (*Representative Men*, 1850), A. Vinet (*Montaigne, the Endless Study and Other Miscellanies*, tr. R. Turnbull, 1850), and G. E. Woodberry (*Literary Essays*, 1910).

Ascham, Roger (1515–68).

I. Born at Kirby Wiske in 1515; educated at St. John's College, Cambridge, where he distinguished himself in the classics; B.A. and fellow, 1534; M.A., 1537; public orator at Cambridge, 1546; tutor to Princess Elizabeth, 1548; resigned and returned to Cambridge, 1550. Secretary to the English ambassador to Charles V, 1550–53, traveling extensively on the Continent; Latin Secretary to Queen Mary, 1553. Married Margaret Howe, and resigned office at Cambridge, 1554; private tutor to Queen Elizabeth, 1558; prebendary of York, 1559. Died in 1568.

II. Works: *Toxophilus*, 1545; *The Schoolmaster*, 1570 (unfinished). Complete Works, edited by Giles, 4 v., 1864–65.

III. *a.* Weidemann, G.: *Roger Ascham als Pädagoge*, Berlin, 1900.

b. Essays by Sir J. G. Fitch (*Educational Aims and Methods*, 1900), S. Johnson (preface to Ascham's *Works*, 1761), S. S. Laurie (*Teachers' Guild Address*, 1892) and R. H. Quick (*Essays on Educational Reformers*, 1886).

Bacon, Francis (1561–1626).

I. Born in London, January 22, 1561, youngest child of Sir Nicholas Bacon, Lord Keeper of the Great Seal; educated at Trinity College, Cambridge, 1573–75; barrister, 1582; M.P. from various constituencies, 1584–93; Queen's counsel, 1596. Largely responsible for conviction of Earl of Essex, his former benefactor, 1601; King's counsel and knighted, 1603. Married Alice Barnham, 1606; attorney-general, 1613; privy councillor, 1616; lord-keeper, 1617; lord chancellor and Baron Verulam, 1618; Viscount St. Albans, 1621. Confessed to "corruption and neglect" and deprived of office. Died April 9, 1626.

II. Philosophical Works: *Advancement of Learning*, 1605 (in English); *Novum Organum*, 1620 (in Latin).

Literary Works: *Essays*, 1597, 1612; in final form, 1625; *History of Henry the Seventh*, 1622; *Apophthegms New and Old*, 1624.

Complete Works, edited by Spedding, Ellis, and Heath, 1857–62.

III. *a.* Church, R. W.: *Francis Bacon*, 1884; Nichol, J.: *Francis Bacon, His Life and Philosophy*, 1888–89; Spedding, J.: *Letters and Life of Bacon*, 7 v., 1861–74 (abridged, 1875).

b. Essays by W. Hazlitt (*Lectures on the Dramatic Literature of the Age of Elizabeth*, 1821) and T. B. Macaulay (*Edinburgh Review*, July, 1837).

Overbury, Sir Thomas (1581–1613).

I. Born at Ilmington, Warwickshire, in 1581. B.A., Queen's College, Oxford, 1598; server to the King and knighted, 1608; traveled in the Netherlands, 1609. Concerned in numerous court intrigues; sent to the Tower, 1613, and there slowly poisoned by agents of Lady Essex, dying on September 15, 1613.

II. Prose Works: *Characters of Vices and Vertues*, 1608; *The First and Second Part of the Remedy of Love*, 1620.

Poem: *A Wife, Now a Widowe*, 1614.

Miscellaneous Works in Verse and Prose, edited by E. F. Rimbault, 1856; reprinted, 1890.

III. See C. S. Baldwin (*Publications of the Modern Language Association of America*, June, 1904), W. L. Cross (*Development of the English Novel*, 1899), C. M. Greenough (*Studies in the Development of Character Writing in England*, 1898), and C. Whibley (*Blackwood's Magazine*, June, 1909).

Earle, John (1601–65).

I. Born at York in or about 1601; B.A., Merton College, Oxford, and fellow, 1619; M.A., 1624; rector of Bishopston, Wiltshire, 1639. Tutor to Charles, Prince of Wales, 1641; D.D., Oxford, 1640; appointed to Westminster Assembly of Divines, 1643; chancellor of Salisbury, 1643. Deprived of office as a "malignant." Chaplain to Charles II in France; at the Restoration, Dean of Westminster; Bishop of Worcester, 1662–63; Bishop of Salisbury, 1663–65. Died at Oxford, November 17, 1665.

II. Works: *Microcosmographie*, 1628; *Hortus Mertonensis* (Latin poem).
III. Greenough, C. N.: *Studies in the Development of Character-writing in England*, 1898.

Browne, Sir Thomas (1605-82).
  I. Born in London, October 19, 1605. Educated at Winchester and Broadgates Hall, Oxford; M.A., 1629; practiced medicine and studied abroad; M.D., Leyden, 1633, Oxford, 1637; settled and practiced in Norwich. Expressed belief in witchcraft, 1664; knighted, 1671. Died October 19, 1682.
 II. Works: *Religio Medici*, 1642 (authorized edition, 1643); *Pseudodoxia Epidemica; or Enquiries into Vulgar Errors*, 1646; *Hydriotaphia: Urn Burial*, 1658; *The Garden of Cyrus*, 1658; *A Letter to a Friend*, 1690.
     Collected Works: edited by Wilkins, 4 v., 1835-36; edited by Morison, Pitt Press Series, 3 v., 1922.
III. *a.* Gosse, E.: *Sir Thomas Browne*, 1905.
     b. Essays by E. Dowden (*Puritan and Anglican*, 1900), W. Hazlitt (*Lectures on the Dramatic Literature of the Age of Elizabeth*, 1821), H. W. Nevinson (*Books and Personalities*, 1905), and L. Stephen (*Hours in a Library, Second Series*, 1876).

Milton, John (1608-74).
  I. Born in Bread Street, Cheapside, London, December 9, 1608. Educated at St. Paul's School and Christ's College, Cambridge; B.A., 1629; M.A., 1632. Lived at Horton, reading classics, 1632-38; traveled abroad, chiefly in Italy, 1637-39. Became tutor to his nephews on return and entered into acrimonious dispute on episcopacy. Abandoned intention of taking orders and married Mary Powell, 1643, who returned to her father after a month. Immediately published pamphlet on divorce. Reconciled to wife, 1645. Wrote various political pamphlets after execution of Charles I. Latin Secretary to Council of State, 1649; became blind but held post until the Restoration. Married Catharine Woodcock, 1656 (died 1658); married Elizabeth Minshull, 1662. Died in London, November 8, 1674. Buried in St. Giles, Cripplegate, London.
 II. Prose Works: *Doctrine and Discipline of Divorce*, 1643; *Of Education*, 1644; *Areopagitica*, 1644; *Tenure of Kings and Magistrates*, 1649; *Eikonoklastes*, 1649.
     Poetical Works: *Comus*, 1637; *Poems*, 1645; *Paradise Lost*, 1667; *Paradise Regained*, 1676; *Samson Agonistes*, 1671.
     Collected editions: *Poetical Works*, 1695; *Poetical Works*, 3 v., edited by D. Masson, 1874; *Complete Poetic and Dramatic Works*, edited by W. V. Moody, 1899; *English Poems*, 2 v., edited by R. C. Browne, 1894.
III. *a.* Garnett, R.: *John Milton*, 1889; Masson, D.: *Life of John Milton*, 6 v., 1859-80; Pattison, M.: *Milton*, 1879.
     b. Essays by J. Addison (*Spectator* Papers on *Paradise Lost*, Decem-

ber 31, 1711 to May 3, 1712), M. Arnold (*Mixed Essays*, 1879; *Essays in Criticism, 2d Series*, 1888), W. Bagehot (*Literary Studies*, vol. 1, 1879), E. Dowden (*Transcripts and Studies*, 1887), W. Hazlitt (*Lectures on the English Poets*, 1818), S. Johnson (*Lives of the English Poets*, 1779–81), J. R. Lowell (*Literary Essays*, vol. 4, 1872), T. B. Macaulay (*Edinburgh Review*, August, 1825), P. E. More (*Shelburne Essays, 4th Series*, 1906).

Taylor, Jeremy (1613–67)
I. Born in Cambridge on August 15, 1613. Perse scholar at Gonville and Caius College, Cambridge, 1628; fellow, 1633; M.A., 1634. Preaching attracted attention of Laud, who sent him to Oxford; fellow of All Saint's College, Oxford, and M.A., 1635. Chaplain to Laud and Charles I; of high repute as casuistical preacher; taken prisoner in Royalist defeat at Cardigan Castle, 1645; returned to Carmarthenshire; preached in London occasionally; Bishop of Down and Connor and administrator of Dromore, 1661. Died at Lisburn, August 13, 1667.

II. Works: *A Discourse of the Liberty of Prophesying*, 1646; *Holy Living*, 1650; *Holy Dying*, 1651; *Worthy Communicant*, 1660. Numerous sermons which rank above his books. Numerous verses.
Collected edition: *The Whole Works of Jeremy Taylor*, ed. R. Heber, 15 v., 1822.

III. Gosse, E.: *Jeremy Taylor*, 1904; Worley, G.: *Jeremy Taylor, A Sketch of His Life and Times*, 1904; Willmott, R. E. A.: *Jeremy Taylor*, 1846.

Cowley, Abraham (1616–67).
I. Born in London in 1616. King's scholar at Westminster; scholar of Trinity College, Cambridge, 1637; fellow, 1640; M.A. 1642. Ejected by Parliament, resided at St. John's College, Oxford. Went to France, 1646; cipher secretary to Queen Henrietta Maria about 1647; Royalist spy in England; M.D., Oxford, 1657. Returned to France and wrote odes on the Restoration and against Cromwell. Died July 28, 1667.

II. Poems: *Poetical Blossoms*, 1633; *Sylva*, 1636; *The Mistress*, 1647; *Poems* (including his " Pindarique Odes "), 1656; *Verses upon Several Occasions*, 1663.
Dramas: *Love's Riddle*, 1638; *Naufragium Joculare* (in Latin), 1638; *The Guardian*, 1641; *Cutter of Colman-Street*, 1663.
Collected Works: *The Works of Mr. Abraham Cowley*, 1668; *Complete Works*, ed. Grosart, A. B., 1881; ed. Waller, A. R., *Poems: Miscellanies*, 1905, and *Essays, Plays, and Sundry Verses*, 1906.

III. Essays by A. W. Fox (*A Book of Bachelors*, 1899), E. Gosse (*Seventeenth Century Studies*, 1883), W. Hazlitt (*Lectures on the English Comic Writers*, 1819), S. Johnson (*Lives of the English Poets*, 1779–81), and T. B. Macaulay (*Miscellaneous Essays*, revised ed., Vol. III).

Dryden, John (1631–1700).

I. Born at Aldwinkle All Saints, August 9, 1631. Scholar of Westminster School and Trinity College, Cambridge; B.A., 1654. Clerk to his cousin, Cromwell's chamberlain, and mourned Cromwell's death in *Heroic Stanzas*, 1659; published *Astræa Redux* and *Panegyric* in honor of the Restoration, 1660–61. M.A., 1668; poet laureate and historiographer, 1670. Between 1668 and 1681 wrote fourteen plays. Involved in several literary controversies; satirised Shaftesbury in verse; defended Anglicanism in *Religio Laici*, 1682; collector of customs for port of London, 1683. Converted to Roman Catholicism, 1686; deprived of laureateship, 1689. Died in London, May 1, 1700.

II. Poetical Works: *Heroic Stanzas, consecrated to the Memory of his Highness Oliver, late Lord Cromwell*, 1659; *Astræa Redux*, 1660; *Panegyric on the Coronation*, 1661; *Annus Mirabilis*, 1667; *Absalom and Achitophel*, Part 1, 1681; Part 2 (with Tate), 1682; *Mac Flecknoe*, 1682; *Religio Laici*, 1682; *The Hind and the Panther*, 1687; *Alexander's Feast*, 1697; *Fables, Ancient and Modern, Translated in Verse from Homer, Ovid, Boccaccio and Chaucer, with Original Poems*, 1700.

Dramatic Works: *The Rival Ladies*, 1664; *The Wild Gallant*, 1669; *The Indian Emperor*, 1667; *Conquest of Granada*, 1672; *Marriage à la Mode*, 1673; *Aurengzebe*, 1676; *All for Love*, 1677–78; *The Spanish Friar*, 1681.

Prose Works: *Essay on Dramatic Poesie*, 1668; *Life of Plutarch*, 1680.

Collected Works, 4 v., 1695; ed. G. Saintsbury, 18 v., 1882.

III. *a.* Garnett, R.: *The Age of Dryden*, 1895; Saintsbury, G.: *Dryden*, 1881.

b. Essays by J. C. Collins (*Essays and Studies*, 1895), W. J. Courthope (*History of English Poetry*, vols. III and IV, 1903), and S. Johnson (*Lives of the English Poets*, 1779–81).

Defoe, Daniel (1660–1731).

I. Born in 1660 or 1661 in the parish of St. Giles, Cripplegate, London. Brought up as a dissenter; sent to academy at Newington Green; went into business. Joined Monmouth's Rebellion, 1685; William of Orange's army, 1688; accountant to commissioner of glass-duty, 1695–99. To Scotland on a secret mission for the state, 1705; author of numerous controversial and satirical pamphlets; on several occasions fined and imprisoned; once pilloried. Condemned to death for treasonable publications but pardoned, 1713. Conducted *The Review*, 1704–13. Died in London, April 26, 1731.

II. Political Tracts: *Argument for a Standing Army*, 1698; *Danger of Protestant Religion*, 1701; *Present State of Jacobitism*, 1701; *Essay upon Loans*, 1710; *Eleven Opinions about Mr. Harley*, 1711; *Reasons Against the Succession of the House of Hanover*, 1713; *And What if the Pretender Should Come?* 1713; *Real Danger of the Protestant Succes-*

sion, 1714; *Secret History of the White Staff*, 1714–15; *An Appeal to Honour and Justice*, 1715; *Reasons for a War*, 1729; etc., etc.

Ecclesiastical Tracts: *An Enquiry into Occasional Conformity*, 1702; *Shortest Way with the Dissenters*, 1702; *More Short Ways With the Dissenters*, 1704; etc.

Economical and Social Tracts: *Essay upon Projects*, 1697; *A Tour Through Great Britain*, 1724–26; *Everybody's Business is Nobody's Business*, 1725; *Street-Robberies Considered*, 1728; etc.

Verses: *The True-Born Englishman*, 1701; *Jure Divino*, 1706; etc.

Narratives: *Apparition of Mrs. Veal*, 1706; *Life and Strange Surprising Adventures of Robinson Crusoe*, 1719; *Memoirs of a Cavalier*, 1720; *Life of Captain Singleton*, 1720; *Moll Flanders*, 1722; *Journal of the Plague Year*, 1722; *History of Colonel Jacque*, 1722; *The Fortunate Mistress*, 1724.

Collected Works: ed. with Life by W. Hazlitt, 3 v., 1840; Oxford edition, 20 v., 1840; *Romances and Narratives*, ed. G. A. Aitken, 16 v., 1895–96.

III. *a.* Aitken, G. A., bibliographical notes to his edition of the *Romances and Narratives;* Chalmers, G.: *Daniel Defoe*, 1790; Lee, W.: Vol. 1 of *Life and Newly Discovered Writings of Daniel Defoe*, 1869; Minto, W.: *Daniel Defoe*, 1879; Rannie, D. W.: *Daniel Defoe*, 1890; Trent, W. P.: *Defoe: How to Know Him*, 1916.

   b. Essays by J. Dennis (*Studies in English Literature*, 1883), C. Lamb (Vol. 1, *Miscellaneous Works*, 1903), L. Stephen (*Hours in a Library*, Vol. I, 1874), and P. F. York (*Occasional Writings*, 1906).

Swift, Jonathan (1667–1745).

I. Born in Dublin, November 30, 1667; educated at Kilkenny grammar school and at Trinity College, Dublin, 1682, where he showed impatience with restraint. Obtained degree by "special grace." Admitted into household of Sir William Temple, serving as secretary; chafed at dependent situation and lack of preferment. Left Temple's household, returned to Ireland and was ordained, 1695. Returned to Temple, 1696. Read deeply in classics; edited Temple's correspondence; wrote numerous satires, polemics, and pamphlets. On death of Temple, 1699, given a prebend in St. Patrick's, Dublin, with other livings; Dean of St. Patrick's, 1713. Frequent visits to England ended after death of Queen Anne, 1714. Complained of treatment of Ireland; adored by the people; attracted to himself a small circle of friends, many of whom were alienated by his ferocity. Died October 19, 1745; buried in St. Patrick's.

II. Works: *A Tale of a Tub*, 1704; *The Battle of the Books*, 1704; *Drapier's Letters*, 1723–24; *Gulliver's Travels*, 1726; *A Modest Proposal*, 1729. Collected Works: 19 v., 1755–1779; Scott, W., ed., 19 v., 1814; *Prose Works*, with introduction by W. E. H. Lecky, 12 v., 1897–1908.

III. *a.* Collins, J. C.: *Jonathan Swift*, 1893; Cordelet, Henriette: *Swift*, 1907; Forster, J.: *Life of Jonathan Swift*, 1875; Stephen, L.: *Jonathan Swift*, 1882.

b. Essays by A. Dobson (*Eighteenth Century Vignettes*, Second Series, 1894), O. Elton (*The Augustan Age*, 1899), and W. M. Thackeray (*English Humourists of the Eighteenth Century*, 1853).

Steele, Sir Richard (1671–1729).

I. Born at Dublin in March, 1671; schoolmate of Addison at Charterhouse; Merton College, Oxford, 1691–94; cadet in life-guards; captain of foot, 1702; married secretly to Mary Scurlock, 1707; wrote various comedies and pamphlets. Began *Tatler*, April, 1709; carried it on with help of Addison until January, 1711; commissioner of stamps, 1710; with Addison carried on *Spectator*, 1711–12. Resigned office and elected M.P. for Stockbridge, 1713; expelled by House for political reasons, 1714; awarded various offices on accession of George I; quarrel with Addison, 1720. Died at Carmarthen, Wales, September 1, 1729.

II. Poetical and Dramatic Works: *The Christian Hero*, 1701; *Poetical Miscellanies*, 1714; *The Conscious Lovers*, 1755.

Essays: *The Tatler*, 1709–11, 271 numbers, about 188 papers by Steele; *The Spectator*, 1711–12, 555 numbers, 236 papers by Steele.

Collected Works: *Complete Plays*, 1759; Political *Writings*, 1715, 1723.

III. *a.* Aitken, G. A.: *Life of Richard Steele*, 2 v., 1889; Dobson, A.: *Richard Steele*, 1888.

b. Essays by J. Dennis (*Studies in English Literature*, 1883), A. Dobson (*Eighteenth Century Vignettes*, 1892), J. Forster (*Historical and Biographical Essays*, vol. II, 1858), W. Hazlitt (*Lectures on the English Comic Writers*, 1819), and W. M. Thackeray (*English Humourists of the Eighteenth Century*, 1853).

Addison, Joseph (1672–1719).

I. Born near Amesbury, Wiltshire, May 1, 1672. Educated at Charterhouse with Steele and at Oxford. M.A., 1693; distinguished as classical scholar; fellow, Magdalen College, 1698–1711; granted pension to enable him to qualify for diplomatic service by travel; traveled on continent, 1699–1703; under-secretary of state, 1706; close friendship with Swift, Steele, and other authors. M.P., 1708 until his death. Married Countess of Warwick, 1716. Died June 17, 1719.

II. Poetical and Dramatic Works: *The Campaign, A Poem*, 1705; *Rosamund, An Opera*, 1707; *Cato, A Tragedy*, 1764.

Essays: *The Tatler*, 1709–11, 271 numbers, about 93 papers by Addison; *The Spectator*, 1711–12, 555 numbers, 274 papers by Addison; resumed, 1714, 24 papers by Addison.

Collected Works, 4 v., 1721; Hurd, R., ed., 6 v., 1811.

III. *a.* Aikin, Lucy: *Life of Joseph Addison*, 2 v., 1843; Courthope, W. J.: *Addison*, 1884.

b. Essays by J. Ashton (*Social Life in the Reign of Queen Anne*,

1883), O. Elton (*The Augustan Ages*, 1899), W. Hazlitt (*Lectures on the English Comic Writers*, 1819), S. Johnson (*Lives of the English Poets*, 1779–81), and T. B. Macaulay (*Edinburgh Review*, July, 1843).

Franklin, Benjamin (1706–90).

I. Born in Boston in 1706; removed to Philadelphia, 1723. Prospered as printer and publisher; rose to position of eminence and influence; founded University of Pennsylvania, 1753; by famous kite experiment demonstrated nature of lightning; deputy postmaster-general for British America, 1753–54; Agent for Pennsylvania and other colonies at British court, 1757–75. Elected to Continental Congress and helped draft Declaration of Independence. Ambassador to France, 1775–85; sat in Constitutional Convention, 1787. Died in Philadelphia, 1790.

II. Works: *Examination before the House of Commons* (published as a pamphlet), 1766; *Rules for Reducing a Great Empire to a Small One*, 1773; *An Edict by the King of Prussia*, 1773; *Poor Richard's Almanac*, 1733–58; *Autobiography* (first five chapters written in 1771; the rest 1784–89), edited by Bigelow, 3 v., 1874.

III. *a.* Ford, P. L.: *The Many-Sided Franklin*, 1899; Fisher, S. G.: *The True Benjamin Franklin*, 1899; Morse, J. T., Jr.: *Life of Franklin*, 1889; Hale, E. E. and E. E., Jr.: *Franklin in France*, 1887.

b. Essay by Sainte-Beuve (*English Portraits*, 1875).

Johnson, Samuel (1709–84)

I. Born at Litchfield, September 18, 1709, son of a bookseller; educated at Litchfield and Pembroke College, Oxford; usher at a grammar school; took pupils at Edial. Married Mrs. Porter, 1735. To London with Garrick, 1737; hack writer; began *English Dictionary*, 1747; *Rambler*, 1750–52. Wife died, 1752. Repudiation of Chesterfield's tardy offer of patronage and M.A. from Oxford on publication of *Dictionary*, 1755. Met Boswell and formed Literary Club, 1763; acquaintance with Thrales, 1764. Published long-delayed edition of Shakespeare, 1765. Traveled with Boswell in Scotland, 1773. Died December 13, 1784. Buried in Westminster Abbey.

II. Works: *Life of Richard Savage*, 1744; *Plan for a Dictionary of the English Language*, 1747; *The Vanity of Human Wishes*, 1749; *A Dictionary, with a Grammar and History of the English Language*, 1755; *Rasselas, Prince of Abyssinia*, 1759; *Works of William Shakespeare, with Notes*, 8 v., 1765; *A Journey to the Western Islands of Scotland*, 1775; *Prefaces Biographical and Critical to the Works of the Most Eminent English Poets*, 1779–81.

Collected Works: 11 v., 1787.

III. *a.* Bailey, J.: *Dr. Johnson and His Circle*, 1913; Scott, W.: *Life of Johnson*, 1821; Stephen, L.: *Samuel Johnson*, 1878.

b. Essays by T. Carlyle (*Fraser's Magazine*, May, 1832), T. De-

Quincey (*Works*, ed. Masson, vol. 4, 1889–90), A. Dobson (*Eighteenth Century Vignettes*, Second Series, 1894), and T. B. Macaulay (*Miscellaneous Essays*, vol. II).

Goldsmith, Oliver (1728–74).

I. Born near Ballymalion, Longford, November 10, 1728, son of Irish clergyman. Entered Trinity College, Dublin, as sizar, 1774; ran away on account of quarrel with tutor; returned and took B.A., 1749. Unsettled life in Ireland until 1752. To Edinburgh to study medicine; on continent, 1755–56; said to have taken medical degree abroad and to have visited Voltaire in France. Reached London destitute, 1756; physician in Southwark; usher at Peckham. Met Johnson, 1761, and became a member of his Club. Hack-writer and playwright. Died April 4, 1774; monument erected to him in Westminster Abbey by the Literary Club.

II. Poetical Works: *The Traveller*, 1764; *The Deserted Village*, 1770.

Dramatic Works: *The Good Natured Man*, 1768; *She Stoops to Conquer*, 1773.

Prose Works, essays, and narratives: *The Citizen of the World*, 1762; *Essays*, 1765; *The Vicar of Wakefield*, 1766.

Collected Works: *Miscellaneous Work of Oliver Goldsmith*, ed. S. Rose, 4 v., 1801; ed. J. Prior, 4 v., 1837; ed. J. N. M. Gibbs, 5 v., 1885–86.

III. *a.* Black, W.: *Goldsmith*, 1878; Dobson, A.: *Life of Goldsmith*, 1888; Forster, J.: *Life and Adventures of Oliver Goldsmith*, 1848.

b. Essays by T. DeQuincey (Works, vol. 6, 1853–60), T. B. Macaulay (Article, "Goldsmith," *Encyclopædia Britannica*, 1856), W. Forsyth (*Novels and Novelists of the Eighteenth Century*, 1871), and W. M. Thackeray (*English Humourists of the Eighteenth Century*, 1853).

Dennie, Joseph (1768–1812).

I. Born in Boston, August 30, 1768; graduated from Harvard, 1790; studied law in New Hampshire, 1790–95; admitted to bar but devoted himself to literature. Edited *Farmer's Weekly Museum* of Walpole, N.H., 1775–78; in Philadelphia as journalist and critic, 1799; editor of *Port Folio*, which published works by Charles Brockden Brown and John Quincy Adams; founded "Tuesday Club." Died in Philadelphia, January 7, 1812.

II. Works: *The Lay Preacher or Short Sermons for Idle Readers*, 1796; *The Spirit of the Farmer's Museum and Lay Preacher's Gazette*, 1801; *The Lay Preacher*. Collected and arranged by John E. Hall. [A new collection, reprinting only one of the 1796 essays] 1817; *New and Original Essays by Joseph Dennie*, 1818 [only one issue known].

III. *a.* Clapp, W. W., Jr.: *Joseph Dennie*, 1880; Ellis, II. M.: *Joseph Dennie and His Circle*, 1915.

b. Essays by Annie R. Marble (*Heralds of American Literature*, 1907),

E. P. Oberholtzen (*Literary History of Philadelphia, 1806*), and A. H. Smyth (*Philadelphia Magazines and their Contributors*, 1892).

Lamb, Charles (1775-1834).

I. Born in the Temple, London, February 10, 1775; educated Christ's Hospital, 1782-89, where he formed lasting friendship with Coleridge; employed in the South Sea House, 1789-92; clerk in the India House, 1792-1825. Mother killed by his sister, Mary, in a fit of insanity, 1796; undertook guardianship of his sister for remainder of his life; himself confined as deranged, 1795-96. Contributed to *London Magazine*, 1820-22, twenty-five essays, signed Elia. Died December 27, 1834.

II. Works: *John Woodvil, A Tragedy*, 1802; *Tales from Shakespear*, 1807; *Specimens of the English Dramatic Poets*, 1808; *Elia*, 1823; *Last Essays of Elia*, 1833.

Collected Works: *Works*, 3 v., 1838; *Complete Works in Prose and Verse*, ed. P. Fitzgerald, 6 v., 1875; *Works*, ed. W. Macdonald, 12 v., 1903; *Works of Charles and Mary Lamb*, ed, E. V. Lucas, 7 v., 1903-05.

III. *a.* Ainger, A.: *Charles Lamb*, 1882; Hazlitt, W. C.: *The Lambs*, 1897; Lucas, E. V.: *The Life of Charles Lamb*, 2 v., 1905; Woodberry, G. E.: *Charles Lamb*, 1900.

b. Essays by A. Birrell (*Obiter Dicta*, Second Series, 1887), T. De-Quincey (*Works*, vols. 3 and 5, 1890), P. E. More (*Shelburne Essays*, Second Series, 1905), and W. Pater (*Appreciations*, 1889).

Hazlitt, William (1778-1830).

I. Born April 10, 1778, at Maidstone; with parents in America, 1783-85; educated for Unitarian ministry; visited Coleridge at Stainey, 1798; married Sarah Stoddart, 1808, whom he divorced in 1822. Lecturer, parliamentary reporter and dramatic critic in London. Contributed to Hunt's *Examiner*; wrote for *Edinburgh Review* from 1814. Married Mrs. Budgewater, 1824, who left him on return from continental tour, 1824-25. Died September 18, 1830.

II. Works: *Essay on the Principles of Human Action*, 1805; *The Round Table* (from the *Examiner*, 1815-17); *The Characters of Shakespeare's Plays*, 1817; *Lectures on the English Poets*, 1819; *Table Talk*, 1821-22; *The Spirit of the Age*, 1825; *Life of Napoleon Buonaparte*, 4 v., 1828-30; *Literary Reviews*, 1836.

Complete Works: Waller, A. R., and Glover, A., ed., 12 v., 1902-06.

III. *a.* Birrell, A.: *Hazlitt*, 1902.

b. Essays by T. DeQuincey (*Works*, vols. 5 and 6, 1889), O. Elton (*A Survey of English Literature: 1780-1830*, 1912), and P. E. More (*Shelburne Essays*, Second Series, 1905).

Irving, Washington (1783-1850).

I. Born in New York City, April 3, 1783. Began study of law, 1799;

traveled in Europe, 1804–06; admitted to New York bar, 1806; appointed military aide to Governor Tompkins, 1814. Resided abroad in England, Germany, France, and Spain, 1815–32; Secretary of United States Legation in London, 1829–31. LL.D., Oxford, 1830. Returned to America and traveled in the Southwest; resided at Sunnyside, 1836–42; Minister to Spain, 1842–46; returned to Sunnyside; died November 28, 1859.

II. Works: *A History of New York, by Diedrich Knickerbocker,* 1809; *The Sketch Book of Geoffrey Crayon, Gent.,* seven parts, 1819–20; *Bracebridge Hall,* 1822; *Tales of a Traveler,* 1824; *Life of Columbus,* 3 v., 1828; *A Chronicle of the Conquest of Granada,* 1829; *The Alhambra,* 1832; *Oliver Goldsmith, a Biography,* 1849; *Mahomet and his Successors,* 1849–50; *The Life of George Washington,* 5 v., 1855–59.

Collected Works: Revised Edition, 15 v., 1849–51; New Knickerbocker Edition, 40 v., 1897–1903.

III. *a.* Irving, P. M.: *Life and Letters of Washington Irving,* 4 v., 1862–63; Warner, C. D.: *Life of Washington Irving,* 1881.

b. Essays by W. C. Bryant (Prose Writings, Vol. 1, 1883–84), G. W. Curtis (*Literary and Social Essays,* 1895), and W. M. Thackeray (*Roundabout Papers,* 1860–63).

DeQuincey, Thomas (1785–1859).

I. Born in Manchester, August 15, 1785; educated at Bath Grammar School and at Winkfield, Wiltshire; sent to Manchester Grammar School, 1801. Left school and wandered in Wales, finally going to London, where he lived a Bohemian life. Met Coleridge, Wordsworth, Southey, and Lamb, 1807–08. Editor of *Westmoreland Gazette,* 1819–20; journalist and hack-writer; died in Edinburgh, December 8, 1859.

II. Works:[1] *Confessions of an English Opium-Eater,* 1822; *Klosterheim,* 1832; *The Logic of Political Economy,* 1844.

Collected Works: *DeQuincey's Writings,* 22 v., Boston, 1851–59; *Selections, Grave and Gay, from Writings Published and Unpublished, of Thomas DeQuincey, Revised and Arranged by Himself,* 14 v., 1853–60; *Collected Writings,* ed. D. Masson, 14 v., 1889–90.

III. *a.* Hogg, J.: *DeQuincey and His Friends,* 1891; Masson, D.: *Thomas DeQuincey,* 1890; Page, H. A. [A. H. Japp]: *Thomas DeQuincey His Life and Writings,* 1877.

b. Essays by A. Birrell (*Essays About Men, Women and Books*), 1892, G. Saintsbury (*Essays in English Literature, 1780–1860,* First Series), 1893, and L. Stephen (*Hours in a Library,* Vol. 1), 1892.

Carlyle, Thomas (1795–1881).

I. Born December 4, 1795, at Ecclefechan, Dumfriesshire; educated at the parish school and Annan Academy; entered Edinburgh Uni-

[1] Most of DeQuincey's writings appeared in magazines and remained uncollected until the end of his life.

versity, 1809; schoolmaster at Kirkcaldy, 1816; studied law at Edinburgh, 1819. Tutored and read German; contributed articles and translations to magazines. Married to Jane Welsh and settled in Edinburgh, 1826; removed to Craigenputtock, where he wrote on German literature. Settled in Cheyne Row, Chelsea, 1834. Publication of *French Revolution* made his reputation, 1837. Gave lecture courses; traveled in Ireland and Germany. Lord rector of Edinburgh, 1865–66; wife died, 1866; Prussian Order of Merit, 1870. Died February 5, 1881; buried at Ecclefechan.

II. Works: Translation of Goethe's *Wilhelm Meister's Apprenticeship*, 3 v., 1824; *Sartor Resartus*, 1836; *French Revolution*, 3 v., 1837; *Critical and Miscellaneous Essays*, 4 v., 1839; *Heroes, Hero-Worship, and the Heroic in History*, 1841; *Oliver Cromwell's Letters and Speeches*, 2 v., 1845; *Life of John Sterling*, 1851; *History of Frederick II*, 6 v., 1858–65.

Collected Works, 16 v., 1856–58; ed. Traill, H. D., 31 v., 1897–1901.

III. *a.* Evans, A. W.: *Carlyle*, 1909; Garnett, R. W.: *Life of Carlyle*, 1911; Nichol, J.: *Thomas Carlyle*, 1892; Perry, B.: *Carlyle*, 1915.

b. Essays by W. C. Brownell (*Victorian Prose Masters*, 1902), R. W. Emerson (*English Traits*, 1856, *Lectures and Biographical Sketches*, 1884), T. E. Kebbel (*Essays upon History and Politics*, 1884), and G. Saintsbury (*Corrected Impressions*, 1895).

Macaulay, Thomas Babington (1800–59).

I. Born in Leicestershire, October 25, 1800; educated at private schools and Trinity College, Cambridge; fellow of Trinity, 1824; barrister, Gray's Inn, 1820. First article (on Milton) published in *Edinburgh Review*, 1828; M.P. Calne, 1830; Leeds, 1831. Member of the Supreme Council of India, 1834–38. Returned to London and engaged in literature and politics; M.P. 1839–47; 1852–56; secretary of war, 1839–41. Proposed and carried the copyright bill which is still a law. Lord rector of Glasgow University, 1849; created Baron of Rothley, 1857. Died December 28, 1859; buried in Westminster Abbey.

II. Works: *Lays of Ancient Rome*, 1842, 1848; *Critical and Historical Essays Contributed to the Edinburgh Review*, 3 v., 1843; *History of England*, 5 v., 1849–61.

Collected Works, ed. Lady Trevelyan, 18 v., 1866.

III. *a.* Jebb, R. C.: *Macaulay*, 1900; Morison, J. C.: *Macaulay*, 1882; Trevelyan, G. O.: *Life and Letters of Lord Macaulay*, 2 v., 1876.

b. Essays by W. Bagehot (*Literary Studies*, 1879), H. Paul (*Men and Letters*, 1901), and L. Stephen (*Hours in a Library*, Third Series, 1879).

Newman, John Henry (1801–90).

I. Born in London, February 21, 1801. Entered at Trinity College,

Oxford, 1816; won a scholarship, 1818; graduated B.A., 1820; elected Fellow of Oriel, 1822. Curate, Oxford, 1824; tutor, Oriel College, 1826–32; friendships with Pusey, Keble, R. H. Froude. Visited Italy, 1832–33; beginning of Oxford Movement, 1833. Became a Catholic, 1845; ordained priest and given degree of D.D., 1846; founded an Oratory at Birmingham, 1848; at London, 1850. Rector Catholic University, Dublin, 1854–58; controversy with Kingsley, 1864; honorary fellow, Trinity College, Oxford, 1877; chosen Cardinal, 1878. Died August 11, 1890.

II. Prose Works: *Tracts for the Times*, 6 v., 1834–41; *Parochial and Plain Sermons*, 1834–43 (8 v., 1868); *Loss and Gain*, 1848; *Scope and Nature of a University Education* (later title, *The Idea of a University*), 1852; *Apologia Pro Vita Sua*, 1864; *Historical Sketches*, 3 v., 1872, 1873; etc.

Poems: *Verses on Religious Subjects*, 1853; *Verses on Various Occasions*, 1868.

Collected Works: Uniform Edition, 36 v., 1868–81.

III. *a.* Abbott, E. A.: *The Anglican Career of Cardinal Newman*, 2 v., 1892; Barry, W.: *Newman*, 2d edition, 1904; Hutton, R. H.: *Cardinal Newman*, 1890; Meynell, W.: *Cardinal Newman*, 1890; Waller, A. R. and Burrow, G. H. S.: *John Henry, Cardinal Newman*, 1901; Ward, W. P.: *Life of John Henry, Cardinal Newman*, 2 v., 1912.

b. Essays by A. Birrell (*Res Judicatæ*, 1892), A. Cecil (*Six Oxford Thinkers*, 1909), J. Jacobs (*Essays and Reviews*, 1891), J. Martineau (*Essays, Reviews, and Addresses*, 2 v., 1890–91), P. E. More (*Shelburne Essays*, Eighth Series, 1913), J. C. Shairp (*Aspects of Poetry*, 1881), and L. Stephen (*An Agnostic's Apology*, 1903).

Emerson, Ralph Waldo (1803–82).

I. Born in Boston, May 25, 1803; at Harvard, 1817–21, A.B., 1821; teaching in or near Boston, 1821–26; at Harvard Divinity School, 1825–28; pastor, Old North Church, Boston, 1829–32. Married, 1829, Ellen Tucker, who died, 1831. Resigned pastorate, 1832; in Europe, 1832–33, 1847–48, 1872–73; residence in Concord, 1834–82; lecturer, 1832–72. Married, 1835, Lydia Jackson. LL.D., Harvard, 1866. Died April 27, 1882.

II. Prose Works: *Nature*, 1836; *Essays* (1st Series, 1841; 2d Series, 1844); *Representative Men*, 1850; *English Traits*, 1856; *The Conduct of Life*, 1860; *Journals*, 10 v., 1909–14.

Poems: *Poems*, 1847, 1865; *May-Day and Other Pieces*, 1867, *Poems*, revised, 1878.

Collected Works: Riverside Edition, 12 v., 1884–93; Centenary Edition, 12 v., with biographical introduction and notes by Edward W. Emerson, 1903–04.

III. *a.* See especially the *Memoir* by J. E. Cabot (2 v., 1887), the lives by R. Garnett (1888) and O. W. Holmes (American Men of Letters, 1885), and the volumes by S. M. Crothers (*Emerson: How to*

Know Him, 1920), M. Dugand (*Ralph Waldo Emerson: Sa Vie et Son Œuvre*, 1907), O. W. Firkins (1915), F. B. Sanborn (Beacon Biographies, 1901), and G. E. Woodberry (English Men of Letters, 1907).

   b. See especially essays by M. Arnold (*Discourses in America*, 1885), Van W. Brooks (*Emerson and Others*, 1927), W. C. Brownell (*American Prose Masters*, 1909), J. J. Chapman (*Emerson and Other Essays*, 1898), T. W. Higginson (*Contemporaries*, 1899), H. James (*Partial Portraits*, 1888), J. R. Lowell (*My Study Windows*, 1871), P. E. More (*Shelburne Essays*, 1st Series, 1904, 11th Series, 1921), G. Santayana (*Interpretations of Poetry and Religion*, 1900), E. C. Stedman (*Poets of America*, 1885), L. Stephen (*Studies of a Biographer*, Vol. 4, 1902), and E. P. Whipple (*American Literature*, 1887).

Holmes, Oliver Wendell (1809–94).

   I. Born in Cambridge, August 29, 1809; graduated at Harvard, 1829; studied law, and then medicine, in Boston and Paris, 1829–35. Practiced medicine, Boston, 1836–39; professor of anatomy, Dartmouth, 1839–40, Harvard, 1847–82. Married Amelia L. Jackson, 1840. Honorary degrees include: LL.D., Harvard and Edinburgh; Litt.D., Cambridge; D.C.L., Oxford. Died October 7, 1894.

   II. Essays and Miscellaneous Prose: *The Autocrat of the Breakfast-Table*, 1858; *The Professor at the Breakfast-Table*, 1859; *Soundings from the Atlantic*, 1863; *The Poet at the Breakfast-Table*, 1872; *John Lothrop Motley*, 1878; *Medical Essays*, 1883; *Ralph Waldo Emerson*, 1884; *Our Hundred Days in Europe*, 1887; *Over the Teacups*, 1890.

   Novels: *Elsie Venner*, 1861; *The Guardian Angel*, 1867; *A Mortal Antipathy*, 1885.

   Poems: *Poems*, 1836, 1846 (London), 1849, 1852 (London); *Urania*, 1846; *Songs of the Class of 1829*, 1854; *Songs in Many Keys*, 1862; *Songs of Many Seasons*, 1875; *The Iron Gate and Other Poems*, 1880; *Before the Curfew and other Poems*, 1887.

   Collected Works: Riverside Edition, 14 v., 1891–92.

   III. *a.* Ball, J.: *Dr. Oliver Wendell Holmes and His Works*, 1878; Kennedy, W. S.: *Oliver Wendell Holmes*, 1883; Morse, J. T., Jr.: *Life and Letters of Oliver Wendell Holmes*, 1896; Townsend, L. W.: *Oliver Wendell Holmes*, 1909.

   b. Essays by S. M. Crothers (*The Autocrat and his Fellow Boarders*, 1910), G. W. Curtis (*Literary and Social Essays*, 1895), Annie Fields (*Authors and Friends*, 1896), Edmund Gosse (*Critic*, Dec. 1, 1894), T. W. Higginson (*Old Cambridge*, 1900), W. D. Howells (*Literary Friends and Acquaintance*, 1900), A. Lang (*Adventures Among Books*, 1905), E. C. Stedman (*Poets of America*, 1885), and L. Stephen (*Studies of A Biographer*, Vol. 2, 1898).

Thackeray, William Makepeace (1811–63).

I. Born at Calcutta, July 18, 1811; father and both grandfathers in employ of East India Company, great-grandfather and cousin fellow and provost, respectively, of King's College, Cambridge; to England, after father's death, 1817; at Charterhouse School, 1822–28; at Trinity College, Cambridge, 1829–30, leaving without a degree. On the continent, chiefly at Weimar, 1830; studying law, Middle Temple, 1831; journalist on *The National Standard* and *The Constitutional*, 1833–37, contributor to *Fraser's*, *The Times*, etc. Married, 1836, Isabella Shawe, who became insane in 1840. Contributor of articles and sketches to *Punch*, 1843——. Lecturer, London, 1851; in United States, 1852–53, 1855–56; editor, *Cornhill Magazine*, 1860–63. Died December 24, 1863.

II. Essays, Lectures, and Miscellanies: *Yellowplush Papers**, 1837–38; *Paris Sketch Book*, 2 v., 1840; *Irish Sketch Book*, 2 v., 1843; *Cornhill to Cairo*, 1846; *The Book of Snobs**, 1846–47; *The English Humourists of the Eighteenth Century*, 1853; *The Four Georges**, 1860; *Roundabout Papers**, 1860–63.

Fiction: *Catherine**, 1839–40; *History of Samuel Titmarsh* and *The Great Hoggarty Diamond**, 1841; *Confessions of George Fitz-Boodle**, 1842–43; *Barry Lyndon**, 1844; *Vanity Fair**, 1847–48; *Pendennis**, 1848–50; *Henry Esmond*, 3 v., 1852; *The Newcomes**, 1853–55; *The Rose and the Ring*, 1854; *The Virginians**, 1857–59; *Lovel the Widower**, 1860; *The Adventures of Philip**, 1861–62; *Denis Duval**, 1864.

Collected Works: *Collected Works*, 26 v., 1869–86; Biographical Edition, with introductions by Anne Thackeray Ritchie, 13 v., 1898–99; Jerrold, W., ed., 13 v., 1901–03; Melville, L. [Benjamin, Lewis S.], ed., 20 v., 1901–07; Saintsbury, G., ed., 17 v., 1908.

III. *a*. Melville, L.: *William Makepeace Thackeray, A Biography*, 2 v., 1910; Melville, L.: *Some Aspects of Thackeray*, 1911; Merivale, H. C. and Marzials, F. T.: *W. M. Thackeray*, 1891; Richie, A. T.: *Chapters from Some Memories*, 1894; Richie, Hester T., ed.: *Thackeray and His Daughter*, 1924; Trollope, A.: *Thackeray*, 1879; Whibley, C.: *William Makepeace Thackeray*, 1903.

b. Essays by S. Axson (*Approaches and Reactions in Six Nineteenth Century Fictionists*, 1916), G. K. Chesterton (*Masters of Literature: Thackeray*, 1909), J. T. Fields (*Yesterday with Authors*, 1872), A. Lang, *Lost Leaders*, 2d edition, 1892), and G. Saintsbury (*Corrected Impressions*, 1895).

Thoreau, Henry David (1817–62).

I. Born in Concord, Massachusetts, July 12, 1817; graduated at Harvard, 1837, school teacher, pencil maker (with his father), land surveyor, lived with Emerson, 1841–43; lived alone at Walden Pond, 1845–47. Died May 6, 1862.

* For starred works the dates of original serial publication are given.

II. Works: *A Week on the Concord and Merrimac Rivers*, 1849; *Walden*, 1854; *Excursions*, 1863; *The Maine Woods*, 1864; *Cape Cod*, 1865; *Early Spring in Massachusetts*, 1881; *The Heart of Thoreau's Journals*, ed. Odell Shepard, 1927.

Collected Works: Riverside Edition, 11 v., 1893; Manuscript Edition (including the *Journal*, 14 v.), 20 v., 1906.

III. *a.* Atkinson, J. B.: *Henry Thoreau, the Cosmic Yankee*, 1927; Bazalgette, L.: *Henry Thoreau, Bachelor of Nature*, 1924; Emerson, E. W.: *Henry Thoreau, as Remembered by a Young Friend*, 1917; Japp, A. H.: *Thoreau: His Life and Aims*, 1877; Jones, S. A., ed.: *Pertaining to Thoreau*, 1901; Salt, H. S.: *The Life of Henry David Thoreau*, 1890; Sanborn, F. B.: *Henry D. Thoreau*, 1882; Sanborn, F. B.: *The Life of Henry David Thoreau*, 1917; VanDoren, M.: *Henry David Thoreau: A Critical Study*, 1916.

b. Essays by John Burroughs (*Essays from "The Critic,"* 1882; *Indoor Studies*, 1889), H. S. Canby (*The Dial*, July 15, 1915), R. W. Emerson (*Atlantic Monthly*, August, 1862; reprinted in collected editions of Emerson and Thoreau), T. W. Higginson (*Short Studies of American Authors*, 1879), J. R. Lowell (*My Study Windows*, 1871), P. E. More (*Shelburne Essays*, 1st Series, 1904, 5th Series, 1908), W. M. Payne (*Leading American Essayists*, 1910), and R. L. Stevenson (*Familiar Studies of Men and Books*, 1882).

Lowell, James Russell (1819–91).

I. Born in Cambridge, Massachusetts, February 22, 1819; at Harvard, 1834–38; graduated Harvard Law School, 1840; practiced law to 1844; contributor to magazines, 1840–50. Married, 1844, Maria White, who died in 1853. In Europe, 1851–52. Professor at Harvard, in succession to Longfellow, 1856–77. Married Frances Dunlap in 1857. Editor of *Atlantic Monthly*, 1857–62, and one of editors of *North American Review*, 1863–72; Minister to Spain, 1877–80, to England, 1880–85; D.C.L., Oxford, 1873. Died August 12, 1891.

II. Essays: *Conversations on Some of the Old Poets*, 1845; *Fireside Travels*, 1864; *Among My Books*, 1st Series, 1870, 2d Series, 1876; *My Study Windows*, 1871; *Democracy and Other Addresses*, 1887.

Poems: *Poems*, 1843, 1848, 2 v., 1849; *A Fable for Critics*, 1848; *The Biglow Papers*, 1st Series, 1848, 2d Series, 1866; *Commemoration Ode*, 1865; *Under the Willows*, 1868; *The Cathedral*, 1869; *Three Memorial Poems*, 1876; etc.

Collected Works: Riverside Edition, 11 v., 1890–92; etc.

III. *a.* Brown, Emma E.: *Life of James Russell Lowell*, 1887; Greenslet, F.: *James Russell Lowell: His Life and Work*, 1905; Quayle, W. A.: *Lowell*, 1906; Scudder, H. E.: *James Russell Lowell: A Biography*, 2 v., 1901.

b. Essays by W. C. Brownell (*American Prose Masters*, 1909), G. W. Curtis (*Orations and Addresses*, 1894), T. W. Higginson (*Old

Cambridge, 1899), W. D. Howells (*Scribner's Magazine*, September, 1900; *Literary Friends and Acquaintance*, 1900), Henry James (*Atlantic Monthly*, January, 1892; *Essays in London*, 1893), C. E. Norton (*Harper's Magazine*, May, 1893), F. P. Stearns (*Cambridge Sketches*, 1905), W. W. Story (*Recollections*, 1903), H. D. Traill (*Fortnightly Review*, July, 1885), E. P. Whipple (*Outlooks on Society*, 1888), and G. E. Woodberry (*Century Magazine*, November, 1891; *Makers of Literature*, 1900).

Ruskin, John (1819–1900).
I. Born in London, February 8, 1819. Precocious and solitary child, elementary education chiefly at home; at Christ Church College, Oxford, 1836–40, where in 1839 he won the Newdigate poetry prize. Traveled with his parents in Great Britain and abroad. To continent for his health, 1840. B.A., Oxford, 1842. Married, 1848, Euphemia Gray; divorced, 1853. Lecturer, 1855–70, before all sorts of audiences on great variety of topics. Slade Professor of Art, Oxford, 1870–79, 1883–84. LL.D., Cambridge, 1867; D.C.L., Oxford, 1893. Died January 20, 1900.
II. Works: *Modern Painters*, 5 v., 1843–60, 6 v., 1888; *Seven Lamps of Architecture*, 1849; *Stones of Venice*, 3 v., 1851–53; *Unto This Last*, 1862; *Sesame and Lilies*, 1865; *Ethics of the Dust*, 1866; *Crown of Wild Olive*, 1866; *Fors Clavigera*, 9 v., 1871–87; *Præterita*, 3 v., 1885–1900; etc., etc.
   Collected Works: ed. Cook and Weddeburn, 39 v., 1903–12; Brantwood edition, ed. C. E. Norton (with valuable biographical prefaces).
III. *a.* Benson, A. C.: *Ruskin, A Study in Personality*, 1911; Collingwood, W. G.: *Life and Work of John Ruskin*, 2 v., 1893; Cook, E. T.: *Life of John Ruskin*, 1911; Cook, E. T.: *Studies in Ruskin*, 2 v.; Harrison, F.: *John Ruskin*, 1902; Meynell, Alice: *John Ruskin*, 1900; Wingate, A.: *Life of John Ruskin*, 1910.
   b. Essays by Anne T. Ritchie (*Records of Tennyson, Ruskin, and Browning*, 1892), J. M. Robertson (*Modern Humanists*, 1895), G. Saintsbury (*Corrected Impressions*, 1895), and L. Stephen (*Studies of a Biographer*, vol. 3, 1902).

Arnold, Matthew (1822–88).
I. Born at Laleham, near Staines, Middlesex County, December 24, 1822, son of Dr. Thomas Arnold, famous headmaster of Rugby. Educated at Winchester, 1836–37, Rugby, 1837–41, and Balliol College, Oxford, 1841–44, where he won Second Class Honors; won Newdigate Prize, 1843; elected fellow of Oriel College, Oxford, 1845. Taught at Rugby, 1845–47; secretary to Lord Lansdowne, 1847–51; inspector of schools, 1851–86. Married, June 10, 1851, Frances Lucy Wightman. Professor of Poetry, Oxford, 1857–67; LL.D., Oxford, 1870; lecturing in America, 1883–84. Died April 15, 1888.

II. Essays: *On Translating Homer*, 1861; *Essays in Criticism*, 1st Series, 1865, 2d Series, 1888, 3d Series, 1910; *On the Study of Celtic Literature*, 1867; *Culture and Anarchy*, 1869; *Literature and Dogma*, 1873; *Mixed Essays*, 1879; *Discourses in America*, 1885; etc.

Poems: *The Strayed Reveler*, 1849; *Empedocles on Etna*, 1852; *Poems*, 1853; *Poems* (2d Series), 1855; *Merope*, 1858; *New Poems*, 1867; *Poems* (collected), 1869, etc.

III. *a*. Dawson, W. H.: *Matthew Arnold and his Relation to the Thought of our Time*, 1904; Paul, H. W.: *Matthew Arnold*, 1902; Russell, G. W. E.: *Matthew Arnold*, 1904; Saintsbury, G.: *Matthew Arnold*, 1899.

b. Essays by A. Birrell (*Res Judicatæ*, 1892), W. C. Brownell (*Victorian Prose Masters*, 1902), E. Dowden (*Transcripts and Studies*, 1887), L. E. Gates (*Three Studies in Literature*, 1899), R. H. Hutton (*Literary Essays*, 1871), A. Lang (*Century Magazine*, April, 1882), J. M. Robertson (*Modern Humanists*, 1891), G. Saintsbury (*Corrected Impressions*, 1895), L. Stephen (*Studies of a Biographer*, Vol. 2, 1898), H. D. Traill (*Contemporary Review*, June, 1888), and G. E. Woodberry (*Makers of Literature*, 1900).

Howells, William Dean (1837–1920).
I. Born at Martin's Ferry, Ohio, March 1, 1837. Common school education. Successively printer, newspaper correspondent, and editor in Ohio, where his father was editor of a country paper. Married Elinor G. Mead, 1862. Consul at Venice, 1861–65; on the *Nation* one year; assistant editor, *Atlantic Monthly*, 1866–72, editor, 1872–81; lived abroad, 1881–85; on staff of *Harper's Magazine*, 1885–1920; Litt.D., Oxford, 1904. Died, May 11, 1920.

II. Essays and Criticism: *Venetian Life*, 1866; *Criticism and Fiction*, 1892; *My Literary Passions*, 1895; *Impressions and Experiences*, 1896; *Literary Friends and Acquaintance*, 1900; *London Films*, 1905; *Certain Delightful English Towns*, 1906; *Familiar Spanish Travels*, 1913; *The Years of My Youth*, 1916.

Novels: *A Chance Acquaintance*, 1873; *A Foregone Conclusion*, 1875; *A Modern Instance*, 1882; *The Rise of Silas Lapham*, 1884; *A Hazard of New Fortunes*, 1889; *The Kentons*, 1902; etc., etc.

Plays: *A Counterfeit Presentment*, 1877; *The Parlor Car*, 1876; *The Register*, 1884; etc.

III. *a*. Cooke, D. G.: *William Dean Howells: A Critical Study*, 1922; Firkins, O. W.: *William Dean Howells: A Study*, 1924; Harvey, A.: *William Dean Howells: A Study of the Achievement of a Literary Artist*, 1917; Howells, Mildred, ed.: *Life in Letters of William Dean Howells*, 2 v., 1928.

b. Essays by W. C. Brownell (*The Nation*, July 15, 1880), S. L. Clemens (*What is Man? and Other Essays*, 1917), H. T. and W. Follett (*Some Modern Novelists*, 1918), E. Gosse (*Living Age*, July 10, 1920), W. L. Phelps (*Essays on Modern Novelists*, 1910), and J. M. Robertson (*Essays Toward a Critical Method*, 1889).

Pater, Walter (1839–94).

I. Born in London, August 4, 1839. Educated at King's School, Canterbury, 1853–58, and Queen's College, Oxford, 1858–62. Elected fellow of Brasenose College, Oxford, 1864. Visited Italy, 1865, 1882; moved to London, 1886; returned to Oxford, 1893. Died July 30, 1894.

II. Works: *Studies in the History of the Renaissance*, 1873; *Marius the Epicurean*, 2 v., 1885; *Imaginary Portraits*, 1887; *Appreciations*, 1889; *Plato and Platonism*, 1893; *The Child in the House*, 1894; *Greek Studies*, 1895; *Miscellaneous Studies*, 1895; *Gaston de Latour*, 1896.

Collected Works: new library edition, 10 v., 1910.

III. *a*. Benson, A. C.: *Walter Pater*, 1906; Greenslet, F.: *Walter Pater*, 1903; Thomas, P. E.: *Walter Pater: A Critical Study*, 1913; Wright, T.: *The Life of Walter Pater*, 2 v., 1907.

b. Essays by A. Cecil (*Six Oxford Thinkers*, 1909), L. Dyer (*The Nation*, August 23, 1894), E. Gosse (*Contemporary Review*, December, 1894), E. E. Hale (Introduction to *Selections*, 1901), R. T. Jacobus (*Fortnightly Review*, March, 1896), L. Johnson (*Fortnightly Review*, September, 1894), and A. Symons (*Studies in Prose and Verse*, 1904).

Hudson, William Henry (1841–1922).

I. Born August 4, 1841, in Argentina; father and mother born in New England; paternal grandfather English. Educated at home; left Argentina for England at age of twenty-eight or twenty-nine; life of poverty and struggle in London. Married Emily Wingrave in 1876; earned a precarious living by writing; many warm friends; won wide recognition in the last decade of his life. Died August 18, 1922.

II. Essays, sketches, and nature studies: *The Naturalist in La Plata*, 1892; *Idle Days in Patagonia*, 1893; *British Birds*, 1895; *The Land's End*, 1908; *Afoot in England*, 1909; *A Shepherd's Life*, 1910; *Far Away and Long Ago: History of My Early Life*, 1918; *A Hind in Richmond Park*, 1922.

Novels and Stories: *The Purple Land*, 1885; *El Ombù*, 1902; *Hampshire Days*, 1903; *Green Mansions*, 1904; *A Crystal Age*, 1906; *Dead Man's Plack and an Old Thorn*, 1920.

III. Galsworthy, John: Preface to *Green Mansions*, 1916; Roberts, Morley: *W. H. Hudson: A Portrait*, 1924.

James, Henry (1843–1916).

I. Born in New York City, April 15, 1843, son of Henry James, Sr., and brother of William James, the philosopher. Private schooling at home and abroad, followed by study at the Harvard Law School. Nearly all his life resident abroad, mainly in England; became a British subject in 1915. Died February 28, 1916.

II. Essays: *Transatlantic Sketches*, 1875; *Hawthorne*, 1879; *A Little Town in France*, 1884; *Portraits of Places*, 1884; *Partial Portraits*, 1888;

Essays in London and Elsewhere, 1893; *The American Scene*, 1907, *A Small Boy and Others*, 1913; etc.

Novels: *Roderick Hudson*, 1875; *The American*, 1877; *The Europeans*, 1878; *The Portrait of a Lady*, 1881; *The Tragic Muse*, 1890; *The Spoils of Poynton*, 1897; *What Maisie Knew*, 1897; *The Wings of the Dove*, 1902; etc.

Short Stories: *Daisy Miller*, 1879; *The Aspern Papers*, 1888; *The Turn of the Screw*, 1898; etc.

III. *a.* Beach, J. W.: *The Method of Henry James*, 1918; Bosanquet, T.: *Henry James at Work*, 1924; Brooks, Van W.: *The Pilgrimage of Henry James*, 1925; Ford, F. M. [Hueffer, F. M.]: *Henry James: A Critical Study*, 1913; West, Rebecca: *Henry James*, 1916.

b. Essays by Theodora Bosanquet (*Fortnightly Review*, June, 1917), W. C. Brownell (*American Prose Masters*, 1909), R. Burton (*Björnson, Daudet, James*, 1903), J. Conrad (*North American Review*, January, 1905, April, 1916), H. T. and W. Follett (*Some Modern Novelists*, 1918), J. Freeman (*Moderns*, 1917), M. Fullerton (*Quarterly Review*, April, 1910), F. Hackett (*Horizons*, 1918), W. D. Howells (*North American Review*, January, 1903, April, 1916), W. L. Randell (*Fortnightly Review*, April, 1916), and S. P. Sherman (*On Contemporary Literature*, 1917).

Gosse, Sir Edmund William (1849–1928).

I. Born September 21, 1849, in London; educated privately in Devonshire; married Ellen Epps. Honorary degrees from Cambridge University, St. Andrews University, Strassburg, Gothenburg, Paris (Sorbonne); Knight of Norwegian, Swedish, and Danish orders; knighted 1925. Assistant Librarian, British Museum, 1867–75; Clark Lecturer in English Literature, Trinity College, Cambridge, 1884–90; Librarian, House of Lords, 1904–14; Chairman of the board of Scandinavian Studies, University College, London, 1917; President of the English Association, 1921. Died May 15, 1928.

II. Criticism: *Northern Studies*, 1879; *Seventeenth Century Studies*, 1883; *History of Eighteenth Century Literature*, 1889; *Questions at Issue*, 1893; *Jacobean Poets*, 1894; *Critical Kit-Kats*, 1896; *French Profiles*, 1905; *Portraits and Sketches*, 1912; *Three French Moralists*, 1918; *Books on the Table*, 1921; *Aspects and Impressions*, 1922; *Silhouettes*, 1925; *Leaves and Fruit*, 1927.

Critical Biography: *Gray*, 1882; *Congreve*, 1888; *Dr. John Donne*, 1899; *Jeremy Taylor*, 1904; *Father and Son* (autobiographical), 1907; *Algernon Charles Swinburne*, 1917.

Poems: *On Viol and Flute*, 1873; *New Poems*, 1879; *Collected Poems*, 1911.

III. *a.* Moore, G.: *Imaginary Conversations: Gosse and Moore*.

b. Binyon, L.: "Edmund Gosse." *Living Age*. 306: 59–61; Noyes, A.: "The Poems of Edmund Gosse." *Fortnightly Review*. 98: 297–303; Williams, S. T.: "Two Victorian Boyhoods." *North American Review*. 213: 819–26.

Stevenson, Robert Louis [Robert Lewis Balfour] (1850-1894).
  I. Born in Edinburgh, November 13, 1850. Educated at private
     schools, 1859-67, and at the University of Edinburgh, 1867-73,
     where he studied science in preparation for his father's profession of
     engineering, then changed to law; admitted to the bar in 1875, but had
     only four briefs, and soon devoted himself exclusively to literature;
     1873-79, living in Edinburgh, London, and abroad; to California in
     1874; married Fanny Van de Grift (Mrs. Osborne), May 19, 1880.
     1880-87, resident in Great Britain and France; 1887-88, in the United
     States; 1888-94, in the Pacific, on account of his health. Died at
     Vailima, Samoan Islands, December 3, 1894.
 II. Essays and Miscellanies: *The Pentland Rising*, 1866; Papers in *Edin-
     burgh University Magazine*, 1871; *An Inland Voyage*, 1878; *Travels
     with a Donkey*, 1879; *Virginibus Puerisque*, 1881; *Familiar Studies of
     Men and Books*, 1882; *Memories and Portraits*, 1887; *Across the Plains*,
     1892.
        Novels and Stories: *New Arabian Nights*, 1882; *Treasure Island*,
     1883; *Prince Otto*, 1885; *More New Arabian Nights*, 1885; *The Strange
     Case of Dr. Jekyll and Mr. Hyde*, 1886; *Kidnapped*, 1886; *The Merry
     Men and Other Tales*, 1887; *The Black Arrow*, 1888; *The Master of
     Ballantrae*, 1889; *The Wrecker*, 1892; *Catriona [David Balfour]*, 1893;
     Island Nights Entertainments, 1893; *The Ebb Tide*, 1894; *Weir of
     Hermiston*, 1896; *St. Ives*, 1897.
        Poems: *A Child's Garden of Verses*, 1885; *Underwoods*, 1887;
     Ballads, 1891; *Complete Poems* (including "New Poems"), 1923.
III. *a.* Baildon, H. B.: *Robert Louis Stevenson: A Life Study in Criticism*,
     1901; Balfour, Graham: *The Life of Robert Louis Stevenson*, 2 v.,
     1901; Chesterton, G. K.: *Robert Louis Stevenson*, 1927; Hellman,
     G. S.: *The True Stevenson*, 1925; Raleigh, W.: *Robert Louis Steven-
     son*, 1895; Stewart, John A.: *Robert Louis Stevenson*, 2 v., 1924;
     Swinnerton, F.: *Robert Louis Stevenson*, 1914; Symons, A.: *Robert
     Louis Stevenson*, 1904.
  b. Essays by J. J. Chapman (*Emerson, and other Essays*, 1898), H.
     James (*Partial Portraits*, 1888), H. W. Nevinson (*From Leith to
     Samoa*, 1905), and L. Stephen (*Studies of a Biographer*, Vol. 4,
     1902).

Meynell, Alice Christiana (Thompson) (1850-1922).
  I. Born in 1850; privately educated by her father, T. J. Thompson;
     lived a good deal in Italy in youth; married Wilfrid Meynell in 1877;
     mother of Everard Meynell, journalist, and of Viola Meynell, the
     novelist. Died November 27, 1922.
 II. Essays: *The Rhythm of Life*, 1893; *The Colour of Life*, 1896; *The
     Children*, 1896; *The Spirit of Peace*, 1898; *Ceres' Runaway*, 1910;
     Selected Essays, 1914; *The Second Person Singular and Other Essays*,
     1921.
        Poems: *Preludes* (republished, as *Poems*, 1893); *Later Poems*,

1901; *Collected Poems*, 1913; *A Father of Women and Other Poems* 1917; *Poems*, complete edition, 1923.

III. *a.* [Meredith, G.]: *The Letters of George Meredith to Alice Meynell,* 1923 (contains Meredith's article on Mrs. Meynell's essays). Tuell, A. K.: *Mrs. Meynell and her Literary Generation*, 1925.

b. Brégy, K.: "Mrs. Meynell: An Appreciation." *Catholic World.* 92: 494–504; Garvin, J. L.: "Alice Meynell." *Living Age.* 316: 103–08; Marks, J.: "Multitude." *North American Review.* 217: 365–73; Moorhouse, E. H.: "Flower of the Mind." *Fortnightly Review.* 119: 64–73; Repplier, A.: "Alice Meynell." *Catholic World.* 116: 721–30.

Conrad, Joseph [Teodor Josef Konrad Korzeniowski] (1857–1924).

I. Born December 6, 1857, in the Ukraine, southern Poland, of a family belonging to the landed gentry; in 1862 his father, banished for revolutionary activity, was accompanied by wife and child to Vologda; mother died in 1865, father in 1870; Conrad educated at Cracow, 1869–74. To sea from Marseilles in 1874, his aim to become master of an English merchantman; to England in 1878; rose from seaman to master by 1884; naturalized, 1884; voyages to Australia, East Indies, Africa. Resigned, 1894, from ill health; first novel, *Almayer's Folly*, written on sea and ashore from 1889 on, accepted for publication. Married, 1896, an Englishwoman; resided in Essex and Kent; visited America in 1923; died August 3, 1924.

II. Essays and Sketches: *The Mirror of the Sea*, 1906; *Some Reminiscences* (American ed., *A Personal Record*), 1912; *Notes on Life and Letters*, 1921; *Last Essays*, 1926.

Novels: *Almayer's Folly*, 1895; *An Outcast of the Islands*, 1896; *The Nigger of the "Narcissus,"* 1897; *Lord Jim*, 1900; *The Inheritors*, 1901, in collaboration with F. M. Ford; *Romance*, 1903, in collaboration with F. M. Ford; *Nostromo*, 1904; *The Secret Agent*, 1907; *Under Western Eyes*, 1911; *Chance*, 1913; *Victory*, 1915; *The Shadow-Line*, 1917; *The Arrow of Gold*, 1919; *The Rescue*, 1920; *The Rover*, 1923; *Suspense* (unfinished), 1925.

Short Stories: *Tales of Unrest*, 1898; *Typhoon and Other Stories*, 1902–03; *Youth*, etc., 1902; *A Set of Six*, 1908; *'Twixt Land and Sea*, 1912; *Within the Tides*, 1915.

III. *a.* Adams, E. L.: *Joseph Conrad, the Man*, 1925; Aubry: G. J.: *Joseph Conrad, Life and Letters*, 1927; Conrad, Jessie: *Joseph Conrad as I Knew Him*, 1926; Curle, R.: *Joseph Conrad: A Study*, 1914; *The Last Twelve Years of Joseph Conrad*, 1928; Ford, F. M.: *Joseph Conrad: A Personal Remembrance*, 1924; Walpole, H.: *Joseph Conrad* (Writers of the Day), 1916.

b. Aubry, G. J.: "Joseph Conrad's Confessions." *Fortnightly Review.* 115: 782–90; Curle, R.: "The Personality of Conrad." *Edinburgh Review.* 241: 126–38; Curle, R.: "Conrad in the East." *Yale Review*, n.s. 12: 497–508; Curran, E. F.: "Conrad, Master of Language." *Catholic World.* 92: 796–805; Galsworthy, J.: "Disquisition on Conrad." *Fortnightly Review.* 89: 627–33; Galsworthy, J.: "Reminiscences of Conrad." *Scribners.* 77: 3–10; Gwynn, S.: "The Novels of Joseph Conrad." *Edinburgh Review.* 231: 318–39; Huneker, J.: "The Genius of Joseph Conrad." *North American Review.* 200: 270–79; Moult, T.: "Joseph Conrad." *Quarterly Review.* 242: 247–61; Moult, T.: "The Life and Work of Conrad." *Yale Review.* n.s. 14: 295–308; Symons, A.: "Conrad." *Forum.* 53: 579–92.

Crothers, Samuel McChord (1857–1927).

I. Born June 7, 1857, at Oswego, Illinois; graduated Wittenberg College, 1873; Princeton, 1874; student at Union Theological Seminary, 1874–77, and at Harvard Divinity School, 1881–82; D.D., Harvard, Litt.D., St. Lawrence, Princeton, Western Reserve. Married Louise M. Bronson, September 9, 1882. Presbyterian minister, 1877–81, with pastorates in Nevada and California. Became a Unitarian minister, 1882; pastorates in Brattleboro, Vermont, St. Paul, Minnesota, and from 1894 at the First Church, Cambridge, Massachusetts. Died November 9, 1927.

II. Juveniles: *Miss Muffet's Christmas Party*, 1901; *The Children of Dickens*, 1925.

Religious Essays: *Members of One Body*, 1894; *The Understanding Heart*, 1903; *The Endless Life* (Ingersoll Lecture), 1905; *Three Lords of Destiny* (Raymond F. West Lectures), 1913.

Criticism: *Oliver Wendell Holmes: The Autocrat and his Fellow Boarders*, 1909; *Emerson: How to Know Him*, 1920.

Miscellaneous Essays: *The Gentle Reader*, 1903; *The Pardoner's Wallet*, 1905; *By the Christmas Fire*, 1908; *Among Friends*, 1910; *Humanly Speaking*, 1912; *Meditations on Votes for Women*, 1914; *The Pleasures of an Absentee Landlord*, 1916; *The Dame School of Experience*, 1919; *The Cheerful Giver*, 1923; *The Thought Broker*, 1928.

III. Brief articles in *Bookman.* 32: 631–33; *Nation.* 125: 589; *Survey.* 59: 535–36; *Atlantic Monthly.* 141: 662–63.

Repplier, Agnes (1858–   ).

I. Born April 1, 1858, in Philadelphia; of French parentage; educated at the Sacred Heart Convent, Torresdale, Pennsylvania; honorary degree of Litt.D., University of Pennsylvania, 1902, Yale, 1925. In recent years spent much time in Europe.

II. Works: *Books and Men*, 1888; *Points of View*, 1891; *Essays in Miniature*, 1892; *Essays in Idleness*, 1893; *In the Dozy Hours*, 1894; *Varia*, 1897; *The Fireside Sphinx*, 1901; *Compromises*, 1904; *In our Convent Days*, 1905; *A Happy Half Century*, 1908; *Americans and Others*, 1912; *Counter Currents*, 1915; *Points of Friction*, 1920; *Under Dispute*, 1924.

III. Anonymous estimate (*Critic.* 47: 204–10); Adams, M.: "Our Miss Repplier" (*Bookman*, 65: 410–12).

Hewlett, Maurice Henry (1861–1923).
I. Born January 22, 1861, at Weybridge, Surrey; student in private schools and at London International College, Spring Grove, Isleworth, to 1878; married Hilda Beatrice Herbert, 1888; admitted to the bar, 1891. Lecturer on medieval thought and art at South Kensington University College. Keeper of Land Revenue Records and Enrolments, 1896–1900; member of Academic Committee, Royal Society of Literature, 1910; Justice of the Peace, and County Alderman, Wiltshire. Contributed to *London Times, Manchester Guardian, Fortnightly Review, Nineteenth Century and After, Cornhill Magazine*, etc. Died June 15, 1923.

II. Essays: *Earthwork out of Tuscany*, 1895; *In a Green Shade*, 1920; *Wiltshire Essays*, 1921; *Extemporary Essays*, 1922; *Last Essays*, 1924.

Poems: *Songs and Meditations*, 1896; *Artemision: Idylls and Songs*, 1909; *Helen Redeemed and Other Poems*, 1913; *Gai Saber: Tales and Songs*, 1916; *Flowers in the Grass*, 1920.

Poetical Drama: *The Masque of Dead Florentines*, 1895; *Pan and the Young Shepherd*, 1899; *The Agonists: A Trilogy of God and Man*, 1911 (composed 1895–97).

Novels and Tales: *The Forest Lovers*, 1898, *Little Novels of Italy*, 1899; *Richard Yea-and-Nay*, 1900; *New Canterbury Tales*, 1901; *The Queen's Quair*, 1904; *Half-way House*, 1908; *Open Country*, 1909; *Rest Harrow*, 1910; *Brazenhead the Great*, 1911; etc.

III. *a.* Bronner, M.: *Maurice Hewlett: A Critical Review of his Prose and Poetry*, 1910; Hewlett, E. J.: *The Letters of Maurice Hewlett ... with Introductory Memoir ...*, 1925.

b. Graham, H. W.: "Maurice Hewlett." *Fortnightly Review.* 124: 47–63; Gwynn, S.: "Maurice Hewlett." *Edinburgh Review.* 239: 61–72; Hervey, J. L.: "Decline and Fall of Maurice Hewlett." *Dial.* 61: 337–39; Squire, J. C.: "Maurice Hewlett, Man of Many Talents." *Living Age.* 318: 362–65.

More, Paul Elmer (1864–   ).
I. Born December 12, 1864, in St. Louis, Missouri, studied at Washington University, St. Louis (A.B., 1887, A.M., 1892), and at Harvard University (A.M., 1893); married Henrietta Beck of St. Louis on June 12, 1900. Honorary degree of LL.D. from Washington University, 1913, and of Litt.D. from Columbia, Dartmouth, and Princeton. Taught Sanskrit at Harvard, 1894–95, and Sanskrit and Classics at Bryn Mawr, 1895–97. Literary editor, *The Independent*, 1901–03; *New York Evening Post*, 1903–09; editor, *The Nation*, 1909–14.

II. Works: *Shelburne Essays*, 11 vols., 1904–21; *Life of Benjamin Franklin*, 1900; *Platonism*, 1917; *The Religion of Plato*, 1921; *Hellenistic Philosophies*, 1923; *The Christ of the New Testament*, 1924; *Christ the Word*, 1927.

Translations: *A Century of Indian Epigrams*, 1898; etc.

III. Brother Leo: "Paul Elmer More." (*Catholic World.* 116: 198–211); Sherman, S. P.: "Paul Elmer More and the Wits." (*The Review.* 2: 54–56); Sherman, S. P.: "An Imaginary Conversation with Mr. Paul Elmer More." (*Americans*, 1922).

Galsworthy, John (1867–   ).
I. Born August 14, 1867, at Coombe, Surrey; educated at Harrow, 1881–86, and at New College, Oxford, 1886–89; admitted to the bar, Lincoln's Inn, in 1890; traveled for about two years; engaged in literary work since 1897.
II. Essays and Sketches: *A Commentary*, 1908; *A Motley*, 1910; *The Inn of Tranquillity*, 1912; *A Sheaf*, 1916; *Another Sheaf*, 1919; *Castles in Spain and other Screeds*, 1927.
   Novels: *Jocelyn*, 1898; *Villa Rubein*, 1900 (new edition with other stories, 1909); *A Man of Devon*, 1901; *The Island Pharisees*, 1904 (revised, 1908); *The Man of Property*, 1906; *The Patrician*, 1911; *The Dark Flower*, 1913; *The Freelands*, 1915; *Saints' Progress*, 1919; *In Chancery*, 1920; *To Let*, 1921; *The Forsyte Saga*, 1922 (including, *The Man of Property, In Chancery, To Let*); *The White Monkey*, 1924; *The Silver Spoon*, 1926; *Swan Song*, 1928.
   Short Stories: *The Little Man and Other Satires*, 1915; *Caravan*, 1925.
   Plays: *The Silver Box*, 1906; *Strife*, 1909; *Justice*, 1910; *The Pigeon*, 1912; *Loyalties*, 1922; etc., etc.   Collected edition, 1928.
III. *a.* Chevrillon, A.: *Three Studies in English Literature*, 1923; Kaye-Smith, S.: *John Galsworthy*, 1916.
   b. Ervine, St. J. G.: "Some Impressions of My Elders." *North American Review.* 213: 271–84; French, E. B.: "Galsworthy's Men of Tranquillity." *Bookman.* 36: 445–47; Macartney, H. H.: "The Novels of Galsworthy." *Westminster Review.* 171:682–93; Martin, D.: "Mr. Galsworthy as Artist and Reformer." *Yale Review.* n.s. 14: 126–39; Willcox, L. C.: "John Galsworthy." *North American Review.* 202: 889–98.

Belloc, Joseph Hilaire Pierre (1870–   ).
I. Born July 27, 1870, near Paris, of French and Irish stock.   Educated in England at Edgbaston Oratory School and Balliol College, Oxford, where he held a scholarship and won a First Class in the Honor Schools in History in 1895.   Served in the French army.   Married, 1896, Elodie Agnes Hogan of Napa, California.   Naturalized British subject in 1903.   Represented, as a Liberal, the South Salford district in Parliament, 1906–10.
II. Essays: *The Old Road*, 1904; *On Nothing*, 1908; *On Everything*, 1909; *On Anything*, 1910; *On Something*, 1910; *First and Last*, 1911; *This and That and the Other*, 1912; *On*, 1923.
   Books of Travel: *The Path to Rome*, 1902; *Esto Perpetua*, 1906; *Hills and the Sea*, 1906; *The Historic Thames*, 1907; *The River of London*, 1912.

Historical works: *Danton*, 1899 (revised, 1911); *Robespierre*, 1901; *The Eye Witness*, 1908; *Marie Antoinette*, 1910.

Novels: *Emmanuel Burden*, 1904; *Mr. Clutterbuck's Election*, 1908; *Pongo and the Bull*, 1910; *The Green Overcoat*, 1912; *Mr. Petre*, 1925; *The Emerald of Catherine the Great*, 1926.

Poems: *Verses and Sonnets*, 1895; *The Bad Child's Book of Beasts*, 1896; *Verses*, 1910.

III. *a.* Braybrooke, T.: *Some Thoughts on Hilaire Belloc*, 1923.
   b. C. Chesterton: "An Estimate." *Living Age.* 251: 689–94; M. Kolars: "Mr. Belloc and English Letters." *Catholic World.* 117: 504–18; T. Maynard: "The Chesterbelloc." *Catholic World.* 110: 145–60; 319–30; 483–95; 617–29; B. Payne: "The Work of Mr. Belloc." *Living Age.* 281: 606–11; T. Seccombe: "The Life and Writings of Hilaire Belloc." *Living Age.* 289: 93–103.

Beerbohm, Max (1872–   ).

I. Born in London, August 24, 1872, son of Julius E. Beerbohm and Eliza Draper, and half-brother of Sir Herbert Beerbohm Tree. Educated at Charterhouse and at Merton College, Oxford, where he matriculated in 1890; visited America in 1895 with his half-brother. Began his literary career by contributing to *The Yellow Book;* became a contributor to London periodicals. Married, 1910, Florence Kahn of Memphis, Tennessee. Has lived in Rapallo, Italy, since 1911. Essayist and caricaturist.

II. Essays: *The Works of Max Beerbohm*, 1896; *More*, 1899; *Yet Again*, 1909; *And Even Now*, 1920; *Around Theatres*, 2 v., 1924; *A Variety of Things*, 1928.

Parodies: *A Christmas Garland*, 1912.

Narratives: *The Happy Hypocrite*, 1897; *Zuleika Dobson*, 1911; *Seven Men*, 1919.

III. *a.* Lynch, B.: *Max Beerbohm in Perspective* (with bibliography), 1921.
   b. Cross, W. L.: "The Humor of Max Beerbohm." *Yale Review.* n.s. 13: 209–27; Lawrence, A.: "Max." *Critic.* 39: 450–56; Littell, P.: *New Republic.* 1: 26; 21: 386; 30: 347; Lynch, B.: "Max Beerbohm." *Dial.* 70: 177–92.

Russell, Hon. Bertrand Arthur William (1872–   ).

I. Born at Trelleck, Monmouthshire, May 18, 1872; son of Viscount Amberley, and heir presumptive to second Earl Russell. Educated at Trinity College, Cambridge, where he took a First Class in Mathematics and Moral Sciences; Fellow and Lecturer at Trinity to 1916. Married (1) Alys Smith, of Philadelphia, 1894; (2) Dora Winifred Black, 1921.

II. Untechnical Works: *Philosophical Essays*, 1910; *The Problems of Philosophy*, 1912; *Justice in War-Time*, 1916; *Why Men Fight*, 1917; *Mysticism and Logic*, 1918; *Practice and Theory of Bolshevism*, 1920; *What I Believe*, 1925; *Education and the Good Life*, 1926.

III. Articles in *Nation*, February 18, 1915; *Living Age*, July 23, 1921, September 3, 1921; *Catholic World*, March, 1923; *American Economic Review*, June, 1924; *Dial*, September, 1927, December, 1927.

Essay by G. Santayana (*Winds of Doctrine*, 1913).

Chesterton, Gilbert Keith (1874–).
  I. Born in London in 1874. Educated at St. Paul's School and at the Slade School of Art; married Frances Blogg, 1901. Began literary career as reviewer of books on art for *The Bookman* and *The Speaker*; has been contributor to the *London Daily News*, the *Pall Mall Magazine*, the *Bystander*, the *Fortnightly*, and the *Independent Review*, the *Illustrated London News*, etc.

 II. Critical Biographies: *Robert Browning* (English Men of Letters), 1903; *G. F. Watts*, 1904; *George Bernard Shaw*, 1909; *William Cobbett*, 1926.

   Critical Essays: *Twelve Types* (American edition, *Varied Types*), 1903; *Dickens*, 1906; *Five Types*, 1911; *The Victorian Age in Literature*, 1913; *Robert Louis Stevenson*, 1927.

   Miscellaneous Works: *Heretics*, 1905; *Orthodoxy*, 1908; *Alarms and Discursions*, 1911; *The Crimes of England*, 1915; *A Short History of England*, 1917; *The Uses of Diversity*, 1921; *The Outline of Sanity*, 1926.

   Fiction: *The Napoleon of Notting Hill*, 1904; *The Club of Queer Trades*, 1905; *The Man who was Thursday*, 1908; *The Ball and the Cross*, 1910; *The Innocence of Father Brown*, 1911; *Manalive*, 1912; *The Flying Inn*, 1914; *The Wisdom of Father Brown*, 1914; *The Man who Knew too Much*, 1922; *Tales of the Long Bow*, 1925; *The Incredulity of Father Brown*, 1926.

   Poems: *The Ballad of the White Horse*, 1911; *Poems*, 1915; *The Ballad of St. Barbara*, 1923; *Collected Poems*, 1927.

III. *a*. Bennett, A.: *Books and Persons*, 1917; Bullett, G. W.: *The Innocence of G. K. Chesterton*, 1923; Scott, W. T.: *Chesterton and other Essays*, 1912; Wells, H. G.: *Social Forces in England and America*, 1914; West, J.: *G. K. Chesterton, a Critical Study*, 1916.

  b. Blackshaw, R.: "Who is Mr. Chesterton?" *Critic*. 42: 459–60; Ervine, St. J. G.: "Some Impressions of My Elders." *North American Review*. 214: 527–37; Firkins, O. W.: "G. K. Chesterton: An Estimate." *Forum*. 48: 597–607; Marsh, E. C.: "Chesterton and Neo-Romanticism." *Forum*. 40: 394–400; Masterman, C. F. G.: "An Appreciation." *Bookman*. 16: 595–97; Prendergast, J. M.: "Gilbert Keith Chesterton." *Catholic World*. 123: 289–97; 493–98; 644–53; "Chesterton and the Revolt Against Modernity." *Current Literature*. 46: 396–99; "Paradox and Pretense in Chesterton's Work." *Blackwood's*. 178: 137–41.

Mencken, Henry Louis (1880–   ).
  I. Born September 12, 1880, at Baltimore, Maryland; educated in private schools and at the Baltimore Polytechnic Institute. On the staff of the Baltimore *Morning Herald* and *Evening Herald*, 1899, 1903–06; *Baltimore Sun* and *Evening Sun*, 1906–   ; war correspondent with the German army, 1916–17. Literary critic, *The Smart Set*, 1908–23, and co-editor, 1914–23; editor, *The American Mercury*, 1924–   ; contributing editor, *The Nation*, 1921–   .
 II. Works: *Ventures into Verse*, 1903; *George Bernard Shaw — His Plays*, 1905; *The Philosophy of Friedrich Nietzsche*, 1908; *The Artist* (play), 1912; *A Book of Burlesques*, 1916; *A Little Book in C Major*, 1916; *A Book of Prefaces*, 1917; *In Defense of Women*, 1917; *Damn! a Book of Calumny*, 1917; *Prejudices*, six series, 1919, 1920, 1922, 1924, 1926, 1927; *The American Credo* (with G. J. Nathan), 1920.
III. *a*. Boyd, E.: *H. L. Mencken*, 1925.
     b. Armstrong, E.: "Mencken and America." *Nineteenth Century*, 101: 117–25; Fitzgerald, F. S.: "The Baltimore Anti-Christ." *Bookman*. 53: 79–81; Genzma, G.: "Mr. Mencken Triumphant." *Nation*. 121: 664–65; Lippmann, W.: "Near Machiavelli." *New Republic*. 31: 12–14; Ratcliffe, S. K.: "Mencken: An English Plaint." *New Republic*. 26: 191–92; Sherman, S. P.: "Mr. Brownell and Mr. Mencken." *Bookman*. 60: 632–34; Swinnerton, F.: "The Great Mencken Fight." *Bookman*. 64: 463–67; VanDoren, C.: "Smartness and Light." *Century*. 105: 791–96; Walpole, H.: "My dear Mencken." *Bookman*. 62: 246–48. (See reply by Bromfield, L.: "My dear Walpole." *Bookman*. 63: 1–2.)

Sherman, Stuart Pratt (1881–1926).
  I. Born October 1, 1881, at Anita, Iowa; educated at Williams College (A.B., 1903) and at Harvard (A.M., 1904, Ph.D., 1906); married Ruth Bartlett Mears of Williamstown, Massachusetts, on December 25, 1906; honorary degree, L.H.D., Williams, 1922. Instructor in English, Northwestern University, 1906–07; in Department of English, University of Illinois, 1907–24 (professor, 1911–24); associate editor, *Cambridge History of American Literature*, 1917; literary editor, *New York Herald-Tribune*, 1924–26. Member American Academy of Arts and Letters, 1923. Died, August 21, 1926.
 II. Works: *Matthew Arnold*, 1917; *On Contemporary Literature*, 1917; *Americans*, 1922; *The Genius of America*, 1923; *Men of Letters of the British Isles* (in collaboration), 1924; *My dear Cornelia*, 1924; *Points of View*, 1924; *Critical Woodcuts*, 1926; *The Main Stream*, 1927; *Shaping Men and Women*, 1928.
     Edited: *Treasure Island*, 1911; *Essays and Poems of Emerson*, 1921; *Leaves of Grass*, 1922; *Poetical Works of Joaquin Miller*, 1923; etc.
III. Brief notices in *Bookman*, 64: 486–87; *Nation*, 123: 188; *New Republic*. 48: 32–33; *Saturday Review of Literature*. 2: 881–82; 3: 65.

Guedalla, Philip (1889–).

I. Born March 12, 1889; educated at Rugby and at Balliol College, Oxford, where he won First Class Honor Moderations (1910) and a final First Class in Modern History (1912). Barrister of the Inner Temple, 1913–23; Liberal candidate for Parliament in 1922, 1923, 1924.

II. Political, historical, and literary essays: *The Partition of Europe, 1715–1815*, 1914; *Supers and Supermen*, 1920; *The Industrial Future*, 1921; *The Second Empire*, 1922; *Masters and Men*, 1923; *A Gallery*, 1924; *A Council of Industry*, 1925; *Independence Day* (American ed., *Fathers of the Revolution*), 1926; *Palmerston*, 1927; *Conquistador, American Fantasia*, 1927.

Morley, Christopher Darlington (1890–).

I. Born May 5, 1890, at Haverford, Pennsylvania; educated at Haverford College (A.B., 1910), and as Rhodes Scholar at New College, Oxford, 1910–13; married Helen Booth Fairchild of New York, June 3, 1914. With Doubleday, Page and Company, 1913–17; *The Ladies' Home Journal*, 1917–18; *Philadelphia Evening Public Ledger*, 1918–20; *New York Evening Post*, 1920–24; contributing editor, *Saturday Review of Literature*.

II. Essays and Sketches: *Shandygaff*, 1918; *Mince Pie*, 1919; *Travels in Philadelphia*, 1920; *Pipefuls*, 1920; *Plum Pudding*, 1921; *The Powder of Sympathy*, 1923; *Inward Ho!* 1923; *The Romany Stain*, 1926; *Pleased to Meet You*, 1927.

Novels and Stories: *Parnassus on Wheels*, 1917; *The Haunted Bookshop*, 1919; *Kathleen*, 1920; *Tales from a Rolltop Desk*, 1921; *Where the Blue Begins*, 1922; *Thunder on the Left*, 1925.

Poems: *Songs for a Little House*, 1917; *Hide and Seek*, 1920; *Parson's Pleasure*, 1923.

Plays: *One Act Plays*, 1924.

III. Canby, H. S.: "Christopher Morley" (*Saturday Review of Literature*. 4: 625–26); Matthews, T. S.: "Christopher Morley" (*New Republic*. 54: 167–69). O'Sullivan, V.: "America and the English Literary Tradition" (*Living Age*. 303: 170–76).

II. GENERAL WORKS OF REFERENCE

Ward, A. W., and Waller, A. R., eds.: *Cambridge History of English Literature*, 14 v., 1907–17.

Trent, W. P., and others, eds.: *Cambridge History of American Literature*, 4 v., 1917–21.

Lee, S., and others, eds.: *Dictionary of National Biography*, with supplements, 70 v., 1885–1921.

Manly, J. M., and Rickert, E.: *Contemporary British Literature*, revised edition, 1928.

Manly, J. M. and Rickert, E.: *Contemporary American Literature*; revised by Millett, F. B., 1929.

New International Cyclopedia, 23 v., 1914–16.
Who's Who.
Who's Who in America.
The Catalogue of the British Museum.
The Catalogue of the Library of Congress.
Cunliffe, J. W.: *English Literature during the Last Half Century*, 1919.
Pattee, F. L.: *A History of American Literature since 1870*, 1915.
Payne, W. M.: *Leading American Essayists*, 1910.

III. THE ESSAY AS A FORM OF LITERATURE

Benson, A. C.: "The Art of the Essayist" (in Rhys, E., ed.: *Modern English Essays*, vol. 5, pp. 50–63).
Benson, A. C.: "On the Essay at Large." *Living Age*. 264: 408–15.
Burton, R.: "The Essay as Mood and Form" (*in Forum Papers*, first series, 1927).
Chase, M. E. and Macgregor, M. E.: *The Writing of Informal Essays*, 1928.
Conway, A. M.: *The Essay in American Literature*, 1914.
Crothers, S. M.: *The Modern Essay*, 1926. (Vol. 24, in *Reading with a Purpose*, American Library Association.)
Eleanore, Sister M.: *The Literary Essay in English*, 1923.
Johnson, B.: *Essaying the Essay*, 1924.
O'Leary, R. D.: *The Essay*, 1921.
Paddock, H. L. and Tainter, S. A.: *On Writing Essays*, 1927.
Rhys, E.: Introduction to *A Century of English Essays* [1915].
Smith, A.: "On the Writing of Essays" (in *Dreamthorp*, 1863).
Tanner, W. M.: *Essays and Essay-Writing*, 1927.
Walker, H.: *The English Essay and Essayist*, 1924.
Wann, L.: "The Development of the Essay in English" (in *Century Readings in the English Essay*, 1928).
Williams, O.: *The Essay* [1914?].